It is thought that some party with a mania for killing people has been stalking the country, and the victims of his lust for blood have simply been those who happened to come his way. This seems to be a plausible theory, and the only one that the police and detectives can arrive at inasmuch as no motive whatever can be discovered for the commission of any of the murders, and all have been executed in a similar manner. It is probably that the identity of the murderer will never be learned unless it is through some accident or confession.

*--- **1911 newspaper report from Monmouth, Illinois***

Traveling about the country like a millionaire or a tramp – no one knows which – striking where he is least expected – no one knows when – this "Billy the Axman" has terrorized the entire country. Sooner or later, the authorities say that he must leave some clew that will lead to his detection, but until that time, no one knows how many people will be butchered with an ax.

*--- **Colorado Springs Gazette, 1911***

It is my opinion that it will be a mere accident if the murderer is ever caught.

*--- **Frank F. Jones, 1916***

Never in the history of crime was pursuit of anybody conducted in this way by a sane man who had honest motives.

*--- **Des Moines Register and Leader, 1917***

Dead Men Do Tell Tales

MURDERED IN THEIR BEDS

HISTORY AND HAUNTINGS OF VILLISCA AND THE MIDWEST AX MURDERS

TROY TAYLOR

A BOOK FROM AMERICAN HAUNTINGS INK

The author with Martha and Darwin Linn in 2006

This book is dedicated to by late friend, Darwin Linn. He was one of the most genuine people I have ever had the pleasure of knowing and from my very first visit to Villisca, he made me feel welcome and happy that I came. He inspired my interest in the story of the murders and inspired the book you now hold in your hands. I miss the dinners that I had with he and Martha whenever I came to town and will always have a place in my heart for the good, kind, fascinating man. Rest in peace, my friend.

© **Copyright 2016 by Troy Taylor & American Hauntings Ink**
All Rights Reserved, including the right to copy or reproduce this book, or portions thereof, in any form, without express permission from the author and publisher.

Original Cover Artwork Designed by
© Copyright 2016 by April Slaughter & Troy Taylor

This Book is Published By:
Whitechapel Press
American Hauntings Ink
Jacksonville, Illinois | 217.791.7859
Visit us on the Internet at http://www.whitechapelpress.com

Second Edition – January 2016
ISBN: 978-1-892523-78-5

Printed in the United States of America

INTRODUCTION:

"SOMETHING TERRIBLE HAS HAPPENED HERE..."

June 9, 1912, was a warm evening in southwestern Iowa, and the town of Villisca stirred quietly in the gloom of the setting sun. The dinner hour had long since passed and many residents escaped to the cool of the front porch after the heat of the day started to settle. Stores locked up for the evening and oil and gas lights began to appear in the windows of homes along the darkening streets. The electricity in town had been shut off because of a dispute between the town council and the electric company, but for most, the evening was too nice to stay indoors anyway.

At the First Presbyterian Church on Third Avenue, music filtered to the street outside, along with laughter and polite applause. The Children's Day program came to an end around 9:30 p.m. and soon the congregation began trickling out into the street, heading home for the night.

Sarah Moore, who had coordinated the program, gathered her family around her as they started walking home. She was joined by her husband, Josiah, known popularly in town as Joe or J.B., and their children, Herman, Katherine, Boyd and Paul. Lena and Ina Stillinger, two young girls who were friends with Katherine and who had also been in the evening's program, came home with the Moores to spend the night. The children were excited after the evening's festivities and Sarah knew that she would have trouble settling them down for the night. She couldn't help but laugh at their antics and jokes, however, especially after J.B. joined in with them. The sound of their laughter could be plainly heard as the group walked along and they waved happily at the other families and friends they passed.

Everyone liked the Moores and no one who waved and smiled at them that night could have imagined that this would be the last time the family would be seen alive.

Early the following morning, June 10, Mary Peckham, the Moores' next door neighbor, stepped out of the back door of her home to hang some laundry on the line. The sun was barely peeking over the horizon, but it was better to finish the outdoor chores early and avoid the heat that came later in the day. Mary went about her business, wringing water from the wash and hanging the wet clothes on

5

the line that stretched across her back yard. As she worked, she had a clear view of the Moore house next door but thought little about how quiet the place was until she finished with the clothes and noticed that the clock in her kitchen now read 7 a.m.

She suddenly realized that not only had the Moores not been outside to start their own chores that morning, but that the house itself seemed unusually still. This was very strange since J.B. Moore always left early for work and Sarah was always up at dawn to start breakfast and the day's chores. The Moore house was full of young children, and so the morning hours were always loud and boisterous. Could the Moores be sick? The house had recently been quarantined twice for small pox. Mary waited for a few more minutes and then decided to go next door and check on her friend Sarah and the rest of the family. Mary approached the house and knocked on the door. It was eerily quiet inside. She waited for a few moments and then knocked again. Once more, there was no answer. She tried to open the door, thinking that she might poke her head inside and call for Sarah, but when she pulled on the door handle she discovered that it was locked from the inside. She found it hard to believe that this was the case, but apparently the Moores had decided to sleep late today.

Mary walked back through the yard, deep in thought. It seemed so unlike the usually energetic family, but who was she to pry? Mary went out to the barn behind the Moore house and let the chickens out into the yard. She felt it was the least she could do to help Sarah, who she was convinced must be under the weather. After she let out the chickens, Mary went back into her own house and tried to get back to her work, but the more she thought about the silent house next door, the more she worried. Finally, when she could stand it no more, she placed a telephone call to J.B.'s brother, Ross Moore, who promised to come over as soon as he could. This was the first step in what would turn out to be one of the most bungled criminal investigations of the era.

When Ross Moore arrived at the home of his brother, he was met by Mary Peckham, who had continued to try and raise someone inside the house. Ross tried the door himself and then leaned up to peer into a bedroom window. It was too dark to see anything, so he returned to the door, banging on it and shouting for his brother and sister-in-law. There was still no answer, so he produced his own set of keys and looked through the ring until he found one that opened the front door. He pushed open the door and stepped into the parlor with Mary Peckham behind him. She stopped at the entryway, however, and did not venture any farther into the house. Moore looked around, seeing no one in the kitchen. He called out but there was no answer. On the opposite side of the parlor was a door that led into one of the children's bedrooms. He carefully opened the door and looked into the room. He nearly cried out when he saw two bloody bodies on the bed and dark stains on the sheets. Moore never even looked to see who was lying there. He ran back to the porch and shouted for Mary Peckham to call the sheriff – someone had been murdered!

Ross sat down on the edge of the porch, trying to grasp what he had seen and what had happened. Mary hurried back to her house and telephoned J.B. Moore's farm implement store. Ed Selley answered and told her that he just saw the city marshal, Hank Horton, walk past. He said he would catch him and be there as soon as he could. Selley, Moore's senior employee, had spoken to Ross Moore earlier that day. After Mary Peckham had telephoned him, Ross called the store and asked if anyone had seen his brother. Selley had not, but offered to send another employee, a man named Carl, to the Moore house to milk the cows. Ross was sitting on the front porch when Carl arrived. They spoke for a moment and Ross told him that he didn't need to worry about milking the cows.

He muttered, "Something terrible has happened here."

Villisca received an unwelcome visitor that humid night in June 1912, leaving the town touched by a horror unlike anything that it had seen before or since. Over the years, the brutal slayings have earned a place in infamy. They remain the most famous in a series of murders that were committed across the prairie during that era.

But Villisca was not the first time that the monster who committed the "Villisca Ax Murders" had tasted blood. He blazed a terrible trail across the region in the years before and after the Villisca slayings, using the railroad lines to carry out his horrific deeds. This book will bring you the story of the Villisca Ax Murders, and the hauntings that followed, but it tells another story as well. It is a tale of madness, murder, horror and blood, and the "transient butcher" who wreaked havoc in the American Midwest and then vanished into history, his name and face forever unknown. Only his dark legacy lingers behind with us today. It remains a chronicle of one of the bloodiest unsolved murders sprees in our history.

The small towns of the American prairie would never be the same again.

1. COLORADO SPRINGS, COLORADO SEPTEMBER 17, 1911

"SIX KILLED IN WHOLESALE SLAUGHTER"

The series of murders began far away from the town of Villisca in Colorado Springs, Colorado, a resort community that had been founded in 1871 by William Jackson Palmer, a Civil War veteran who had come to the territory as a surveyor with the Kansas Pacific Railroad. While searching for possible railroad routes south of Denver, Palmer stumbled across a valley in the shadow of Pikes Peak that he believed would be the perfect location for a town. He was unable to convince the Kansas Pacific to follow the route that he wanted, so he secured the funding to start his own railroad, the Denver & Rio Grande, which he intended to run all the way to Mexico City. Palmer founded Colorado Springs as the first stop on his line on July 31, 1871. He had the intention of creating a high-quality resort community, and the stunning mountain view, as well as the nearby Garden of the Gods, made the city's location the perfect choice. Within two years, Palmer had opened his flagship resort, the Antlers Hotel, and began welcoming travelers from all over the world. Health-seeking individuals were attracted by the high altitude, sunshine and dry climate of the area and soon Palmer's visions for a thriving resort town were coming true. Colorado Springs developed into one of the most popular travel destinations in late nineteenth-century America.

Among those who flocked to the city were tuberculosis patients, lured by the mineral waters and the extremely dry climate, which was advertised to ease their condition. It wasn't long before the city became one of the most sought-out recuperative locations in the country.

Travel, scenic beauty, and nearby gold and silver strikes all contributed to the development of the city and Colorado Springs gained a reputation as a peaceful,

Colorado Springs, circa 1910

almost tranquil place – but that peacefulness was shattered on September 20, 1911, when the bodies of six people were found slaughtered in their homes.

That afternoon, Nettie Ruth left her home on South Sierra Madre Street in Colorado Springs and walked to the cottage where her sister, May Alice Burnham, lived with her husband, Arthur, and their children, Nellie Emma, six, and three-year-old John. She brought some sewing with her that she had planned to work on with her sister. Nettie had visited with May on Sunday evening and both women had complained of being behind in their mending. May invited her sister to return the following day, but Nettie was busy until Wednesday, so they made plans to meet that afternoon. Nettie later told the newspapers, "I wasn't in any particular hurry, knowing we had all afternoon to sit and talk and sew. But I never felt anything was wrong until I tried the door and found it was locked. I started around the house to try the other door, when I noticed all the window blinds were drawn."

Nettie assumed that her sister had gone to the home of her friend, Anna Merritt, who lived a half-block away on Pine Street, and she walked over to meet her. But when Anna answered the door, she said that she had not seen May in several days. At that point, both women began to fear that something was wrong.

Nettie decided to call her brother-in-law and see if he knew where his wife might be. Albert Burnham was employed as a laborer at the Modern Woodmen of America tuberculosis sanatorium, which was located about 12 miles outside of Colorado Springs. He was also a patient at the sanatorium and had lived there on and off for years. Over the summer of 1911, his condition had worsened, and between his labors at the hospital and his health, he usually only spent one day a week with his family. Nettie telephoned the sanatorium and spoke with Burnham, who told her that he had not been home since the previous Wednesday and had no idea where May might be. Nettie later stated that he sounded worried.

Nettie and Anna decided to go to the Burnham house and take a look inside using the spare key that May had given to Anna some time before. They hurriedly walked to West Dale Street and, feeling worried and upset, climbed the steps to the back door. The stench of death swept over them as Anna turned the key in the lock. Nettie exclaimed, "Oh, suppose we find May and her babies dead in the house. It would be terrible, terrible!" In her fright, Nettie had an unknowing premonition of the horror that the two women were going to find inside.

The lock stuck and it took a minute or so for Anna to work the key loose. Finally, it opened and they stepped into the gloom of the cottage's interior. On a table in the little rear room that the family used as a combination kitchen, dining room and bedroom, were the remains of Sunday evening's supper. Nettie later declared that the room looked just the same as it had when she had left the house on Sunday evening around 8:45 p.m. Unknown to Nettie at the time, a grocer's boy, trying to collect on a bill, had called on the Burnham house on Monday morning. He had knocked on the door several times, but had not received an answer. He returned on Tuesday and again on Wednesday, but still no one was home. He thought nothing of the fact that the house was closed up and tacked a copy of the grocery bill to the front door, assuming that the family was away and would return. If not for Nettie's insistence that something was wrong, it might have been even longer before the crime was discovered.

The bed in the back room had not been disturbed. The women pushed open the door leading to the front bedroom – half expecting to see some signs of tragedy – but with no idea of the carnage that awaited them.

The bed in the room was soaked with blood. At first, Nettie and Anna did not see the bodies that were tangled in the pile of sheets and blankets on top of the mattress. They could only gape at the blood – huge great stains and torrents of gore splashed on the walls and lying in puddles on the floor. Then Nettie saw the body of her niece, little Nellie, lying on the edge of the bed with her skull crushed, and began to shriek in terror and grief.

The two women could look no more and both ran screaming from the house. Two men who were passing by on the street went inside while the women waited. A moment later,

Arthur Burnham, his wife May Alice, and their children, Nellie Emma and John

they also rushed outside. Soon, news of a triple murder spread through the streets of Colorado Springs.

The coroner, police and sheriff's office were notified by telephone and investigators converged on the scene. People from the neighborhood began flocking to the house. People in automobiles, buggies, motorcycles and bicycles began arriving almost at the same time as the police. Later, they were followed by people on foot, and the street car company did a booming business hauling men, women and children on the Tejon and Spruce street lines to Dale Street. Packed into the crowd were friends and neighbors of the Burnham family, but the majority of the onlookers were what one officer called "the morbid curious." The street in front of the house was soon filled with people, automobiles and vehicles of every size and description.

The crowd watched with great excitement as the coroner, policemen and officers from the sheriff's department searched the area for evidence. They pushed forward to look into the windows of the house, hoping to catch a glimpse of the bodies that were reported to be inside.

According to reports, May and the two children had been sleeping in bed together when the killer entered the house. All three had been savagely beaten with the flat edge of an ax. May and John had been killed before they could awaken but Nelllie, judging from the position in which her body was found, had woken up during the attack and had tried to escape. The killer had struck her down and she fell partly across the body of her mother.

As the crowd pushed and gaped at the house, a neighbor of the Burnhams noticed something odd and brought it to the attention of the police officers on the

A newspaper photograph of the crowds gathering outside of the Burnham cottage as news spread of the murders.

scene. Almost everyone in the area had come out of their homes to see what was going on – except for the Wayne family. Their cottage was directly behind the Burnham home and it was silent and dark. The blinds had been drawn over the windows and no one was stirring.

No one knew much about the Waynes. They had moved to the area only about a month before. The household consisted of Francis Wayne, who went by his middle name, Henry, his wife Blanche, and their eighteen-month-old daughter, Lula May. Henry had heard about the rental cottage from Arthur Burnham, a fellow "lunger" at the sanatorium. The Waynes had been living in Indiana when Henry was diagnosed with tuberculosis and was advised to move west to a healthier climate. As a member of the Modern Woodmen of America, he had come to the sanatorium near Colorado Springs, living there as a patient for several weeks and becoming acquainted with Burnham, who mentioned that there were a number of vacant rental cottages in the neighborhood where he and his family lived. Wayne subsequently rented one of the houses on Harrison Place, around the corner from the Burnhams' home, and moved his family from Indiana to join him.

After receiving the ominous warning about the house, police officers decided to investigate. They walked over to the Wayne cottage, where earlier a neighbor woman had found an ax that she had loaned Mrs. Wayne leaning against the house. The ax blade was bloodstained but the neighbor later told police that she had thought nothing of it, assuming that it had been used to kill chickens. The police learned otherwise when Assistant Police Chief Springer forced open the door and found Henry Wayne, his wife and baby lying dead in the same bed. Their skulls had been crushed by the flat side of an ax. They had, like May and John Burnham, been killed in their sleep.

With six murders in two different homes, the authorities grew frantic. Police officers swarmed over the two cottages, while more and more spectators descended on the scene. Men swore and cursed and threatened a lynching if the murderer could be found. Women and children, their faces white and streaked with tears, huddled in groups and whispered of the terrible tragedy.

The police, sheriff's deputies, and investigators from the district attorney's

Henry and Blanche Wayne

office searched both houses for clues. They came to believe that robbery had not been a motive in the murders. Mrs. Wayne was still wearing her jewelry and a gold watch was in plain sight in the Burnham home. Nothing appeared to have been taken and nothing in either home was disturbed. The doors of both houses had been locked and the police believed that the killer had exited through a window. The rear door of the Wayne house was thought to have been opened by a skeleton key made with twisted wire. The killer had also opened a screen door, which had been latched with a hook, by cutting the screen. He then locked the door from inside, killed the Waynes and their daughter, and climbed out a window. He had done the same thing at the Burnham house, but when leaving through a window on the east side of the house, he had knocked over a bottle of ink, which had been sitting on the sill. The killer left black fingerprints on the metal bowl that he used to wash his bloody hands.

The police questioned everyone who lived in the area, but no one had seen anyone going in or coming out of either house on Sunday night. They became convinced that while robbery was not a motive in the crime, it could hinge on jealousy, revenge or perhaps both. It wasn't long before detectives began looking toward the victims to provide some sort of answer.

The Waynes had moved to Colorado Springs from Medaryville, Indiana, arriving only a few weeks before the murders. No one in the quiet neighborhood knew much about them. Henry had married Blanche McGinnis in 1908 and their daughter, Lula May, was born in 1909. Henry had been a photographer in Indiana and suffered from tuberculosis, an all-too-common ailment at the time. He was a member of the Modern Woodmen of America, which had opened a 1,000-acre sanatorium in Colorado Springs. Henry made the trip to the hospital in September 1910, and his health began to improve. He met Arthur Burnham while staying there and Burnham told him of empty houses for rent in his neighborhood. According to Burnham, this was the extent of their relationship, but according to

police interviews, Wayne actually obtained a job at the sanatorium and began working in the kitchen, replacing Burnham, who worked as a part-time cook. Wayne worked for a few days and then went to Indiana to bring back his wife and daughter. On August 23, Wayne placed a call with an operator to Burnham and asked about the empty cottage that was behind Burnham's place. On August 31, the Wayne family arrived in Colorado Springs and moved into the house on Harrison Place. Henry made a bank deposit that day of $55 from the sale of their furniture in Indiana.

One avenue of investigation into the murders was that they might have been the result of some sort of love triangle. The theory was that Wayne, away from his family for so long, had been friendly with another woman and that he had broken things off when his wife and daughter arrived from Indiana. This prompted Denver Chief of Police Hamilton Armstrong to surmise that the killer was a woman, but there's nothing to suggest that this was true. In fact, it's likely that Wayne spent almost all of his time at the sanatorium before he was released. According to interviews, he had no friends in the city and only a few acquaintances at the hospital. The only solid evidence that Wayne interacted with anyone outside of the sanatorium was an argument that he was seen having in his yard with an unidentified man. The argument occurred about one week before the murders. It was a brief incident and witnesses stated that no punches were thrown. No one could say what the dispute was about and the man was never found.

The Waynes moved into the cottage on Harrison Place near the railroad tracks where the rent was $6 per month. Wayne paid two months in advance. Lula May and the Burnham children played together in the yard behind their respective houses a few times and May Burnham told her husband that [Blanche was] a nice little woman." In the weeks after they moved in, Blanche was often seen in the neighborhood with her daughter, walking to the corner store or to the park a few blocks away. Nearly everyone in the area said that while they recognized the pretty young woman with the toddler, they didn't know her or her husband very well. The only exceptions were apparently May Burnham and Grant Collins, the owner of the nearby grocery store. Collins told detectives that he saw the Wayne family almost every day, but hadn't really talked to them until the Sunday afternoon before their deaths. The Waynes had gone to church that morning and were later seen walking in the park. A few hours later, the family stopped in at the grocery store, which was across the street from the Burnham cottage. According to Collins, business was slow that day and he and Henry Wayne had started talking. He invited them into the back room and they visited until about 5 p.m. This was the last time that Collins saw them alive.

When the murders were discovered, the Burnhams were found first. As a crowd began to gather around their house, a neighbor realized that the Waynes were not around and that their house was dark and closed up. When the police broke in, they discovered the crime scene. Unfortunately, there are no original documents or reports about what they found, only notes in the newspapers of the time, which stated that the bodies were "nearly nude." There are few other details, but a fingerprint and crime scene expert (called a "Bertillon expert" for Alphonse

Bertillon, a French detective who first implemented the idea of fingerprints and mugshots for criminal investigations) was called in from Leavenworth, Kansas. He made a special point to examine what he described as "the chimneys of two lamps," which the killer was believed to have handled.

The murders of the Burnhams were just as puzzling. Arthur J. Burnham grew up in Michigan and lived for about 12 years in Leavenworth with his grandmother and a cousin. During that time, he drove a mail wagon for the post office, but the tuberculosis that he had long been suffering from grew worse. Like Henry Wayne, Burnham was a member of the Modern Woodmen of America and had been told about the healing properties of the Colorado Springs air and sunshine. His health did improve after his arrival and he met and married May Alice Hill in 1904. When the sanatorium was opened in 1909, Burnham became an inmate and was given a job variously described in subsequent newspaper reports as "yardman" or "laborer." He also worked part-time as a cook at the sanatorium and, on his one day off each week, baked at Tucker's restaurant in Colorado Springs. On that day, which was usually a Thursday, he stayed with his family at their cottage. By 1911, though, Burnham's tuberculosis had become severe again and he had trouble just walking the grounds of the sanatorium without assistance.

May Alice Burnham was the oldest daughter of John and Emma Hill. John met Emma while working for the railroad, making wooden ties, and they were married in 1882. John's job required him to move his family along the line as the railroad was being built. May and her younger sister, Nettie, were born in Kansas, and by 1890, Emma had reached her limit with their transient lifestyle. She wanted a house and wanted her daughters to go to school. The Hills moved to Colorado Springs, where John purchased a house and took a job as a wagon maker. May and Nettie were always very close, likely because of relocating so often when they were young, and this closeness remained strong even after both of them were married. John Hill went back to work for the railroad after Nettie was married and he traveled south into Mexico, which is where he was at the time of May's murder. Shortly before this, Emma petitioned for divorce and took a job making pastries for one of the local hotels.

May married Arthur Burnham, who was recovering from tuberculosis, in 1904. When Arthur relapsed and he moved into the sanatorium almost full time, May essentially became a single mother. She and her children moved in with Emma for a short period, and then in the middle of 1910, Arthur was deemed well enough to live outside the sanatorium again. He maintained his job there as yardman, but was able to live again with his family. He moved his wife and children out of Emma's house and into some rooms that were rented from Anna Merritt, who operated the upstairs section of her home as a boarding house. It was during this time that May and Anna became good friends. In the early part of 1911, Arthur discovered the small rental cottage not far from Anna's house, and moved his family into it. Later that year, when Arthur's tuberculosis became severe again, he spent little time at home, leaving his wife to care for the children and the house by herself.

To make ends meet, May took in sewing and she also accepted the overflow from Anna Merritt's boarding house when someone needed a bed for the night. This often involved renting the extra bed in the kitchen. The door between this room and the front room had a lock on it and could be secured from the room where May slept with the children. May also allowed overnight guests to rent the hammock on the front porch. This regularly brought her into contact with strangers and with transients, who passed by thanks to the proximity of the Denver & Rio Grande Railroad. During the few weeks that the Waynes lived behind the Burnhams, they came into contact with the same itinerant strangers --- one of whom likely ended their lives.

On Sunday morning, September 17, May took the children to church and then was seen in different locations throughout the neighborhood during the day. They also stopped into Grant Collins' store that afternoon. May's sister, Nettie, often visited with May and the children on Sunday evening and had supper with them. Both women had sewing that needed to be completed and made plans to get together again on Wednesday afternoon. Nettie left the Burnham cottage around 8:45 p.m.

She was not to see her sister or her niece and nephew alive again.

The *Colorado Springs Gazette* offered a better description of the Burnham crime scene than it did of the Wayne crime scene, but not by much. May and the children were found in the bed in the front room. May and John were covered with bloody sheets, but Nellie was lying across her mother's legs, at the foot of the bed. From her position, the police inferred that she had awakened, tried to run away, and was struck down. It's also possible that her body may have been moved after she was killed. Elmer Prettyman, the superintendent of detectives at the Pinkerton's Denver office worked on the case and, for unknown reasons, he referred to the killer as a "moral pervert." We are left to wonder if the body of the little girl was molested in some way, but without any existing notes or documents related to the crime, we may never know.

In the back room of the house, the Sunday night supper dishes were still on the table and the bed had not been slept in. On the floor in front of the stove was a small pile of ashes. A bowl containing bloody water was also found in the kitchen. A bottle of ink had been knocked off the window sill as the killer was leaving the house and an attempt had been made to clean up, which accounted for the fingerprints that were left behind.

In the front room, a crumpled piece of the Sunday newspaper was found partially burned, as was the lower part of one of the window curtains. Investigators at first believed that the killer had attempted to burn down the cottage and erase all evidence of the crime, but they were mistaken. It was later discovered that a photographer had used too much flash powder when photographing the scene and a spark had caught the curtain on fire. The newspaper had been another casualty of the near blaze.

The police frantically pursued the evidence in the case, but as with any sensational crime, there were scores of people who imagined that they heard or saw something or someone threatening. The case created panic in the city and the investigators were forced to run down each and every report in an effort to satisfy the public and the press. The fact that there was no direct connection between the victims and the alleged suspects made no difference at all. The police, feeling the pressure to get the madman responsible for the murders off the streets, began rounding up every drifter, transient and stranger they could find, grilling them for hours before releasing them. In all honesty, they had little else to go on. There were no forensic investigations in those days, no analysis in labs and even the fingerprint expert that was summoned could do little to help them because he had nothing to compare the killer's prints to. The investigators were floundering in the dark, looking for anything that might offer a solution to the crimes.

The best suspect that the authorities could come up with in the beginning was Arthur Burnham, the only survivor from both households. He had a solid alibi, but the police didn't want to take any chances. Burnham's alibi was his health. According to his roommate and Dr. J.A. Rutledge, the superintendent at the sanatorium, Burnham was at the hospital when his family was killed. His tuberculosis had grown worse and he wasn't even close to being healthy enough to swing an ax as many times as would be needed to kill six people. In spite of this, he was held for two days. He was allowed to attend the funeral of his family on September 22, and then was returned to his cell. Later that same evening, he was released and allowed to stay with his in-laws, who believed him to be innocent of the crime.

During Burnham's questioning, he was able to offer the police the name of a man who might have a connection with his wife, an Italian named Tony Donatel, a childhood friend of May's and the Hill family. When Burnham had met May, Donatel was his only competition for her hand in marriage.

Donatel was about 40 years old when the murders occurred and worked as a laborer. He had been married once before but his wife had left him in 1893 and he had divorced her. He was said to have an eighteen-year-old son. He lived alone in a one-room cottage and frequently visited with the couple that lived next door. He reportedly owned a number of other properties that he rented out. Other neighbors described him as being a little peculiar and said he was frequently seen scrubbing the outside of his home to wash away "marks left by witches." A few historians have made much of this seemingly odd behavior, surmising that perhaps he was paranoid or suffered from delusions. A more likely explanation would be that as a landlord overseeing cheap properties, Donatel had frequent disagreements with some of his tenants. It would not be strange for many of them to scrawl unkind messages on his house. Another theory was that the marks were made by hoboes, who had developed a series of pictograms that were chalked on houses and fences to let others know of places to avoid, or where they would be likely to get food or a bed. This was especially common near the railroads, where Donatel's rental homes were.

May told Burnham that Donatel had been one of her suitors before Arthur had arrived in Colorado. She insisted that he no longer had any affection for her outside of friendship, although May's sister, Nettie, told investigators that Donatel still had feelings for May and that she once overheard him saying that May had no business marrying Burnham. By Donatel's own admission, he was friendly with May, even after her marriage, but added that he hadn't seen her "in a long time" and didn't know where the Burnhams lived. The week before the murders, Donatel was working on a sewer line within a half block of the Burnham cottage, but claimed that he only knew the Burnham house was somewhere in the neighborhood.

In the newspaper, Burnham expressed surprise when Donatel was arrested for the murders, even though he was the one who gave the investigators his name. He came to Donatel's defense in a newspaper interview and stated that he didn't believe he had anything to do with the crime.

Unfortunately for Donatel, things didn't look good. He could not sufficiently account for his whereabouts on the night of the murders. He said he ate supper with neighbors and stayed with them until 9:30 p.m. After that, he went home and went to bed, where he stayed until morning. He visited his neighbors on Monday and Tuesday and was said to be acting normally, never mentioning the Burnhams. It wasn't much of an alibi, but things got worse. An unnamed incident had occurred in 1910 that caused Donatel's sanity to be questioned. He was examined by County Physician E.L. McKinnie and was released soon after. Investigators also found drops of a red substance on his pants that was originally thought to be blood (it later turned out to be ink). Donatel swore to the police that he had nothing to do with the murders and his friends that lived next door to him defended him in print. He was later released after the Bertillon expert from Kansas stated that his fingerprints did not match those on the ax, the wash basin or the window sill.

After Donatel was released, no other serious suspects were ever found. The murder investigation grew cold and was eventually shuffled off into the files of the unsolved.

The Burnham family was buried in Evergreen Cemetery in Colorado Springs, while the battered bodies of the Waynes were loaded on a train and shipped east to Indiana. The caskets were opened for an informal viewing on Saturday, September 23, and then the family was laid to rest in the Medaryville Cemetery.

Arthur Burnham was admitted to the St. Francis Hospital in November 1911, suffering from the late stages of tuberculosis. He left the hospital at some point in December but was re-admitted on January 26, 1912, after his condition worsened. He died alone at the hospital, wasted away from tuberculosis, asthma and Bright's disease, an old-fashioned term for acute kidney disease. He was buried near his family at Evergreen Cemetery a few days later, closing a chapter on the case.

Who killed the Burnham and Wayne families?

His name will likely never be known, but at least two people may have seen him. Soon after midnight, during the early morning hours of Monday, September 18, C. Marshall, a worker at the Golden Cycle mill, stated that he saw a man acting suspiciously in the vicinity of the Burnham house. Almost two hours later, a milkman who was starting his route also saw what sounded like the same man. They both described him as tall and wearing a light-colored hat. He was never found by the police.

Was he the killer? And if so, was he the same man that left Colorado Springs that night, bound for Illinois, Kansas, Iowa, and beyond?

2. MONMOUTH, ILLINOIS
OCTOBER 1, 1911

"THREE SLAIN IN BED BY FIEND"

Death called next in the small town of Monmouth, Illinois, a quiet railroad and farming community in the northwest area of the state. The town had been established in 1831 and its name was literally drawn out of a hat. It was first called "Kosciusko," but town leaders feared that it would be difficult to spell and pronounce so they settled on Monmouth.

Unusual history touched Monmouth several times over the years. Western lawman and gunfighter Wyatt Earp was born there in 1848 and controversial Civil War General Eleazar Paine – reprimanded for brutalizing civilians in Kentucky during the war -- practiced law there for many years. Mass murderer Richard Speck lived in Monmouth for a short time as a child and then returned in the spring of 1966, months before slaughtering a group of nursing students in Chicago.

But horror came to Monmouth one night in October 1911, when a killer entered the home of a man named William E. Dawson, murdering Dawson, his wife, and his daughter in their beds. Their skulls were crushed, their bodies covered with bloody sheets, and an eerie link was left behind that seemingly connected the murders to the Burnham and Wayne killings in Colorado Springs.

The killer had tasted blood once more.

Of all the crimes linked to the "transient butcher" that gained infamy in Villisca, the murders in Monmouth are the hardest to document. There are few resources available and even newspaper articles are scarce. The official records, even the report from the coroner's inquest, have apparently been destroyed. This is perhaps because the case was officially "solved" and no one wanted any lingering questions to remain behind. Unfortunately, the guilty verdict in the case was controversial at best and, at worst, an outright miscarriage of justice.

During the early morning hours of October 1, 1911, William and Charity Dawson and their twelve-year-old daughter, Georgia, were murdered in their home near the corner of South First Street and East Ninth Avenue. Their small, five-room cottage was located in what was then known as the "colored district" of town, a section of rundown older homes that were owned predominantly by African

Americans.

Dawson was not a wealthy man and had spent time at the Illinois Penitentiary for horse theft nearly 20 years before. By all accounts, though, he had reformed and was well liked by people in town and at the church where he worked as the caretaker. He had proven himself to be honest and hard working, which had won him a job at the First Presbyterian Church. The fact that he didn't show up to unlock the church on Sunday morning, October 1, was what alerted Reverend J.C Greene that something was wrong. Dawson had always been reliable and Reverend Greene feared that he had been taken ill.

William and Charity Dawson were originally from Indiana and were married on June 6, 1875. They had 11 children together, three of whom lived with their parents in Monmouth. Dawson had moved his family to Monmouth eight years before, after he was released from prison. On the night of the murders, two of the daughters were staying away from home. One was at the home of a sister in the country and the other spent the night with a girlfriend from church. The latter was a member of the choir and was actually singing at church when the bodies of her parents and younger sister were found.

On Sunday morning, after failing to unlock the church and not appearing for the 11 a.m. services, Reverend Greene became worried. A telephone call was placed to the Dawson house, but there was no answer. Finally, two men from the church went over to the house to find the front door was locked. They knocked several times but there was no answer. One man went to the kitchen door and knocked again. Still no answer, but when he tried the knob, the door swung open.

The interior of the cottage was gloomy and dark. All of the windows were closed and the curtains had been pulled shut. The men cautiously walked through the kitchen and the living room to the front bedroom where Georgia Dawson slept. They were stunned to find her bloody body sprawled across the bed. Terrified, one of them stumbled into a bedroom across the hall to find that it was mercifully empty. However, a horrible scene greeted them in the other room. The walls were spattered with blood and two still forms were lying on the bed. William and Charity Dawson had been murdered in their sleep!

The police were immediately called to the scene and a crowd began to gather outside. Rumors and accusations flew. A white family had been murdered in the "colored district" of town and people were upset and angry. Care had to be taken to control not only the crowd, but the rumors that were being spread around town. The last thing that the police wanted was a riot or a lynching on their hands.

The investigation began right away, but once again, the police had little in the way of clues or evidence to pursue. The Dawson house was located several blocks from the railroad tracks in a low-income neighborhood. Georgia's body was found in her bedroom. The bodies of her parents were found in the room next to it. The empty bedroom across the hall belonged to the two daughters who were absent at the time. All three victims had been beaten to death with some sort of blunt instrument, their skulls crushed. The curtains on all of the windows in the house had been tightly closed and the bodies of William and Charity had been covered with bed sheets. They appeared to have been killed when they were asleep, but

Georgia's body was found in a different position. She was found in the center of the bed, with her head shoved down off the pillow and one arm raised above her head. The sheet was tangled in her hand, as if she had pulled it over herself. Had she struggled? Or had her body been moved by the killer? There were rumors that Georgia had been raped, but there are no documents to support this. We are left to wonder if perhaps she had been molested in some way, as some believed little Nellie Burnham had been.

Initially, the police believed that the murders had been committed for revenge. One theory suggested that the killer had been a former crony of Dawson, who had been engaged in horse stealing with him. Dawson had apparently given testimony against this man and had been rewarded with a shorter prison sentence. The man swore that he would get even with Dawson when he was released and investigators thought that perhaps he had made good on this threat. It was soon learned that the man in question had been paroled a year before and was living in Danville, Illinois, about 200 miles from Monmouth. He also had a solid alibi. He had been in Danville on Saturday night and Sunday morning and could not have made the round trip to Monmouth in such a short amount of time. Other than this man, the authorities were unable to find anyone who could be considered an enemy of the Dawsons.

Another theory discussed was the idea that a group of blacks had slaughtered the family because William Dawson paid too much attention to their women. There is no indication of where this ludicrous idea came from, but it would be revived in 1915 when three lawyers "cracked" the case and a black man was convicted for the murders. His alleged motive? Dawson had shown too much attention to his female relatives.

But before the police gave up on the investigation in 1913, they came to believe the murders were the work of a "bloodthirsty maniac," who may have killed before. The *Daily Free Press* wrote:

There is a reign of terror throughout the city of Monmouth since the murder, the people fearing that a bloodthirsty maniac is at large and that any of them are likely to meet the same fate as the Dawson family at his hands at any time. As a consequence, many of the citizens have their houses guarded at night and people generally are afraid to go out after dark.

The police and detectives have been working on the case constantly since the murder, and it is a matter of much wonder to them that such an atrocious triple murder could have been committed outright under their very eyes and the murderer get away without leaving any trace whatever.

On Monday, bloodhounds that belonged to Deputy Sheriff Roy Bendure from Macon County, Illinois, were brought to Monmouth to search for the killer's trail. Unlike at the scene of the Burnham and Wayne murders in Colorado Springs, the murder weapon was not immediately located and was at first believed to have been a hammer or the flat side of an ax. The dogs followed a trail from the Dawson house to a pond west of town, which was located near the southbound railroad tracks. On the bank of the pond, they discovered a two-foot length of one-inch gas pipe that was covered in blood and hair. The pipe was later sent to Chicago for analysis and the blood and hair turned out to be human. In those days, there was no way to match the samples to the victims, but reports did say that it appeared to match the hair of the Dawsons. There were also bloody fingerprints on the weapon and they were supposedly photographed. Unfortunately, there was nothing to compare them to – no prints were found at the scene.

Interestingly, while there were no lamps reported at the scene that the killer might have touched, he did apparently light the house by another method. Several months after the murders, a wire fence was removed at the back of the Dawson property and a pocket flashlight was found where it had apparently been dropped. The flashlight was taken to the police and, under examination, it was discovered that the words "Colorado Springs" had been scratched into the metal of the flashlight's case. Of course, it cannot be proven that the flashlight belonged to the killer, but it does seem to be an eerie link between the two cities – and the two murder scenes.

The discovery of the flashlight led to the belief that the Dawson murder may have been perpetrated by the killer of the two families in Colorado Springs. The theory had already been advanced by the police in Denver and the discovery of the bloody pipe and the flashlight strengthened the idea. Newspapers in Denver and Colorado Springs jumped on the connection, the similar methods used in each case, and the fact that no motive for the murders was ever discovered. Editorials added:

It is thought that some party with a mania for killing people has been stalking the country, and the victims of his lust for blood have simply been those who happened to come his way. This seems to be a plausible theory, and the only one that the police and detectives can arrive at inasmuch, as no motive whatever can be discovered for the commission of any of the murders, and all have been executed in a similar manner. It is probably that the identity of the murderer will never be learned unless it is through some accident or confession.

The Dawson case soon went cold. The clues that were discovered led nowhere. The county sheriff tried to pass the case off to the Pinkerton Agency, but they refused to take the case since they were convinced they would not be paid. By 1913, the Dawson murders were unofficially dismissed as unsolvable.

But then in March 1915, Monmouth police chief G. W. Morrison went to St. Louis to gather information on a black man named Lovey Mitchell, who had been working at the roundhouse for the Monmouth & St. Louis Railroad at the time of the murders. It was believed that Mitchell was living in Kansas City, so Morrison was surprised to find that he was in St. Louis. He was questioned about the murders and surrendered to arrest without incident. He was escorted back to Monmouth, but locked up in nearby Galesburg because it had a stronger jail. The arrest of Mitchell was the result of a continuing "investigation," primarily carried out by a Monmouth attorney named John H. Hanley. He had never been satisfied with the police investigation and believed they should not have given up. With help from two other lawyers, he began his own search for the killer.

Little information is available about Lovey Mitchell, before or after his arrest. The case against him was weak. A former co-worker at the roundhouse, John O. Knight, who was already serving a prison sentence for burglary and larceny, had reportedly "confessed" to taking part in the murders with Mitchell. His wife was brought into the case as a witness and was put in jail in Peoria in order to "protect" her. Reports from Peoria claimed that Chief Morrison was telling reporters that Mitchell had confessed to the murders, but the Monmouth newspaper denied that this was the case. Mitchell was denied a lawyer and was not allowed to speak to reporters. While Morrison would not state whether he felt Mitchell was guilty of the Dawson murders, he did state he "did not believe [Mitchell] was guilty" of the murders in Colorado. L.A. Ryan, the editor of the *Monmouth Review-Atlas*, didn't believe that Mitchell was guilty of anything. Newspapers reported that Mitchell would face a grand jury in April 1915, but it never took place. His arrest made national headlines, but there was little coverage of the fact that all of the charges against him were later dismissed and he was released. Mitchell is believed to have died in January 1979, near East St. Louis, Illinois.

But the story didn't end there. With Mitchell released from jail, efforts to prosecute someone for the crime were turned toward John O. Knight, who had claimed to have committed the crime with Mitchell. His "confession" was used to railroad him into a 19-year prison sentence. According to the *Monmouth Daily Review* for February 2, 1918, he was found guilty of the Dawson murders and forced to add the additional term onto the two years and eight months that he was still serving on the earlier burglary charges. Although records are far from complete, there appears to have been little evidence against Knight, other than the fact that he was black and lived in the same neighborhood as the Dawsons at the time of the murders. His "confession," which had likely started out as an attempt to shave some time off his earlier sentence, turned out to be his undoing.

Of all of the murders carried out by the "transient butcher," this was the only one that was successfully prosecuted. Tragically, though, the authorities got the wrong man. The murderer was free to continue his dark deeds – and he would soon taste blood again.

3. ELLSWORTH, KANSAS OCTOBER 15, 1911

"FOULLY SLAIN IN THIS CITY SUNDAY NIGHT"

Six weeks later, the "transient butcher" struck again, this time to the west in the former cattle town of Ellsworth, Kansas. While a quiet and peaceful railroad town at the time of the murders, Ellsworth made a reputation for itself in the 1870s. Abilene was known as the first cattle town in Kansas and Dodge City was said to be the last, but Ellsworth was known as the wickedest. One newspaper of the era once stated, "As we go to press, hell is still in session in Ellsworth."

Ellsworth was destined for a troubled reputation for the state. Fort Ellsworth had been established on the edge of the frontier in 1864 to deal with the Cheyenne, who were attacking settlers on their way into the Colorado Territory. The Cheyenne refused to willingly stop their raids. They attacked wagon trains, stole horses, and battled with the ill-equipped soldiers who chased them across the prairie. In 1866, the outpost was renamed Fort Harker, and it was relocated one mile to the northeast in 1867.

Fort Harker became a major supply post for military campaigns against the Plains Indians. During this era, Ellsworth City was conceived with the idea of making money from the soldiers stationed at the fort. A town site was platted nearby and when the railroad came through, it overflowed with settlers, shopkeepers, and gamblers of every kind. As soon as a new saloon opened for business, the place was nearly overrun with soldiers, gamblers, railroaders, cowboys, and the inevitable "soiled doves," who serviced them all.

But only months after it came into existence, Ellsworth was struck by a series of near-fatal blows. The Smoky Hill River flooded and left the town standing in nearly four feet of water. A cholera outbreak at Fort Harker spread to Ellsworth. Cheyenne attacked railroad workers west of town and stole work horses right out of town. Those who endured started over again, moving the town site to higher ground to the west.

The town soon began to prosper again and business -- wicked and legitimate -- thrived. Gunfire and revelry in the streets could be heard at all hours of the day and night. James "Wild Bill" Hickok ran for sheriff in 1868, but was defeated by former cavalryman E.W. Kingsbury. Hickok and a friend, Jack Harvey, rode the

Ellsworth, Kansas, once known as the "wickedest town in Kansas"

district as deputy U.S. Marshals.

By 1872, the Texas cattle trade had abandoned Abilene, and Ellsworth became the new destination where longhorn cows could be shipped out from the Kansas Pacific stockyards. Cowboys ran wild through the town after every cattle drive and stories of shootings, brawls, and drunken parties became part of the town's legend. In 1873, Ellsworth geared up for the largest drive of Texas Longhorns to date. Expecting trouble, they beefed up the police force to five men and settled down to wait. The summer was quiet, though, with only one killing – until one hot day in August when a gun battle occurred that would mark the beginning of the end for the cattle era in Ellsworth.

The city marshal, "Happy Jack" Morco, sided with a gambler against Texas gunfighter Ben Thompson in a dispute over the winnings of a card game. Thompson and his brother, Billy, went out to the middle of the plaza near the train depot and called for the others to meet them in the open. With the city marshal already embroiled in the dispute, Ellsworth County Sheriff Chauncey Whitney went out into the street to talk to the Thompsons. He calmed things down and convinced the two men to come to Brennan's saloon and have a drink with them. As they started to walk away, Marshal Morco charged down the street with his guns drawn. Thompson fired and narrowly missed Marco, but Billy stumbled and his shotgun accidentally went off, killing Sheriff Whitney. Thompson and a group of Texas cowhands managed to hold off the townspeople so Billy could make his escape. Over the next couple of weeks, "Hell was in session in Ellsworth" as Morco was fired and then was gunned down in the street. The new city marshal, Ed Crawford, pistol-whipped a Texan to death, and vigilantes roamed the streets and warned Texans to get out of town. Then Ed Crawford was shot to death in a local dancehall. Ellsworth soon became known as a place that the cowboys from Texas wanted to avoid. The shipping pens were finally closed down in 1875.

By 1911, Ellsworth had left its "wickedest town in Kansas" reputation behind. It began to grow into a pleasant western community, connected to larger cities across the region by the busy railroads. Goods were shipped through town on a daily basis and the trains ran around the clock from the Ellsworth stations and depots.

But death also rode those same rails – and came calling on October 15.

Night had fallen in Ellsworth. A Union Pacific train roared through the crossing, just steps away from the house where the town's marshal, Morris Merritt, lived. The supper hour had long since passed and Merritt was sitting in his front room reading the newspaper. As he sipped from a steaming mug of tea, the pages of the paper rustled in his hand, breaking the stillness of the otherwise silent house. Merritt sighed and leaned back in this chair to place the tea mug back onto the small table next to him. It had been a long day and he was tired. Soon, he would turn out the lamp and go to bed. He turned his attention back to the newspaper and that's when he heard the strange sound -- a peculiar, scratching sound that was coming from the back of the house. It sounded as if an animal was clawing and scraping at the back door.

Merritt looked up from the paper, gazing toward the back of the small cottage. A moment later, the sound stopped. He wondered what it might have been for a second or two and then dismissed it. It was likely just an animal or even something stirred up by the wind. The house had certainly seen better days and he made a promise to himself to do some work on it before winter set in. He opened the paper again and went back to reading.

Less than a minute later, the sound returned. Merritt again heard the scratching and this time the marshal decided to investigate. He picked up the lamp off the table and went to the back room. Almost as soon as he walked into the room, the sound stopped again. Merritt waited but whatever it was, it didn't return. It must have been an animal after all, he thought. It heard me coming and I must have frightened it off.

Soon after this, Merritt put out the lamp and went to bed. When he got up the next morning, he dimly recalled the odd incident from the previous night and went around to the back of the house to look things over. He was surprised by what he found --- the screen had been removed from the back window and an attempt had been made to try and pry open the window itself. Someone had tried to break into the house! Perhaps when they heard him inside, they had run off. The marshal was happy that he had decided to stay up and read the paper. Who knows what might have happened if he had been asleep?

Later that afternoon, Merritt would find out just how lucky he had been…

On Monday, October 16, Laurie Snook got up in the morning and took care of her usual chores. She made breakfast for herself and her child and went quietly about her daily routine. Laurie's husband worked nights and slept during the daytime, so she took special care not to bother him with noise from the kitchen and the front room. She took care of some of the washing and then went outside to hang the clothes on the line. While she was pinning up the wash, she looked up and saw a bird dog lurking at the edge of her yard. She recognized the animal right away for it belonged to her friends, the Showmans, who lived two blocks away. Will Showman, his wife, Pauline, and their three children, Lester, Fern and Fenton, were friends of the Snooks and often came over in the evening to keep Laurie and her baby company while her husband was working. In fact, they had called on her just the night before and had gone home around 9 p.m.

Will Showman

Laurie had no idea why their dog had wandered down to her house, but she shooed the animal out of her yard and told him to go home. The dog trotted toward the Showmans' and Laurie thought no more about him until dinner time, when she saw the dog in her yard again. Laurie once more chased the dog off toward home and then went back in the house to make dinner for her husband, who would be getting out of bed soon. She still needed to pack his supper pail so he could take it with him to work that night. Before she did, she telephoned the Showmans to let them know about the dog, but there was no answer.

The afternoon was fading by the time Laurie went back outside to bring in the washing. Mr. Snook had just left for work and she was prepared for another lonely night at home. She took the clothing off the line, folded it into her basket and was prepared to go inside when she noticed the Showmans' dog was lying down in her yard again. Laurie picked up the telephone and called the Showmans again, but there was still no answer. Perplexed, she then called Will's place of work, but his employer told her that he had not shown up for work that day. Concerned and worried that they might be ill, she decided to walk over to their house. The dog jumped to his feet when she came outside carrying the baby, and when he realized that Laurie was following, he sprinted ahead to the Showman house.

It didn't take long for her to walk the two blocks to the house. Will Showman had purchased the little cottage in a tax sale four years before. The previous owners had failed to pay the taxes they owed and Showman had gotten a good deal on the house. It sat perched on a small hill overlooking the railroad tracks, a short distance from the front door. Showman had done some work on the place, most of it after the addition of his two youngest children. Lester was seven years old, and Fern and Fenton were four and two respectively. The growing family had forced Showman to add an additional angled-roof room on the back of the house, which was now used as a kitchen. The family slept in the front room with their beds on opposite sides of the room.

Showman was the youngest son of David and Sarah Showman. David was a veteran of the Civil War and had served in Company H of the Maryland Volunteers. He moved his family to Ellsworth in the middle 1870s and took a job as a mail carrier. He died in April 1898. Will's wife, Pauline, was the youngest daughter of John and Theressia Kratky and was born in Ellsworth County in 1884. Her family had immigrated to America from Bohemia (now the Czech Republic). They joined scores of other Bohemian farmers living in the area. Will and Pauline had married in 1904 and Showman found work as a chauffeur. Unfortunately, it was a job that did not pay well in a rural town like Ellsworth. However, the family was well liked in town. They regularly attended church and Showman was a member in good standing of the local Redmen Lodge, a fraternal organization.

When Laurie Snook walked up to the Showman house, she carried her baby around to the back door. She saw that the door and the outer screen door were both hanging open. The bird dog that she had followed down the street was crouching anxiously just inside the door. He left out a soft whine as she approached him. Laurie leaned into the darkened house and called out for Pauline and Will. There was no reply and she cautiously stepped inside. The house was silent except for the soft sounds made by the baby in her arms. She called out again as she passed through the kitchen and into the front room. The room was dark, but there was still enough light for her to see the horror that awaited her in the room.

The walls, floor and ceiling were covered with blood. The battered and bloody bodies of the Showman family were flung upon the beds. Two of the children had been killed sitting up and their bodies lay tangled on one of the beds. A stained sheet had been pulled over them. Will Showman had been slaughtered in his sleep, his head bashed in and a sheet pulled over him, leaving only the top of his head and a tangle of blood-soaked hair visible. Fenton, the youngest child, was next to his father on the bed. Like the rest of his family, his skull had been crushed. Only Pauline's body was clearly visible on the bed. Her head had been crushed, her body mutilated and then posed in a manner like nothing Laurie had ever seen before....

She clutched her baby to her breast and ran screaming from the house. Terrified, she rushed home and called John Showman, Will's brother. Crying and gulping, she managed to choke out what she had seen in the charnel house. It was John who finally summoned the police to the scene. The sheriff and his deputies were, like other inexperienced law enforcement officers in small towns of the era, completely overwhelmed by the crime scene that confronted them.

Investigators immediately examined the scene. The crime, it was decided, had taken place at some point during the night. Marshal Merritt reported the strange sounds at his back door, as well as the removal of the window screen, and it was surmised that the murders took place soon after. Merritt's house was just two houses away from the Showman house.

The murders had been carried out with the flat side of an ax. As with past scenes in Colorado Springs and Monmouth, the killer had used a weapon that was found at the scene. In this case, the ax had belonged to the Showmans next door neighbor, Bill Miller. The ax had been embedded in a tree stump in his front yard.

A few days before, Miller and some of his friends had a contest to see which of them could drive the ax head the deepest into the stump. Fred Boyer won the contest, driving it in so deeply that it took several men to remove it with another ax, chipping the blade in the process. The ax was left in the stump, which was the last place that Miller had seen it.

When the sheriff arrived at the Showman house, the ax was discovered leaning against the wall between the front room and the kitchen. It had been washed off with water, but there was sufficient blood on the blade and handle to show that it had been used for the murders. There were also strands of hair stuck in the blood that matched that of Pauline Showman.

The bed had been positioned against the wall of the room. Will had been lying next to the wall and had been killed first. Two-year-old Fenton had been sleeping next to his father and was killed next, which had evidently roused Pauline from her sleep. She attempted to fight off the attack but was also killed, waking the other children. As they tried to get out of their bed, the killer pounced on them, killing both with the ax.

After the family was dead, the killer completed his grim tasks by the light of an oil lamp. He removed the glass chimney from the lamp, working carefully in the dim light that it offered without the glass. The chimney was later found under a chair in the kitchen. In the near darkness, the murderer used a bucket of water to wash off his hands and clean the ax. The bucket, still filled with blood-tinged water, was found the next day by the investigators. He also took a dress that belonged to Pauline and for some reason, draped it over the telephone in the kitchen. It's possible that he hoped to muffle the sound of the ringing in case anyone called to check on the Showmans. If the neighbors could not hear the telephone, no one would question why they were not answering it.

Finally, the killer staged the scene, posing the body of Pauline in a sexual way. The *Ellsworth Reporter* noted, "From the positions of the bodies it would seem that they had no warning of their terrible fate, as there was no evidence of any struggle, and the bodies, with the exception of Mrs. Showman, however had been subjected to treatment that clearly indicates that the fiend was possessed of an abnormal hatred towards her." There are no details available as to exactly what was done to Pauline Showman's body, but it seems that the "moral pervert" was at work once again.

After Sheriff Rufus W. Bradshaw and Marshal Merritt had done everything that they could at the scene, the bodies were removed to the Hutchinson Undertaking parlor. The investigators were at a loss. They were used to dealing with drunks, noise complaints, and perhaps the occasional burglary or theft. The mass murder of an entire family was beyond their capabilities and unlike anything they had dealt with before. But the investigators were not going to give up easily.

Sheriff Bradshaw wired to Abilene for bloodhounds, which arrived on the 11:57 p.m. train on Monday night. Sheriff Young of Dickinson County accompanied the dogs and they were taken to the scene of the crime. The dogs were given a scent from a cloth on which the murderer had dried his hands, took the trail and followed it to where the Union Pacific and Frisco lines crossed, about a half mile west of town. The crossing was only a short distance from the Showman house. At that point, the dogs stopped and began barking and walking in circles. The trail seemed to end at that point. Still determined, though, Sheriff Young returned them to the Showman cottage, offered them the scent again and this time, let them off the leash. Howling and barking, the dogs circled the house several times and then darted off into some bushes behind the house. Moments later, they were back and ran off on the same trail they had followed earlier, which ended at the railroad crossing. The officers believed that the killer walked to the crossing and then boarded either a Frisco or a Union Pacific train. They had no clue as to where he might have gone from there.

They followed every lead available to them, including searching for a stranger who had asked for a room at the Baker Hotel on Monday morning between the hours of 1 and 2 a.m. The man registered under the name "John Smith" from Junction City and said that he was going to work in one of the salt mines in Kanopolis. This was the last time he was seen in Ellsworth. He left a hat and a bundle of clothing, containing a blanket and other bed clothing in the hotel office, which he did not return for. In the morning, when he didn't check out, his room was searched and more clothing was found on the floor. One of the items was a shirt, which was smeared with blood. Whether the man brought the bloody clothing with him to the hotel when he first came in, or whether he went out, committed the murders and then returned to his room to change, was unknown. However, the man apparently did go to Kanopolis and ate breakfast at a restaurant in town on Monday morning. He went to the Royal salt mine and applied for a job. When he left, after being told there was no work available at the moment but there would be shortly, he said he was walking to Salina. That was the last that was heard of him. Since the man had signed the hotel register with a note that said he was from Junction City, Sheriff Bradshaw contacted the authorities there with his description --- he was almost six feet tall, weighed about 170 pounds with light hair and light blue eyes.

It took nearly a week but on Saturday, October 20, John Smith – who also went by the name of John Smitherton – was tracked down in Kanopolis. Sheriff Bradshaw received a telephone call that let him know that a man fitting the suspect's description had just stepped off a train in town. Bradshaw hurried to Kanopolis, arrested him and brought him back to Ellsworth. Smitherton was so drunk at the time that he was unable to answer questions. He was locked up to sleep it off so that he would be able to account for his movements around the time of the murders. By Monday, he had sobered up enough to talk. His story was to the effect that he had left Junction City on Sunday afternoon, October 15, and ended up in Ellsworth late that night, around the time the murders had taken place. When he got off the train, he was intoxicated and picked up a bundle of clothing that did not belong to him. He carried the clothing with him to the Baker Hotel. During the night, he had a serious nosebleed, and took a shirt from the bundle of clothes to staunch the bleeding. The following morning, he walked to Kanopolis, leaving the clothes behind at the hotel. He applied for work at the mine and was promised a job, after which he left, saying that he would be back.

Smitherton then returned to Junction City and brought his wife and five children to Kanopolis, intending to go to work at the salt mine. When he arrived in town, though, he was recognized and arrested soon after.

Smitherton's story was corroborated in every detail by his wife. She stated that her husband was often afflicted with nosebleeds when he drank too much. Mrs. Smitherton had no idea why her husband had been arrested, so she couldn't have lied for him as to where he was and what he was doing. Smitherton didn't even know why he had been arrested. He said after sobering up that he thought it was due to his having taken the bundle of clothes from the train. He was shocked and surprised when he was told the real reason. After serious questioning by the authorities, assisted by private detectives, his story could not be shaken or disproved. Smitherton was released on Monday afternoon.

The search for Smitherton may have sent the Ellsworth authorities on a wild goose chase, but he was not the only suspect they had for the murders.

Charles Marzyck

In fact, Smitherton was not even the most serious suspect – that was a man named Charles Marzyck, a brother-in-law of Pauline Showman. Marzyck was a con artist who had been sent to the state penitentiary in January 1906, for the theft of some wheat. At the time, he had been married to Minnie Kratky, Pauline's sister. She obtained a divorce while Marzyck was serving his sentence and married an Ellsworth man named James Vopat. Marzyck was released from prison in 1910 and immediately went back to his criminal ways. Even while married to Minnie, he was not averse to living outside of the law. In Denver, he carried out a series of check forgeries that were said to have netted him several hundred dollars from saloonkeepers and grocers. He fled from the city before he could be arrested. He was arrested again in St. Joseph, Missouri, for forgery and fought extradition to Colorado for his earlier crimes, getting released on a technicality. After that, he allegedly went to San Francisco, where he was said to be living at the time of the murders.

So, if no one had seen Marzyck in Ellsworth, how did he become a suspect? According to rumor, Marzyck blamed Minnie's family for his arrest and subsequent prison sentence and had vowed revenge. Marshal Merritt was convinced that Marzyck was out to get him as well. He had been the main witness against him at his theft trial and Merritt believed that he had been the killer's first target on the night of the murders, but had frightened him off. He was sure that it had been Marzyck who tried to break into his house that night, but was it? Probably not...

Regardless, the authorities started a nationwide manhunt for Charles Marzyck, who was quickly nicknamed "Billy the Axman" by inventive members of the press who were always up for a lurid story. The police, as well as the newspapers, had linked Marzyck to not only the Showman murders, but the killings in Colorado Springs and Monmouth as well. Detectives had the right idea, but the wrong man. Marzyck's connection to all of the murders was later discredited, which is likely why the idea of a single transient killer in all of the cases was ignored for so many years.

The *Colorado Springs Gazette* was especially keen to pin all of the murders (and a few more) on Marzyck. They came right out and accused him of the crime and guessed, based on their timeline for the other murders, that he would kill again by the end of October. According to their theory, "Billy the Axman" had murdered a family of three in Portland, Oregon; eight people in Rainier, Washington; the Waynes and Burnhams in Colorado Springs; the Dawsons in Monmouth; and the Showman family in Ellsworth – 35 people in eight weeks! (Note: Some of these murders were later solved, but the fact remains that one person did commit many of these killings – and later, more – but it was not Marzyck) The newspaper grimly added:

Two weeks separated each of these five murders – the worst known in America. The fiend's next crime is due for execution October 29. No one knows where, but those who have studied the five murders fear that within the next two weeks, the murderer will add another to his long record.
Traveling about the country like a millionaire or a tramp – no one knows which – striking where he is least expected – no one knows when – this "Billy the Axman" has terrorized the entire country. Sooner or later, the authorities say that he must leave some clew that will lead to his detection, but until that time, no one knows how many people will be butchered with an ax.

The newspapers were quick to connect the missing Marzyck to any similar attack that might occur, like one that took place on October 31, 1911, in Mt. Pleasant, Iowa. Shortly after 5 a.m., Belle Jordan, whom the newspapers were to describe as "a fine-appearing woman" of about 40, was attacked in her sleep by someone wielding an ax. She was struck twice in the head with the flat edge of the weapon, fracturing her skull and injuring her right eye. Her husband had left for work not long before the attack (he was a fireman at the Gheen ice plant near their home) but her son, Albert, heard the commotion and ran into the room. When he opened the door, the intruder had already fled. No clues were found as to the killer's identity or the reason for the attack since the Jordans had only recently moved to the city from Salem, Iowa, and had no enemies. The house had not been robbed. Although it looked like Mrs. Jordan was going to die from her wounds, she eventually recovered, albeit with the loss of sight in her eye.

The authorities told the newspapers that the crime had all of the earmarks of recent killings in Colorado Springs, Monmouth and Ellsworth and, of course, blamed the attack on Charles Marzyck, who the papers had already turned into "Billy the Axman."

Unfortunately, those who had been promoting Marzyck as a fiendish killer looked rather silly when he was eventually captured in Manitoba, Canada, in April 1912. He had a solid alibi for the time of the murders (he was living in Colorado at the time) and had not been in the country when other the attacks took place. Regardless, he was brought back to Ellsworth and put on trial for the murders. Despite a number of witnesses who spoke against him none of them actually placed him in Ellsworth at the time of the murders. Despite planted evidence in the form of a cigar cutter that he supposedly left in the Showman house, Marzyck was cleared of the crimes and a not guilty verdict was returned by the jury.

The newspapers still couldn't let it go, though. They were sure that he had gotten away with something. According to reports, Marzyck had always been a "clever man" and "many speculated that he had been cleverest in his career to come out of the trial with an acquittal." A private investigation report from 1917 implied that no other arrests were made in the Showman case because the majority of the investigators believed that Marzyck really had committed the crime. What was more likely was that during the time that the authorities were tracking down Marzyck, the real killer was able to get away and the case grew cold.

The murders of the Showman family were never solved. Once again, the killer carried out his bloody crimes, hopped a passing train, and moved on to the next town before anyone even knew a murder had taken place. Nothing new had been learned about the "transient butcher" after the Ellsworth murders, but at least now he had a name – Billy the Axman.

And Billy would strike again eight months later in a small town south of Kansas City, staining himself once more in the blood of his innocent victims.

4. PAOLA, KANSAS
JUNE 5, 1912

"SLAIN IN A MOST BRUTAL MANNER"

Strangely, in the contemporary newspaper reports and the theories of the crimes created by detectives and other investigators, the murders that occurred in Paola, Kansas, in 1912 were never linked to the crimes that took place in Colorado Springs, Monmouth, Ellsworth, and Villisca. It has not been until recently that it's become generally accepted (by those who believe that a "transient butcher" was at work) that Paola was part of the string of Billy the Axman murders.

Investigators at the time didn't link the Paola crime to the ones before and after for several reasons, one of which was undoubtedly the publicity afforded the killing. Each of the previous crimes was followed by at least two weeks of stories, reports and follow-up articles. As the crimes continued to go unsolved, the newspapers increased their demands that the authorities needed to find the killer and the rewards grew larger. But by the time the murders in Paola occurred, it had been eight months since the last crime connected to the Axman and many people had forgotten about the others. Then, just five days later, any attention that the murders might have gained were overshadowed by the slaughter in Villisca.

In addition to the delay between possible connecting crimes, people were still reeling from a huge tragedy that had taken over the nation's headlines for the last month and a half – the sinking of *Titanic* in the North Atlantic. When the ship went down in April 1912, the world mourned the loss of the "unsinkable" ocean liner and the 1,500 people who had gone to their deaths in the icy water. The story dominated public interest for six weeks, and then the Paola murders occurred, followed by those in Villisca. There simply wasn't time for most people to connect to the Kansas tragedy when another one in Iowa followed so closely on its heels.

The third reason was Anna Hudson herself. Anna's reputation was a poor one, whether it deserved to be or not, and this probably did more to derail the investigation than anything else. The police were looking for a scorned lover or a violent point of a love triangle, not a "transient butcher."

Make no mistake, though, as the similarities between the murders will show, Billy the Axman was almost definitely at work in Paola, Kansas. And when he failed to satiate his bloodlust, he struck again just a few days later in a small town in Iowa.

In 1912, Paola was considered a railroad town. The arrival of the Kansas City-Fort Scott and Gulf Railroad in 1870 changed the way of life for the residents of the quiet community located south of Kansas City. The new rail line ran north and south connecting Hillsdale, Paola, and Fontana with Kansas City, Fort Scott, and points beyond. Soon, the whole world was open to the people of Paola but, unfortunately, anyone from anywhere could also slip into the little town and then disappear again just as easily.

The first inhabitants of Paola were the Native Americans who established communities throughout the area. They were followed by Spanish explorer Coronado, French missionary explorers Marquette and Joliet and, finally, the settlers who began streaming west along the Santa Fe, Oregon, and Mormon Trails. Between 1827 and 1832, forced resettlement of Indians from the eastern lands – the Kaskaskia, Peoria, Wea, and Piankishaw – arrived in the Paola area and called their new home "Peoria Village." The Piankishaw and Wea Tribes were granted 250 sections of land within the boundaries of the current Miami County. The tribes formed the Confederated Allied Tribes led by Baptiste Peoria. Of French and Indian ethnicity, Baptiste spoke six or seven Indian languages as well as English and French. He, along with the Paola Town Company, was influential in founding and developing the town that followed later.

The original name for Miami County, of which Paola became the county seat, was Lykins County. It was named for Dr. David Lykins, the first white settler and a member of the Territorial Council. Lykins came west from Indiana in 1844. He was a Baptist missionary and started an Indian school in 1848 that lasted until the start of the Civil War. The name of the county was changed to Miami after Kansas was admitted to the Union in 1861.

In addition to Lykins, other missionaries also came to the area, including several Catholic priests. One of them, Father Paul M. Ponziglione, an Italian, moved to the area in 1851 and was given credit for naming Paola after a town on the western coast of Italy.

A large influx of settlers began arriving in 1854. The town plat for Paola was laid out in early 1855. On August 23, 1855, the First Territorial Legislature incorporated the Paola Town Company. Members included Baptiste Peoria, Isaac Jacobs, A. M. Coffey, and Reverend David Lykin.

In 1861, Kansas was admitted to the Union, ushering in the most violent period of the state's history. Confederate raider William Quantrill was held briefly in the town's jail, charged with grand larceny in April 1861. After his infamous raid on Lawrence, Kansas, he came back to Paola for revenge, but bypassed the town when he learned that a force of Union soldiers was waiting for him.

Excitement came to Paola in 1888 when oil was discovered north of Reverend Lykins' old school. The first oil well west of the Mississippi River was drilled there soon after and a small refinery was built to handle the oil in the early 1890s.

In 1912, Paola was a quiet, peaceful town. That peacefulness was shattered in June 1915, when the bodies of a troubled couple were found slaughtered in their homes.

JUNE 5 – 9:00 P.M.

The man walked down the street, his intentions clearly focused on the home of Rollin and Anna Hudson, relative newcomers to Paola. They had arrived in town on April 10, 1912, from Massillon, Ohio, perhaps hoping for a fresh start. The couple boarded with G.W. Cole and his family for a short time after coming to Paola. Rollin Hudson knew Cole when the two of them had worked together on a railroad section at Centerville, Kansas, the year before. It's possible that Cole had talked to the younger man about the virtues of living in Paola, convincing him to move west from Ohio. After a week or so, the Hudsons moved across the street to a five-room rental cottage at 710 West Wea Street.

It was to this house that the man walked on the evening of June 5. The man was memorable to the people who saw him in Paola. He had been in town for a couple of days, staying at a rooming house, and several people recalled him asking about the Hudsons and where they could be found. The man was a stranger but he didn't dress like a hobo or a drifter. He was recalled wearing a blue serge suit and a straw boater hat on the night when he walked up to the Hudsons' front door. He also had, according to several witnesses, a "pig face." It's unclear from the newspaper reports of the time exactly what this meant, but perhaps it was meant that he had an upturned nose. Regardless, witnesses later felt sure they would remember him if they saw him again. Of course, that didn't matter since he disappeared without a trace after leaving the Hudsons' cottage that night.

When the young man knocked on the door that night, he was "greeted like a friend," witnesses later stated. And perhaps he was an old friend. That's what he claimed to be when he asked about the Hudsons around town. Perhaps he was just an old acquaintance from Ohio who stopped at the Hudson home on his way to the train station, leaving after a short visit. Items that were later found in the house were left in such a way that they suggested some brief reminiscing. A photo album was left open on a table, along with a box of letters. The supper dishes had not been cleared and it looked as though washing up had been interrupted. It seemed to be a hurried, unplanned visit. The man in the blue suit was invited inside and Anna may have quickly put together a small meal. They all sat down together to look at photographs from Ohio. The stranger may have asked about old friends and so the Hudsons pulled out a box of letters in order to find out their current addresses. The neighbors never saw the man leave, but they could have been occupied with something else and not paying attention to something that was really not all that interesting. The stranger boarded his train and left the area. With the way that the news traveled – and since the Paola murders received little press compared to the other killings – he may not have known that the Hudsons had been killed for a year or even longer. It's possible that he had no idea that he was the last person, other than their killer, to see the couple alive.

The blue-suited stranger was a suspect in the murders, at least for a time, although he seems an unlikely one. He did nothing to hide his presence in town.

He walked up to the house in full view of the neighbors and knocked on the door. He was greeted by a young couple who appeared happy to see him. It's more likely that he called on the Hudsons at what turned out to be an inopportune time and if he had not been leaving town, and had chosen to stay the night at their cottage, he might have been even more unlucky.

As it was, even though the neighbors never saw the man leave, the Hudson house was dark by 10 p.m. The blue-suited stranger's short visit was over, but another visitor would come calling before the night was over.

JUNE 6 – 12:01 A.M.

The sound of shattering glass echoed through the house. Mrs. Joseph Longmeyer, a woman who lived near the Hudson cottage, sat bolt upright in bed. Had a window been broken? Had something fallen? Where was Sadie? Without putting on her robe, she sprang from bed and stumbled out into the dimly lit hallway toward the front parlor. Suddenly, a flicker of movement caught her eye and she turned toward the kitchen. There was a loud banging noise and she saw the back door fly open. The figure of a man, indistinguishable in the darkened room, fled out the door. She heard his footsteps as they crossed the wooden porch and then he was gone. Mrs. Longmeyer was still groggy and stunned from being awakened from her sleep, but a new terror filled her heart, jolting her awake.

What was the man doing in her house? And where was Sadie?

Running, panicked and breathing heavily, she hurried toward her eight-year-old daughter's bedroom. The door to the room was standing open and Mrs. Longmeyer rushed inside to see that Sadie's bed was empty! Before she could call out, she heard crying from the corner of the room. Sadie was crouched there, curled up in terror. There was a man, she said, he had been leaning over her mother's bed!

Perhaps realizing that he had been seen, the man darted out of the bedroom. A few moments later, there was the sound of breaking glass in the dining room, which had awakened Mrs. Longmeyer. She had entered the front part of the house just in time to see the man as he ran out the door. When Mrs. Longmeyer investigated the dining room, she found broken glass, as well as a woman's kimono-style dressing gown. It looked as if it had been draped over a chair, but had fallen off onto the floor. It would later be learned that the gown belonged to Anna Hudson – it had been taken from the scene of her murder.

And the broken glass? It was the chimney that had been removed from an oil lamp. The lamp was sitting nearby, its wick turned down low so that it gave very little light, but the killer had apparently dropped the glass chimney and it had shattered on the floor.

JUNE 6 – 3:20 P.M.

On the afternoon of June 6, two excited and worried women walked around the little yellow house on West Wea Street that was rented by Rollin and Anna

Hudson. The house had been strangely silent all day. The two women, Mrs. Sherman Stump and Mrs. S.J. Musick, were both neighbors of the Hudsons, and after hearing of the late-night intruder at the Longmeyer house, had become unsettled by the eerie quiet. They walked around the cottage, trying to peer through the drawn curtains of the bedroom until finally, courage and curiosity rising above their sense of dread, they began calling to the Hudsons again and again. Their voices drew the attention of Mrs. William Pryor, who lived next door to the Hudsons on the east side, and she hurried over to the house. Bolder than the others, she walked up onto the porch and pushed open the front door. She went inside, but only stayed there for a few moments. Mrs. Pryor quickly burst back through the door, her face as pale as milk. She took a few steps toward her own home before she fainted in the Hudsons' yard.

Herman Hintz, a deputy marshal for the west side of town, happened to be passing by the house in a buggy when he saw the commotion taking place in the yard of the little yellow house. He was hailed by two women in front of the house, who seemed frantic and upset. A third woman was lying in the grass. Hintz stopped his buggy and agreed to take a look inside the house. He entered slowly, aware of the pale faces and the clenched hands of the women outside. He looked about in the darkened house, taking a moment to get his bearings. The door to the bedroom yawned open and he stepped into the shadowy room. Moments later, he hurried back out of the front door. His arms were raised above his head and his face was ashen. "My God, they have been murdered! They have been killed in their bed!" he cried and bolted down the street to get help.

Finally, one of the women outside went to the front door and peered into the gloom. She could see into the bedroom and saw the two bloody forms on the bed. Blood spattered the walls and soaked the blanket on the bed. It was a horrible, gruesome sight. The woman began to scream.

When the police arrived at the scene, they seemed to bring half of the town of Paola with them, all hoping to catch a glimpse of the killer's work. Not surprisingly, when those curiosity-seekers finally went home, they went to bed that night with all of the lights still burning. Things like that were not supposed to happen in little country towns and, once again, the authorities were overwhelmed by a crime they were not equipped to deal with.

The Hudsons had been brutally murdered on Wednesday night, June 5. The murder weapon was never definitively named. Some said it was a coal pick, likely stolen from the Frisco rail yards, which was only two blocks away. Others said it was a rock hammer, or an ax. Regardless, Rollin and Anna's skulls had been crushed and their faces were barely recognizable. There was no evidence of a struggle, as they had been apparently killed in their sleep. They lay upon the same pillow in the center of their small iron bed, their arms clasped partly around one another. The killer had left no traces behind. He had entered the home through an east window, removing the screen and leaving it propped up against the side of the house. The window led into an unused bedroom, through which he passed, moving through a sparsely furnished dining room, through the front room and into the bedroom where the young couple slept. Nothing had been taken from the

A crowd gathered outside of the Hudson home for a newspaper photograph

house – Anna still wore all of her jewelry – except for the dressing gown that had been left behind in the Longmeyer house at some point after the Hudsons had been killed. He had carried out his macabre work with the light of an oil lamp, from which the glass chimney had been removed. The lamp was discovered near the foot of the bed.

The bodies of the Hudsons had been covered with a blanket. Rollin was barely recognizable. The left side of his skull had been torn away and a dozen other blows had rendered his head into a bloody, pulpy mass. The coroner believed that the first blow that struck Anna caused instant death. She was struck over the left temple, leaving a gash three inches long. There was also a gash across her forehead and another over her left eye that scrawled downward, gouging out her eye. After the killer covered the bodies, he continued to strike them, hammering so hard that the blanket had been ripped in several places.

The interior of the house led the police to the conclusion that household routine had been interrupted the night before, as if the appearance of an unexpected visitor had been the excuse for leaving everything untouched until the next morning. This seemed to fit with the arrival of the blue-suited stranger, who was reported by the neighbors. Whatever Anna's shortcomings as a wife might have been, the *Miami Republican* reported that she was "a neat, careful housekeeper." It was apparent that the Hudsons had visited with someone known to them both on Wednesday night, judging by the box of photographs, the postcard album, and the letters that had been left out. The police surmised that the visitor might have been the killer, but this seemed unlikely. Even so, the man was never found.

The authorities searched the five rooms of the house. In the dining room, the remains of the evening meal were still on the table. Three places had been set. On the cold stove was a coffee pot. An apron was hung over the back of a chair. In the room that had been used for laundry and storage, a large washtub was still filled with water and wet clothing. A pan of strawberries was resting on a pantry shelf and on the parlor table was a pile of sewing, the pieces unfinished and looking like they had been suddenly set down.

Who had killed the Hudsons? And why?

The police immediately began looking into the backgrounds of Rollin and Anna Hudson, hoping to find some enemy that might have wanted to do them harm. And, unfortunately, as with the mistaken pursuit of Charles Marzyck after the Ellsworth murders, this is where the investigation went off the rails. While the police and detectives were busy prying into Anna's sordid past, the murderer slipped away and went on to kill again.

Most of the investigation began to center around the Hudsons' unhappy married life. They had been married for two years, but there were many problems and they had separated at least three times. Rumors that Anna had been involved in an affair with another man deepened the mystery – and added another suspect to the list.

The Hudsons had moved to Paola in April 1912. They had been married the year before in North Industry, Ohio, and by all accounts, their marriage was a turbulent one. Anna was a vivacious, flirty woman and she gained a reputation for being "loose." Unfortunately, Anna may have lived up to that image, since there seems to be quite a bit of circumstantial evidence to say that she actually had an affair. Rollin, 21, was a year younger than his wife and was the son of Jonathan and Emma Hudson of North Industry. His father was a justice of the peace in Stark County, Ohio, and was reportedly an important man in the state Republican party. Rollin worked for a time in an automobile factory in Ohio before coming west to labor in the Frisco coal chutes. This new employment was gained during one of the separations from his wife.

The source of most of the young couple's marital problems seemed to be a man named Roy "Hooky" Adams, a friend of Anna's from Akron, Ohio. In the short time they were married, Rollin left Anna three times and they were often seen arguing in public. When they first moved to Paola, they lived with the Cole family only a few blocks from the Missouri-Kansas-Texas railroad line and the Frisco coal chutes. Rollin was a hard worker and rarely missed a day of work. He was always trying to better his position, but he had a volatile temper and sometimes left town with no warning. One day, he walked down to the Frisco chutes to get some coal and vanished for a week. He had ridden the rail line to the town of Beagle to take a coal job there and hadn't told anyone. It's likely that Rollin's temper and Anna's flirtations made for some interesting conversation among their neighbors – and created a situation that confused the search for their killer.

Friends and neighbors were quick to tell the police about the things that they had heard and seen take place between the couple. George W. Cole had met Rollin in July 1911, when he had first come to Kansas. He told Cole that he and his wife had recently separated and he had come west to forget about her. He mentioned another man and told him that his wife had not been true to him. Cole later told the police, "He cried while telling the story and I did not press him for details. He seemed to be deeply in love with the woman."

A short time before the murders, Rollin left his wife again. A few days later, he was back in town and ran into Cole at the Missouri-Kansas-Texas coal chutes. The two men talked and Rollin expressed his unhappiness with his marriage. Cole told him that he should return home to his wife. But Hudson didn't appreciate the suggestion and hotly replied, "You wouldn't want to live with a woman who proved herself to be false on three separate occasions, would you?" He again referred to a man in Ohio, but he didn't give a name. He drew a letter from his pocket and said that it contained facts related to Anna's former meetings with the man. It was addressed to Anna Hudson, general delivery, Paola, Kansas. Rollin had taken the letter from her, which had been the reason why he had left home once again.

More details were later learned about the letter. On the morning it arrived, Anna met James A. Jones, a substitute mail carrier, two blocks east of her home. Jones noticed she seemed excited when she asked if he had a letter for her. He recollected handing her the letter and remembered that she became even more animated as she tore open the envelope and continued walking toward downtown. Somehow, Rollin had gotten hold of the letter, which led to another violent argument between the two of them.

Rollin did not report to work the day after the letter arrived. Neighbors recalled that he spent most of the day on the front porch. That evening, the couple was seen at the local cemetery, where they were heard arguing. Rollin's voice rose to an angry pitch, they said, while his wife's tone was conciliatory. When they returned, Rollin, still angry, scribbled a note to her on a paper bag and stormed out of the house. The poorly spelled note read:

Anna – I am going to K.C. Leave my clothes and those too pictures with Charley. I will be back next faul and get them. You will not be bothered with me eny more. Good-bye. Rollin

Rollin told his wife that he was walking down to the chutes to get some coal, but he just kept going. He didn't stay away for long. On Sunday night, he was back in town and saw G.W. Cole at the chutes. While the two men were talking, Anna approached them. She had been weeping. Cole remembered that she asked Rollin if he would come back home and live with her. Rollin again accused her of infidelity, which brought about a fresh bout of tears from his wife At that point, Cole excused himself and left the couple to talk privately. He later saw them going into their home together, and while he did not speak with the Hudsons again, he saw them sitting on the porch together the next evening with their arms about each other. Once again, their quarrel appeared to have been resolved.

The Hudsons' relationship was so confusing that even their families did not know what was going on. When Rollin's father, J.S. Hudson, arrived in Paola to take charge of the bodies and return them to Ohio for burial, he was surprised to learn that Anna had been with his son in Kansas. He told the newspapers, "I did not hear from Rollin and supposed that his wife was still at her home in Massillon [Ohio]." Hudson spoke to reporters about the times that Rollin and Anna had separated, connecting each circumstance with Roy Adams, Anna's former lover from Akron. Two weeks before, Mr. Hudson had spoken to Anna's father, Jacob Axxe, who informed him that Roy Adams had left Akron. It was believed that the man had come west, which encouraged the police to send out a bulletin asking for information as to his whereabouts. It was later discovered that Adams did indeed leave Akron, but he only went to Canton, Ohio, to take a job in a rubber plant. He was nowhere near Paola when the murders occurred and, apparently, had not had any contact with Anna in quite some time.

With the blue-suited stranger having vanished and Roy Adams being ruled out, the police were desperate to find other suspects in the case. Naturally, they began delving into Anna's "unseemly" private life, looking for current and former lovers who might have committed the heinous crime.

On June 10, it seemed that the missing link had been found. A rambling, three-and-a-half-page letter was discovered on a stairway between Charles Mundell's restaurant and the W.T. Potts grocery story which led up to the office of the local justice of the peace. The letter, dated May 27, was addressed to Anna Hudson and had been mailed from Kansas City. Pinned to the envelope was a note which said the enclosed letter should be turned over to the authorities. The letter was found by William Wilgus and Jack Lyon, who turned it over to Judge Israel Kent, who read portions of it before giving it to Sheriff Marion Chandler. Kent noted that the letter was incoherent, adding, "It was evidently written in a burst of jealous passion."

The letter was never published or even seen in public again. It was apparently given to J.L. Ghent, a detective from Kansas City who had been hired to work on the case. A small section of the letter was "re-created" by the newspapers from the memory of one of the men who saw it. This portion read:

My dear sweetheart: I am becoming desperate. You must arrange a meeting. True love cannot be trifled with in this fashion. You know my love for you and I cannot stand this thing much longer. People have been killed for less, and more my follow. Don't get the idea this is a threat, or that I mean it that way, because it is the real thing. Be true to me. I love you.

No one knows how the letter ended up on the staircase, or even if it was authentic. It's possible that it had been stolen from the crime scene by some curiosity-seeker, or perhaps someone made up the whole thing for fun, we'll never know. The police never put as much stock in the letter as a motive for the murders as the newspapers did. After the paragraph was printed, the papers speculated wildly about the "affinity letter," as they called it, and this invited more speculation and questionable reports from the public, further muddying the investigation.

A few days before the murders, John Powell and Dock Reed said they had been out driving with their wives when they passed a woman they claimed was Anna Hudson two miles southwest of Paola. It was Sunday morning (the same day that Rollin returned and patched things up with her) around 9:30 a.m. and the woman seemed very agitated. When they stopped to see if she needed help, she refused and only asked for the shortest route back into town. She told them that she did not want to take the main road so they told her to cross a field and follow the Missouri Pacific Railroad tracks. Powell and Reed could not say for certain that the woman was Anna Hudson, but they did note that there was no man in the vicinity. Regardless, the newspaper suggested that it had been a "secret meeting" between Anna and her lover.

And it was not the only assignation they claimed took place. The publicity generated more sightings, like the one reported by John Dageforde of East Valley. He was in Paola on the morning of Memorial Day and was sure that he saw Anna on the Hanna Bridge, about a mile and a half southeast of town. There was a man with her whom Dageforde described as about six feet tall and wearing overalls that were turned up at the bottom. Dageforde told the newspaper, "They were quarrelling and seemed greatly excited about something. After I passed them, I turned around and saw the man shake a fist in the woman's face. I didn't think much about the occurrence until I saw Mrs. Hudson's picture in your paper last week. I am positive the woman on the bridge was Mrs. Hudson."

Meanwhile, the police were still following whatever leads they could find. On the Monday morning after the murders, a coal pick was discovered beneath the Frisco Railroad lunch room by Charles S. Gibson. The building was within 200 yards of the Hudson house. The handle of the pick was missing and rumors spread that it was covered with blood and hair and that the murder weapon had been found. It wasn't. According to a railroad worker named Sid Rawson, he had tossed the broken tool under there himself. He had found it more than a year before and used it frequently to dig for worms when he wanted to go fishing.

After this discovery, a group of men went to work in a vacant lot west of the crime scene, searching the weeds and underbrush for clues. Three men, using scythes, cut the long weeds and grass, under the direction of the sheriff, mowing down more than three acres behind the Hudson, Stump, and Longmeyer houses. No clues were discovered and the murder weapon was never found.

Soon, the case went cold. The nation was traumatized by the mass murder in Villisca (not too distant from Paola) on June 10, and the deaths of Rollin and Anna Hudson were almost forgotten. Interestingly, a comment appeared in the *Western Spirit*, the Miami County newspaper, which was attributed to Sheriff Chandler. He was quoted as saying that he was satisfied that the "axe-man" who had slain whole families in different parts of the country over the past year was also guilty of the Hudson murders.

Did Billy the Axman also slay the Hudsons? I believe that he did, despite a few differences in the crime. The most glaring difference was the disappearance of the murder weapon. In every other case, Billy used a weapon of convenience – something that he had found on the property – and left it behind at the scene. In this case, he undoubtedly took it with him to the Longmeyer house, where he attempted to carry out more murders, just as he did in Colorado Springs and attempted to do in Ellsworth. When he broke the lamp chimney, he heard Mrs. Longmeyer stirring and realizing that someone in the house was awake, he fled the scene. This was the same thing that he did in Ellsworth when he realized that Marshal Merritt was awake.

In Paola, the victims were slain in their beds and then covered with a blanket. A coal oil lamp, its glass chimney removed, was used to light the room. The curtains had been pulled closed. The killer had entered the house by removing a screen and climbing in through a window. However, there was no evidence that he tried to wash up, although there was a laundry tub still filled with water in a back room. What happened to the murder weapon is unknown, but it's possible that it was simply tossed away in the railroad yards and never found. Or, if it was, no one realized that it had been used in a murder.

Billy the Axman – if it truly was Billy, and I think that it was – vanished from Paola in the early morning hours of June 6. He likely rode away on one of the dozens of trains that steamed through town each night. The railroads carried him northeast, past Kansas City and on into Iowa, where just four nights later, he committed the most famous (and perhaps final) murders of his bloody spree.

On the night of June 9, Billy the Axman came to Villisca.

5. VILLISCA, IOWA
JUNE 9, 1912

"VILLISCA'S DARKEST NIGHT"

Tucked among the rolling hills and fields of southwestern Iowa is the tiny town of Villisca, a quiet, peaceful home of a few hundred families – and home to a tragic and enduring mystery. It was here, in June 1912, that a horrific mass murder took place, wiping out an entire family and their two young guests. The murder was never solved, casting a pall over Villisca that still lingers today. And this dark cloud may not be the only thing still lingering there. There are many who believe that the spirits of the murdered family may still remain here, as well, their ghosts haunting the old house where they once lived and tragically died.

Villisca is located in a remote corner of Iowa, far off the modern interstate and a good distance from any town with a population of more than a couple of thousand souls. It's an isolated place, accessible only by an old, two-lane highway. Believe it or not, this is in great contrast to how it was back in the early 1900s. In those days, Villisca was a booming town with more than 2,500 residents. The streets were lined with flourishing businesses, and several dozen trains pulled into the depot every day. It was a popular destination in Montgomery County in those days, offering not only stores and shops of just about every kind but restaurants and a theater, as well.

The history of Villisca began in 1859 when D.N. Smith, an agent for the Burlington & Missouri Railroad, laid out the course of a new rail line and platted a town that he called "Villisca." The name is thought to be derived from "waliska," meaning "evil spirit" in the language of the Sac and Fox Indians. Judging by what happened there later, perhaps the Native Americans were on to something. Somehow, the white settlers got the impression that the word meant "pretty place" or "beautiful view." At the time, there was a small settlement located at the site of the future town, which locals called "The Forks" because of its proximity to the junction of the Middle and West Nodaway Rivers. The structures included a log cabin, a frame house and a small store owned by Thomas Moore, who supplemented his living as a farmer by selling supplies to area residents and travelers.

The Civil War slowed down the construction of the railroad, but it didn't dampen

Frank Jones

local enthusiasm for its eventual arrival. In the fall and winter of 1861-1862, a steam-powered sawmill was set up in what would later be the south end of town. The town slowly began to grow and by 1865, Villisca had two stores, a blacksmith shop, a doctor, and a handful of new homes. In 1867, the railroad surveyors returned and finalized the route of the line. Within two years, trains were passing through Villisca on a regular basis. The town began to thrive and would continue to do so for the next 50 years. Much of the growth in town could be attributed to a hardworking young man named Frank Jones.

Jones was born in Steuben County, N.Y., in 1855 and lived an eventful and productive life. He was a farmer, schoolteacher, accountant, merchant, banker, state legislator, and political operator. He traveled in Europe, met with presidents, and wrote legislation regulating the insurance industry that is still in effect today. He worked to form the Iowa Department of Transportation, chaired the House Appropriations Committee, served on the state board of education, and worked for prison reform. He spoke out against socialism and the government control of banks and utilities, advocated conservative politics and warned against wasting natural resources. He also became embroiled in a horrible murder case, which is how he is best remembered in Villisca today.

Jones spent the first few years of his life in the Finger Lakes region of New York. His father, a farmer and carpenter, decided to move his family out west, and in 1862, they moved to southern Michigan and a year later, to a farm in Bureau County, Illinois. In Illinois, Jones attended school for the first time and his teacher became his role model, encouraging the boy to continue his schooling. In the fall of 1871, he left home to attend high school in the northern Illinois town of Princeton, graduating with honors. He was almost immediately offered a job as a teacher.

In the spring of 1875, Jones' father decided to move farther west. Accompanied by Frank and an uncle, they traveled to Iowa looking for land. There was an abundance of rich farmland in the Nodaway River valley around Villisca, but apparently they were unable to afford it. Instead, they purchased a plot of thin, hilly land near the tiny community of Guss, about 10 miles south and east of Villisca. In his later memoirs, Jones called it a "poor buy."

But Jones had no interest in moving to Iowa with his parents. He had a good offer for a teaching job in Illinois and only planned to be away long enough to help his parents move and get settled at their new farm. When the people of Guss learned that young Frank was a schoolteacher, however, they made him an attractive job offer, hoping to entice him to stay. Jones reconsidered his plans. He hadn't yet accepted the position in Illinois so, after weighing his options, he decided to stay in Iowa and start teaching in Guss.

He quickly gained a good reputation as a teacher. He was an enthusiastic young man who was strict in the classroom but had a good sense of humor. This tempered the demands that he made on his students to work hard. For the next seven years, he farmed in the summer and taught school the rest of the year in Guss, or in the nearby small towns of Brooks and Hawleyville. In January 1880, he married Maude Hanes, who would remain his wife until his death, 61 years later.

After Jones married, he decided to try and make his living as a farmer. With help from his father and father-in-law, he built a new home on a small farm that he purchased and did not return to teaching school the following autumn. As luck would have it, the good corn crop of 1880 was followed by a particularly poor one in 1881. He had little choice but to return to teaching once more. He also started working as a bookkeeper for the Villisca hardware and farm implement store that was owned by the firm of Banes & Waterman. The work suited him and at the end of the school year, in the spring of 1882, Jones and Maude moved to Villisca and he went to work for Banes & Waterman full time.

Villisca was in its heyday in the 1880s, enjoying the prosperity that came with the railroads. It was a busy, bustling place. New buildings were being constructed and opportunities abounded. Jones went to work for an agricultural firm at a time that historians have referred to as the Golden Age of Farming in the Midwest. Land wasn't cheap in those days, but it was affordable. A man could make a living and raise a family on 80 acres of land, perhaps more if he was willing to take on a hired hand or two. The railroads had already made it possible to ship products from coast to coast, and soon, markets all over the world would be open. Field work was powered by horses and mules, so as long as there were crops and pasture, there was always fuel. New advances in farm machinery made the hard work easier, giving farmers the chance to prioritize their time. A typical farmer milked cows, kept chickens and made his grocery money each week by selling off the extra eggs, milk and cream. He could also make more money each year when his cattle, hogs, and sheep were shipped by rail to Kansas City or Chicago. For most, farming wasn't a way to get rich, but it offered a good life and was the main reason why towns like Villisca were able to thrive.

More and more people moved to the area and new farmhouses and barns were raised all around the town. The arriving farmers needed plows, rakes, and cultivators and their wives needed cloth, sewing machines, stoves, pots and pans, and dishes. There was enough business in a town like Villisca to support several hardware and implement stores.

Farmers also needed credit. Farming was a way of life where most of the money tended to be made at one time of the year, mostly in the fall, after the harvest. It was common for farmers to take out a loan in the spring so that they had the funds to buy seed and livestock, as well as for everyday expenses. After the fall harvest, the loan was usually paid back. Many businesses also offered credit to farmers, usually under similar terms. Frank Jones dealt with these types of credit accounts in his job as a bookkeeper. Banes & Waterman sold every type of hardware and implement needed by the local farmers and a good share of those items was sold on credit. Jones' new employers were pleased with his work, not only because he was a skilled accountant, but also because he soon proved himself to be a productive bill collector. Merchants like Banes & Waterman, who had been in business for many years, recognized the need to sell on credit and to collect on their accounts, but they also knew how important it was to treat their customers well. They never wanted to offend or make enemies of the customers who were slow to pay, so they left their collections to affable men like Frank Jones. He had been well liked as a local schoolteacher, but those who owed money to the company came to know him as a ruthless and unsympathetic bill collector. He took his collection work seriously and, not surprisingly, there were some who ended up with hard feelings toward him after he pushed them to pay what they owed.

During the winter of 1882-1883, J.S Banes and F.G. Waterman had some sort of falling out and decided to close the business. They divided the inventory and bid against one another for the real estate. Jones could have gone with either man but decided to stay with Banes. He was the older of the former partners, and even though Jones didn't feel that Banes always used the best judgment when issuing credit, he did offer Jones the chance to supplement his bookkeeping income by also selling equipment on commission. It was an opportunity that Jones quickly took advantage of. The following summer, he went door-to-door selling a new model of sewing machine and also worked with Banes to introduce the Minneapolis Twin Binder to area farmers. The mechanized binder offered a fast, labor-saving method to assist with reaping, and this device, along with the new sewing machine, sold well. Jones made money from the sales, and in 1886, he invested some of it in a choice piece of real estate, a corner lot on Fifth Avenue in Villisca. This was considered the most fashionable part of town. He would not build on the lot for several years but what was important was that he was moving up and making plans for the future.

In early 1890, Jones left J.S. Banes and went into business with J.L. Smith, who owned a hardware store. The two men bought out the implement business of J.S. Boise & Son and expanded on the hardware company that Smith owned. Most of the young men who had been Jones' students when he was a teacher were now established farmers in the area and made a reliable customer base for the new business. The new company thrived and Jones was on his way to becoming one of Villisca's wealthiest men.

Two years later, in 1892, Smith bought out the hardware store of Jones' former employer, F.G. Waterman, and went back into the hardware business on his own. He sold his half of Smith & Jones to Jones, and on September 1, 1892, Frank Jones had his own business. For the next 40 years, his location on the south side of the Villisca town square would be known at different times as Jones of Villisca, the Jones Store, and Jones & Company.

In the early 1890s, the steam thresher came on the market, and in 1893, Jones

Villisca in the early 1900s

sold the first one in Villisca to a farmer named C.C. Moore. It was also in 1893 that Jones went into an agreement with the McCormick Company to handle their binders and mowers. It was a profitable move and one that earned McCormick the lifelong loyalty of Frank Jones. Jones of Villisca, as the business was then known, was booming, and in 1894, Jones expanded into the banking business.

The co-owners of the Citizen's Bank of Villisca decided to open a new bank, and Jones became the fifth partner in the Farmer's Bank of Villisca. Jones tapped his list of customers and friends who had also supported his foray into the hardware and implement business. Many of them became depositors in the new bank.

In 1898, Jones decided to focus on the bank and he sold the implement business to the Farlin Brothers. He was now a widely respected man in the community, and he and his family were considered the cream of local society. Bowing to pressure from his wife, he finally got around to building a home on the corner lot on Fifth Avenue. Construction was started in 1898 on a grand Victorian-style home. It was a large, sprawling affair with a wide porch that stretched all the way across the front, as well as an upper verandah, pitched roofs and elaborate gingerbread trim. It was a home that fit the social status of the Jones family.

Over the next three years, Jones began to miss the farm business, and he decided to buy back a half share in the implement store from the Farlin Brothers. In 1902, he bought the other half and became the sole owner again.

Josiah Moore, known as J.B. or Joe, had been hired by the Farlins to run the store for them. Moore, then in his early thirties, was an outgoing, well-liked family man, married to Sarah Montgomery, the daughter of a prominent local farmer. Moore was a natural salesman, and he had been promoted by the Farlins to manage the store. Jones saw no reason not to keep him on.

By that time, Jones likely had little to do with the day-to-day operations of the store. At the age of 45, he was one of the most successful men in the area. His children, Albert and Letha, were good students and looking forward to attending college. Albert planned to study business and work with his father, while Letha planned to follow in her father's footsteps and become a teacher. In addition to being a banker and merchant, Jones was a pillar of the local Methodist church where he taught Sunday School, and had served on the town council. Thanks to his status and influence, he also became interested in politics, and in 1903, he ran for a seat in the Iowa House of Representatives. He won easily and was later appointed chair of the Committee on Penitentiaries and Pardons. Jones, along with Representative Fred Maytag (from the appliance manufacture family) was also responsible for overseeing the management of the University of Iowa. He was re-elected twice, each time by comfortable margins. However, knowing that senators had more influence than representatives, he decided to run for higher office in 1912.

Jones worked hard to make a better life for himself and his family, as did J.B. Moore. He worked for Jones at the store for a few years, but when he learned that the John Deere Company was looking for dealers that would handle their equipment exclusively, he made a deal with them. His new John Deere dealership opened directly across the street from Jones' store. No one can say whether Jones and Moore were friendly competitors or not, but this business climate has been the subject of much debate over the years. It was a situation that some believed gave Jones a motive for the killings. Could animosity towards his former employee have boiled over into murder?

J.B. Moore was born in Hanover County, Illinois, and came to Iowa with his parents while still a child. He grew up in Page County and was one of 16 children, although four of his siblings died very young. Another, Willie, died at age 20, and Moore's sister Anna died in November 1910. At the time of the murders, J.B had been a resident of Villisca for 13 years, having been employed by Jones for nine of those years. He was known as a hard-working man, generous with credit and kind to friends, neighbors, and customers alike.

Sarah Montgomery Moore seemed to have even fewer enemies than her husband. She had been born in Knox County, Illinois, in 1873, and had moved to Iowa with her parents and her sister, Mary, in 1894. She was also an active member of Villisca's First Presbyterian Church, and was beloved by the children she taught in Sunday school. Sarah was considered to be a generous and kind-hearted person and a devoted mother to her children. The Moores' first child, Herman, was born in 1901, followed by Katherine two years later. The two youngest boys, Boyd and Paul, were seven and five years old respectively in the summer of 1912.

The last day of J.B. Moore's life was a Sunday. After milking the cows and doing some chores, he had breakfast and then walked downtown. Although the post office was not open on Sundays, the lobby was and he retrieved his late mail from Saturday. Moore then went to his store, exchanging greetings along the way with several people on the street. After reading the mail and doing a little bookwork, he returned home.

The Moores had purchased their small, two-story frame house in 1903. Although it was located not too far from the home of Frank Jones, the two houses were nothing alike. The Moore house dated back to 1868 and had no indoor plumbing or electricity. It was a happy home but it was a tight fit for a family of six. The downstairs consisted of a kitchen with a small pantry, a parlor, and one small bedroom where Katherine slept and Sarah used for sewing. Upstairs were two bedrooms and an unfinished attic that was used for storage. Boyd, Herman and Paul shared the larger upstairs bedroom on the south side of the house and J.B. and Sarah used the low-ceilinged, cramped room at the top of the stairs. It was in the attic storage room, accessible through a small door, that some believe the murderer hid and waited for his victims to go to sleep that night.

The Moores were regular attendees at the Presbyterian church a few blocks west of their home. It was a short walk for Sunday morning services, and at Sunday School that morning, Katherine met two of her friends, sisters Lena and Ina Stillinger, aged 11 and 8 respectively. They were the daughters of Joe and Sarah Stillinger, who lived on a farm about two miles south of town.

Joseph Stillinger, the father of the two girls, had come to Villisca when he was 14 years old. His father died during the Civil War and his mother settled a few miles north of Villisca on land that was given to her as the widow of a soldier. His brother, George, bought another farm nearby. When Joseph married Sarah Hastings, he built a large home across the creek from his mother and brother and did so well with his farm that he eventually bought out his brother's land and incorporated it into what came to be known as Doddy Hollow Farm. Stillinger became an expert in horticulture and the farm boasted several fine orchards of fruit and nut trees. He also raised sheep and Angus cattle that had been imported from Scotland, operated a seed corn business, and was involved in a small coal-shipping venture. He received the most acclaim for his orchards, however, and traveled widely to speak to farmers under the sponsorship of Iowa State College. On a number of occasions, he appeared before the state legislature to discuss a statewide horticulture program. In spite of being respected for his hard work and efforts on behalf of the state's farmers, his was not an appealing personality to most of those who knew him. He had little time for anything but work, never socialized, and refused to attend church. These were traits that failed to make him likable in a small town such as Villisca where being sociable counted for a great deal. On Sunday, June 9, Stillinger refused to take his daughters to church and quarreled with his Sarah when she let them walk into town. Stillinger's bad nature led some to consider him a suspect in the murders, and he was among the people that C.W. Tobie, an agent with the Burns Detective Agency, investigated in July 1912. He wrote:

This morning in resuming this investigation, I took up the report concerning Joe Stillinger and made inquiry concerning his character and general reputation, which I find to be that of a close fisted hard working farmer, who is quite prosperous; that he made his money by hard work and close attention to his business. He is a wicked man, but I was unable to learn that there was anything really detrimental to his character except that he is an awful man to curse and believes that work alone is about all any young farmer needs. He is reported to be a man of his word and strictly honest. I was unable to verify any quarrel between he and his wife on the day prior to the murder or concerning his objection to his children attending church services.

That particular Sunday was the traditional date of the annual Children's Day program. It was always held in the evening, starting at 8 p.m., and the Sunday School classes had been practicing for weeks. The Stillinger girls planned on having dinner with their grandmother in town, spending the afternoon there, and then returning to her house that evening to spend the night. After talking to Katherine, though, they decided that it would be more fun to spend the night at the Moore house. Katherine asked her parents for permission and Sarah promised to check with Lena and Ina's parents.

On that same Sunday, Frank Jones, like J.B. Moore, had gone to the post office and spent some time at his store. He wrote and received a lot of letters that summer, most of them connected to his senate campaign. He was not well known outside of the immediate area, but he did know a number of implement dealers and bankers in places like Mills County and knew he could count on them for support. That morning, he sent several letters to ask not only for their votes, but for their assistance in arranging speaking engagements in their towns.

Letha Jones was living with her parents that summer. She would not resume teaching until the fall and so she planned to visit with friends, help her mother with the house and garden, and catch up on her reading.

Albert Jones was in the second year of his marriage in 1912. His wife, the former Dona Bentley, was considered to be one of the area's most beautiful women. Dona had an oval face with classic features and lively brown eyes. Her fashionable bouffant hairstyle, spirited personality, and shapely figure made her the epitome of the era's standard of young female perfection: the "Gibson Girl," popularized by the drawings of Charles Dana Gibson. Many suspected that the dark-haired beauty had married the plodding and portly Albert for his family's money. Albert was not seen as particularly ambitious or intelligent. Despite the grand plans that he had espoused when he was younger, he never took over his father's business. When Albert and Dona met, he was the only son of a wealthy businessman and heir to a growing fortune. Dona was teaching school at the time and, according to rumor, the family with whom she boarded was upset by her scandalous behavior. It was said that she and Albert often went off together for the night, something that was considered taboo for unmarried people at the time. Gossip had it that her questionable behavior continued after her marriage.

On Saturday, June 8, Albert and Dona had taken the train to Clarinda to spend the night with some friends. They returned on Sunday evening at about 6 p.m. Their home was the first one north of the alley behind the Moore house. While Albert was outside that evening, he ran into J.B. Moore. The two men met in the alley and part of their conversation was overheard by three youths, one of them Lawrence Gridley, 17-year-old farm boy who had just come into town and was putting his buggy into the barn owned by a relative who lived next door to Albert. The conversation would later be recounted – and would be of much interest to the authorities.

Around 7 p.m., while J.B. was still in conversation with Albert Jones, Sarah Moore called to her husband from their yard and asked him to come home and get ready to return to church for the evening program. He walked into the house and before changing clothes, telephoned the Stillinger farm and asked if it was all right for the girls to spend the night with them. A sister, Blanche, answered and told J.B. that her parents were outside. J.B. explained that the street lights were not working that night and Ina and Lena didn't want to walk to their grandmother's house in the dark. They were welcome to stay with the Moores, he told her. Blanche said that she was sure that her parents wouldn't mind and that she would tell them where the girls were.

At the Presbyterian church, Reverend Wesley J. Ewing began the Children's Day program promptly at 8 p.m. After a prayer and a few opening remarks, the program was turned over to Sarah Moore. She introduced the Sunday school teachers, who in turn presented their classes. The children sang, recited scriptures, and put on short skits based on Bible stories.

Seated in the back of the church was a minister that few of the congregation knew. His name was Reverend Lyn George Jacklin Kelly, and he had traveled from his home in Macedonia on Saturday to preach at two country churches in the area, Pilot Grove and Arlington. He had then been brought to Villisca, where he watched the program and planned to spend the night with Reverend Ewing and his wife, Nora, before returning home on an early morning train.

Across the street in the Methodist Church, Frank Jones was seated in the back row, which was unusual for him. Normally, the Jones family sat up front. Although it was not raining outside, Jones had brought a raincoat with him to church. The humid air had turned the sky dark and rain threatened. It was not a typical Sunday evening service at the Methodist Church. An outdoor revival meeting by a boisterous sect known as the "Holy Rollers" was being held in town that week. Because of the threat of rain, the Methodists had offered them the use of their building. There was a good crowd on hand, including the Holy Rollers, Methodists who usually came to church on Sunday evening and probably a few who showed up out of curiosity. The Holy Rollers were a Pentecostal-type group who were reputed to go into religious frenzies in which they spoke in tongues, tore off their clothes, and rolled up and down in the aisles. No one probably expected anything so outlandish to happen, but they hated to miss it if it did. As it turned out, the service was quite orderly. The only odd incident to occur – and it was barely noticed – came near the end of the evening when Frank Jones got up and walked. Maude and Letha Jones had left for church a few minutes before Frank, their evening stroll taking them past the home of Albert and Dona. Like many others in town on that warm night, Albert and Dona were sitting on the front porch, so Maude and Letha stopped for a moment to visit. Letha asked if they were coming to church. They were not. Both said they were tired from the long weekend and planned to go to bed early.

The Villisca Presbyterian Church

The Children's Day program ended at 9:30 p.m. and it was nearly 10 p.m. before the Moores and their two overnight guests got home. J.B., Sarah, their children and the two Stillinger girls noisily and happily entered the house and closed the door behind them. They didn't bother to lock it. Who locked their doors in such a quiet, peaceful little town?

The Ewings and Reverend Kelly left the church and walked across the street to the parsonage. They sat down in the parlor and visited for a few minutes before getting ready for bed. Ewing was bothered by nasal infections (he was later to die due to complications from surgery to remove a nasal polyp.) Nora Ewing suffered from asthma. On some nights the only relief they found was to sleep outside in a tent. Reverend Kelly would sleep upstairs in the guest room and the Ewings went out to their tent in the back yard.

Late that night, the peacefulness of the town was shattered, leaving behind eight bloody corpses in a little house along one of Villisca's tree-lined streets – streets that were darker than normal. Thanks to a squabble between the town council and the company providing electricity to the community, the electric power had been shut down on June 9. Even though the street lights in town were dim, and only located in the downtown area, even the small amount of light they offered was absent. Electricity was quickly restored when the bodies at the Moore house were discovered the next day, but the crime and the absence of street lighting led at least one newspaper reporter to refer to June 9 as "the darkest night in Villisca's history." And it truly was...

What happened on that "darkest night"? Who killed the Moore family and the Stillinger sisters? And what occurred to cause at least some of the spirits of this terrible crime to linger behind?

6. BLOODY MURDER

On the morning of June 10, 1912, Mary Peckham rose from her bed around 4 a.m. It was laundry day. In addition to her usual chores, she reserved every Monday morning as the day of the week to wash and dry the clothing belonging to herself and her husband, Elmer. She did not have as much laundry as she did when her children were young, which was a good thing since Mary was starting to feel her age. Her health had not been good of late. in fact, she would not survive the year. It was a death, some said, that was hastened by the events of that day.

Mary started the water heating in the kitchen and may have had some breakfast, or coffee, before she went outside at just after 5 a.m. Her husband had already left for his job at the town cemetery. Mary's work would take her in and out of the house several times over the course of the next two hours. She went about her tasks, wringing water from the wash and hanging the wet garments on the line that stretched across her back yard. As she worked, she had a clear view of the Moore house next door, but thought little about how quiet the place was until she was nearly finished with the wash and saw that the clock in her kitchen now read 7 a.m.

Mary and Elmer had been neighbors of the Moore family for nearly 10 years. She knew J.B. and thought the world of Sarah, as almost everyone else did. Mary was especially fond of the four children. She had last seen the family the previous evening around 8 p.m., as they were leaving for church.

Now, she realized there was something strange about the Moore house. She would later call it an "odd stillness." J.B. was usually outside early in the morning, tending to a few chores before leaving for work. Sarah was always up at dawn to start breakfast and her own chores for the day. The Moores were all early risers, and with a house filled with young children, mornings were always hectic. But on this day, the curtains were all drawn and there was no movement of any kind. The livestock in the barn was growing restless. The cows needed to be milked, the horses needed to be fed, and the chickens should have been let out by now.

Could the Moores be sick? Mary waited for a few more minutes and then finally decided to go next door and check on the family. She was unable to shake the idea that something was wrong. Mary approached the house and knocked on the door. It was eerily quiet inside. She waited for a few moments and then knocked again. Once more, there was no answer and so she tried to open the door, thinking

The J.B. Moore house in 1912

that she might poke her head inside and call for Sarah. She pulled on the door handle and discovered that it was locked from the inside. Perhaps the Moores had simply overslept. It had been a busy night for them, and despite the fact that this was entirely against their nature, perhaps they were still in bed.

Mary went back into her own yard, deep in thought and still very troubled. She knew that J.B.'s father, who lived on a farm south of town, was in poor health. Perhaps he had gotten sick or died during the night and the Moores had been called there. Mary returned to the Moore yard and went out to the small barn behind the house. She could at least let out the chickens, she thought, knowing that Sarah would not mind. She shooed the chickens out into the yard and then went back home. But the more she thought about the silent house next door, the more she worried.

Finally, when she could stand it no more, she placed a telephone call to J.B.'s brother, Ross. He had already left for the drug store owned by Dr. Lomas that he managed. His wife, Jessie, answered the telephone. Mary asked about J.B. and Ross' father, and then explained why she was so concerned. Jessie rang up the drug store and Ross then called his brother's implement store. Ed Selley, Moore's senior employee, said that he had not seen J.B. that day, but offered to call out to the farm of the senior Moores on the Mutual line to see if he was there. Villisca had two phone systems at the time: the Mutual system and the Bell system. Ross was on the Bell line and his parents had a Mutual telephone. J.B., like many other businessmen of the time, had installed both lines at his store. Selley made the call and spoke to Moore's mother. He learned that there were no problems that she knew of and that they had not heard from J.B.

Selley had his own concerns about J.B.'s whereabouts that morning. He was supposed to go out into the country and make sales calls on local farmers that day and he couldn't leave until Moore arrived with the horse and buggy that was normally used for such trips. He was watching the clock and waiting for J.B. to arrive when Mary Peckham called Ross. Selley decided that he would walk over to the Moore house and see what was going on for himself. He met Mary in the yard and after talking with her for a moment, went into the barn and fed the horses. He agreed with Mary that the Moores didn't seem to be around, but had no idea where they might have gone or even what he should do about it. Mary asked if he would milk the cows and he told her that he had better not take the time since he needed to get back to the store, but he would send a man named Carl, who worked at the implement store, to take care of it. Carl usually did the milking for the Moores whenever J.B. was out of town. Selley returned to the store, still planning to make his sales calls that morning.

Ross Moore, like Mary Peckham, was bothered by the situation. There was something not quite right about it. After worrying for a while, he left the drug store and walked across the town square to his brother's store. He arrived just a few minutes after Selley had left. When told that Selley had gone to tend the livestock at his brother's house, Ross followed after him. He took a different route, though, and the two men did not see one another. Selley was on his way back by the time Ross left the store.

When Ross Moore arrived at J.B.'s house, he was also disturbed by the eerie stillness of the place. He went to the barn, checked on the horses and saw that they had just been fed. As he was walking out of the barn, Mary Peckham came over to meet him. She told him that Selley had been there and planned to send someone to do the milking. Mary was quite flustered by this time. She had continued to try and raise someone at the neighboring home, but to no avail. Ross tried the door himself and then leaned up to peer into the downstairs bedroom window. It was too dark to see anything inside because the curtains were drawn. He rapped hard on the window, but there was no answer. He returned to the door, banging on it and shouting for his brother and sister-in-law. There was still no answer, so he produced his own set of keys and looked through the ring until he found one that opened the front door.

Ross stepped into the parlor with Mary Peckham behind him. She stopped at the entryway, however, and did not venture any farther into the house. Ross noticed how neat and clean the front parlor was. Even though he did not regularly visit his brother's house, he knew Sarah prided herself on keeping the place spotless. The downstairs had just three main rooms. The front door opened into the parlor and adjoining this room was a small downstairs bedroom, which was Katherine's room. Another doorway from the parlor led into the kitchen, which included a pantry and a side porch. There was a doorway in the kitchen that opened to the narrow stairs that led up to the second floor.

Mary Peckham had noticed an "odd stillness" about the house, and to Ross, the heavy silence was ominous. He knew that something was wrong, but he was not prepared for what he was about to see. Ross looked around, finding no one in the kitchen. He called out but there was no answer. A few steps away was the door to the downstairs bedroom and Ross passed through the doorway and entered the room. The window shades were closed, but even in the murky darkness, he could see that the top sheets had been tightly pulled up to the top of the bed. There were two figures under the sheet, which he suddenly realized was covered with dark stains. The room stank of copper and death. He could see a small hand dangling limply from beneath the edge of the sheet.

Ross frantically backed out of the room, pounded out to the porch and told Mary Peckham that it was bad and that she should call the police, summon Marshal

Horton, anyone…. there were dead people in the house!

Ross sat down on the edge of the porch, trying to grasp what he had seen. Mary hurried back to her house and telephoned J.B. Moore's store. Ed Selley answered and told her that he just saw the city marshal, Hank Horton, walk past. He would catch him and be there as soon as he could. Carl was already on his way to the Moore house to do the milking when Mary Peckham called. Ross was sitting dazed on the front porch when he arrived. They spoke for a moment and Ross told him that he didn't need to worry about milking the cows.

He muttered, "Something terrible has happened here."

Ed Seeley and Marshal Horton arrived a few minutes later. They went into the house through the front door and Seeley only glanced into the parlor bedroom before hurrying back outside again. He wanted no part of what had happened in the house.

"I was scared there, I admit it," he later said. "Hank, I'll get out of here. Those were the words I used. I remember them very well."

As Selley stepped back onto the porch, Harry Moore, another of J.B.'s brothers also arrived. Even though Ross tried to stop him, Harry pushed his way inside but Marshal Horton ordered him back outside. The others waited on the porch while Horton searched the rest of the house by himself.

Horton returned to the small bedroom off the parlor. The room was dark and filled with gloom. He struck a match and approached the bed, looking down at the two still forms that had been covered with the bloody bed sheet. Horton had never had to deal with a murder before – such things just didn't happen in towns like Villisca. Likely nervous about what he had to do, he blew out the match and decided to open the curtain and let some light into the room. As he did so, he saw that a black cloth covered the mirror in the room. He also saw a rusty ax leaning against the bedroom wall.

Horton backed out of the room and went into the kitchen. He took a quick glance about the room and then turned to the arrow stairs that led to the second floor. He lit another match as he climbed, making a sharp right turn and then carefully going up the creaking steps. It was darker in the stairwell than it had been in the parlor bedroom. As he reached the second floor, he looked through the railing and could see a bed in the dim light. There were tangled forms on the bed and dark splashes that he feared could only be blood. He stepped over to the window and raised the shade, his stomach clenching as he saw the bodies of J.B. and Sarah Moore, their heads smashed into the pillows. He looked down and saw a lamp sitting on the floor. There was blood spattered all over the walls of the small bedroom.

Horton continued on into the south bedroom. He raised the shade and looked at the three beds in the room. In the southeast corner was a bed containing the body of a child and another small body was lying in a bed in the northeast corner. In the third bed tucked into the northwest corner, blood-soaked blankets covered the forms of two more bodies.

Everyone in the house had been murdered in their beds. Their heads had been crushed with terrible force and their bodies carefully covered with sheets and blankets. At some point, probably later in the day, Horton saw marks in the upstairs ceiling that he realized were made from the swing of an ax. Whoever had killed the people in the house had likely been filled with rage. The murders were brutal and all of the victim's skulls had been crushed with an ax.

Hank Horton left the house, shaken and upset. He came back out onto the porch, his chest heaving, fighting for breath. But he had a job to do and he was determined to do it. John Henry "Hank" Horton was just a few days shy of his fifty-first birthday at the time of the murders. He had lived in the area his entire life and was the son of early settlers to Villisca, who raised him just outside of town. He

Villisca town marshal Hank Horton

farmed, or worked for farmers, until becoming a carpenter. The city was looking for a night watchman and, for a few years, Horton supplemented his income by walking the streets and alleys at night, checking doors and locking up drunks. It was a part-time job that he shared with several others, but he liked it well enough that he applied for the city marshal position when it opened in 1911. It was an era when law enforcement officers in small towns were hired to simply keep the peace. They were not expected to have expertise in performing criminal investigations – serious crimes rarely happened in such places. His job was to check doors in the business district to make sure they were locked, break up fights, and run undesirables out of town. He was a tough, ready-for-anything kind of man and he was fully capable of doing what he had been hired to do. But on the morning of June 10, Horton left the Moore house knowing that he was totally out of his depth. He told the few people standing outside not to let anyone into the house and then went downtown looking for Dr. Cooper.

Dr. J. Clark Cooper was a local physician and surgeon. He was 39 years old and a graduate of the College of Medicine at the University of Iowa. He had stopped at the post office that morning, where he picked up his mail and the newspaper before walking over to his office. He settled down to read the newspaper before his first patients arrived but was interrupted when Hank Horton rushed in and demanded that he come with him to a murder scene. We can only imagine his surprise at the request. Dr. Cooper, a small town physician in rural America, had never been called to a murder scene before. Such things just didn't happen in his town...

Almost as soon as the murders were discovered, the news of the massacre traveled quickly throughout Villisca. Word spread, first to the Moore family and then beyond. Another medical doctor, E.C. Hough, and Reverend Ewing had both been called and arrived at the house before Horton returned with Dr. Cooper. Mary

Peckham was making telephone calls, as was Jessie Moore, and probably everyone they told reported it to someone else. The telephone operators heard all of the details and they passed along the news to others they thought should know.

Frank Jones was at the construction site of the new First National Bank building that was going up on the Villisca town square when he heard the news. He hurried over to the house but was not allowed inside. He shook Ross Moore's hand and tried to offer some comfort. He stood around for a few minutes and then went to the town hall. As an elected state official and former city councilman, he wanted to do what he could to make sure that the investigation ran smoothly. He was on hand while Horton made telephone calls to Montgomery County Sheriff Oren Jackson, County Attorney William Ratcliff's office, and to a private detective to help with the case.

The Moores were a large and popular family with a wide circle of friends, customers, acquaintances, and relatives. People from all over the county either knew J.B. or Sarah, or one of their family members. If they didn't know them, then just the rumor of a mass murder being discovered in Villisca was enough to make people drop what they were doing and head into town. Farmers later remembered getting word of the murders while working in their fields that morning. One couple from Villisca left on a 7 a.m. train to Clarinda, a few miles to the south, and the news of the murder beat them there. The speed at which the news traveled was important later, as investigators tried to sort out who, if anyone, spoke of the crime before the bodies were discovered.

People from all over the area began to descend on the Moore house. They were filled with a mixture of shock and curiosity that morning – terror would come later that night.

Hank Horton, Dr. Cooper, Dr. Hough, Dr. F.S. Williams (who had been brought to the scene by Ed Seeley), and Reverend Ewing were among the first to go through the house and later testified at the coroner's inquest. Dr. A.L. Linquist, the county coroner, lived in Stanton, and he arrived at the scene around 9 a.m. He would provide the most detailed investigation of the scene.

When the group went into the house, they turned back the sheets over the two bodies in the downstairs bedroom. The faces of the two girls were smashed and unrecognizable, but by now everyone knew who they were. The bed had been pushed into the corner of the room and Ina Stillinger, eight years old, was closest to the wall. She was lying on her back, her nightgown undisturbed. The investigators believed that she was killed instantly by a blow from the flat edge of the ax, and then, like the others, was struck in the head several times after she was dead. A gray coat belonging to a little boy, possibly taken from the closet in the room, was used to cover her face.

Lena Stillinger lay on the side of the bed by which the killer had stood. She was found with her nightgown pushed up and no undergarments on. Her body was drawn into an odd position, possibly positioned that way by the killer. Dr. Williams noted that she was lying on her right side, her leg protruding sideways from the bed and her right hand and arm shoved up under her pillow. He believed that she had been turned that way after her death because blood had already seeped through the pillow and onto the bed before her arm had been placed there. There was also a smear of blood on the inside of her right knee, suggesting that someone had perhaps turned the body slightly after she had been killed.

The white dresses the girls had worn the night before were at the foot of the bed. Some underclothing and other garments lay on the floor. The doctors all agreed that the girls had not been raped (nor had anyone else in the

A modern photograph of the downstairs bedroom where the bodies of the Stillinger sisters were found.

house) but the position of Lena's body and the removal of her underwear led to speculation that some sort of act of sexual perversion had taken place.

The girls were too badly beaten to be immediately recognized, but Bibles on the nightstand next to the bed bore their names. In addition, almost everyone that had been at the church the night before knew that the Stillinger girls had gone home with the Moores after the program was over. News had already spread around town that the girls were the two extra victims in the house. Tragically, Sarah Stillinger had called the Moore home early that morning, wondering when her daughters would be coming home, but no one answered. When she tried to place the call again, later that morning, the telephone operator told her, "Everyone in that house is dead." This offhand remark was how Mrs. Stillinger learned that her daughters had been murdered.

Lena and Ina left behind seven living siblings and Mrs. Stillinger was pregnant at the time of the murders. She was to give birth to a stillborn son, yet another tragedy in a family that had already suffered far too much.

Dr. Cooper spoke later about the white dresses, the bloodstained sheets, the ax leaning against the wall, the oil lamp with its glass chimney removed and the battered faces of the two little girls, but he also admitted that he was not as observant as he should have been. He often spoke of seeing Lena's hand dangling out from under the sheet and the ruined features of the girls. He admitted that these things shook him to the point that he was "dazed and merely did what I had to do." He followed Horton upstairs, plodding behind him and already sickened by death. He counted six more bodies but failed to examine them closely. The one thing he did note was that J.B. seemed to have been struck more times than the others. The doctors pointed out that the victims had all been struck first with the flat side of the ax, then later with the blade. A few were only struck a few times, but J.B. had been hit over and over again – and with such ferocity that marks had

J.B. and Sarah's bedroom at the top of the stairs

been cut into the ceiling by the backswing of the ax.

Dr. Williams later recounted that he had discovered J.B. on the south side of the bed, his head facing west. He was on his back, his left hand on his chest and his face obliterated by blows from the ax. Sarah was also on her back, with deep gashes in her face and head, but Dr. Williams noted that the damage was less than had been done to J.B. Dr. Linquist reported:

> Mr. Moore's face was cut worse than [Sarah's]. The top of the skull was crushed and the face was cut. The eyes were gone and the cheeks were cut but the cheekbones were not crushed in. The children were cut in about the same way. The tops of their heads were broken and crushed in and it looked as if the brains had been chopped out by some instrument.

After examining the Moores, Dr. Williams went into the south bedroom. It was there that he found the slaughtered children. His notes read:

> Just at the left hand, east side of the room was a cot, another bed standing there with a little boy in it, he was sleeping on his stomach, top of his head was all beaten in, there was a gauze undershirt on top of his head, soaked up with blood and I lifted that off, lifted it to see which one it was, then in the bed, angling at the foot of the bed, southeast corner of the room was another bed with a little girl, and her head was all beaten in, and on top of her bed was a little dress and it was all blood spattered, and I think it was partly curled up over her head and covers pulled up over her face, and in the southwest corner of the room were two little boys lying with both of tops of their heads beaten in, and blood spattered on everything, and blood over the pillows, did not look as though they were moved at all.

The most detailed investigation of the scene was performed later that day by Dr. Linquist, the county coroner, but even his examination left much to be desired. It would be easy for us to say that the murders were never solved because of mismanagement by local law officers, or because of carelessness on the part of the investigators, but this really is not the case. In 1912, such a crime would have been difficult to solve no matter where it occurred. At that time, fingerprinting was still a new idea, crime scene photographs were rarely taken and DNA testing would be unimaginable for decades to come. In short, investigators in rural areas like Villisca simply did not encounter crimes of this magnitude in 1912. In spite of this, the investigators managed to make some notes of the scene, or all of the clues would have been completely lost. As it was, though, any evidence left in the house was likely destroyed – either by the investigators or the hordes of curiosity-seekers that descended on the scene.

Modern photographs of the kitchen and the front parlor of the Moore house, looking much like they did in 1912.

Dr. Linquist and other investigators put together a list of clues but, at the time, little of it made sense. In fact, they managed to make the mystery even more perplexing. What was known for certain was that all eight people in the Moore house had been bludgeoned to death in their sleep at some point between midnight and 5 a.m. Doctors who examined the bodies guessed that the murders had occurred closer to midnight.

It is unknown whether the adults or the children were murdered first but none of them stirred while the killer was at work.

In the south bedroom, two of the Moore children, Herman and Katherine were sleeping in separate beds. The room held three beds. The younger boys, Boyd and Paul, were sleeping in the third bed. According to testimony given in the coroner's

63

inquest by Dr. Cooper, the children were also killed in their sleep. Dr. Cooper testified, "Not a face was exposed. The windows were all down, the curtains were all down and when I went into the south room, I reached up to run the curtain up, and in so doing I knocked that curtain down, I did not put that back up. It seems there was sort of a three-window effect, one big window and one little window on each side. I gave it a quick jerk, and I knocked it off, it was so dark in there, and the other in the back room, I ran that up myself."

The murder weapon was presumed to be the bloody ax that had been left behind in the downstairs bedroom occupied by the Stillinger girls. The ax belonged to J.B. Moore. It was smeared with blood and it looked like the killer had made an effort to wipe it off.

A kerosene lamp was found sitting on the floor at the foot of J.B. and Sarah's bed. The glass chimney had been removed and placed under the dresser and the wick had been turned down almost all of the way. Another lamp, with its chimney also removed, was found at the foot of the bed where the Stillinger girls had been sleeping. With the wicks turned down the way that they were, the lamps would have provided only a very small amount of light.

The ceilings in the upstairs bedrooms had gouge marks in them that had apparently been made by the upswing of the ax. This would imply that the killer had used a fairly decent amount of force when striking his victims. It would also suggest that the striking of the victims' skulls, as well as the contact with the ceiling would have made a fairly loud noise. Strangely, no one in the house seems to have been awakened during the murders. There is no indication how the killer could have managed this during an obviously frenzied "spree" murder, but somehow he did.

In each case, the faces of his victims were covered with bed sheets or clothing after they had been killed. Modern criminal psychologists would suggest that indicated the killer either knew the victims or that he felt guilty for what he had done. Some have suggested that this means that the killer could not have been a stranger to the victims. But this is short-sighted thinking because it's possible that the killer possessed a mental condition that caused him to immediately regret the murders, even though he was incapable of stopping himself from committing them. Or it's possible that someone other than the killer covered the bodies – someone who stumbled onto the scene later. This is part of the theory that I personally subscribe to and which will be explored later.

Whatever his state of mind might have been, the killer did not immediately leave the house when he was finished with his work. There were a number of oddities about the scene that were either left behind by the killer or by someone else after the murders had been committed.

In addition to the bodies being covered, all of the mirrors in the house were covered too. The curtains were drawn on all of the windows. Two of the windows did not have curtains. These were found covered with clothing from the Moores' closets. This may have allowed the killer (or someone else) to light the lamps so he could see what he was doing without any light being visible from the outside. If lights were seen burning in the house in the very early morning hours, it could have attracted attention from the neighbors.

A pan of bloody water was found in the kitchen, possibly where the killer had attempted to wash up. Next to it was a plate of food that he had prepared but had not eaten. The killer spent quite some time in the house, likely calming down after the murders. But why prepare a meal if he did not plan to eat it? It's possible that he may have realized the lateness of the hour as the sun began to lighten the sky, and left the food untouched. Investigators also found a slab of bacon, weighing about two pounds and wrapped in a dishcloth, lying in the kitchen. Another slab of similar size was found in the icebox.

Dr. Linquist noted that one of Sarah's shoes had been moved after the murder. The shoe, he said, was on J.B.'s side of the bed. Blood was inside it, and it was found on its side with blood under it. He inferred that after J.B.'s head had been crushed, blood flowed from the pillow into the shoe and on the floor around it. He also found a magazine on the floor of the downstairs bedroom with what he thought was a heel print on it. There was no indication as to whether or not this was a clue left by the killer.

Before the killer – or anyone else that was there – left the house, he locked all of the doors. This was something not usually done in Villisca at the time, ensuring that there would be some delay before the bodies would be discovered.

The investigators compiled an impressive list of evidence from the scene, but with no fingerprints to match and without the technology to analyze hair and blood samples, footprints or trace evidence, there was little to go on. The most promising physical item of evidence was a piece of a keychain that was found on the floor in the downstairs bedroom. It did not appear to belong to anyone in the house and the police deduced that it must have been left behind by the killer.

But was it? We may never know, for the killer has undoubtedly taken his gruesome secrets with him to the grave. Why were the murders committed? Were the Moores targeted by someone they knew? Or were they random victims – as I believe? Or does the apparent randomness of the killings complicate the mystery even further?

Hank Horton traveled back and forth between his office in the town hall and the Moore house several times that morning. Besides trying to make sense of what had happened and what he needed to do about it, he spent quite a lot of time placing telephone calls and conferring with Frank Jones. He had contacted the county sheriff, who recommended a private detective named Thomas O'Leary, employed by the Kirk Agency. O'Leary agreed to come and was expected in Villisca later that night or the next morning. Horton also asked about bringing in some bloodhounds from the town of Beatrice to try and track the killer but hesitated to authorize it because he was afraid there would be a problem with getting the bill paid. Jones told him to go ahead and bring the dogs in, that he'd guarantee the payment if necessary.

Sheriff Jackson had arrived early at the scene but, unfortunately, he was almost as poorly skilled at criminal investigation as Horton was. He had traveled widely and had worked at various jobs over the years, including as a prospector in Alaska in the late 1890s. He spent two years there but found no gold and returned to Montgomery County a wiser man, but not a wealthier one. After serving a term as deputy, he was elected sheriff, but his daily duties consisted mostly of serving papers and tending the jail, not tracking down murderers.

Horton and Jackson were the only lawmen that the area had to offer. County Attorney Ratcliff was on business in eastern Iowa and would not return until late Monday night. Thomas O'Leary was an experienced investigator, but he would not arrive for many hours. So, on the morning of June 10, Horton and Jackson suddenly found themselves in charge of dealing with a crime the like of which neither of them had ever before seen. Neither of them was even remotely prepared.

The state of Iowa could not be relied on for help, at least not in the short term. In those days, there was no state police force of any kind. The attorney general was the top law enforcement official, but his staff did not include any investigators. When the state needed detectives, they got them from the same place that private individuals did: from private agencies. The leading agencies at the time were Pinkerton, Burns, and Kirk. There were also many smaller agencies in large cities and most medium-size ones. They worked for wages and reward money. Some waited for calls while others took it upon themselves to work a case hoping they might be hired or rewarded for the information they uncovered. Detectives of this sort were in great demand and, until state and local governments began training their own investigators, they were the closest thing to experts when it came to investigating crime scenes. Detectives, especially those from the major agencies, were given a great amount of respect by both the public and by police officers, but the quality of their skills varied widely. Some of them were good, some bad, and many of them were downright corrupt. It would be the Villisca murders that would finally push the state of Iowa to put together a state-operated criminal investigative agency.

Detectives began arriving in Villisca within hours of the murders and dozens more began showing up over the course of the next few weeks. Some of them were asked to come, most were not, but all of them came with the hope of solving the crime. The good detectives merely wanted justice to be done while others hoped for financial gain or simply the fame that would come with solving the mystery.

After making the call to detective O'Leary and a plea for bloodhounds, Horton returned to the Moore house and was dismayed to see that the scene was overrun with onlookers. Horton had ordered the town's night watchman to keep out everyone who had no business in the house, but he hadn't done it. Horton hurriedly called in the Villisca unit of the Iowa National Guard, and by noon the scene was roped off and an organized effort was made to control who got in and out. By then, the damage had already been done. No one knows how many people were in the house that morning, or worse, how many took souvenirs with them. Horton later estimated that perhaps 20 people went through the house, but other estimates – likely more accurate ones – numbered the curiosity-seekers at 100 or more. Even if they didn't steal anything, they undoubtedly touched objects that they shouldn't have, picking them up and putting them down somewhere else. Even after the National Guard enclosed the yard with ropes and posted soldiers every few feet, people still managed to get inside. Jessie Moore was allowed into the house to get photographs of J.B., Sarah and the children for the newspapers. Doctors, undertakers and their guests walked in and out. The guards knew that only authorized people were to be allowed in the house, but just who was authorized and who was not remained open to debate.

This was likely how a shady character named W.B. "Bert" McCaul got into the house. McCaul had a reputation as a drinker, a gambler, and a womanizer. He operated a pool hall and an automobile livery service. His wife was from a farm family who lived near Missouri Valley in the west central part of the state. When things started to go bad for him locally, a couple of years after the murders, he returned to that area to farm, but in June 1912, he was still trying to make a living in Villisca. McCaul hoped to go into partnership with Albert Jones selling automobiles. Despite his father's objections, Albert had befriended the man and often hired him to drive him out into the country. He loved the idea of being chauffeured around town in an automobile when so many people at the time didn't have one.

McCaul spent the evening of June 9 as he usually did, playing cards at the Knights if Pythias building in downtown Villisca. It was the one place in town where men could together, drink whiskey and play poker. Among the regulars that night was Captain C.J. Casey, commander of the local National Guard unit.

On Monday morning, McCaul and Albert Jones left town together, although where they went and what they were doing remains unknown today. What is known is that they traveled north and were told about the murders from some farmers around 9 a.m. They hurried back to Villisca and went immediately to the Moore house. Albert talked to a few people and stayed out in the street, but McCaul was determined to get inside. He was turned away, but returned later in the day and tried to talk his way inside. After a scuffle with one of the soldiers, he appealed to his pal Captain Casey, who allowed him to go inside and look around.

In his pool hall a few months later, McCaul displayed a chunk of bone with flesh still clinging to it that he claimed was a piece of J.B. Moore's skull. Later, after McCaul gave up on the pool hall, his successor found the bone, which had been wrapped in a cloth and tucked away in a glass case. His wife made him throw it away because she thought it was disgusting.

But, as mentioned earlier, the lack of crime scene security was common in the early years of the twentieth century. There were no well-trained, heavily equipped criminologists. There was no way to lift fingerprints, analyze blood spatter, or examine the uncompromised scene in detail. What was available was poorly utilized. A local druggist thought that it would be a good idea to photograph the scene and managed to get his bulky photographic equipment into the house. The photographs would have been useful, but unfortunately, Dr. Linquist caught him and threw him out.

By noon, the town square, pool hall, restaurants, and the street in front of the Moore house, were filled with people. More people arrived throughout the day.

Many of them knew the Moores or the Stillingers, but most simply came because they heard about the murders and wanted to somehow be a part of a momentous event. Most of the onlookers were local people on the first day, but in the days that followed, people traveled to Villisca by train from all over the state. The hotel rooms and boarding houses in town quickly filled up. Before long, even the hotels in nearby towns were filled and within a few days, an out-of-town reporter was liable to find that the closest available room might be an hour's train ride away.

People watched the detectives, the authorities and the doctors as they went in and out of the house. They talked, gossiped, and spread their own theories of the crime. Just about anyone could get attention if he talked loud enough, and anyone who could claim to have actually been inside the house was given more importance than he probably deserved. Theories and potential suspects were plentiful. Some people, finding it hard to believe that anyone could sleep while others nearby were being murdered, suggested that perhaps the victims had been drugged or poisoned. Others named potential suspects who lived in town.

One of the people considered as a possible suspect that first day was Sam Moyer, husband of one of J.B.'s younger sisters. Moyer was a shiftless, itinerant gambler who had married Anna Moore, and had a couple of children with her, but had little interest in staying at home with his family. J.B. and his brothers were left to provide financial support for Anna and her offspring. J.B was not happy with the situation and often said so, but whether or not he and Moyer ever had words is unknown. Some of Moore's employees were under the impression that J.B. had once written the footloose Moyer (who was living in Oregon at the time) a stern letter reminding him of his responsibilities as a husband and a father. Others believed that the two men had a physical altercation at the time of the annual Old Settlers Days event a few months before. Few local residents outside of the Moore family knew much about Moyer, but there seemed to be some reason to consider him a potential suspect.

There were also questions being asked about Lee Van Gilder, the divorced husband of one of Sarah Moore's sisters. Van Gilder was known for being a violent man who harbored bitter feelings toward his ex-wife. He'd had several run-ins with the law and rumor had it that he and J.B. Moore had been involved in a quarrel, which led to he and his wife separating and their eventual divorce.

Joseph Stillinger's name was also whispered. It was said that he had recently had problems with some of his hired men. However, the idea that one of them could have hated Stillinger enough to kill his daughters and the entire Moore family was quickly dismissed as unlikely.

Not surprisingly, everyone wondered about strangers who had been in town in the days leading up to the murders. There was no way of keeping track of everyone; Villisca was a railroad town and on any given day, a dozen or more passenger trains brought hobos, sightseers, businessmen, salesmen and scores of other people to town. Men passed through on their way to jobs, farms, and military service. Some stayed a few hours, others stayed for days. In addition to the railroads, people came to town in automobiles, buggies, and on horseback. Some of them simply passed through, others stayed longer. The local people had no idea

An older photograph of the Moore family, taken before Boyd and Paul were born. J.B. and Sarah and shown here with Herman and Catherine.

who most of them were, where they had come from, or where they might be going next. The list of possible suspects seemed to get larger with each passing hour, which encouraged the curious to talk, accuse, and speculate even more.

It was on the afternoon of the first day that rumors spread claiming that Frank Jones might be involved in the murders. It was Jones himself who inadvertently contributed to the stories. Dennis Meyerhoff, a long-time acquaintance of Jones who had worked with him on political issues, happened to be in the area on business on June 10. He sought Jones out and told him that he had heard about the murders on the train that morning and one of the men spreading the news had hinted that Jones might have something to

do with them. Both Meyerhoff and Jones later said that they laughed at the absurdity of the suggestion, but any humor that Jones found in being considered a suspect was short-lived. Jones made the mistake of repeating what his friend had told him, never thinking that anyone would take it seriously, but it was too late. The seed had been planted and it would not be long before the off-hand comment grew into a storm of conspiracy, alleged corruption, and murder. Suspicion was one thing -- but it would be a charismatic detective who would lay waste to the life of Frank Jones once and for all.

Later in the afternoon, search parties made up from the ranks of the National Guard and volunteers began examining outbuildings, starting with the Moores' barn and working outward. They were looking for discarded clothing with blood on it or any kind of clue. There was also the remote possibility that the killer might be hiding somewhere nearby. Hotel registers were checked and agents for the Chicago, Burlington & Quincy Railroad questioned their conductors and searched their ticket sale registers for anything out of the ordinary. Thomas O'Leary, the Kirk Agency detective, arrived on Monday afternoon and took a look inside the house.

Dogs known as the Beatrice Bloodhounds, brought in from Beatrice, Nebraska, and well-known for their tracking abilities, arrived in town about 9 p.m. Sheriff Jackson took the dogs and their owner, Elmer Noffsinger, to the Moore house. Even though it had been handled by an unknown number of people since the murders, the ax was used to give a scent to the dogs. At first, the hounds seemed to have a trail. They raced out of the front door, turned north on Fourth Avenue, and then headed west to the edge of town. The dogs then turned south toward the Nodaway River, but when they encountered heavy brush along the riverbank, they lost interest. They were taken across the river, but the trail seemed to be lost.

Dr. Linquist convened the coroner's jury late on Monday afternoon but it was not until evening that he took them into the Moore house to view the bodies. Several undertakers had been called and were ready to begin their solemn work once Linquist allowed the corpses to be taken from the scene. County Attorney Ratcliff arrived around 10 p.m. and was satisfied that the bodies did not need to remain in the house any longer. Around midnight, the bodies were carried out one by one, placed in a wagon and taken to the fire station, which was serving as a temporary morgue. The grim task took nearly two hours. It was noted that the final body was placed on a cot in the fire station at 2 a.m. Armed members of the Villisca National Guard unit were stationed at the door.

By suppertime, most of the locals had gone home to their families, who were eagerly awaiting news. As darkness fell over Villisca, the shock and excitement over the murders was replaced by the sobering realization that a killer was at large, possibly right there with them in the community. The men who had speculated in broad daylight about who had it in for J.B. Moore, now began to realize that a killer might be in their midst – one who perhaps chose his victims at random and just might strike again. Men sat up all night with loaded guns. Doors were locked and lamps were left burning. People who lived alone sought out neighbors with whom to spend the night. Closets were searched and many looked under their beds before they climbed into them.

In the days to come, the hardware stores sold out of hasps and locks, ordered more, and had those spoken for before the new locks even arrived. In a town where no one had ever needed to lock their doors, people were filled with fear. Many who had never owned a gun bought one as soon as they could. Many locals got into the habit of carrying a gun with them and continued to do so for many years after the murders. Residents began using their chamber pots again, something usually only done on the coldest winter nights, rather than make the dark and lonely walk to the outhouse at night.

There were very few people in Villisca who slept well that first night – or for many nights afterward.

On the morning of June 11, Elmer Noffsinger's bloodhounds were brought back to the Moore house and this time, they were given their scent from the downstairs closet where some thought the killer might have waited. It was there where a heel print had been found on a magazine that had been tossed on the floor. Dozens of people showed up at daybreak to watch the dogs as they bounced off on a tight leash, following the same trail they had followed the evening before. Once again, they found nothing.

Among the bystanders that morning was Frank Jones. He reportedly told someone standing next to him that the dogs were going in the wrong direction. Jones would later swear that he said nothing of the sort and even if he had, nothing was made of it at the time. Three years later, though, his comment was brought up again and the forgotten remark became another small piece of a larger conspiracy that was created by a detective who took on the case.

Many wondered if the bloodhounds really had a legitimate trail, but since they had gone to the Nodaway River twice, the possibility seemed worth following. County Attorney Ratcliff and Sheriff Jackson organized groups made up of National Guardsmen and about 100 volunteers from the Villisca area. They fanned out on both sides of the river and marched to the south. Another group of about the same size was organized in Clarinda and it worked its way north. The search failed to turn up any clues of value.

On Tuesday, more people flocked to Villisca. Probably every train that pulled into station brought at least a few people who were there because of the murders. Some of them were detectives – or would-be detectives – reporters, free-lance writers, and curiosity-seekers who had heard the news of the murders and wanted to see where they happened for themselves. They questioned the locals, walked the streets, stood outside of the Moore house and milled about in the town square.

The biggest rumor of Tuesday was that partially burned papers that linked a "prominent local merchant" to the murders had been found in the Moores' kitchen stove. No one knew what the papers actually were, but this didn't stop people from talking about them and speculating. In reality, the papers didn't exist. Nothing of that sort was found in the house. The authorities told the press, then and later, that no partially burned papers or any kind of documents that might shed light on the killer's identity had been discovered. The story might have been forgotten altogether if one of the local newspapers, the *Red Oak Sun*, had not used the fictional papers to illustrate the fact that many of the "yellow journalists" that had flocked to Villisca were not above making up stories and printing gossip and speculation. The newspaper used the burned documents story as an example. The article did not mention the name of the "prominent local merchant" and said that the story was untrue, but by bringing it up at all, it presented the rumor to hundreds of people who had not heard it before. Once again, another seed was planted. Although his name was never mentioned, locals were convinced the story was referring to Frank Jones.

One of the men who became a central figure in the investigation of the murders was a criminologist named M.W. McClaughry, special agent in charge of the Department of Justice, Bureau of Criminal Investigation for the U.S. Federal Prison in Leavenworth, Kansas. He was a fingerprint expert and a member of a family that was distinguished in law enforcement circles. His father was Major R.W. McClaughry, the warden at Leavenworth, and his uncle was C.C. McClaughry, the warden of the Iowa State Reformatory in Anamosa. McClaughry was a well-educated man with experience in the emerging science of criminal investigation. He wrote the most detailed crime scene report from the Moore house, which included detailed measurements and observations. He claimed to have gone over the entire house with a magnifying glass. However, according to Hank Horton and Dr. Linquist, when McClaughry stepped off the train in Villisca, he was staggeringly drunk. He was taken to the house anyway, but was so inebriated that Linquist ordered him to his hotel room to sleep it off. McClaughry returned later and spent the next two days attempting to find fingerprints in the house. He examined lamp globes, mirrors, panes of glass, the bloody washbasin, the ax -- anything that might have been touched by the killer -- but ended with the conclusion that there "were no finger marks of any kind of judicial value." McClaughry would later put forth his own suspect in the murder, whom we will explore later in the book.

Another important figure in the case – a suspect rather than an investigator – was Reverend Lyn George Jacklin Kelly, who was mentioned earlier as an attendee at the Presbyterian church on the night of the Children's Day Program. Kelly was undoubtedly one of the strangest suspects to emerge in the case. People who met him seldom forgot him. He was a twitchy little red-haired man who stood only five feet two inches tall. He had a reputation as a peeping tom and was variously described as "eccentric," "peculiar," "somewhat insane," "perverted," and "unquestionably out of his mind." Kelly had been born in England in 1878 and at the age of 26, came to America with his wife, Laura. He was a religious zealot who, after many failed attempts, eventually managed to become a Presbyterian minister.

Kelly was odd-looking, with protruding ears, a large nose, high forehead and a wide mouth with rubbery lips. People always seemed to remember his piercing blue, deep-set eyes, which many described as "crazed," but they were disturbed more by the way he acted rather than how he looked. He was easily excited and often ranted and spoke so fast that he was impossible to understand. He was also said to drool excessively and spray spit all over those who were unwise enough to stand close to him when he talked.

Kelly was moved from place to place by the church, unable to find anywhere where he really fit in. He was said to be an enthusiastic preacher, but his bizarre personal behavior and his habit of borrowing money and failing to repay it was not what most congregations expected from their pastor. In 1912, Kelly and Laura settled in Macedonia, about 40 miles west of Villisca, after several years of preaching throughout the Midwest. He continued to work as an itinerant preacher and on June 8, while Laura remained at home, Kelly took the train to Villisca. He attended the Children's Day program and was on the 5:19 a.m. westbound train out of Villisca the following morning.

Kelly returned to Villisca a few days later. Home in Macedonia, he had talked incessantly about the crime to anyone who would listen and was anxious to get back to Villisca so he could share his views with the authorities. After he returned to town, he visited the Moore house with Reverend Ewing and told investigators about a strange man he claimed to have seen at the train depot on Monday morning. Kelly said he had arrived at the station early and encountered a shabbily dressed man who he assumed was waiting for the same train. He said that the man acted nervous, paced the floor and seemed anxious to get out of town. Kelly said he assumed the man had gotten onto the train, but he never saw him again. Within a few days, though, Kelly began to embellish the story. He then claimed that he had seen the man sitting in the back row of the church during the Children's Day program. The story was checked out, but no one else who had been present recalled seeing anyone who fit the description that Kelly gave. Passengers on the early morning train that day recalled seeing Kelly, but not the stranger he described.

Initially, Kelly was dismissed as a crank, but he later confessed to the murders and was put on trial. In my opinion, Kelly did have a connection to the case, but it was not what the authorities thought at the time. The arrest, trial and my own theories will be featured in a later chapter.

The authorities weren't just looking for Reverend Kelly's mysterious stranger – strangers all over southwestern Iowa were being carefully checked out. Sheriff Jackson received countless reports about suspicious characters in and around Villisca. One reported a black man who was seen south of town. An area farmer had seen a man walking through his fields and another believed that someone had slept in his barn. Investigators were also searching for a lace curtain salesman who had been in town for a couple of days and who had checked out of the Fisher Hotel shortly before the murders were discovered. He had called on Sarah Moore, as well as many others in town. The man had registered as M.J. Rourey (or Kourey; the handwriting was poor) from Chicago. He was eventually found and, not surprisingly, there was nothing to connect him to the murders other than that he was, according to the *Villisca Review*, a "mysterious foreigner."

But in Villisca, Iowa, in June 1912, that was enough to make someone a suspect in the most horrific crime in the history of a town that was now paralyzed with fear.

The funerals for the Moore family and the Stillinger sisters were held on Wednesday, June 12. It turned out to be a beautiful day and the services were held in the town square. The caskets containing the bodies were arranged in a semi-circle in the town hall building. The caskets were closed and even family members had not been allowed to view the devastated remains of their loved ones. The casket of Lena Stillinger was on the far right. Next to her was her sister, Ina, then J.B. Moore, Sarah, Herman, Katherine, Boyd, and Paul on the extreme left. Floral arrangements had poured in from relatives, neighbors and friends of both families. There were also flowers from John Deere, local businesses, the Presbyterian church, the board of education, schoolteachers, customers of J.B.'s store, classmates of the children and literally scores of others. The arrangements filled the room and overflowed out onto the sidewalks. Armed soldiers were posted both inside and outside the town hall, keeping everyone out. Captain Casey also posted guardsmen in the park at the center of the square and along the procession route to the cemetery.

More than 7,000 people crowded into the park that day. In addition to the mourners, there were journalists from newspapers and magazines across the country. There were also hundreds of morbid curiosity-seekers, some of them local, but most having traveled great distances to be a part of what was now being called the most heinous mass murder in Midwest history. The crowd was also sprinkled with detectives, all curious to see if the killer would return to the scene of the crime. There is no indication as to how they would have known who he was if he really did turn up for the funerals that day.

A platform had been built in the park and Reverend Ewing presided at the service, with several ministers from other area churches on hand to offer prayers and words of comfort. Although most of the crowd was unable to hear what he said, Ewing spoke about the Moores, their lives and the affection that he felt for the family. The surviving Moores, Stillingers and Montgomerys were seated directly in front of the platform and wept as he spoke, especially when he talked about the six children who had died. John Montgomery had gone to the temporary morgue the day before, insisting on seeing his daughter and grandchildren, but he was turned away. Charles Moore, seated with his wife and surviving children, was ailing and would die a few months after the funerals. It was said that he was not fully aware of what had happened to J.B. and no one in the family wanted to tell him.

Reverend Ewing spoke for about 20 minutes and closed with the words:

Asleep in Jesus, blessed sleep
From which none ever wake to weep
A calm and undisturbed repose
Unbroken by the last of foes.

Sadly, many believe that the victims of this horrible crime would not rest "calm and undisturbed" in the years to come.

After prayers and hymns, the service in the park came to an end. The caskets were carried from the town hall by pallbearers, all of whom were current or former farm implement dealers with whom J.B. Moore had worked. Among them was Albert Jones.

The funeral cortege was the longest ever seen in Villisca, before or since. Two horse-drawn hearses were used, as well as six new farm wagons that had been draped in black. They were followed by an estimated 50 carriages and by hundreds of people who walked, making a procession that was nearly one-quarter mile long. The hearses arrived at the cemetery on the north side of town at about the same time the last of the cortege was leaving the downtown square. After a long delay while everyone assembled, Reverend Ewing spoke again at the gravesides.

There was other work being carried out at the same time as the funeral. Hank Horton had hired Sylvester "Ves" Cooney and a day laborer named Carl Peterson to clean up the Moore house while everyone was busy with the services. Horton unlocked the house and conducted the pair through, showing them what needed to be done. Peterson took a look around the gore-splattered rooms and wanted no part of the job. Feeling sick, he went outside to wait by the wagon. Cooney had a stronger stomach. He folded up the blood-soaked downstairs mattress and bed covers, wrapped the bundle with wire and carried it outside to the wagon. He did the same with the mattresses upstairs, but being unable to navigate around the turn in the stairs, he heaved the bedding out the triple window, leaving a bloody stain on the siding that Peterson later eradicated with whitewash.

After loading the mattresses and bedding in the wagon, Cooney drove to the city dump. He placed a sheet on the ground and shook all of the bed covers over it. He later said that several pieces of bone and flesh fell onto the sheet. One bone fragment, a square piece that was about three inches in diameter, came from the bed where J.B.'s and Sarah's bodies had been found. Cooney then started a fire and burned it all -- bloody sheets, mattresses, and pieces of skull.

Little had been done to preserve the scene, no useful fingerprints were ever collected and now, the physical evidence had been destroyed. At this point, the murders in Villisca could never really be connected to any other crime or traced to any one killer. The murders remain unsolved a century later.

7. SUMMER OF FEAR

One of the things that the summer of 1912 would be remembered for was the terrible storms that raged across southwest Iowa. Damaging winds and violent electrical storms pounded the area, and at least a half dozen farm buildings near Villisca, including two houses and several barns, were destroyed by wind or burned after being hit by lightning. Several unlucky farmers lost their entire crop of oats, and a new house built by John Slack burned to the ground.

But the weather was not the most prominent topic of conversation that summer. People were still speculating about the Moore and Stillinger murders. Fear still loomed over the small town. Doors were still being locked at night, and after dark, the streets of Villisca were nearly deserted.

The Stillingers had more sorrow that summer. A few days after the funerals, Sarah Stillinger lost her unborn son, and before the year was over, the family home was destroyed by fire.

Iowa Governor Beryl F. Carroll announced in June that the state was offering a $500 reward for information leading to an arrest in the Villisca case. He was soon criticized for what many saw as a paltry sum. While $500 was a large amount of money in 1912, it seemed an inadequate reward for finding the killer of eight people. Villisca residents were angry and vowed to raise more money locally, which they did. In fact, the money, which grew into thousands of dollars, was deposited in the First National Bank in Villisca, which was owned by Frank Jones. Governor Carroll defended the reward, pointing out correctly that he was limited to $500 per case by statute and couldn't legally offer more. But what most people didn't know then was that the state was doing much more than was assumed.

Carroll had given approval to Attorney General George Cosson to hire a detective from the famed Burns Detective Agency. Based in Chicago, the agency had branch offices all over the country and overseas. The agency had been founded by William J. Burns, who became known as "America's Sherlock Holmes" after a private investigation that cleared Leo Frank of the sensational murder of Mary Phagan in 1915. Burns had been born in Baltimore, Maryland, and was educated in Ohio. As a young man, he had been a Secret Service agent and used his reputation to form his own detective agency. A combination of natural ability as an investigator, combined with an instinct for publicity made Burns a national figure. His exploits made national news, the gossip columns of New York newspapers, and the pages of detective magazines, in which he published true crime stories based on his exploits. Iowa state officials believed that the investigation was in good hands with the Burns agency involved.

A detective from the Burns office in Kansas City named C.W. Tobie was assigned to the case. Tobie had insisted that he work undercover for a time and so in July, when he arrived in Villisca and people were complaining that nothing was being done in the case, Carroll was unable to admit that a detective had been hired.

Tobie identified himself only to Ratcliff, Jackson, Horton, and a handful of officials that he thought needed to know of his presence in town. There is no indication that Tobie and O'Leary, the detective brought in by Hank Horton, had any problems with one another, even though they were in direct competition, or that they had any contact at all. Both of the men were hopeful of tracking down the killer, claiming the growing reward, and making front page news as the detective who caught the Villisca murderer. They did not share any information with one another, or with any of the other professional and amateur detectives that were roaming the countryside.

Tobie, like all other Burns detectives, traveled with a typewriter that he used to file daily reports that were mailed to both the Kansas City and Chicago offices. Another copy was sent directly to Governor Carroll. Tobie felt that he had a huge break in the case only days after his arrival in town, but what happened illustrates the problems that occurred with competing investigations at the time.

Mike Kearns was one of two night watchmen in Villisca. The other watchman, Henry "Mike" Overman, had seen someone he didn't recognize in the town square on the night of the murder and let the man pass without checking to see who he was. He was later chastised for letting this happen and so Kearns undoubtedly had instructions to check out any stranger that he encountered. On the night of July 6, he approached a raggedly dressed man at the railroad depot and began to question him. The man began acting strangely and then suddenly fled into the darkness. Kearns and Horton searched for the man all night, but he was not found. However, they did discover that he had checked his baggage. He had given the name Otto Mattusbak and his suitcases were checked through to Chicago. Horton contacted Sheriff Jackson and agent O'Leary, who was working for the county. Even though Tobie was in town, and had made himself known to law enforcement officials, they didn't bother to tell him about the Mattusbak incident. Jackson contacted authorities in Chicago and asked them to apprehend whoever came to the express window to collect the baggage for Mattusbak. Three days later, on July 9, Chicago police officers picked up the man and it was only then that Tobie was told about the suspect. The only reason he likely heard about it at all was because he was with Horton when the telegram from Chicago arrived.

Tobie was irritated by the local police officer's failure to communicate with him, but he made the best of the situation. In his report that night, he noted that he had spoken with Jackson and Ratcliff about the situation and had confirmed with the Chicago police that Jackson would be leaving in the morning to pick up the prisoner. The next morning, knowing that a letter would reach Governor Carroll faster than his report – and probably worried that none of his recent reports had mentioned a man that locals considered a prime suspect – he quickly sent a letter to the governor. He began it with "We have under arrest..." and went on to explain that Mattusbak fit the description of one of the men seen in town on the weekend of the murders. He asked the governor to keep everything under the strictest confidence and added that he was hopeful that "this arrest may straighten out affairs here."

But as it turned out, it was established that Mattusbak had been working in Missouri for the previous three months. He had been there at the time of the murders and had left on July 6 to return to Chicago. He had stopped in Villisca only to change trains. No one knows why he ran from Kearns that night, but after he had established his alibi, he was released from custody.

Tobie continued his investigation during July and August, only leaving in September after he was promoted to the position of manager at the Burns office in Chicago. He ran down dozens of leads and investigated a number of remote possibilities, but in the end, he turned up nothing of value. He heard the rumors about Frank Jones' involvement in the case, but dismissed them. He also heard about Reverend Kelly doing some strange things, but he had little interest in the odd little man as a suspect. It seemed obvious to Tobie that the killer was no longer in Villisca.

By July, Reverend Kelly was referring to himself as a detective, claiming that he had trained as a criminologist while living in London. His theories about the crime varied from time to time, but in some of his letters, he stated that he believed the killer was a member of the Moore family. He never named a suspect, but in letters written in the weeks after the murders, his ideas seemed to coincide with the early speculations about Moyer. Regardless of what he wrote, though, Kelly would talk to anyone who would listen to him about the murders. One night, he became so agitated in the lobby of a Villisca hotel that frightened guests asked Mike Kearns to come over and settle him down. Kelly was ranting about the manner in which he believed the killings took place, going into a vigorous re-enactment of the attacks.

Detectives Tobie and O'Leary dealt with Reverend Kelly in different ways. Kelly wrote to and spoke with both men and offered to work with them. He insisted on telling them about the ideas that he received from visions and dreams. Tobie wanted nothing to do with such an obvious oddball and eventually wrote him a very sternly worded letter saying so. O'Leary, on the other hand, cultivated the relationship. He apparently felt that Kelly had something worthwhile to offer.

Tobie remained in Villisca until his move to Chicago. At that point, a Burns detective named W.S. Gordon took his place in town. Gordon called the case "one of the greatest, if not the greatest, crime mystery in the history of the United States." He said that the Burns agency had never faced a bigger challenge. He spent the fall of 1912 helping the police to eliminate suspects in the case. That period marked the high point of the relationship between the Burns agency and the state of Iowa. It would continue into 1915, but it became increasingly volatile over time, especially after an incident in the fall of 1912.

Most of the people in the Villisca area spent the summer of 1912 going about their usual routines during the daytime. But at night, it was a different story. The initial terror had passed, but it was still common to find two or three families sleeping in one house. Many farmers took their wives and children to a home of a friend or a relative after the evening chores.

Sheriff Jackson probably hurt the situation more than helped it that summer, making frightening newspaper statements like, "This is the most terrible and deadly menace with which society has ever had to deal. Heaven only knows where these fanatics may strike next. It may be my family, it may be yours." He also told the press that, "When the next family is found murdered by an ax, and that discovery of this kind will be shortly made I am certain, the police and the entire country should cooperate in running down the perpetrator." It took only a matter of weeks for his prediction to come true. Another ax murder in Illinois occurred in September, and even though it had no connection to Villisca, it sent shockwaves through the investigation and nearly ruined the relationship between the Burns Detective Agency and the state of Iowa.

8. MURDER IN QUINCY

"SIMILAR TO VILLISCA HORROR"

"Murdered in Home!" screamed the headlines in Quincy, Illinois, on September 30, 1912, as news began to spread about the quadruple murders of Charles Pfanschmidt, 46; his wife, Mathilda; their 15-year-old daughter, Blanche; and a young schoolteacher who boarded with the family. The bodies were discovered in the Pfanschmidt home, about 12 miles outside of Quincy after a fire swept through the residence on Sunday, September 29. The police guessed that they had been killed on Friday night and the fire set to destroy the evidence. Telephone lines to the house had been cut, making it impossible for friends to reach them on Saturday.

Neighbors spotted smoke coming from the house very early on Sunday morning and alerted the authorities. By the time they arrived, it was burning nearly out of control. The fire nearly destroyed the house, and when the metal roof was removed, the bodies of three women were found lying on blood-soaked mattresses in what would have been the upstairs bedrooms of the house. The roof had preserved the corpses well enough to reveal that the women had been bludgeoned with an ax while they were sleeping. The bodies were those of Matilda and Blanche Pfanschmidt and Emma Kaempen, 21. Miss Kaempen taught school in Quincy and boarded with the family.

Another body was discovered in the ruins of the cellar. There was so little remaining of the charred corpse that it was impossible to determine its sex. The flesh and bones of the head, arms, shoulders, upper trunk, legs and half of the lower trunk were gone. Only one thigh remained. A doctor later testified that the body had been dismembered with knives and a saw before it was burned. It was eventually determined that the body belonged to Charles Pfanschmidt.

Near the body in the cellar was an ax head with what was later determined was human blood baked on it from the intense heat of the flames. The handle of the ax had been completely burned away.

Police officers and sheriff's deputies immediately descended on the scene, gathering law enforcement personnel and armed citizens to search the countryside for the killer. Bloodhounds were brought to the scene in an effort to trace the murderer who, it was believed, had driven to the home in a buggy on Saturday night, a few hours before the fire was discovered.

It was no surprise that the police believed that Billy the Axman had struck again. According to newspaper reports, they were seeking the "degenerate who had perpetrated similar ax murders in Iowa and Colorado recently." They also noted that the crime was "similar to the horror in Villisca." And unfortunately, it would not be only the local police who believed this to be true.

As news of the murders in Quincy spread, there was a fear that the Villisca killer was still at work. Iowa's attorney general asked the Burns Detective Agency to send someone to look into it. C. W. Tobie, who had worked the Villisca case for a few weeks in July and August before going on to manage the agency's Chicago office, assigned himself to the investigation. Detective Thomas O'Leary from the Kirk's Detective Agency and was still embroiled in the Villisca case, also went to Quincy to investigate. The two men were soon to clash, causing a situation that managed to help the killer escape prosecution.

Before either detective arrived in Quincy, the Adams County sheriff had arrested Ray Pfanschmidt, 20, the only surviving offspring of the murdered couple. The young man had moved out of the family's home in August to start work on an excavation project for the Chicago, Burlington & Quincy Railroad. He was living in a tent near the worksite. The main evidence against him was a set of buggy tracks that led directly from the Pfanschmidt house to the work camp and bloodstained clothing that belonged to him.

The clothes had been discovered by accident. J.L. Freese, who lived near the work camp, was making improvements on his property and moved an outhouse to a new location. When the structure was moved, he found a bundle of bloody clothing hidden beneath it and called the police. The khaki shirt and pants were splattered with blood, the largest stains measuring about two inches in diameter. They were identified by Esther Reeder, Ray Pfanschmidt's fianceé, as belonging to him.

Charles Pfanschmidt owned a considerable amount of real estate and his wife owned large tracts of land that she had inherited from her father. Upon the deaths of the Pfanschimdts, their land and money was to go to their children, meaning that Ray stood to gain a large inheritance after the murders. It was known that he had money problems. In the weeks prior to the murders, Charles received two notes from his bank informing him that his son's accounts were overdrawn. Charles had allegedly complained to a friend about Ray's spending habits. The young man's need for money provided all the motive that the authorities needed to arrest him.

Detective Thomas O'Leary, who was still working for Montgomery County, arrived in Quincy and looked into the case. He quickly decided that the evidence was overwhelming – Ray Pfanschmidt was the killer and the murders had nothing to do with Villisca. Detective Tobie, though, saw things differently. While his bill was being paid by the state of Iowa to determine if the crimes in Villisca and Quincy were related, he talked to a few people and visited Ray Pfanschmidt in jail. After meeting with the Burns detective, Pfanschmidt hired Tobie as an "expert witness" to testify that the murders could have been committed by the roving ax maniac who had slaughtered people in Colorado, Kansas, Illinois, and Iowa. Tobie, considered an expert in the other cases, was supposed to provide an element of reasonable doubt for the defense. And in the end, it worked.

At the initial trial in March 1913, Ray was convicted for the murder of his sister and sentenced to the gallows in October. The evidence against him was circumstantial, but Ray was perceived as being greedy and spoiled. It didn't help his prospects when his grandfather testified in court about his constant demands for money.

"I told him, Ray, you are going to the dogs and you are going there damn fast," the old man was quoted as saying, no doubt with grim satisfaction.

His lawyers appealed the case, stating that a change of venue request should have been granted due to extreme prejudice against the defendant expressed by people living in Quincy and the surrounding area. They argued that some of the evidence (including letters from the bank regarding overdrafts) should not have been admitted. In February 1914, Pfanschmidt was granted a new trial by the Illinois Supreme Court. He was retried for the murder of his sister and found not guilty. He was then put on trial for the murder of his father and reasonable doubt won out again. The case for the murder of his mother was dismissed and the authorities didn't try and convict him again. Pfanschmidt collected his inheritance and left Adams County for good.

Some believed he had gotten away with murder. If so, C.W. Tobie helped him. For a time, the Burns detective was on the payroll of not only the state of Iowa, but was also being paid by the man he had been hired to investigate. It was an ethical situation that greatly bothered the attorney general and nearly ended the state's relationship with the agency. Things were eventually smoothed over and the agency would continue to work for the state until 1915, although no hard evidence was really ever obtained by Burns detectives.

The Quincy case stunned the people of Villisca. They had been hoping for a solution to their own murders, but that turned out not to be the case. There was no connection between the two crimes and only one element (ax murders committed while the victims slept) was the same. But it should be noted how quick people – including law enforcement officials – were to believe that a single killer was at work. Billy the Axman had now taken on the role of a Midwest bogeyman, lurking behind every murder where an ax was used and in some where it wasn't.

Near Council Bluffs, Iowa, in the summer of 1912, a Danish farmer named Martin Thompson, his wife and their eight-year-old son were found dead in their home. Their throats had been cut with a butcher's knife and the heads of the woman and boy had been smashed with a hammer. Early reports incorrectly stated that all of them had been killed by an ax. Newspapers and local gossip immediately speculated about a connection to the Villisca, Colorado, Kansas, and Illinois murders and Sheriff Jackson and County Attorney Ratcliff went there to pursue it. When they arrived, their hopes were dashed when local authorities showed them a suicide note written by Thompson. He had killed his wife and son and then turned the knife to his own throat.

At the time of the Pfanschmidt murders, the authorities in Villisca were still anxiously looking for clues and were quick to leap at the chance that the killer had struck again in Illinois. Things had become so desperate that they were willing to try anything, even spreading the word that Lena Stillinger could identify her killer. According to a newspaper report, detectives had somehow acquired a photograph of the murderer from an image preserved on the retina of one of Lena's eyes. She had apparently awakened during the attack and her body was found with its eyes open. They were checking the image now, they said, and planned to make an announcement about the killer's identity soon. Needless to say, no announcement ever came. It's believed that the story was planted by one of the detectives in the case, hoping that it might force the murderer to identify himself in some way if he thought that his name was going to be revealed.

Billy the Axman continued to strike fear in the hearts of people all over the Midwest, but where was he? And would be soon strike again?

9. FRANK JONES

Over the days of that summer, a number of suspects were named and then dismissed. And as summer turned to fall, and fall turned to winter, there were still dozens of theories, but genuine leads were getting harder and harder to find.

Frank Jones had problems of his own in the summer and fall of 1912. Gossip was circulating in town about the possibility of an affair between J.B. Moore and Dona Jones, Albert's wife, who already had a reputation as a loose woman. There was also talk about the "bad blood" that supposedly existed between Jones and Moore over business matters. At the time that J.B. quit working for Jones and went into competition with him at the new dealership, little was made of it. Jones, of all people, understood how business worked. It's possible that he felt a little betrayed by Moore, but he never publicly expressed any hard feelings against him. After the murders, though, people in town began to talk, inventing trouble where there hadn't been any before.

But it was only small town gossip at this point. Jones had bigger things to worry about, namely his run for the Senate in the Eighth District, comprised of Mills and Montgomery counties. Jones' only political experience up to that point were the three terms he had served on the city council. His biggest threat in the race came not from his Democrat opponent, W.S. Reiley, but from former President Theodore Roosevelt.

Roosevelt had gone from the New York governor's office to the White House in a matter of a few years. A dynamic man with a lot of public relations savvy, Roosevelt had made a name for himself in Cuba during the Spanish-American War and took the vice-presidential ticket next to William McKinley during the general elections of 1900. When McKinley was assassinated a few months after taking office, Roosevelt became president. He was by and large popular, and he pleased many in the Democrat party by leaning to the left during his time in office, taking on big business on behalf of labor interests. He won re-election in 1904 but said that two terms were enough. He groomed his vice-president, William Howard Taft, to take his place and stepped down in 1908. After Taft's victory, Roosevelt went on an extended safari in Africa. Over the next few years, however, Roosevelt came to believe that Taft had failed in his leadership duties to the country. By the time of the 1912 primaries, Roosevelt decided to seek the Republican nomination once more. Taft won in the majority of states and, much to Roosevelt's displeasure, the nomination went to his rival. He left the convention with plans to run on a third-party ticket.

A few days after the Villisca murders, Roosevelt announced that he was the candidate of the Progressive, or "Bull Moose" party. Progressive Party members in Iowa were elated by the news. They began to scramble for local candidates to fill out the Iowa ticket. For a few weeks, the Senate race remained with Jones as the Republican candidate and Reiley for the Democrat party. Reiley was a well-known and respected businessman from Red Oak and it would be a close race. Republicans outnumbered Democrats in the area, so if the vote went along party lines, Jones had the edge – unless he either made some sort of mistake, people started believing the gossip about him, or if the Progressive Party managed to take away some of the Republican votes by bringing in a viable candidate.

Progressive Party members predicted a Bull Moose landslide, but more conservative analysts knew that they were likely to do more than split the Republican vote, which would hand the election to the Democrats. The *Villisca Review* was among the first newspapers to announce that the Progressive Party had a candidate to run against Jones and Reiley: Alvin C Gustafson of Red Oak. The front page article on his candidacy was a glowing story about the Bull Moose candidate and in bold print just below the headline, "Means Defeat of F.F. Jones." Jones frequently complained that the editors of the Villisca paper were biased against him and he had valid reasons to believe this was the case. This time, though, Gustafson was one of their own and they didn't bother to try and be impartial. Gustafson was a newspaperman, the former editor of the *Stanton Call*. At the time when he decided to run for office, he was the editor of the *Weekly Record*, a sales publication of the Thomas D. Murphy Company, which printed calendars and was one of Red Oak's largest employers. The article lauded Gustafson's qualifications and made him look attractive to crossover Republican voters by stating that he would vote for U.S. Senator William Kenyon in the elections. In Iowa in 1912, U.S. senators were elected by state senators and Kenyon was popular with both parties. Kenyon had a lot of support in Montgomery County, thanks to the fact that he had pledged to bring federal law enforcement officials into the Villisca murder case. He announced in late summer that Secret Service agents were working on the case, as were U.S. Postal Inspectors. Assistance from these agencies never really added up to much, although the postal service did assist investigators with the glut of mail they received about the case, mostly crazy confessions and lunatic ramblings.

Jones also planned to vote for Kenyon, but knew the Villisca newspaper wasn't going to run a story about it. It was shaping up to be a difficult race and Jones had no idea what the outcome was going to be.

By fall, the senate race was still too close to call. There were no scientific polls in those days. The political contest was talked about in pool halls, saloons, restaurants and drug stores, at public events, and over the back fence with the neighbors.

The hoopla over Gustafson's candidacy had faded by October and his supporters had come to realize that he was unlikely to win. The question then became whether or not he would snag enough Republican votes to put a Democrat into office. Jones was working hard to prevent this from happening, but Reiley was working hard too. Many observers expected the three-man race to end with Gustafson third, drawing enough of the votes away from Jones to give Reiley the victory.

But that wasn't the way things happened. On Thursday, October 24, Alvin Gustafson announced that he was withdrawing from the race. He told the newspapers that he was not doing so at the suggestion of Jones (which seemed to imply that Jones had contacted him) but because it had become apparent to him that neither he nor Jones could win and Gustafson did not want to take the blame for putting a Democrat into office.

That same night, Jones was toastmaster at the Villisca Commercial Club banquet, which was held at the Methodist Church. It was an important event, made even more special by Gustafson's announcement. Now, Jones could speak to his friends and colleagues and feel more confident about the fact that he might actually become a state senator.

Many of those that took part in the dinner that evening became intertwined in the troubles that faced Frank Jones in the years to come. Albert F. Davie performed a musical number that night. He was considered to be one of the premier vocalists in the area, widely known as the "songbird of Villisca." He sang at hundreds of weddings, banquets, church services and funerals over the years. He was also one of the men that would soon be accused of having an affair with Dona Jones. Whatever the case, when Albert died in 1935, Davie sang as his funeral. When Frank died in 1940, Davie was one of his pallbearers.

Schoolteacher turned real estate and insurance agent F.A. Glackemeyer spoke at the banquet that night about Villisca's recent building boom. He was a neighbor of Jones and would later testify in two separate trials. Mayor F.M. Kelsey, a dentist who was not running for re-election and would be replaced by L.E. Lewis, would be instrumental in the hiring of the detective who would ruin Frank Jones' life nearly two years later. Lewis, an attorney, would become embroiled in that investigation and would end up as a witness in one of the trials that followed.

But on the night of the Commercial Club banquet, all of that was still in the future. The main thing on Jones' mind in late October 1912 was the election, which was literally days away.

The dust soon cleared and it became apparent that even without Gustafson, the race was uncomfortably close. In Montgomery County, Jones got 1,596 votes. Reiley received 1,454 and the Socialist candidate, J.F. Christie, ended up with 84. Even though he had withdrawn, 332 people still voted for Gustafson. Red Oak overwhelmingly went to Reiley, but rural districts and small towns put Jones over the top. In the end, it was Villisca – the town where rumors could have hurt him the most – that handed the election to Frank Jones.

10. THE CASE TURNS COLD

A few weeks before 1912 came to a close, another brutal ax murder took place in the Midwest. This time, it happened in Columbia, Missouri. The victims were two elderly women, Mary J. Wilson, 82, and her daughter, Georgia Moore, 61. They were hacked to death in their home on Moore's Boulevard, a short distance west of North Seventh Street. An old ax with a blunt edge and a broken handle had been used to commit the crime. It was found in a ravine about 50 feet from the house. Mrs. Wilson had been murdered in her bed and her daughter's partially undressed body was found lying near the back door with a horrible gash in her neck and a deep cut in her forehead that had splintered her skull.

An arrest was quickly made. Henry Lee Moore, Georgia Moore's son and Mrs. Wilson's grandson, was charged with the murders. Moore was 38 years old and worked in the blacksmith department of the Wabash Railroad car shops in Moberly, Missouri. He lived a rough life and had been sentenced to the Kansas State Reformatory in Hutchinson, Kansas, on a forgery charge. He was released in 1911 and later testified that he lived with his mother and grandmother during the winter of 1911 and the summer of 1912. That fall, he left for Moberly to take the job with the railroad.

When questioned, Moore claimed that he had left Moberly at 6 a.m. on the Wednesday morning after the murders, arriving in Columbia at 8:15. He stated that he then went to the house shared by his mother and grandmother, but he got no response when he knocked on the door. Mrs. A.J. Coats said that Moore had stopped by her house that morning and asked how his folks were doing. He told her that he was going to hurry over to their house because he wanted to arrange Christmas with them. A short time afterwards, Moore went to the home of another neighbor, Mrs. Sam Cornelison, and asked about his family. He told her that no one seemed to be home. Moore then went to the back door and pushed it open, "finding" the two women dead. He ran back to the Cornelison home and other neighbors were notified and went to the scene of the crime.

The police searched the house and surrounding area. It was at this time that the bloody, broken ax was found. The bodies were taken to the undertaker and an inquest was held, during which Moore was questioned.

Soon after the inquest, it was learned that Moore had actually arrived in

Columbia on Tuesday afternoon, the day of the murders. He arrived at 3:45 p.m. and spent the night at the Central Hotel, placing him in the city when his mother and grandmother were killed. Slowly, the rest of his story unraveled, and when it was learned that his grandmother had recently sold a farm for a sizable amount of money, Moore was arrested. He was tried and convicted to a life sentence at the state penitentiary in Jefferson City.

Eventually, Henry Lee Moore became a potential suspect in the Villisca murders, but few took the claims against him seriously. Regardless, it was another tragic and shocking crime that came in the wake of Villisca. It certainly attracted the attention of some of the detectives looking into the Villisca case, ending 1912 on a dark and bloody note.

The year 1913 turned out to be a time of almost complete inactivity in the Villisca murder case. Few new leads were discovered and the investigation began to grow cold. That's not to suggest that the murders had been forgotten, though. Lawmen, detectives, doctors, and family members were all haunted by the night of June 9, 1912 – as were the people of Villisca, who still felt a twinge of fear when the sun went down each day.

Early in 1913, Charles Moore, J.B.'s father, passed away. Moore had settled in the Villisca area in 1869 and had raised 15 children. He had been sick for some time and his death was not a surprise, but it meant more sorrow for the family.

As the case grew colder, Attorney General George Cosson stopped dealing directly with the Villisca investigation, the family, and the detectives. He delegated it to an assistant attorney named Henry E. Sampson, who began hearing a lot about what a strange fellow Reverend Kelly was. In the early spring of 1913, he received a letter from a private detective that detailed information about the case and provided some lurid information about Kelly. The letter reported the minister to be a "window-peeker" with unnatural sexual tendencies. He also ran up numerous debts and took loans with no intention of repaying them. Kelly talked incessantly about the murders, the letter added. Perhaps of more substance was the claim that he had taken a bloody shirt to a laundry in Council Bluffs, Iowa, a day or two after the murders. Sampson checked with County Attorney William Ratcliff and was assured that the authorities knew about Kelly and that they were checking into the story of the bloody shirt. It was soon learned that a Bluffs City Laundry employee named Cora Marquard had seen the shirt. She stated that it was wet when Kelly brought it in. The bloodstains had soaked all of the way through the fabric and it looked to her like it had been soaked in water, likely in an attempt to wash out the stains before it was brought into the laundry. She described it as a white shirt, designed for a detachable collar, with cuffs and a front pleat -- the type of shirt a minister would wear.

But the reason for the letter about Kelly? One of the detectives in the case was looking for more money to continue his investigation into the strange little minister and hoped that the state of Iowa would provide it.

Sampson decided that Kelly, who was living in Nebraska by then, needed to be questioned by someone else before any additional funds could be allocated. By this time, the budget for investigating the case had been all but exhausted. Sending another paid detective on a trip that might be a waste of time was out of the question. So he contacted J.A. Tracy, Iowa's assistant state fire marshal, to go to Nebraska and have a talk with the minister.

Tracy may have seemed an odd choice to be recruited as an investigator, but strangely, he wasn't. The state fire marshal's office had been created two years earlier and funds allowed for the marshal and one assistant. An accountant with political ties to the governor was appointed as fire marshal and Tracy, who had been a U.S. Deputy Marshal for northern Iowa, was named as the assistant. Tracy was in constant demand by local police departments and fire officials who wanted him to look into their suspicious fires. It had not been the intent when creating the fire marshal's office, but Tracy became the first full-time employee of the state who was primarily a criminal investigator. Thanks to his experience, he was a good choice to interview Kelly.

Tracy's report to Sampson was brief and noncommittal. He traveled to Omaha, spoke with Kelly and learned where he was on the day of the Moore murder, what he had been doing in Villisca, what happened at the church that night. Kelly also told him about the man with the dark complexion he claimed was sitting behind J.B. After the service, Kelly said that he had gone home with Reverend Ewing, but didn't sleep that night because he felt very restless and uneasy. He left for the railroad depot early and there, he encountered the same man from the church, now wearing a different suit and hat. He left on the 5:19 a.m. train for Macedonia and the man got on the same train.

His report may have been non-committal, but privately, Tracy was disturbed by the odd little man. He had learned of some of Kelly's antics in Villisca and read the reports of his strange proclivities. Tracy and Sampson both felt Kelly was a suspicious character who was worth watching, but they agreed that there was not enough evidence for an arrest. Sherriff Jackson had a different opinion and felt more strongly about it. He was satisfied that Kelly had nothing to do with the crime. Like others (then and now), he saw Kelly as an eccentric, mentally unbalanced man, but a harmless one. There was no evidence, not even an allegation, that Kelly had ever harmed anyone and to think that his first violent act was a multiple ax murder seemed difficult – if not impossible—to believe. At that time, Sheriff Jackson favored the idea that it had been some sort of religious cult murder and if not that, then a traveling maniac, riding the rails, killing and then drifting through the Midwest until he decided to strike again.

Detective Thomas O'Leary also leaned in favor of the "transient butcher," but he had an open, analytical mind and was willing to consider any evidence and see where it led. O'Leary wasn't perfect, but unlike the Burns detectives on the case like Tobie and later, James Wilkerson, he would never be accused of being more interested in money than in justice or of using unethical practices and arriving at conclusions and then twisting the evidence to fit them. He became an advocate of the serial murderer theory, but was never quite sure the Villisca killings weren't the work of a single group or individual. In March 1913, he wrote to Henry Sampson to let him know that he had looked into the ax murders in Columbia and was convinced they had no connection to Villisca. He added, "I assisted the county attorney a few days and there is no doubt in my mind that [Henry] Lee Moore, the man under arrest, killed his mother and grandmother and we will be able to prove the motive." But he did tell Sampson that he had received a number of letters from Reverend Kelly similar to ones that he had received while in Villisca. At that time, he had been interested in what the minister had to say and this hadn't changed. He told Sampson, "Recently, I have given this fellow some thought and sometimes think he might be the guilty man."

O'Leary ended the letter with an offer to work with Sampson if he was needed in the future. While it's impossible to say what direction O'Leary's investigation might have eventually gone, events would have almost certainly been different if O'Leary had been given the case when the family and friends of the Moores decided to hire their own detective in 1914. Unfortunately, though, that didn't happen. By late 1913, the relatives were beyond their initial shock and grief and their mood had changed to frustration and anger. They needed to know who had been responsible for the crime and that someone would be punished for it. But as the first anniversary of the killings came and went, the authorities were no closer to a solution than they had been during the previous fall. In disgust, they sought the attorney general's help in 1914. He directed them to the same source that he had been using since the crimes occurred: the Burns agency. The Moores would live to regret taking his advice.

Meanwhile, Frank Jones came home at the conclusion of the 35th General Assembly, his first as state senator. Albert had taken care of business in his father's absence, but through letters, telephone calls and frequent trips to Villisca, it was Frank Jones who made the decisions. Farm implement sales had been strong that summer and most farmers found it was a better year for crops than 1912. The bank was also doing well, although Jones was not generally involved in the day-to-day operations. He established policy, made decisions on officers and reaped the financial rewards of his investment.

But all was not perfect for the Jones family. Rumors about their involvement in the Moore-Stillinger murders persisted. People whispered that J.B. Moore had been seen with Albert Jones' wife, Dona, in places they shouldn't have been. The telephone operators told of listening in to calls that J.B. had made to Dona in which she told him, "It is all right to come over now." They claimed that Moore had given them boxes of chocolate as a bribe to keep the calls a secret. The Moores were reluctant to accept the fact that J.B and Dona had been having an affair and the claims that business rivalry had been a motive for murder were never very convincing, but the rumors continued.

People loved to gossip and when sex was involved, the stories became irresistible. It's likely that not everyone believed the stories, but the tales were told and re-told anyway, and as time passed, many began to accept them as the truth.

11. "AGENT 33"
DETECTIVE WILKERSON ENTERS THE CASE

In the early spring of 1914, a contingent from Villisca made up of Ross Moore and Dr. F.M. Kelsey, the town's former mayor, traveled to Des Moines to meet with the attorney general, George Cosson, and his assistant, Henry Sampson. Kelsey managed the reward fund for the Moore-Stillinger murders and he had taken a personal interest in trying to get the lagging investigation started again. He was likely involved when the Moore family decided that it wanted to hire its own detective to work the case. It was his idea to meet with the attorney general, both to seek advice in hiring an investigator that state officials would work with and to ask for additional funding from the state. They were prepared to use the proceeds from J.B. Moore's insurance policy, plus a few hundred dollars in contributions that were on deposit. Sarah's father, John Montgomery, had pledged another $250, if needed. Even so, a top detective costs at least $8 to $10 per day, plus expenses, and they had no idea how long the investigation might take. They were hoping the state might be able to help, even though Cosson's budget was limited. In the meeting, he did agree to offer more funds as long as the work that was being done was productive. He wanted to see a solution to the case as much as anyone. Cosson had put a lot of time and energy into the investigation, but had seen little happen with it, outside of it becoming a political liability. As far as recommendations for detectives went, Cosson had only one – the Burns agency. Ross Moore had met with many of the others, including Tobie and O'Leary, but respected Cosson's opinion. A request was put in and a new detective was assigned to the case.

This was how a Texan named James Newton Wilkerson became a part of the Villisca case. No one knew it when he arrived in town but he would be the man who would literally destroy the investigation, warping it for his own gain, turning, twisting and concocting evidence to inflate his own theories in the case, and in the process, becoming an embarrassment to law enforcement in Iowa. In all honesty, the Villisca murders would probably have never been solved – unless Billy the Axman had been arrested after a future crime and confessed to them – but Wilkerson ensured this would be the case.

Wilkerson was 48 in the summer of 1914. He had studied law in Texas and had been admitted to the bar in 1890, but never practiced law in any conventional manner. He decided to become a detective instead and went to work for William

Detective James Wilkerson

J. Burns, who thought highly of him. He commanded a higher wage than most detectives working at the time and managed to bring in a greater number of rewards. When he arrived in Villisca, he claimed to be a Texas land agent, representing a group of investors who were interested in buying farmland in Iowa. It soon became obvious to most people, though, that he was asking more questions about the murders than looking at land. He spent his first few weeks listening to all of the rumors that had been going around town and re-working leads that had been exhausted by other detectives. Wilkerson also managed to make peace with Sheriff Jackson, who had been angered by another Burns detective, C.W. Tobie, who had criticized the sheriff before an earlier suspect had been found and cleared. However, he was unable to patch things up with town constable Hank Horton, who disliked Wilkerson from the beginning. As time passed, the animosity grew, in part because Wilkerson eventually announced that Frank Jones had been responsible for the murders, a position that Horton didn't agree with.

Wilkerson spent time with Ross Moore and with J.B.'s former employees. He sought out those who spread rumors of an affair between J.B. and Dona Moore. Other detectives had heard the gossip that named Jones as a suspect, but had dismissed it. Wilkerson, however, did not and became determined to find any kind of evidence that he could to make his theory fit the crime. I believe that Wilkerson was drawn to the idea of a "Jones conspiracy" because Jones was an important man -- a wealthy businessman and state senator. It would be quite an addition to Wilkerson's resume for him to be able to say that he brought down such a powerful figure in a murder case. And there was also the reward, which was growing all the time. Jones was an easier man to find than some elusive nameless killer who had slipped out of town years before, never to return. Jones was right there in Villisca and in some ways, Wilkerson had public opinion on his side since there were those in town who were more than willing to believe the gossip that was going around about the Jones family. At that point, Wilkerson just needed something that he could "hang his hat on," so to speak, a damning witness or piece of evidence that would kick the case against Jones into full gear.

The search started slowly. Wilkerson was still traveling in the early stages of his investigation, wrapping up cases that he had been working on when he was assigned to Villisca. During April and May, he spent as many days as possible in Montgomery County, learning about events and people and spending a lot of time with Sheriff Jackson. He was gathering facts and possibilities and spent much of his time watching Frank Jones. He visited his store, staked out his house, and followed him around. He even once sat near him in church. At the end of the service, they shook hands, but Jones barely noticed him. He had no idea who the man was and certainly had no foreshadowing of the fact that the detective was going to make every effort to ruin his life.

His first break came in late May. A woman contacted the attorney general's office in Des Moines and later met with Henry Sampson. His details about the meeting are vague and it was never clear if the woman actually had information about the murders, or knew someone who did. The woman wished to remain anonymous and Sampson never recorded her name. After the meeting ended, Sampson contacted the Burns agency and told them that someone needed to look into her story. Wilkerson, in Villisca, made the trip to Des Moines, met with Sampson and then two days later, traveled to Marshalltown, Iowa, a small town northeast of Des Moines.

It seems nearly unbelievable today that Wilkerson would have based his entire case on the bizarre story that was going to be told to him by Vina Tompkins. But he was looking for a story, any kind of story, no matter how weird and colorful it was, upon which he could build his case against Frank Jones. It's hard to believe that the unconvincing tale would be enough – combined with accusations, gossip, and smears -- to ultimately ruin a man's career and reputation. But Wilkerson was determined and his defense and embellishment of the story proves it.

The fact that Wilkerson visited Marshalltown at all shows that he was willing to pursue wild stories that had already been dismissed by other investigators, especially when they pertained to Frank Jones. Vina Tompkins had already been checked out by Hank Horton and Villisca's mayor, L.E. Lewis. A man named Fred Houghkirk, who claimed to be a detective from Marshalltown, had visited Villisca a few months earlier and let it be known that he knew someone who might be able to provide important information about the murders – for a price. Hoping for a reward for himself, Houghkirk told Horton about Vina Tompkins. A few days later, Horton and Lewis traveled to Marshalltown to talk with her. Lewis was a practicing attorney and while young, was a well-educated man. He believed that between himself and Horton, they would be more than qualified to decide if the witness was believable. They learned that Tompkins and her family had been camped in Villisca in the fall of 1911 while her husband worked on a city street paving crew, but little else. They concluded the interview with Tompkins feeling that she had no valuable information to offer.

Wilkerson later contended that Tompkins wouldn't talk to them because Horton threatened her and that she was afraid of him because she knew that he had been bought off by Jones and was actually a part of the conspiracy.

On June 2, Wilkerson took a train to Marshalltown, where he met with Houghkirk and, eventually, with Vina Tompkins. According to Houghkirk, Tompkins had told his wife that she knew a terrible secret about the Villisca murders, including the identity of the people involved. When he was told this, Houghkirk went to see Tompkins, but she was very secretive and vague about what she knew. Houghkirk then shopped her around, hoping for a reward, but she would never tell anyone what her "terrible secret" was until she met Wilkerson. Even then, he had to drag it out of her – or at least that's the way he presented it, probably to brag about his investigation skills.

Wilkerson later told Tompkins' strange story in a detailed report to the attorney general. He described the 36-year-old Tompkins as a "remarkable witness," with little formal education but very smart. Her family name was Whipple and she had grown up in Guthrie County, Iowa. She had lived most of her life in Iowa, moving from place to place, and had spent a few years in North Dakota. When she was 16, she married a man named Dave Clark and had two sons with him. After years of cruel treatment and abuse by Clark, she took her youngest son and fled to North Dakota. She remained there for a few years and then returned to Iowa and sued Clark for divorce. She obtained custody of her sons, but Clark took the oldest boy to California and out of the court's jurisdiction for some time. Eventually, she agreed not to press charges against him for kidnapping the boy as long as Clark returned to Iowa and allowed her visitation rights. She told Wilkerson that she had been denied this privilege and only saw her son when she could arrange secret meetings. She was very afraid of possible continued violence by Clark, Wilkerson said, and this led the detective to make some promises to her in return for her testimony.

Wilkerson was either moved by her story, or more cynically, he claimed to be in order to obtain the information that he wanted from her. According to Tompkins, she was born and raised in an atmosphere of crime and had never been free of criminal influences, which she claimed to hate. Her entire family was made up of criminals and many of them, as well as people where she grew up in Guthrie County, were part of a wide-reaching criminal organization that spread throughout the Midwest. She claimed to know the names and addresses of over 100 members of the gang, including Joe Matthews (alias Jake Weems and several other names), Jack Uviats, Parson Rainey, Jack Ballinger, and many others. She was currently living with a gang leader named Elmo Tompkins and had several brothers who were also part of the gang, Clint Whipple, Harry Whipple, and another named, of all things, The Whipple.

Wilkerson claimed that after Hank Horton and L.E. Lewis interviewed Tompkins, she had received a letter from Jake Weems, an alleged gang leader, warning her that "she was talking too damn much" and that she had better stop. He supposedly also enclosed a letter that she was to give to Fred Houghkirk, which threatened him and told him that he would never be able to break up the gang. There is no indication that this small-time "detective" ever tried to tangle with the "gang" and the alleged letter seems to have been concocted to make Houghkirk seem like someone with whom hardened criminals would not want to tangle. The letter was signed "96," which Tompkins claimed was Weems' number. She explained to Wilkerson that all of the gang members had secret numbers assigned to them and that they frequented communicated in code, using only the numbers to identify themselves to one another. It was like a fantasy spun from the popular Nick Carter secret agent stories of the era, but Wilkerson apparently swallowed all of it – including the fact that Vina had a brother named "The."

Tompkins was also aware, she claimed, of many murders committed by the gang. One murder was alleged to be of a man the gang called only "Old Whiskers." When the gang found out that he was an undercover detective, they lured him across the country and he was never seen again. She said that she knew of many other murders committed by the gang, "many of which have always been shrouded in mystery." They were involved in many other crimes as well, including stealing livestock, passing worthless checks, raiding boxcars, blowing safes, wrecking trains, forging mortgages, and more. Their usual method of operation was to work in teams of four and then split the spoils of the crime four ways. The larger gang did not share in the split from individual crimes. They only banded together for mutual protection and to intimidate witnesses, pay off corrupt officials, and provide getaway arrangements when needed. She further told Wilkerson that it was agreed upon that if any of the gang members were arrested "he takes his medicine and never squeals." She added that this rarely happened, since the organization had a number of law enforcement officials in their employ who protected them and tipped them off to danger.

Tompkins said she knew of members in the gang with connections to Villisca, including a man named Jack Ballinger, who she said was in jail in Red Oak at the time of Wilkerson's interview. Ballinger had kept his wife in a house on the outskirts of Villisca and he rented her out for sex to anyone who wanted to pay. He treated her badly and once had carved his initials into her breast with a knife. Later, he did jail time for incest (or another statutory offense, she wasn't sure) and had been "giving the officers around Villisca trouble ever since."

The man she was living with and whose name she had taken was Elmo Tompkins, who worked as a bricklayer and laborer around Marshalltown. He was also a peripheral member of the gang. Tompkins had been laying bricks on a job in Villisca, which is what brought Vina into contact with the Moore family before the murders. At the time, she was living in a camp along the East Nodaway River on the outskirts of Villisca. She became acquainted, she claimed, with the Moore family and had been in their house. Around the time of the murders, she had been in Corning with her husband, who was working there. However, several members of the gang, including her brothers Harry and The, had been in the vicinity of Villisca. She said that soon after the murders, she and Elmo went to live in Redfield, Iowa, then Perry, where they stayed for a time, and then several other places, before finally ending up in Marshalltown about six months before she met with Wilkerson.

Tompkins told Wilkerson that she knew all of the details about the murders in Villisca, who did it, who paid to have it done, why it was done, and everything about them. She had waited so long to come forward because soon after the murders had been committed, she left Elmo Tompkins due to his drinking and physical abuse. She had only delayed in leaving him because she had been unable to find out where her former husband was holding her eldest boy. After she learned of his whereabouts, she left, but the gang soon found her and brought her back, threatening her with death if she left again. When she told them that she would rather die than be involved with them again, her children were threatened, so she reluctantly agreed to remain with them.

All this was very melodramatic and there was more to come.

It was Houghkirk who finally convinced her to come forward, Wilkerson stated. Soon after the detective began investigating her, he moved into a house near where she lived, cultivated her friendship and ingratiated himself with her family. A short time later, someone broke into his house at night and attacked him, clubbing him in the shoulder when they missed his head in the darkness. Houghkirk chased them into the yard and fired a few shots after the attacker, but he got away. Wilkerson believed the attacker was either Jake Weems or Elmo Tompkins, trying to force him off the case.

According to Wilkerson, Vina Tompkins agreed to confess to all she knew on two conditions, namely that he would rescue her son from her former husband, Dave Clark, and get her and the boys to safety somewhere out of the reach of the gang. After that, she said she would tell him everything.

In his report, Wilkerson told the attorney general that he was sure that Tompkins was telling the truth and that her account fit with other facts in the case that she had no knowledge of. He added, "I conclude that since her life and the life of her two boys will be the pledges for her faithful performance of her part of the contract that I can safely negotiate with her." He then dramatically noted, "With just how much personal safety to myself from the gang will depend somewhat upon judgment, discretion, cunning, but largely upon luck."

Cosson and Sampson were interested in the tale that Tompkins had to tell. However, it's also likely they had reservations about her and some elements of her story. Her character was in question and it appeared she had a wild imagination. There was also the issue of Wilkerson having promised Tompkins safety in exchange for her information. In spite of this, Cosson felt the story needed to be looked into further and he agreed to underwrite half of the expenses of the investigation. He may have warned Wilkerson about promising Tompkins safe haven, since it's barely mentioned in Wilkerson's reports after that. He used other methods to get the story, which turned out to be even more questionable.

The closing words of Wilkerson's report, which warned of the danger to himself that he was about to take on, became typical of his melodramatic style. For instance, when he wrote of his second meeting with Cosson and Sampson in Des Moines, he referred to two other men in attendance: "Manage JAG" and "Dr. K" The first man was J.A. Gustafson, manager of the Burns Detective Agency's Kansas City office and the other was Dr. Kelsey, the Villisca dentist and former mayor who was working with the families and providing funds for the investigation. There was no real need to conceal their identities in his report, aside from being dramatic. He also began signing his reports with a made-up code name that he gave himself – "Agent 33." It was a bad sign of things to come.

Wilkerson met with Tompkins again on June 10, but "Agent 33" stated in his report that she wouldn't talk with him due to a remark that he made to Houghkirk implying that the relationship between Houghkirk and Tompkins was not strictly platonic. Houghkirk told Tompkins and she supposedly took offense. Wilkerson met with her again the next day, writing that it took "a lot of persuasion," but he got back in her good graces again. However, she still refused to tell him her "secret." He made plans to visit her again on June 12, but it rained that day so Elmo stayed home, canceling Wilkerson's visit. He seems to have avoided Elmo Tompkins completely. He often wrote about him, but never mentioned meeting him.

Wilkerson spent the day with Houghkirk, discussing the case. As the two men were sitting on Houghkirk's front porch, watching the rain, Wilkerson saw a saleswoman going door-to-door in the neighborhood. This gave him an idea. He recalled an experience that Vina Tompkins said she had with a fortune-teller. She claimed that she had visited a psychic, who had "looked into my palm and told me I had a terrible secret on my mind." Her need to share this secret about the Villisca Ax Murders had led her to tell Mrs. Houghkirk about it, who told her husband and eventually brought Wilkerson to her door.

Wilkerson followed the saleswoman to the boarding house where she was staying and found out that she was part of a crew of women in town selling household remedies and cosmetics. The manager of the group was a woman from New York named Mrs. McEntire, who he described as "brilliant and talented." Wilkerson's plan, which was agreed to by Mrs. McEntire, was to have her go to Vina Tompkins' house the following day under the pretense of selling her wares, but to also let Tompkins know that she possessed certain psychic powers. Wilkerson filled Mrs. McEntire in about Vina's background – her previous marriage, her children, her troubled past and more. Armed with this information, Mrs. McEntire was to convince her of her occult powers, gain her confidence, and then tell her that she should tell her secret to a man in whom she could trust completely – James Wilkerson.

Mrs. McEntire called on Vina on Friday, June 19, and Vina Tompkins easily took the bait. Wilkerson never stated how much he paid McEntire for her work, but to him, it had been well worth the money.

In his next report, Wilkerson said that he stayed away from Vina over the weekend so that she could mull over the "psychic's" advice. He waited until Monday, a day that he knew she went downtown. He followed her and "accidentally" bumped into her outside a store. She told him that she wanted to see him. He arranged to come by her house at 1:30 on the following afternoon. The meeting lasted for four hours. Wilkerson said that they mostly talked about fortune-tellers, especially about the one who told Tompkins that she had been sent by God to tell her she should trust the detective. Their meeting lasted until 5:30, close to the time when Elmo would be home, so there was not enough time to talk about the murders. They made arrangements to meet the next day at a nearby cemetery. It was in the graveyard that Vina Tompkins finally told her story, which in turn was passed on by Wilkerson. How accurate was his summary? That's a question that many people would ask in the days, months, and years to come.

In the fall of 1911, Elmo and Vina Tompkins, Vina's brother, Harry Whipple, his wife, Edith, and one child from each family, traveled to Villisca. The men were looking for work on the crew that was paving Third Avenue, the town's main street. They camped along the East Nodaway River, about a half-mile east of town. The men were hired and worked long days in town while the women spent their time at the camp, cooking, washing, and taking care of the children. Near the camp was an old building that had once been a slaughterhouse, which many of the local merchants used as a place to dump discarded crates. Vina and Edith went there often to get wooden crates that could be broken up and used as firewood.

One day, which Vina thought was in mid-September, Vina, Edith and Edith's daughter were walking to the slaughterhouse when the little girl stepped on a thorn. Edith returned to camp with the child and Vina continued on to look for crates. As she neared the site, she heard voices and ducked down to hide behind some thick brush. She said she was very close to three men, but they never saw her. She described them in a general way: the first was in his fifties with gray hair and a beard, the second was slender and clean-shaven and appeared to be his mid-twenties, and the third was a rough-looking man that she didn't see clearly.

According to the report, she heard the older man say, "He deserves killing, he must be killed, he has got to be killed. If it can't be done any other way, it has to be done while he is asleep, if he has to be chloroformed."

The third man talked of "getting Levi to do the job." He made several references to a gang and mentioned the name "Whipple." This attracted Vina's attention. Whipple was her maiden name and Levi Wood was a member of the gang that she often talked about. There was talk about money and the older man said he had it, but would have to be careful and not take it out of the bank all at once. There was also discussion about an escape route and dealing with the city marshal. At that point, she claimed the older man said, "The marshal is fixed. He will never bother anybody that does it, and he will see that nobody else bothers while they are getting away."

After the men left, Vina returned to camp. She said she didn't sleep that night. She cried and pleaded with Elmo to leave Villisca. She wouldn't tell him about what she heard because she feared that her brother, Harry Whipple, was involved and was afraid that if Elmo found out he would get dragged into a murder scheme. Elmo was drunk and beat her, but he eventually agreed to leave.

The women went to town the next day to get some things for the trip and while there Vina said they encountered a "big fellow, and he had a mean look on his face, and he began to look closely at Edith and I." She asked and learned that the man was Marshal Hank Horton. The next day, they were preparing to leave when the mules that drew their wagon got stuck in the mud at the riverbank. The women and children were on the bridge when two men came by and asked if they were alone. The men were the oldest and youngest of the three men that Vina had heard planning the murder. Vina said she was rude to them, hoping they would leave, and they did. Moments later, a man came by driving a wagon with a load of coal and she asked him who the men were that had just passed by. She said she thought he told her their names were "Jones or Stone," she wasn't sure exactly.

The mules were pulled out of the mud and the families left for Clarinda. A few days later they traveled to Corning, where Elmo again found work laying bricks. They relocated every few months, mostly living out of the wagon, until eventually settling in Marshalltown. Months after leaving Villisca, she read about the murders in the newspaper and knew the plot had been carried out. When she saw the location of the house, she realized she had been inside, having been given a drink of water, and had met the Moore family.

Wilkerson's report states that Vina Tompkins told him that after her initial conversation with the Houghkirks about the murders, she had two more encounters with Hank Horton. She said the first took place a few months after the murders. She and her husband were sleeping and heard their dog barking downstairs. Elmo refused to go and investigate, so she went herself. She claimed that she found Horton sitting in her living room and that he tried to grab her. She fled upstairs and Horton left. She said she next saw the marshal a few weeks later when he and Mayor Lewis came to see her, asking what she knew about the murders.

Another incident that Tompkins believed was connected to the murders occurred when Elmo took her along on a visit to Guthrie County, where his family still lived. She didn't want to go, she said, because she knew Elmo would take up with the gang, which he did. One night, her brother Harry, Levi Wood, and Elmo came to the house where they were staying. It was late and all three men were very drunk. They said they were going to kill Vina's brother-in-law, George Green. When she asked why, they replied, "He has squealed about the murder." They left the house, followed by Vina and Edith. The women took a shortcut and made it to George's houses before the three men. They warned him and he hurriedly packed his gear to leave. In order to stall for time, Vina said she raced down the road and met the three would-be assassins on a bridge. She asked them again why they planned to kill George. "God damn him," one of them reportedly told her, "he has squawked and tipped off that Villisca murder." She answered that it hadn't been George who talked, that it had been her. Harry then pulled a knife and came at her, but Vina took it away from him and threatened her brother with it. He was still sober enough to know she intended to use it and backed away. George Green escaped and hid out in Omaha for a few months. By then, the matter seemed to have blown over and he returned.

Vina said she had another conversation with Levi Wood that she believed further incriminated him. The two of them got into some sort of argument over money and Vina told him that he had none. Wood replied that he had more money than she knew about. She asked him if he had got it in Villisca and Wood went into a rage. He told her to never say anything about that "Villisca deal" or she and her boy would be killed. Vina refused to back down and told Wood that she had police officers that would protect her and her son and Wood laughed. They couldn't protect her, he said, the people who had committed the murders had walked right past two police officers after it was done and weren't even questioned. Tompkins was sure that Levi Wood was the murderer and that other members of the gang had participated.

Wilkerson's report to the attorney general contained a statement that he attributed directly to Vina Tompkins. According to Wilkerson, she said:

You are the first living person I have told this to. I have always been afraid for my life. I will have to depend on you to do the right thing for me. I do not want any money for telling this story, but I want to get away from the gang. I don't want you to put me on the witness stand because they will outswear me. Use this information in any way you see fit, any way that it will do any good, but please do not tell anyone under the shining sun who told you. I will depend on you to protect me in this. I believe I can trust you. I do not know why they waited so long after the plot. I don't know if Harry was used. I feel certain that Levi Wood is the one who actually did the deed.

Wilkerson's report stated his own belief that the third man at the slaughterhouse that day had been number "96," aka Jake Weems. He said that he thought Vina knew this, but refused to name him because he had assisted her with some domestic problems. He expressed the "unreserved opinion" that Weems was the "other corner of the triangle in the slaughterhouse murder plot."

There is no record to show how Cosson and Sampson felt about the sensational report. The two men were interested and agreed that the story needed to be looked into further, but there were parts of it that were beyond belief, making the entire thing questionable. The two law enforcement officials must have also questioned Wilkerson's shady tactic of hiring a phony fortune-teller, then taking the subject to a graveyard for the interview, where nothing could really be written down and recorded. This created a dilemma that was apparently not considered by the attorney general – that the report was Wilkerson's embroidered version of what Vina Tompkins said, not necessarily what she actually told him. Much of it, she would later deny. But whether Wilkerson influenced her or distorted her story, he had a report in his hands that outlined a murder conspiracy masterminded by men identified as "Jones or Stone" who matched the general descriptions of Frank Jones and his son, Albert.

Wilkerson's theory would later change. He later focused on the slaughterhouse plot with Frank and Albert Jones being involved with Harry Whipple, discounting Levi Wood. He also had different ideas, at different times, about Jake Weems. By the time that Vina Tompkins appeared in court to set the record straight about Jones, Wilkerson didn't need her. He had other witnesses and evidence that he believed would convict Jones. Vina Tompkins was merely a tool, a means to an end, and a way for Wilkerson's real investigation to begin.

On June 16, 1914, he traveled to Villisca with the intention of confronting Frank Jones, or so he claimed. When he got there, "Agent 33" learned that Jones was in New York, attending his daughter's graduation exercises. A short report to the attorney general about the failed interrogation was accompanied by his expense account and a bill for his services.

Wilkerson offered no clue as to how he intended to approach Jones, but later when he questioned Albert Jones and Burt McCaul, he began by learning what he could by engaging in friendly conversation and then watching their reactions after asking a few surprise questions. Wilkerson was an expert at asking carefully phrased, very leading questions and twisting around the answers. He later printed and sold to the public a list of 100 questions that he wanted Jones to answer, a few of which he likely would have asked on June 16, if the senator had been in town.

After failing to find Jones, Wilkerson went to his office and wrote another report to the attorney general, which he titled "Corrections, Memoranda and Suggestions." Wilkerson wrote that he had made a number of conclusions in the Villisca case and he offered information that he noted should be "assumed" was true about the murders. Point by point, he wrote:

First: That the murderer was stark naked when these lives were taken, except he wore gloves.

Wilkerson explained that he thought the killer was naked (except for gloves) because no bloody clothing was ever found. It would have been impossible, he said, for the murders to have occurred without soaking the perpetrator's clothing with blood. He was convinced that the killer had walked boldly away from the house, in plain sight, so he could not have been carrying a bundle of clothing with him. He had cleaned up, Wilkerson believed, and then had gotten dressed again. He wore gloves, Wilkerson concluded, because no fingerprints had been left behind on the ax. Even if there had been fingerprints, the local officials lacked the methods or the knowledge to collect and analyze them. More likely the ax was simply wiped off.

Second: It is my further opinion that the draping of the mirror in the room where the main portion of the family was killed was an act of superstition.

Wilkerson's theory about the superstition surrounding the mirror had nothing to do with spirits of the dead, as some people assumed when they learned the mirrors and reflective surfaces were covered. He stated that he had heard of a belief where it was bad luck to see oneself naked in a mirror. He also cited the idea that many killers were superstitious, citing an example of Sicilian Mafia killers, who kissed their victims on the lips to keep their ghosts from pursuing them after death.

Third: I am of the further opinion that the meal prepared in the kitchen and partially consumed was prepared by a party not in any way connected with the dead.

Believe it or not, thanks to the many disparaging comments that I have written about Wilkerson so far (with more to come), I agree with his theory on this one – although I believe he named the wrong person as the intruder who ate the meal. I don't believe that the killer prepared the food either, mostly because it doesn't fit the pattern for any of the other murders that came before Villisca, but Wilkerson believed that the food was eaten by Lee Van Gilder, a nephew of J.B. Moore, who entered the kitchen through the back door, never realizing what was happening in the house. Wilkerson surmised that the young man had been in the kitchen eating and was discovered by the killer. He rushed out of the house, barely escaping with his life, and was so thoroughly frightened that he refused to speak about it afterwards. Supposedly, Van Gilder was seen in the park around midnight on the night of the murders. The murders were alleged to have taken place around midnight, or soon after, based on the time when the victims arrived home after church. Wilkerson heard around Villisca that Van Gilder had told his girlfriend that, "had he not been drunk on the night of the murder, he could have prevented it." He was also informed that the young man had been uneasy about his personal safety ever since it happened.

As mentioned, I don't agree with all of Wilkerson's suppositions on this point. I think that a second person was in the house that night and this person not only ate the food but covered the mirrors, as well. I'll talk more about this later on.

Fourth: It is my further opinion that the main actor in the instigation of these terrible murders had an extra incentive of extreme jealousy, besides the hatred that he bore for the head of the murdered family, on account of known business disagreements, and when I say the main actor, I mean not the husband of the woman whose lack of chastity is at the bottom, doubtless, of this awful tragedy, but her father-in-law.

Since this was a private report to the attorney general, there is no reason why Wilkerson – or perhaps we should say "Agent 33" – needed to refer to the Jones family in such obscure terms. The "main actor" was Frank Jones; the "husband of the woman" was Albert Jones; and, of course, the flirtatious Dona was the woman with the "lack of chastity." Wilkerson had been listening to all of the gossip that had been swirling about town for the last two years and had created his own scenario from it. He believed that Frank Jones was in love with, and possibly having an affair with, his daughter-in-law. Since J.B. Moore was not only rumored to be having an affair with Dona, he was also a business rival, which gave Jones two reasons to hate him. Wilkerson based his belief in the affair on the fact that Jones' wife never accompanied him to church, but Dona often did and Frank occasionally accompanied her home. After following Jones for some time, he also came to the conclusion that Jones was "an amorous individual" and claimed he once saw him trying to make a date with a woman who was a stranger in town.

Jealousy about Dona's affairs would not have affected her husband, Wilkerson thought. Albert knew about Dona's dubious morals when he married her and Wilkerson wrote, "I am also reliably informed that she has doubtful associations but with undoubted purpose, among numerous male admirers, which the young man must know and has taken no steps to prevent." The real character of Frank Jones, Wilkerson said, when brought to light, will show that he is "a man of strong passion, unscrupulous instinct, extreme cunning, and one when stirred by jealousy in love affairs, added to extreme jealousy in business affairs, will be ferocious in the extreme."

Fifth: I am of the further opinion that the man who occupied the pulpit of the First Methodist Church that fatal night, in the guise of a Holy Roller preacher, was connected with the crime, if not the actual perpetrator of the deed.

This is probably the strangest of Wilkerson's allegations. There is nothing to say where he came up with the idea, but it could have been influenced by Sheriff Jackson's belief that the Moores had been killed by a group of religious fanatics. Wilkerson couldn't really connect religious maniacs with Frank Jones, but connecting them to Jones' church seemed to be the next best thing.

It's also obvious from his report that Wilkerson – like many other people at the time – had a prejudice against the Holy Rollers, a sect that was definitely outside of the norm of mainstream Christianity in that era. The Holy Rollers were an offshoot sect of Pentecostalism, a part of the Christian church that places special emphasis on the direct experience of God through the baptism of the Holy Spirit, or "speaking in tongues." The idea of speaking in tongues (glossolalia) became a basic tenet in Pentecostalism and it is still practiced today.

There are several different types of the Pentecostal faith but the most conservative are members of the Apostolic branch, who are separated from many of the other "charismatic" churches. Apostolic church services can be very lively, placing great emphasis on testifying, praise for the Lord, fiery sermons, and almost hypnotic music. It is during these music and prayer sessions that members of the congregation sometimes become possessed by the Holy Spirit, which can result in speaking in tongues, dancing, jumping up and down, running through the church, shouting, crying, falling to the ground and passing out. It's not surprising that the outsiders who witnessed these sessions found them both bizarre and a little frightening.

While it may seem a little strange that the staid members of the First Methodist Church of Villisca would offer the use of their building to the exuberant Holy Rollers, it can be explained by a simple impulse of generosity to fellow Christians. To Wilkerson, though, nothing was ever simple. He believed that the use of the church somehow figured into the Jones conspiracy. He wrote in his report:

It is a well known fact that the Methodist Church is an aristocratic institution. It is one of the two leading and fashionable churches in Villisca. The Holy Roller people and those of their ilk are of a very low type. They are actually to be classed as religious maniacs. Their doings become practically intolerable, and have caused trouble in many localities. In some instances, they have walked stark naked through streets in towns and cities. They writhe upon the ground in a religious frenzy, and pronounce curious incantations; they pretend to speak in strange tongues, calling it a confusion of tongues; they emit horrible shouts, cut fantastic capers and otherwise deport themselves in a way far from who might be in any manner considered approaching the formal, or, to put it stronger, they can't strictly be called decent.

Now it is unthinkable that the Pastor of the Methodist Church in Villisca should have vacated his pulpit in favor of a man of this stripe had not a strong and favorable influence been brought to bear to accomplish this purpose.

And who did Wilkerson believe pushed the pastor into loaning the use of the church to the Holy Rollers? Frank Jones, of course. In Wilkerson's opinion, Jones practically ruled the church as the superintendent of the Sunday school and the dictator of its policies. Because of his wealth, he donated heavily to the church and in return, was allowed to run it as he saw fit from his customary pew near the front. It was this particular pew, Wilkerson pointed out, that he had occupied during every service except for the night of the murders. On that night, he sat near the door and left the service early, which was unprecedented for him. Wilkerson believed that he went outside early to check on the progress of the Children's Day Program and to find out when the Moores might be leaving for home. A simpler explanation might be that Jones was just as annoyed with the Holy Rollers' form of worship as other people were at that time. He most likely wanted to be there to keep an eye on things, and he chose to sit near the door so he could leave early, which he did. It was very unlikely that there was anything more sinister to it than that.

The way that Wilkerson twisted around Jones' behavior that night was just as ridiculous as his claim that the leader of the Holy Rollers revival killed the Moores and the Stillinger girls. He had absolutely no evidence to back up such a claim, but he didn't care. All he wanted to do was to plant the seed of doubt, get people talking, and then fan the flames into something that he could pretend was evidence.

Wilkerson threw out this information to the attorney general and then followed it up with a blatant attempt to solicit more work and generally make himself appear indispensable. He pushed for the questioning of two local farmers who claimed to have seen Albert Jones with two strange men on the morning after the murders. He wanted to nail down the whereabouts of Harry Whipple, Dave Weems, and Levi Wood at the time of the murders. He wanted to dig through Jones' financial records and look for unexplained expenditures around the time of the murders, especially funds drawn from a bank in Morton Mills, in which he maintained Jones had a secret interest. He also wanted to question those who saw Jones at church that night and press Van Gilder for the truth about what happened at the Moore house.

Wilkerson was also very concerned with getting a confession out of Hank Horton, whom he disliked and distrusted. He was convinced the lawman had something to do with the conspiracy. He wanted the marshal's movements on the night of the murders thoroughly researched and wanted to know why he had been harassing Vina Tompkins. "The marshal, at the proper time, should be handled with a view of getting a confession," he wrote to the attorney general. "He, in my opinion, is a low browed, cowardly individual, who would squeal if the right pressure is brought."

"Agent 33" was also sure that he could force a confession from Albert Jones, if given the chance. He told the attorney general that he had heard a rumor that Albert was out of the house on the night of the murders and that his mother heard a sound, went to investigate and found her son sneaking inside. "This should be thoroughly investigated," he stated. In closing, he wrote:

I would also suggest that local officials be kept away as much as possible. This case ought to be handled through the attorney general's office strictly... local officials have always acted strangely.

And who was the primary investigator for the attorney general's office at that time – none other than James Wilkerson! He was simply pushing for more work. The report held little of any substance; Wilkerson was simply showing that the rumors that had been around for two years had grown a little, but were basically still the same and were just as baseless. And not only that, Wilkerson proved that he was spending too much time chasing down rumors to do proper research. He wrote that Jones "might" have an interest in a bank at Morton Mills (where he allegedly kept his conspiracy slush fund) but everyone knew about Jones' involvement with the bank: he was its president. This fact was posted in the bank's regular front page newspaper advertisements.

Henry Sampson, who dealt directly with Wilkerson, must have questioned the whole unlikely premise that the detective was putting forth, as well as the impossible complexity of the plot, but he grudgingly admitted that Wilkerson was asking questions that needed to be answered – like, did Van Gilder really say that he could have prevented the murder? Did Senator Jones behave oddly at church that night? Was he really having an affair with his daughter-in-law? Sampson recommended to his boss that the investigation continue. Attorney General Cosson, who certainly didn't know at the time that Wilkerson's growing conspiracy theory was soon to include him, read the report, paid the bill, and agreed that there was still work to be done.

Meanwhile, Reverend Kelly was getting into more hot water during the summer of 1914. He had been arrested earlier that year in South Dakota, charged with using the U.S. Mail to try and entice a teenage girl to pose nude for him as inspiration for a religious book that he was writing. He was later transferred to a federal mental asylum in Washington D.C. for evaluation.

Interest in Kelly's connection to the Villisca murders was renewed, mostly due to his behavior while jailed in South Dakota. He not only spoke frequently about the murders, both to the jailers and to the other prisoners, but he also implied that he was responsible. On at least one occasion, he told a guard that he had actually committed them. According to the statement of a cellmate, an Indian named Baptiste Takes the Knife, Kelly groped and made attempts to perform oral sex on other inmates. He also ranted, begged to be killed, and one report claimed that he attempted suicide. Sheriff Jackson was contacted and he made the trip from Red Oak to South Dakota, accompanied by County Attorney Ratcliff. Both men sat down with Kelly and once again ended the interview believing that he was definitely an oddball, he was not the killer.

Regardless, word reached the newspapers that Kelly had made incriminating statements in jail, and that Jackson and Ratcliff had looked into them. Several reporters pursued the story and published articles that included some of the circumstances that had made Kelly a suspect in the first place. The result was that, while at the asylum in Washington, Kelly and his doctors consented to an interview. The minister emphatically denied any involvement in the murders and his doctors seemed to agree that he hadn't committed them. Kelly said that he had witnesses who could account for his whereabouts at the time of the murders (he didn't) and that he wouldn't have killed anyone. Doctors at the asylum are quoted as saying that Kelly had a violent temper, but they doubted that he was capable of the slayings in Villisca. Kelly told the no doubt astonished reporters that he had become a target of the investigation because he was a detective himself, and had looked into the crime and developed his own theories. Because some of his theories were close to the mark, the real killer was trying to frame him. Kelly turned out not to be thrilled with the press coverage that resulted from his interview. He thought the stories made him look like a lunatic, which was not surprising.

He ended up spending a few months being evaluated at the asylum before his doctors released him on the grounds that he was basically harmless. He returned to preaching soon after his release. Because of his disturbed mental state at the time, the charges against him for using the mail to solicit a minor female were dismissed.

Frank Jones took time that summer to write a lengthy piece on Iowa road law, which appeared on the front page of the *Villisca Review*. The arrival of automobiles in southwest Iowa had made good roads a priority. The problem at the time was the question of which agency was going to build and maintain them, where they would be located, and how they would be paid for. The statute that established the state highway commission in 1904 gave some responsibilities to the state and others to the counties and townships. The majority of voters were unhappy with how the law was working and felt the state should not play a role in building roads. They wanted the law to be repealed. Jones thought the law could be fixed with some of the amendments that he had in mind and wanted to let the voters know what they were. He would eventually be successful in getting the amendments enacted and was later recognized by the governor for his work on the new plan.

The issue, though, was a divisive one and upset both the local citizens and many career politicians. County Attorney Ratcliff decided not to seek re-election that fall and instead started making preparations for a run for Jones' senate seat in 1916. It would be an election where new roads would become a major issue.

The rest of the summer kept Jones busy with the implement store and with his responsibilities at the bank, unaware that he would soon become the target of a smear campaign launched by James Wilkerson.

As for Wilkerson, he spent several weeks that summer talking to people, refining his theory in the Moore-Stillinger case, eliminating some conspirators and adding others. He went about his work quietly and methodically, gaining supporters as time passed. A few were people who had always suspected that Jones was in some way involved, others just wanted to believe that someone, somehow, would finally get to the bottom of the mystery. More than two years had passed since the murders and other detectives had given up. Wilkerson said that he believed that the reason the murders were never solved was because officials had been bought off by Jones and were covering it up. There was a segment of the population that believed what he had to say. These people were indignant that the wealthy senator thought he could get away with murder.

But there were still many who were not receptive to the story that Wilkerson was spreading. Many people knew and liked Frank Jones and those who knew him best were disgusted and outraged by the allegations. The two factions were growing – one side wanted Wilkerson's work to continue and the other felt that Jones was being maliciously persecuted. There was a lot of unrest in the town over the case and it was becoming harder and harder for people to remain neutral.

Wilkerson had worked hard to implicate Jones in the crime, mixing and matching the various rumors to build a somewhat coherent, if improbable, case against Jones. He had tried to put the murder weapon in the hands of a particular person, but that had not worked out well. Jones was the mastermind, he believed. All he lacked was the actual murderer.

But then, another major ax murder occurred that summer – perhaps the final crime of Billy the Axman. On July 5, Jacob Mislich, his wife, Mary, daughter Martha, and her infant daughter Marie, were murdered in their beds in the Chicago suburb of Blue Island. Initial speculation linked Martha's estranged husband, William Mansfield, to the murder. However, police investigated Mansfield's whereabouts at the time and found that he had been working in a Milwaukee packing house when the killer struck.

But Wilkerson was not so easily satisfied. He visited the scene and reported that the Blue Island and Villisca cases were nearly identical – and they were. However, from that point on, he insisted that Mansfield was the perpetrator of both crimes, having been hired by Frank Jones to do away with J.B. Moore.

12. BLUE ISLAND, ILLINOIS JULY 5, 1914

"FOUR MURDERED ASLEEP IN BED"

More than two years passed between the murders in Villisca and the slaughter that occurred in Blue Island in 1914. It was the longest period of time between murders during the spree that was perpetrated by the killer we have been referring to as Billy the Axman. For some reason, the murders in Blue Island have been largely ignored by historians with an interest in the Midwest ax murders, and by those who have researched the Villisca case. Most likely, it was the propaganda spread by Wilkerson that caused this case to be overlooked. Wilkerson would forever maintain that it was William Mansfield who murdered his estranged wife, their baby, and his in-laws, despite the fact that he was elsewhere at the time and was cleared by the authorities for any involvement in the crime. It was true that Mansfield had an unsavory reputation, he had been involved in other crimes, and treated his wife badly, but he was not, as far as has ever been proven, a murderer.

I believe that the Mislich murders may have been the final killing spree carried out by Billy the Axman. What happened to him afterwards? Did he die? Or was he the man who walked into a police station and confessed to the murders a year later? Could the man who was arrested and locked up in a mental asylum have been the same man who had murdered dozens of innocent people and struck fear into the hearts of Midwest residents over a three-year period?

Blue Island, located south of Chicago in Cook County, was a working class suburb in 1914. The city took its name from a large hill that was once an island during the last ice age. Early pioneers gave the ridge the name because at a distance it looked like an island set in a trackless prairie sea.

Established in the 1830s, the town was originally a way station for settlers traveling on the Vincennes Trace from Indiana. It prospered since it was conveniently situated less than a day's journey from Chicago. In the 1840s, it enjoyed notable growth during the construction of the feeder canal (now the Calumet Sag Channel) for the Illinois & Michigan Canal and as a center for the brick-making industry. In the 1850s, Blue Island became known as the "brick-making capital of the world." In the early years, the bricks were made by hand and created mostly for local use. But by 1866, the Illinois Pressed Brick Company began employing about 80 men and using what was described as "steam power and machinery" to produce about 50,000 bricks per day. By 1900, the Clifton Brickyard alone, which had opened in 1883, was producing 150 million bricks every year. It was still a thriving industry in 1914 and a major part of Blue Island's economy.

Businesses, hotels, and restaurants flocked to the city, eager to reap the dollars that were being made by Blue Island's residents. The town's central business district (known as Uptown to locals) was regarded as one of the most important commercial centers south of Chicago. With stores like Woolworth's, Kline's Department Store, Sears, and Montgomery Ward, there were always plenty of places to shop. Until Prohibition put them out of business in 1919, Blue Island was home to several breweries that used the east side of the hill from which Blue Island took its name as a place to store their products before the advent of artificial refrigeration.

Beginning in 1883, Blue Island became the home to the car shops of the Rock Island Railroad. Even today, it is a busy hub for railroad lines running into Chicago and beyond.

The main railroad tracks in Blue Island were just one block from the house where the Mislich family was slain.

On July 5, 1914, a Sunday night, the "ax murder fiend" visited Blue Island and left a bloody trail of four victims, virtually wiping out an entire family. Jacob Mislich, age 75, his 65-year-old wife, Mary, their daughter, Margaret, age 22, and her six-month-old daughter, Marie, were slain as they slept in their beds at the Mislich home at 67 Broadway in Blue Island.

The murders were eerily similar to the others that had occurred across the Midwest over the previous three years, a fact that was quickly pointed out by the newspapers. No clues had been left behind in the house, except for the bloody ax, which had been used to crush the skulls of the family members. The ax had been left in the bedroom where the two women and the infant slept. It was covered in blood and had been picked up in a neighbor's back yard and brought into the house by the killer. After slaying each of the victims with the flat side of the ax, he had pulled the bed sheets up over the bodies, hiding them from view – just as he had in all of the other cases.

The bodies had been discovered by Mislich's son, Jacob Mislich, Jr., who had entered the house on Monday morning. The younger Mislich also lived in Blue Island and was at work on the railroad line near the house that morning. He walked over to his parent's house around 10 a.m. to get a pail of water. The back door was partially open and he pushed it open the rest of the way. Darkness lay beyond and he called out to his mother several times. When he received no reply, he walked inside. The first thing that he noticed was the gloom of the house. All of the window curtains had been pulled closed and the blinds were down. He called

Newspaper photographs from the Mislich case, including the home in Blue Island; Jacob Mislich and his daughter, Martha; who was married to William Mansfield.

out again and then started across the kitchen.

After a few steps, he entered the main part of the house and noticed that his feet were sticking to the floor. He looked down and was startled to see that a trail of blood ran from a bedroom off the kitchen to the front hall. It was too dark to see where the trail came to an end. His heart pounding, he pushed open the door to the bedroom.

There were several forms under the bloody sheet on the bed. The walls had been spattered with blood and pools of it congealed on the floor. A few steps away, a blood-soaked ax was lying on the wooden floorboards. Jacob walked slowly to the edge of the bed. He later told the newspapers:

I pulled back a part of the bed sheet and there lay my mother, her head cut and bleeding. I pulled the sheet back a little further and saw the body of my little niece. Her head had been severed. Beside her lay my sister. She too, was dead. I then ran into the street and called several passerby, [sic] who accompanied me upstairs where my father slept. He too, was dead, having been killed in the same manner as the others.

Several people who knew Jacob's parents were outside. They followed him back into the house and helped him search the place. His father had been sleeping upstairs in what the newspapers called the attic, but was actually a part of the second floor with a slanted ceiling. The Mislich house was not large and the family was not well off, but they were on good terms with their neighbors and were liked by the other German-Americans in Blue Island. There was no indication that the doors had been forced open. Instead, the police surmised that the killer had entered and departed through an open window where bloody handprints were found on the sill.

The police arrived to investigate the scene. Lieutenant William Miller of the Blue Island police took charge. His first thought was to look for Margaret's estranged husband, William Mansfield, who had a police record. Lieutenant Miller was initially the only one who suspected Mansfield. The newspapers were shouting that the "degenerate ax murder" had struck again – claiming more innocent lives. The Mislich murders were immediately connected to not only the Villisca murders, but to the earlier cases in Colorado Springs, Paola, Ellsworth, and Monmouth.

And newspaper reporters looking for a sensational story were not the only ones who believed the "transient butcher" was still at work. Chicago Assistant Chief of Police Herman Schuettler, a well-known and experienced officer who had been involved in the famous Luetgert murder case in 1897, was a strong proponent of the idea that all of the murders were connected. He was quoted in the newspaper on July 7, stating that, "The mad axman, whose trail of tragedy runs through five states, has reached the outskirts of Chicago." Captain Schuettler was quick to add that the Mislich case, like nearly all of the others, occurred on a Sunday night. He also publicized the belief that the killings had taken place when the moon was passing from the last quarter into the dark, or emerging into the first quarter. This would come up again in the future when Schuettler named a possible suspect.

The case rapidly went nowhere. On July 7, the Chicago police arrested a suspect named Peter Buchanow, who had escaped from an insane asylum in Kankakee, Illinois. A bulletin had been issued about his escape from the asylum before the murders had taken place. Buchanow was picked up by two police detectives at a boarding house at 4333 South Hermitage Avenue. When they searched his room, they found a bundle of clothing and some shoes that looked as though they had bloodstains on them. The detectives both thought of the Mislich murders – which the assistant chief of police stated had been committed by a madman – and brought Buchanow in for questioning. He was eventually cleared. Even though he had passed through Blue Island by train on the night of the murders, Buchanow was able to provide an alibi. He had been staying with a farmer, who had been kind enough to offer him a meal and a place to sleep.

This left only William Mansfield, whom Lieutenant Miller considered his prime suspect. Mansfield was an unsavory character, to say the least. He had twice joined the military and twice deserted. He'd done time in Leavenworth and after he was paroled, had moved to Chicago, where he met Margaret Mislich. He was working in a meat packing plant as a sausage stuffer. Although he was courting Margaret, he was also seeing a woman who worked in the plant named Kate Romanofski. Both women became pregnant around the same time. He married Margaret, but just as he had done with the military, he quickly abandoned her. Shortly before Margaret's baby was born, he and a very pregnant Kate left town together. A few months later, his wife, their baby and her parents were slaughtered in their beds by someone wielding an ax.

While Mansfield was a suspect in the crime, he really had no motive. Besides

William Mansfield's booking photograph from Leavenworth Prison. It would create a prejudice against him, despite a solid alibi.

that, no one had seen him in Blue Island for months. He was eventually tracked down and was able to prove that he had been working in Milwaukee at the time of the murders. The police lost interest in him and continued with their investigation – an investigation that soon went cold.

It would be a year before another suspect emerged. In July 1915, a man was arrested in Buffalo, New York, who confessed to the Mislich murders. His name was Casimir Arciszewski, a Polish immigrant who had once boarded with the Mislich family. The Mislichs were poor, a situation made worse by the fact that William Mansfield had abandoned his family and the elderly couple was forced to support their daughter and granddaughter. To help with finances, they occasionally took in boarders, one of whom was Arciszewski. He was alleged to be mentally ill and to have made unwanted advances toward Margaret. For this, as well as the fact that he failed to pay his rent, he was evicted from the house.

Soon afterwards, Arciszewski dropped out of sight. He later told the police that had roamed the country both before and after the murders, traveling by rail and drifting aimlessly. Then, one day, he walked into a police station in Buffalo and confessed to the Mislich murders. Two Chicago detectives and the mayor of Blue Island traveled to New York and brought him back, intent on learning if he was connected to the other ax murders that had been taking place since 1911. If he was, he never told them. He was judged to be insane and incompetent to stand trial. He was committed to a mental asylum in 1915. After that, he vanished into history, leaving many unanswered questions in his wake – questions we will look into further later on.

Soon after the news of the Mislich murders broke, James Wilkerson traveled to Blue Island to look into the case. There was no denying that the murders were nearly identical to the crime in Villisca, as well as the other ax murders. Even the crime scene was similar. The three women were killed in the downstairs bedroom and had been struck in the head two or three times with the head of an ax. Jacob Mislich was sleeping upstairs and was killed in the same manner. The ax had been left behind in the downstairs bedroom. The killer had entered the house by a window and left the same way. All of the curtains in the house had been pulled shut and all of the bodies had been covered with sheets. The only thing missing seemed to be an oil lamp with the glass chimney removed, but nothing like that was found in the house.

While in Blue Island, Wilkerson learned about William Mansfield, who would become a key piece in the case the detective was putting together. The police later dismissed him as a suspect, but Wilkerson refused to forget about him. Whether he had an alibi or not, Wilkerson knew that people would be quick to believe the worst about an army deserter, adulterer, and a man who abandoned his family. He would make the perfect addition to the case that Wilkerson really wanted to build – a case against Frank Jones.

13. LOVE, SEX & MURDER
WILKERSON AND THE NELLIE BYERS CASE

By 1915, Wilkerson was still plowing ahead with his case against Frank Jones. He was making progress, he believed, with proving his conspiracy theory. He had at least one motive, the statement from Vina Tompkins, and the alleged wielder of the ax -- William Mansfield. He had also worked the colorful Guthrie County gang into the mix. There were still a lot of loose ends and pieces that didn't make sense – his theory was never a finished product – but he had the basic plot for a document that he would later call his "dope sheet" in the language of detective stories of his era. He continued to work on the potential witnesses and, perhaps most importantly, was continuing to find local financial support to continue the investigation. The state of Iowa had started to balk at providing funds. They'd paid the Burns Detective Agency about $800 at that point, but only about $107 of that was paid in 1915. Burns was paying detectives around $100 a month (probably more for Wilkerson) and they charged $10 per day for his services, plus expenses, which means that the attorney general paid for only a few days of Wilkerson's work in 1915. The rest was covered by the county and by a group of family and friends of the victims.

Wilkerson later claimed that the state backed out when it became evident that he was building a case against Senator Jones, but this was not true. Even after reviewing Wilkerson's reports from the Vina Tompkins interview and his letter written after the failed interview with Jones, the state continued to fund a portion of the investigation. Attorney General Cosson and his assistant Henry Sampson were interested in the Jones investigation, and there's no indication that they ever did anything to obstruct it. But the operation was funded by the legislature, whose members had occasion to meet Frank Jones in the state capitol when the senate was in session. This likely caused some mixed feelings.

In addition, they had very good reason to question the methods and ethics of the Burns operatives, which likely led them to prefer local funding for the investigation rather than providing the money on state level. And, by the time the summer of 1915 was over, Wilkerson would destroy any chance for future cooperation from the attorney general.

Perhaps because there was little money coming in from the Villisca case, Wilkerson worked on another case in 1915. He made a trip to Kansas that summer to investigate the murder of a young woman named Nellie Byers. Also that summer, in a courtroom in Missouri, he obtained a divorce from his wife, Minnie Wilkerson. The couple had divorced once before and remarried. While none of this had anything to do with the Villisca murders, the time would come when Frank Jones would start an investigation of his own and both the divorce and the Nellie Byers case would figure into it strongly.

Nellie Byers was an attractive young woman from Grant County, Kansas. She obtained a teaching certificate in the late summer of 1915 and accepted a position at a country school in the southwestern part of the county. As many teachers did in those days, Nellie made arrangements to board with farmers who lived in the area. At the time of her murder, she was living with the Eidson family, but had been invited to stay with others in the area as well. The Eidson house was about two miles from the school, down a narrow road that crossed the Cimarron River. Nellie's daily walk to school each day took her past the farm of an elderly couple named Hensen.

A few weeks before her death, a young man named Archibald Sweet came to live with the Hensen family. He and the Hensens' son, Clint, had met in jail and when Sweet got out and needed a place to live, the Hensens took him in. Sweet did little to better himself after getting out of jail. During the time he lived with the Hensens, he drank a lot, but did little else. Rumor had it that he consumed nearly a quart of liquor every day – as he later admitted he had on the day of the murder.

Nellie's walk took her past the Hensen farm and she soon started telling friends that she was afraid of Sweet. She didn't like the way that he stared at her or the way he talked to her. She thought he was going out of his way to watch her as she passed each day. As often as she could, she caught a ride with children who drove a horse and buggy to school or arranged to walk with someone else.

On October 22, 1915, the Hensen family, including Clint, was away from the farm. Sweet stayed there alone, doing a few chores, drinking whiskey, and walking the fields with Hensen's shotgun, hoping to scare up some jackrabbits. Nellie walked to school alone that day and as Sweet was believed to have studied her routine, investigators assumed that he knew she would be walking alone when she returned.

The Eidson family was also away from home that day, returning just before evening chores. When they realized that Nellie was not home, they assumed that she was working late. When she had not arrived by 8 p.m. they grew worried. Mr. Eidson saddled a horse and rode to the school. He found the building closed and locked and guessed that Nellie was staying the night with another family. When he hadn't heard from her by morning, Eidson was concerned enough to check with other families with whom she might have boarded. He soon found that no one had seen her since school had let out the previous day. He gathered some neighbors and started a search for the missing teacher. Members of the search party noted later that Archibald Sweet seemed to be watching them closely as they examined the roadsides between the Eidsons' house and the school. They thought it was odd that he never approached them to ask what they were doing.

Around mid-morning, the naked body of Nellie Byers was found in some brush near the Cimarron River, about 100 yards from the road. The authorities were sent for and Sheriff Bert Ladner, County Attorney H.W. Stubbs and a doctor arrived in a short time.

A few hours later, the Hensens arrived home. Clint Hensen joined Sweet in watching the group of people who had gathered around the body. While the doctor examined the body, Sheriff Ladner and County Attorney Stubbs noted the marks of a struggle on the road, then drag marks to near where Nellie was found, and then more signs of a struggle indicating where a sexual assault might have taken place. Two sets of tracks were found, including Nellie's and those of a man that were later determined to match the size and shape of shoes worn by Sweet. When they saw him nearby, Ladner and Stubbs confronted Sweet. They told him he was a suspect and he consented to a search. He was stripped in a nearby outbuilding, and then taken into custody, charged with the murder of Nellie Byers.

County Attorney Stubbs was convinced that Sweet had raped, beaten, and strangled Nellie Byers and had a lot of circumstantial evidence to support his belief. Sweet had been watching Nellie for weeks and she had become afraid of him. One of his previous convictions was for the sexual assault of a young girl. Stubbs believed Sweet had watched Nellie walking to school that morning and spent the day drinking whiskey and making plans to attack her on her way home.

Sweet denied any part in the murder, but during questioning he admitted that he had been near the scene of the attack that day. However, he saw and heard nothing. Several people later testified that Sweet told them that he saw Nellie walking that afternoon but that he turned away rather than meet her on the road. If he had looked over his shoulder, he said, he might have seen the killer. Sweet was carrying a shotgun that day and Nellie had been struck with a blunt instrument that could have been the barrel of a gun or the blackjack found hanging from a nail in Sweet's bedroom. There were no marks found on Sweet and the clothes that he was wearing on the day of his arrest were clean and fresh. Sweat-stained clothing and underwear were found in his bedroom, soaked with perspiration from what Stubbs believed was his struggle with Nellie. In addition to her head wounds, Nellie had also been strangled. Her sweater, which had been wrapped around her neck and used to drag her, was found next to her body. The rest of her clothing was found the next day, folded and hidden in a location between where her body was found and the Hensen house.

Stubbs had a case, but it was mostly circumstantial. There were no witnesses, limited physical evidence, and even though Sweet was uneducated, he knew the criminal system well enough that he was unlikely to confess. Stubbs was sure that Sweet's family would spare no expense in hiring good defense attorneys, so he needed to build the best case against him that he could. He decided to hire a detective to help put the prosecution's case together. He contacted the Burns Detective Agency and they sent him James Wilkerson.

According to sworn statements given by Stubbs and Sheriff Ladner after the trial, what took place after Wilkerson arrived was quite different than what the county attorney expected. Stubbs met Wilkerson at the train station and spent time going over the case with him. They made a brief visit to the crime scene and then Wilkerson asked to be taken to the jail so that he could interview Sweet. During the ride, Wilkerson asked Stubbs if there was a reward being offered. When Stubbs replied that there was not, Wilkerson suggested that he try and arrange for one, promising Stubbs half of what he managed to drum up. Stubbs told Wilkerson that he didn't think a reward would be offered, and if it were, it wouldn't make sense because Sweet had already been arrested and charged.

Wilkerson spent three hours alone with Sweet in his jail cell and when he was ready to leave, he shocked Stubbs by telling him that Sweet was not guilty, but that he had provided enough information to identify the person who was. Wilkerson suggested that Stubbs contact the governor, tell him the wrong man had been jailed and that a reward was needed to expand the investigation. According to Stubbs, Wilkerson again offered to split the reward with him.

Stubbs was not the only one surprised by Wilkerson's actions that day. In 1918, long after his trial was over, Sweet signed an affidavit stating that Wilkerson told him that several prominent citizens of the area didn't have alibis for the day Nellie was killed. The detective suggested Sweet should name one of them as being in the area on the afternoon of the murder. Sweet said he refused, but he did agree to participate in a plan to elicit a confession from Clint Hensen.

Stubbs was upset and would soon become angry. He didn't know the details of Wilkerson's conversation with Sweet, but he did know that the detective that he had hired to help convict Sweet was not cooperating. After only being in town for a few hours, he was insisting that Sweet was not the killer. In Stubbs' opinion, Wilkerson was more interested in the reward money than in justice for the murdered girl.

Wilkerson plowed ahead with a plan that he promised would get a confession from Hensen. First he worked on Stubbs, convincing him to send a telegram to the governor saying that the wrong man had been arrested and it was imperative that a reward be put together as an incentive to find the real killer. Against his better judgment, Stubbs agreed.

Wilkerson's plan was to arrest Hensen and soften him up over a few days. According to the jailer, Wilkerson directed the other prisoners to work Hensen over with a piece of rubber hose which the detective provided. The prisoners were promised privileges for administering the beatings. In the meantime, Wilkerson met with Sweet daily, coaching him for eliciting a confession out of Hensen. Wilkerson scripted out the meeting and, if Sweet's statement is believed, told Sweet to punch his former friend Hensen in the face, if necessary. The detective assured Sweet that the conversation would be monitored and help would be nearby if Hensen started to fight back. On the evening before the confrontation was to take place, Wilkerson had his hotel deliver a porterhouse steak dinner to Sweet's cell.

Wilkerson arranged everything at the jail. A dictating machine was hidden outside the cell and a court reporter was on hand to quickly transcribe the conversation between the two men. The reporter, in a sworn statement, described the experience as "strange." He said that Wilkerson told him in advance what he would hear and, indeed, the words, emphasis, and manner of speaking where exactly what he heard from Sweet. There was no doubt in the court reporter's mind that Sweet was repeating exactly what Wilkerson told him to say.

With everything in place, Hensen was taken to Sweet's cell. Sweet first played on Hensen's ego, then turned to direct accusations, shouting and threats. He bullied him, pleaded with him, and then threatened him. Hensen refused to confess. Sweet, having repeated what Wilkerson told him to say, and unsure what to do next, just sat and waited for Hensen to be taken away.

Angry, irritated, and embarrassed, Stubbs fired Wilkerson from the case. But the detective refused to leave town right away. He stayed for another day and, according to Stubbs' statement, met with newspaper reporters and told them that Sweet was innocent and that an injustice was being done. Wilkerson's pride had been wounded when he was fired and he wanted to do everything he could to sabotage Stubbs' case.

In spite of Wilkerson, Stubbs won the case against Sweet. He received angry messages from William Burns himself when he refused to pay the bill for the agency's investigative services. Wilkerson's supervisors defended his conduct and threatening to sue if the bill was not paid. They had no idea that their legal problems with Wilkerson were just beginning. Stubbs was resentful about what he saw as unethical behavior by the detective and was more than happy to share information with Frank Jones and later, with Attorney General Horace Havner.

Another murder case made headlines that summer. Once again, it had nothing to do with Villisca. The case took place in Taylor County, a few miles from Villisca. It brought Attorney General George Cosson to the area. It was an unusual crime, dating back 47 years, and it attracted the attention of a newspaper reporter named Jack Boyle, who was to strongly influence events in Villisca in the months to come.

The Taylor County crime dated all the way back to 1868. A cattle buyer from St. Joseph, Missouri, named Nathaniel Smith came to Iowa to buy livestock. He was allegedly carrying with him between $60,000 and $90,000. He made the first part of his trip by train and then, upon reaching Iowa, by horse and wagon. He was traveling with his son, who was 12 or 13 at the time. A group of Taylor County outlaws heard about the large amount of cash Smith was carrying and decided to rob him. They killed him and his son, burying the boy's body in a grove of trees and dropping Smith's body down an abandoned well. They decided to wait before dividing up the money, burying it near the shallow grave of the boy.

The story became part of the local folklore, including the fact that the map to the buried cash was lost when the home of one of the killers burned down. The gang was never able to find the money again. Over the years, scores of people had searched and failed. Most locals began to doubt that the treasure existed at all, but some held out hope. One of the believers was a man named Samuel Anderson, who bought the land that where he believed it was buried. After looking for 15 years and finding nothing, he became convinced that someone from the original gang had trespassed on his land and dug the money up. He let it be known that he wanted his share. When he didn't get it, he went to a lawyer.

The attorney, W.W. Bulman from Chariton, claimed that four local men, then in their late seventies, had killed Smith and his son 47 years before and had later recovered $43,000 of the loot. He claimed that he had evidence, including the bones of the two victims. He took the case to the county attorney, who in turn passed it on to the state's attorney general. Cosson, who planned to run for governor in 1916, may have been influenced by an opportunity to get some free publicity when he ordered the four old men arrested. He took the case before a grand jury and presented what little evidence there was, but the panel decided there was not enough to warrant an indictment. The four old men went home to their farms and Cosson went back to Des Moines.

The whole thing was over in just a few days, but it was a big story for awhile, attracting reporters from a number of major newspapers. One of them was Jack Boyle, who then worked for the *Kansas City Post*. Wilkerson later described Boyle as "an old time murder story writer of the premier class. A mighty good detective too." Such high praise coming from the disreputable detective makes one shudder, considering what Boyle must have done to get some of his stories.

Boyle became famous as the creator of "Boston Blackie," a fictional reformed thief turned detective. Boyle wrote about Boston Blackie's exploits for a number of publications, including *American Magazine, Cosmopolitan,* and *Redbook.* Boston Blackie was later featured in radio shows and serial films, the character enduring long after Boyle's death in 1928. During his reporting days, Boyle's writing style can best be described as sensational. In other words, he never let the facts get in the way of a good story.

Boyle traveled to Taylor County to look into the buried treasure story. While there, he learned about the Villisca murders. It's surprising that a reporter for a Midwestern paper would have missed the Villisca case, but according to Wilkerson, Boyle was working on the West Coast in 1912 and simply missed the story. But now, three years after the murders took place, Boyle was determined to follow up on it. He asked a Taylor County resident to suggest someone whom he might contact in Villisca to get information about the murders and was given Frank Jones' name. Boyle then called Jones. The reporter would later say that Jones was so angry with him on the telephone that he decided to investigate further.

Boyle took a train to Villisca. He asked questions around town and learned there were those who suspected that Jones had something to do with the murders. He also found out that a detective from the Burns agency was working the case. After returning to Kansas City, Boyle contacted the Burns office, and according to Wilkerson, he was first told that no Burns agent was investigating the case. Boyle reportedly told them that there should be. He said he was going to do a story about the crime, apparently implying that he planned to slant it so that suspicion fell toward a state senator. When this information was passed on to Wilkerson, he immediately got in touch with Boyle and allegedly worked out a deal with him. If Boyle wrote the story now, he told him, it would ruin the case. If he would agree to hold off, Wilkerson would let him into the case and give him some "inside dope" on the investigation.

Boyle got more than just information. He was taken in as an active participant in the investigation. Shortly after making the deal with Wilkerson, he went with the detective to find Bert McCaul, the former pool hall owner and friend of Albert Jones. McCaul was then living on a farm near Missouri Valley, Iowa. Wilkerson said that they "sweated McCaul for two days," but didn't get anything out of him. They tried to entice Albert Jones to the hotel where they were grilling McCaul, but he refused. He did answer a few questions, though, but nothing that he told them led to anything.

Soon after, "Agent 33" and Boyle decided to go to Villisca's Old Settlers Day to continue their investigation. The celebration was Villisca's biggest event of the year. It drew more attendees than the summer livestock shows or the town's Fourth of July celebration. Old Settler's Day started out as a reunion of early residents of the area and soon became much more, doubling, even tripling the population of the town for one summer weekend. In 1915, the day included various musical performances, a horseshoe-pitching contest, a baseball game, a boomerang-throwing contest, a contortionist, a sack race, a tug of war contest, and massive quantities of food. The featured speaker at the city park that day was Attorney General George Cosson, whose topic was "The Condition of the U.S. from an Attorney's Perspective." He was introduced that day by Senator Frank Jones.

In Wilkerson's words, Jones and Cosson were obviously "pissing through the same quill" and the two of them together presented an opportunity for him and his new partner, Jack Boyle, to do... well, something. Just what they planned to do was subject to change. The original plan had Wilkerson staying out of sight at the Fisher Hotel while Boyle brought Jones there under the pretense of conducting an interview with him. Wilkerson would hide his Dictaphone in the room and record everything as the two men "put the horse to him in such a way that he would loosen something."

Boyle approached the stage where the attorney general was waiting to speak, and Cosson, remembering him from the Taylor County proceedings a few weeks earlier, readily agreed to be interviewed. After Jones introduced Cosson to the crowd, Boyle asked the senator to step aside with him. In Wilkerson's version of the encounter, Boyle is said to have drawn Jones away from the crowd and flatly announced that he was investigating the murders and he was convinced that Jones was involved. As Cosson's speech continued, Boyle and Jones walked over to Jones' store. Boyle asked Jones several times to come to his hotel room, but Jones refused. In true yellow journalist fashion, Boyle told him that he was giving him the chance to tell his side of the story, otherwise, he was going to run a story about the murder based on the information that he currently had. Jones invited him into his store to talk about it, but Boyle refused to go inside and Jones ended the conversation. He turned his back on the reporter and went back over to the park, where Cosson was still speaking.

Jones was near the podium when Cosson finished his speech and he apparently warned Cosson about the false interview because instead of going to the hotel, Cosson went home with Jones. When Cosson didn't show up for the interview, Boyle called the telephone operator and asked her is she knew where the attorney general was. She did, and she rang the Jones house. Boyle got Cosson on the telephone and asked him again to come to the hotel for the interview. Cosson reluctantly agreed but when he arrived at the hotel, Boyle was as blunt with him as he had been with Jones. According to Wilkerson, Boyle accused the attorney general of making a deal with Jones, agreeing to protect him from a murder investigation if Jones promised not to run against him in the governor's race. Wilkerson had the dictating machine running during this conversation but he conveniently failed to record Cosson's reply. The attorney general stormed out of the hotel. After Cosson left, Boyle again telephoned the Jones home. Frank and Albert drove to the hotel, but refused to go inside. Harsh words were exchanged outside, with Boyle again threatening to print a story accusing Jones of murder. Jones told the reporter that he would never get away with it.

Soon after the Old Settler's Day incidents, a separate occurrence took place that Jones would call blackmail and Wilkerson would claim had been merely an investigative technique. Based on the detective's behavior during the Nellie Byers case, I would say that Jones was likely more accurate in his description. There are no questions about the basic facts: Wilkerson arranged for an itinerant newspaper writer named Bell (using the name Daley) to go to Jones and offer to sell him Wilkerson's investigative reports. It's easy to understand why Jones would consider this blackmail. Only a few days before, Boyle had accused him of murder, implied there was considerable evidence against him, and threatened to print a story about it. Now, Bell – by both Wilkerson's and Jones' accounts – was demanding $25,000 in exchange for the reports. Jones said that Bell not only offered the reports, but told him that if he paid up, all investigation activities against him would stop at once. Jones had at least two conversations with Bell. During the second, they met in Jones' home, where the senator had friends concealed in the next room to listen in on the conversation.

In 1915, $25,000 was a fortune, nearly the equivalent of $1 million today. If the plan was extortion and Wilkerson had succeeded, he could have cut Boyle in on the money and still been a very wealthy man. Since it failed, Wilkerson was quick to claim that it had just been an investigative tactic. He said he had no intention of collecting the money; he only wanted to see what Jones' reaction to the proposition was. He also claimed that Sheriff Jackson, who never commented on it, was aware of the scheme. If Jones had agreed to buy the reports, it would be seen as an indication that he had something to hide.

Wilkerson's version of the second meeting with Bell also differed from Jones'. He said that Bell had dropped the price for the papers during the first meeting from $25,000 to $5,000. Jones said he might be interested and set a second meeting in a few days. Bell, carrying an enveloped stuffed with blank papers, went to Jones' home, but when he got there, Jones was no longer interested. Instead, he produced a letter from Attorney General Cosson, allegedly assuring that the state would discontinue pursuit of the Villisca murder case.

No one can say for sure what happened with this blackmail / investigative incident. If Jones really had friends hidden in the next room to listen to his second conversation with Bell, none of them ever filed affidavits about what they heard. There is also no proof that Wilkerson arranged the scheme with Sheriff Jackson's approval, so he could have easily taken the money and no one would have been the wiser. Jones' supporters saw the whole episode as extortion, while Wilkerson's supporters saw it as valid investigative strategy.

There was one other incident that occurred in 1915 that had an effect on the Villisca case, although no one knew it at the time. It happened in late December on a particularly frigid night, during a season that became known for low temperatures that sometimes dipped into the 20 below zero range. Around 2 a.m., a fire broke out at Jones' National Bank Building. It was discovered by the night marshal, who sounded the alarm by firing his revolver into the air as he ran down the street to ring the town's fire bell.

The bank, a two-story stone building that had been under construction at the time of the murders, also housed several office spaces. The fire was put out without any structural damage, but smoke, heat and water damage occurred in a print shop and in the offices of two doctors and a dentist. The fire destroyed the contents of a photography studio owned by John Warren Noel. Luckily for Noel, he had $1,500 in insurance coverage on his studio equipment.

Noel was a relative newcomer to Villisca. He was 25, with a wife and two small children. He had been working late in his studio that night, as he often did, and had apparently left only a short time before the fire was discovered. The cause of the fire was designated as unknown and the insurance company paid off on the damage. But as people in town learned more about Noel – his financial situation, his tendency to live beyond his means, his arrest record, and his role as a star witness in the Wilkerson investigation – they began to wonder about exactly what happened on the night of the fire.

14. FRANK JONES AND POLITICS
THE 1916 ELECTION BATTLES BEGIN

In the early days of 1916, it became apparent to Frank Jones that he would have even more difficulties during the 1916 senatorial election than he'd had in 1912. Four years before, Jones was confronted with the early rumors that he was somehow involved in the Moore-Stillinger murders as well as the loss of Republican votes to a third party, Bull Moose candidate, and yet he went on to win. In 1916, he was facing a much tougher situation. The rumors were still around and, in fact, were much worse, since Wilkerson was telling people that he was developing serious evidence against the senator. In addition, there was a residency arrangement that had been reached between Mills and Montgomery counties, along with the fact that Jones had been appointed to a six-year term on the state board of education. The two county governments had agreed that the office would be held by a resident of one county for eight years, and by the other for the next eight. Jones, or any other candidate from Montgomery County, was only supposed to serve one term. This, along with the fact that Jones' position on the state board of education would keep him out of his senate seat during the 1917 General Assembly, led many people to assume that he would not run again.

William Ratcliff had considered entering the race against Jones in the 1912 primary, but decided against it and ran for another two-year term as county attorney instead. He did not run in the 1914 elections and decided to try for the senate seat in 1916. It was likely that he didn't think that Jones would run in the primary. It's also likely that local Republican leaders, knowing Ratcliff was going to be a candidate, would have asked Jones what his plans were for the coming elections. If they did, he didn't give them any information for quite some time. He may have accepted the board of education post as a way of keeping his options open, or he may have taken it thinking that he wouldn't run again, and then changed his mind. Regardless, Jones had not yet made any of his plans public when Ratcliff announced his candidacy for the Eighth District senate seat in February 1916.

Jones stayed silent for the next two months. When he had been offered the state board of education post, he wrote the governor saying that he would accept it only with the understanding that he might choose to run again for the senate and would resign if he were re-elected. He knew after Ratcliff announced his intentions that the primary would turn into a nasty fight if he got in. Even without the rumors, Ratcliff had been a popular county attorney with many influential supporters. Jones also knew that he would be criticized for taking the board of education position if he planned to run again, but was prepared to fight. Jones finally announced his candidacy in April.

When Ratcliff had announced that he planned to run, the front page of the *Villisca Review* printed his photograph and a lengthy story about his accomplishments. Thanks to his long-standing unpopularity with the newspaper, Jones knew that he would receive far less. There was no photograph and only a small article on page two. The final paragraph was a correction for an article in a previous edition that stated that Jones had resigned his senate seat. The *Red Oak Express* had endorsed Ratcliff and questioned Jones' commitment to Prohibition. The *Villisca Review* had stopped short of a public endorsement, but the quality of their news reports left little doubt as to the political preference of the editors.

Because Jones entered the race so late, the campaign was short but hostile. Ratcliff was not at all reluctant to attack Jones over his voting record and for the bills that came out of his committee. He spoke about it during his speeches and in a series of paid newspaper advertisements that forced Jones to also purchase ad space to defend himself. As the candidates took the battle to the voters, the issues of paved roads and Prohibition emerged as the two most important. Jones had already been forced to justify his work in helping to establish the Iowa Highway Commission. By 1916, the commission was working toward a statewide system of paved roads, but many voters would have preferred mud roads to higher taxes, a side that Ratcliff took. He blamed Jones for a recent increase in property taxes, money that had been used, in part, to pay for new roads. Their differences on the road issues were clear and it was easy for voters to decide which side of the fence they were on.

The issues over Prohibition were more complicated. Montgomery County was "dry" at the time and Jones was unquestionably in favor of temperance. Both in his career and personal life, he advocated abstinence. He sided with groups that also shunned liquor, but he knew there were varying opinions on whether or not Prohibition should be the law of the land. During the 1914 legislative session, Jones questioned the advisability of a proposed bill to repeal the law making provisions for saloons, saying the measure would be ineffective and fall short of what was needed. When he voiced this view, and his opposition to the bill, he aroused the anger of the Iowa Anti-Saloon League, a powerful temperance organization that went to Jones' constituents and urged them to write letters to the senator. In the end, Jones bowed to pressure and voted the way the Anti-Saloon League wanted him to, but the incident made the league feel that he was soft on the issue. This caused him problems during the 1916 campaign. Ratcliff urged voters to "play it safe" when it came to alcohol. He ran a series of ads telling voters that the Anti-Saloon League had branded Jones as a man who was "not safe" on the issue, while Ratcliff was absolutely opposed to alcohol and favored national Prohibition.

Jones referred to Ratcliff's ads and speeches as "mudslinging," but he had been around long enough to know that it was simply politics. Ratcliff was simply putting forth every effort to try and defeat Jones and Jones undoubtedly respected him for it. The primary election was scheduled for Monday, June 5, and Ratcliff had far outpaced his opponent. The rumors may have hurt Jones, but legitimate issues and his own failure to enter the race earlier had cut into his popularity, too. The outcome had almost certainly been decided and neither candidate needed what happened on the weekend before the primary vote.

The letters were mailed from Kansas City on Saturday afternoon, meaning that they would be delivered on Monday or made available on Sunday to those who picked up their mail from a post office box. Whoever sent the letters knew they would be read on Sunday or Monday, the day of the election. The dozen or so anonymous letters contained a photograph of a man that turned out to be William Mansfield, an ex-convict whom James Wilkerson was just about to introduce to the people of Villisca. These startling lines appeared above his mugshot:

This is the ax murderer. He murdered the Moore family at Villisca. The hypocrite whose dirty money paid for the hellish job wants your support for the state senate. Will he get it?

When the letters arrived they started a wave of excitement. While only a handful of people in Villisca and Red Oak received the letters, hundreds saw them before the polls even opened that morning.

One of the letters was shown to Frank Jones, who promptly came out with a statement challenging the person responsible for the charges to come forward. He added that this was the first time that any accusation of this sort had ever come to him in a way that a public statement could be made.

When Ratcliff learned of the letters, he immediately came to Villisca with Ralph Pringle, a lawyer from Red Oak. The two called at the Jones house, looking for the best course of action to find the letter writer and bring him to justice. It was also likely that Ratcliff came to assure Jones that he'd had no connection to the letters. Frankly, Ratcliff didn't need to stoop to such things to win the primary. Jones was already beaten and both men probably knew it. Later on that day, Ratcliff announced that he would pursue federal charges against the letter writer. This was probably another example of Ratcliff trying to do the right thing. He and Jones likely knew who had sent the letters – James Wilkerson – but neither had any idea of how to prove it.

The letters may have influenced some voters, but it really made no difference in the outcome. Ratcliff carried every precinct in the county except for the three wards in Villisca. And even those had been close – Jones won by two votes in one precinct in Villisca, seven in the second and by 27 in the third. Ratcliff carried Montgomery County by a margin of four-to-one. Ratcliff's victory turned out to be a rout and although Jones would complete his term with the state board of education, his years as an elected official had come to an end.

In an edition that appeared a few days after the primary, the *Villisca Review* ran a lengthy editorial about the letters and the rumors about Frank Jones. In the piece, there was a mention of the "honest differences of opinions" with Jones, but went on to say that "when his standing in the community as a moral character and a respected citizen is brought into question that's an entirely different matter, and Mr. Jones will find the *Review* loyally and earnestly protesting his evidence until positive guilt has been PROVEN." In other words, the editors at the newspaper didn't like Jones personally, but they thought that the letters were a dirty trick that he hadn't deserved.

Jones was likely pleased by the unexpected support, although he probably wondered about some of the wording that had been used. In the editorial, there had been the phrase, "until positive guilt has been proven," instead of "*unless* positive guilt has been proven." This probably left him wondering just how genuine the newspaper's support actually was. But there was one thing the newspaper editorial did do – it reiterated the statement that Jones had made on the day the letters had been received, promising that he'd start proceedings against anyone who publicly accused him.

It was a promise that he eventually kept.

15. THE "BLACKIE" MANSFIELD FIASCO

On a cold Tuesday night in January 1916, the county clerk, auditor, and recorder met at the courthouse and drew the names of twelve men who would serve a one-year term on a grand jury for Montgomery County. The jurors would call witnesses, hear sworn testimony, and sort through the rumors and gossip that had been buzzing around the area since 1912. The jury would finally hear the case that Wilkerson had built against Frank and Albert Jones, and by mid-summer, they would get their first look at the man that Wilkerson believed had carried out the Villisca murders, as well as several others.

By the time the grand jury convened, the Wilkerson investigation was completely out of control, but at least *something* was happening, which was more than could be said for the past four years. It must have seemed like a relief to know that the case was finally moving forward – but soon that sense of relief would be overwhelmed by dread.

When the anonymous letters were sent out in early June, they contained a photograph of William Mansfield that was taken at the time of his arrest for desertion. Wilkerson had obtained the photograph and was using it in his attempt to connect Mansfield with the Villisca murders. He had probably gotten the photograph from Jack Boyle, the newspaperman with whom he had been working since the previous summer. Boyle had written a story that would provide all of the links between Villisca, Mansfield, and Jones – links that Wilkerson had created. The story was ready to go and Boyle had been waiting for months to release it. They would later maintain that the anonymous letters prompted Boyle to release the story when he did, fearing that some competitor might beat him to the punch. Of course, it's more likely that Wilkerson and Boyle were the ones responsible for the letter and then used it as justification they could present to Boyle's editor and get him to run the story. Boyle's story was a perfect ploy for Wilkerson, who loved to shake things up to see what might happen. Having a story that he had almost written himself printed in a major Midwestern daily like the *Kansas City Post* would definitely shake things up.

On June 11, Boyle's story appeared in the *Kansas City Post*. It was quickly picked up and reprinted by newspapers all over the country. The headline read:

"'Insane Blackie' Wanted! Warrant issued for him – Charged with the Murders of Sixteen People! Including Villisca Victims! Police of Every Large City Notified by Wire to Arrest Man Supposed to be Ax-Murderer!"

B.C. Hullinger, the editor of the *Villisca Review*, debated on whether or not to run the story. In the end, he decided to do so with a preface that expressed doubt as to its veracity. The story finally ran in Villisca on June 14. Ahead of the story, Hullinger wrote:

The following story, which is now thoroughly going the rounds of the daily and weekly press, together with the pictures of Mr. and Mrs. J.B. Moore and two of their children and the man who is supposed to have committed the Villisca crime of four years ago, appeared in Monday's Kansas City Post *under flaring headlines. The* Review *would much prefer to ignore the story entirely (which simply consists of the most part of statements made by a Burns detective who, though claiming to be in possession of a lot of facts, has not backed up any of them by making a single arrest up to this time), but it will be published in surrounding papers, and, then, too, we believe that the sooner the people know the supposed grounds for all the talk that has been indulged in during the past months, the sooner the whole matter will be cleared up for all time to come, which will be a welcome relief to everyone in this community. Insofar as there being anyone in Villisca who is connected directly or indirectly with the crime, the* Review *prints it with due reservation as to its authenticity.*

The rambling, fantastical article that ran in the newspaper was pure "Agent 33." There were few indications of Boyle's having a hand in the story at all, it read almost identical to the wild reports that Wilkerson sent to the attorney general in the past – declaring that he had single-handedly solved the case and naming William "Insane Blackie" Mansfield as the killer of the ax murder victims in Paola, Kansas; Villisca, Iowa; and Blue Island, Illinois. The evidence mostly boiled down to Wilkerson's theories about the case, and not much else. It was no surprise that he had managed to convince Sheriff Jackson to issue an arrest warrant for Mansfield, since the two had worked together on the case for years and Jackson was definitely one of Wilkerson's supporters. The letters that were sent out before the political primary "ended all hope for secrecy" in the case, so Wilkerson claimed that he had been forced to obtain the arrest warrant and make his case public.

The article started off with the results of Wilkerson's investigation:

1.   The murder of Joe Moore, and the seven other occupants of this home in Villisca, Iowa, was committed by Mansfield, alias Blackie, for hire.

Keep in mind that Wilkerson had absolutely no proof that this was true. There was nothing to link Mansfield to anyone in Villisca. As usual, what Wilkerson was stating as a "conclusion" was nothing more than a theory that he had cooked up.

2.   The victims of the Blue Island, Illinois ax-murders, until now an unsolved mystery, were the wife, the infant child and the father and mother-in-law of Mansfield. He was in Blue Island on the night of the murders. The motive attributed is that Mrs. Mansfield had obtained a felony warrant for her husband charging abandonment.

Once again, Wilkerson had made another statement that was only partially true. The facts were that the victims in Blue Island had been Mansfield's family, but he was not in Blue Island when the murders occurred. His alibi had already been checked out and confirmed by the Blue Island and Chicago police, and he had ruled been out as a suspect. Yes, he was a disreputable character, but detectives had already shown that he was not the killer. Mansfield would also be able to provide an alibi for where he was at the time of the Villisca murders. Once more, it was thoroughly checked out and he was cleared.

3.   *"Insane Blackie" was in Paola, Kansas on the night of the ax murders there. This was four days before the Moore murders.*

Mansfield was absolutely not in Paola at the time of the murders. This was another "fact" that Wilkerson had engineered on his own to build the case and take advantage of the similarities between the murders.

4.   *He was in a notorious "joint" in Aurora immediately after the murders of Jennie Peterson and Jennie Miller and was seeking to buy cocaine.*

The murders of Jennie Peterson and Jennie Miller remain a mystery to most researchers of the Villisca crime. Most of them choose to ignore this reference made by Wilkerson and never mention it at all. Those who only do light research into the history of the case merely re-print the mention from other sources and it gets mixed into the story, making it appear that perhaps there was some justification in Wilkerson's accusations against Mansfield. So, I decided to start digging into some old newspapers and try and track down these crimes. As it turned out, Wilkerson's inclusion of them in his list of Mansfield's "crimes" became even more mysterious. I have no idea why he included them, other than they were young women who were bludgeoned to death in a town that was not too far from where Mansfield lived and they happened to fit into a convenient timeline for his manufactured case.

The murders that he mentioned were actually two of three murders that took place over a period of several months in Aurora, Illinois. The first victim was Theresa Hollander, who was beaten to death with a wooden club on February 16, 1914. A former boyfriend was twice tried and acquitted. The second victim was Jennie Miller, who was beaten to death with a heavy iron pipe on November 19, 1914. She was the daughter of a former mayor of Aurora. Her murder was also never solved. On February 25, 1915, a young woman named Emma Peterson (not Jennie) was also killed. Her head was also beaten in, probably with a metal pipe, although the weapon was never found. Her empty purse was discovered a short distance from her body and the police surmised that she had been killed in a robbery. There were no connections between any of the murders and nothing to connect them to Mansfield. I can only assume that Wilkerson added them to his list of charges because he wanted to inflate the "crimes" of William Mansfield.

Needless to say, there was nothing to realistically link Mansfield to the Aurora murders. There was also nothing that proved he ever used cocaine.

5.   All of these murders were committed in precisely the same manner, indicating strongly that they were the work of the same man.

I do believe that the murders in Paola, Villisca, and Blue Island were probably committed by the same man – just not by William Mansfield. I think that the methods used in each of the murders included in this book show very strong similarities that would have made the existence of a "copycat" killer unlikely at a time when news traveled much slower than it does today.

However, the case against William Mansfield was completely manufactured by Wilkerson, including the fact that, as the newspaper story stated, detectives believed that the killer had been a maniac or "a man with a brain distorted by drugs." While this is not a recurrent theme throughout the investigations, Wilkerson decided to run with it and create a past history of drug abuse for Mansfield. He also created a biography for Mansfield – and a sinister nickname – that was mostly fiction, as well. Wilkerson maintained that Mansfield, who was known as "Insane Blackie" by his criminal friends, also used the names George Worley and Jack Turnbaugh. The fact that he was a two-time deserter from the Army was true. It wasn't true that he had a long history of using cocaine and other drugs and "planned a long series of murders with more cunning that can be attributed to a drug-sated mind."

Wilkerson gave part of the credit for his discovery of Mansfield as the killer to Vina Tompkins, who overheard the plot that day behind the old slaughterhouse on the Nodaway River in Villisca. Even though the identity of the actual killer changed several times in Wilkerson's theory, he always maintained that Frank and Albert Jones were involved. The article detailed Wilkerson's discovery of Vina Tompkins, how he managed to gain her trust by using a phony fortune-teller and how she told him of her terrible secrets in the graveyard that day. In this version of the story, though, he claimed that Tompkins had recognized the voice of the other man who met with the Joneses as that of a professional killer from Chicago who had often had secret business dealings with her husband. Of course, as stated in Wilkerson's own report, Tompkins told him nothing of the sort. This story was completely made up by the detective and Jack Boyle, who invented the nickname "Blackie." Boyle would later pen tales of an imaginary thief-turned detective named "Boston Blackie." According to the newspaper story, Tompkins gave him Mansfield's two aliases -- George Worley and Jack Turnbaugh -- names that Mansfield never used. She claimed – in the version of the story printed in the newspaper – that Mansfield had visited her a year after the murders and that he had written one of his aliases on a matchbox and had given it to her, which led

Wilkerson to discovering his true identity. Vina Tompkins later stated under oath that the account Wilkerson attributed to her in 1914 was not accurate. What Boyle has her saying in 1916 goes well beyond that.

Wilkerson then claimed that he was able to obtain Mansfield's photograph from Leavenworth Prison (where Mansfield did serve time for desertion) and took it with him to Blue Island after the Mislich murders. In actuality, it was in Blue Island where Wilkerson first learned of Mansfield's existence. But for the sake of his story, he claimed that he not only knew about him in advance, but he questioned the Blue Island chief of police about him. The article claimed that the police chief was stunned to see the photograph and said that he had been looking for Mansfield for months because he was a suspect in the Mislich murders. Once again, this detail sprang from the imagination of either Wilkerson, Boyle, or perhaps both. By the time Wilkerson arrived in Blue Island, the police had already cleared Mansfield as a suspect in the murders, since his Milwaukee alibi had checked out.

The article also put Mansfield in Aurora, Illinois, when "Jennie Peterson" was murdered. There is no record of anyone by that name being murdered, so we have to assume that he meant Emma Peterson. Regardless, Mansfield was not in Aurora at the time, buying cocaine or anything else. This was another element of the story that Wilkerson or Boyle created and its inclusion makes little sense. Nevertheless, it was put into print and added another sensational element to the story.

The entire story was pretty suspicious and the *Villisca Review* editor was correct about being hesitant to print it. Unfortunately, though, since it was printed as news, a lot of people believed it. In Red Oak, County Attorney Gillett, still hoping to be re-elected, confirmed the warrant had been issued and announced that a grand jury would hear the case against Mansfield as soon as he was arrested and brought to Iowa.

Two days after the story was published, Mansfield was arrested by Wilkerson himself. There was no need for a nationwide manhunt. Mansfield was working as a sausage stuffer in Kansas City. Wilkerson arrested him at work, and in his "Dope Sheet" account, he told of allowing Mansfield to draw his pay and take it home to his common-law wife. Wilkerson wrote that Mansfield and Kate Romanofski were living as husband and wife in a shabby, one-room shack in the Stockyards district. The couple and their baby had little in the way of possessions. Kate was left in the shack with the baby and Wilkerson took her husband to the Kansas City jail.

With Mansfield in jail, many people believed the newspaper headlines and thought the Villisca murders had been solved. Sheriff Jackson was awaiting orders to bring Mansfield to Iowa, and County Attorney Gillett was looking for anything of substance to present to the grand jury, other than the newspaper article. Gillett was an inexperienced prosecutor working through his first term, and he let Wilkerson and Jackson bully him into presenting the case. All that he could do was to take the information that Wilkerson gave him and present it the best that he could – not realizing that the vast majority of it was a mass of supposition and outright lies. The detective promised him that he would have more, but all he had to start with was Wilkerson's "Dope Sheet."

In it, Wilkerson recounted the Blue Island murders, referring to "Stanley

William Mansfield at the time of his trumped-up arrest

Mislich," even though the victim's name was Jacob, and claiming that his head had been severed, which it hadn't. Wilkerson then recounted the similarities of the murders, which was fairly accurate, but then swerved into the realm of fiction as he expanded on his biography of Mansfield, literally making up the story as he went along to paint the suspect in the worst light possible.

According to Wilkerson, Mansfield had been born in the "slums of Chicago" in 1885, learned the cattle butchering trade from his father, and then joined the Navy when he was 16. He deserted soon afterwards, waited four years for the statute of limitations to run out, and then joined the Army in April 1908. He was initially stationed at the Jefferson Barracks in St. Louis and then sent to Fort Vancouver in Washington, where he deserted again. He went back to Chicago, where he was arrested, court-martialed, and sentenced to 18 months in Fort Leavenworth military prison. He was released in July 1910. Prison records, Wilkerson claimed, characterized Mansfield as a troublemaker.

A man named George Wilson allegedly told Wilkerson that he got Mansfield a job working with an extra gang on the Burlington Railroad at St. Joseph, Missouri, after he was released from prison. He worked for a while and then quit, dropping out of sight for several months. Wilson saw Mansfield again in late 1910, working on an extra gang for the Rock Island Railroad in Manhattan, Kansas. He said that the former convict worked there for a few weeks before disappearing once again. Wilson then saw him again in late 1911, working at a construction camp in eastern Iowa. Mansfield worked there for about six weeks and then Wilson said he didn't see him again until shortly after the Villisca murders. He was running an employment office in Kansas City by that time and Mansfield came to him looking for work, hoping he could be sent to Chicago. Wilson had no work for him and Mansfield left. He said he did not see him again until September 1915. He came into the office one day and Wilson asked him where he had been – he assumed Mansfield had been in jail. When Mansfield asked him why he wanted to know, he told him that he'd heard his entire family had been murdered in Blue Island. Mansfield claimed that he could account for his whereabouts at the time of the murders, but he never told Wilson where he had been.

Continuing with Wilkerson's timeline, Mansfield went to Blue Island in July 1912, moving in with his sisters, Minnie Showitz and Annie Mansfield. He got a job checking freight for the Rock Island Railroad and remained employed for a few weeks. Around this time, he met Martha Mislich and the two began seeing one

132

another. Her brother Jacob allegedly hated Mansfield from the time he met him, believing that in addition to being an army deserter, he was a thief and a violent man. He told his sister that Mansfield had syphilis (he didn't) and begged her not to marry him. Martha didn't listen and she and Mansfield were married on Thanksgiving Day 1912. They moved into a small house near the stockyards and Mansfield got a job making sausages for the Omaha Packing Company.

It was while working at the meat packing company that he met Kate Romanofski, later deserting Martha in October 1913 to leave town with Kate. They moved to Milwaukee and Mansfield took a job packing sausages for the Plankington Packing Company. According to Wilkerson's report, he worked there steadily for more than a year, except for a few days that he missed in early July 1915. The Blue Island murders had occurred on July 5 and Wilkerson stated that Mansfield missed work on the days leading up the murders. However, as it would turn out later, this was not the case.

Wilkerson swore that he had been looking for Mansfield for months. His claim was backed up by Vina Tompkins, who supposedly told him that a photograph of Mansfield bore a close resemblance to a man she knew as "Jack," who had worked on the street paving crew with her husband while they were in Villisca. Wilkerson caught up with Mansfield on June 13, 1916, when he received a message from a man named Bill Lane at the Swift meat packing plant in Kansas City. Lane said he knew Mansfield and that he had worked at Swift until recently. He thought he was now working at the Cochran plant.

Wilkerson passed along to County Attorney Gillett a couple of conversations that Mansfield allegedly had with workers at the plant, both of which were supposed to show that Mansfield had somehow gotten away with killing his wife in Blue Island and that he had gone to Iowa to take care of some "private business." The conversations – if they happened at all and weren't simply invented by Wilkerson – don't amount to any sort of proof of anything, something even an inexperienced county attorney like Gillett would have known.

Wilkerson also presented a strange account from a man named W.R. Tilson:

W.R. Tilson is the County Treasurer at Maryville, Missouri says that on the 31st day of May 1916 a fellow walked into his office and says "Have you got any money here for me[?], walking up to his counter. Tilson pays the witness fees in criminal cases. He thought that he came in to collect money, that he was a witness in a criminal case, and picked up his fee book and says, "What is your name?"

"My name is Bill Mansfield."

"What case were you in, Bill?"

"Oh I was not in any case at all."

He says "There was a party from Villisca was going to leave some money for me in town and I have not been able to connect with it and I thought maybe he left it here."

Tilson said, "Villisca, Iowa? That is where the Moore murders was committed. Did you know the Moores?"

Bill says, "Yes, I knew him. I knew Joe Moore and he has a brother up there named Ross and another one named Charlie and he has another one named Van Gilder, and they suspicion Van Gilder killed him." And he says, "More than that, they have suspicion me, and they have also suspicioned a rich old banker up there."

He says, "Suspicioned you? What did they suspicion you for, Bill?"

Well he said, "I have had some trouble, shot at my brother-in-law once. Been in the penitentiary. Been in the army. My record is not very good. They suspicioned me but I won't do anything about it."

He says, "Say, do you know that there was a hell of a poker game going on in town that night?"

"What night?"

"Why, the night of the murder up there."

Tilson said "why no, I don't know anything about a poker game. How should I know anything about it? I don't live up there."

Well he said, "There was, all right."

At that time a woman came in to be waited on and this party left.

The rambling story seemed to lock Mansfield into some connection with the Villisca murders, especially coming from a public official like Tilson, a former sheriff. But there was more to it than first met the eye and I suspect that Tilson was tricked by someone who wanted him to believe that it had been William Mansfield who came into the office that day.

The interrogation of William Mansfield began the afternoon he was arrested and continued until the detectives went to supper. After they had eaten, Wilkerson wrote that they had returned "and had an all-night session with him." Jack Boyle was allowed to sit in and may have even taken part in the questioning. Exactly what happened during the interrogations didn't become clear until Mansfield told his side of the story in a subsequent lawsuit, but even Wilkerson admitted that it was an aggressive attempt to solicit a confession. He went hard after Mansfield and kept the prisoner from seeing anyone, calling a lawyer or speaking to anyone but the detectives. Wilkerson later stated that he had called Sheriff Jackson on the night of Mansfield's arrest and told him to come to Kansas City right away. Wilkerson planned to take him out of the jail and transfer him to Iowa, even though this would have been illegal. Jackson told him that he would come, but then changed his mind; perhaps having second thoughts about railroading a man whose guilt he doubted. Wilkerson was angry and wrote, "That is the only time that Jack's wind failed him. He did not come down like he ought to. He sent that damn little Gillett down there."

County Attorney Gillett arrived on the morning of June 15, and by then, Mansfield had signed a waiver of extradition that would allow the authorities to send him to Iowa. But before arrangements could be made to take him out of state, an attorney named Jacob Detweiler intervened in the case. Detweiler withdrew the waiver, maintaining that Mansfield had signed under duress and without understanding what it was. He succeeded in getting the matter in front of Kansas Governor Arthur Capper.

Detweiler was a serious problem for Wilkerson, both at the time of Mansfield's arrest and later, when he filed a lawsuit on Mansfield's behalf. The detective and some of his supporters spread the rumor – and perhaps some of them even believed it – that Frank Jones had hired the attorney. Jones denied this, as did Detweiler, who said that he read about the situation in the newspaper, thought Mansfield was being railroaded, and offered to represent him at no charge. He was the best thing that ever happened to William Mansfield. He helped him obtain records that showed he was not in Iowa at the time of the murders and could not have been on the road crew in Villisca when Vina Tompkins was camped along the river. Detweiler denied that his client had ever called himself Jack Turnbaugh or George Worley, or used the nickname "Blackie." He also secured convincing evidence that the person dubbed "Insane Blackie" was someone else entirely. Governor Capper ultimately decided that Mansfield should be sent to Iowa, but thanks to Detweiler, a month had passed since his arrest and the defense was prepared.

In mid-July 1916, Mansfield was finally brought before the grand jury. The proceedings were sequestered and tightly guarded. A small army of reporters waited impatiently outside the courthouse, drumming up any kind of story they could find. One story was given to them by County Attorney Gillett, who said that three key witnesses in the case had died mysteriously since the murders. Two of them were neighbors: Mary Peckham and Mrs. W.E. Crop. It was Mary Peckham who had first became alarmed about the lack of activity at the Moore house and called J.B.'s store. Although both of them were questioned in the weeks after the murders, neither ever offered any information that would incriminate Frank Jones or anyone else. Both died of natural causes, but that didn't prevent gossip from circulating that they had known something and told someone, leading to them dying "mysteriously." The third dead witness, according to the story that spread outside the courthouse, was an unnamed man who supposedly could confirm what was said to be a startling account by an unknown female witness. Who that witness might be, what she had to offer, and the identity of the man who was supposed to be able to corroborate her story were all matters of rumor, guesswork, and gossip.

The reporters were able to question the witnesses as they came and went. Some of them talked to the press and others didn't, but as the days passed, enough information leaked out to give the news writers a good idea of what was happening during the proceedings.

To those who expected a quick indictment of William Mansfield, things were not going well. Detweiler presented photographs of payroll records that proved Mansfield was working in Montgomery, Illinois, on June 9, 1912. Wilkerson swore, then and later, that the records were forged, but the grand jury believed them to be authentic. Detweiler also told them that if there was a "drug-crazed dope fiend" out there named "Insane Blackie," it was someone other than Mansfield.

W.R. Tilson came up from Maryville, Missouri, and related his story about the man who came into his office on May 31, 1916, and had identified himself as Bill Mansfield. But it must have been someone else with the same name, or someone masquerading as Mansfield. Work records proved that Mansfield was at his job in Kansas City that day, and when Tilson saw him in court, he said that he was not the man who came into his office. He told the same thing to the reporters outside.

The authorities weren't sure what to make of Tilson's story. He was a former sheriff and a reliable witness and few doubted that the incident had taken place. But who would go to Maryville four years after the murders, call attention to himself by mentioning the murders, say that he was expecting money from someone in Villisca, and mention an "old banker" as a suspect? The answer to that is easier than one might think – it could have been done by someone trying to frame Mansfield by placing him within 50 miles of Villisca and making it look like he had a connection to the crime. Was it a coincidence that four days after the incident in Tilson's office the letters with Mansfield's picture and the accusation that Jones had hired him were mailed out? Sheriff Jackson told reporters "when we lay our hands on the man who was in Maryville looking for a shipment of money from Villisca, and who took the pains to use Mansfield's name, we will have the final solution of the Moore murder." Not likely…. To the Jones camp – and to this author – the Maryville incident looked like part of an elaborate frame-up attempt with Wilkerson and Boyle at the bottom of it.

Wilkerson, using Gillett as his mouthpiece, laid out his case to the grand jury, asking not only for an indictment of Mansfield but also, as he told reporters, of "another man." But the witnesses were not as dependable as Gillett had hoped they would be. Vina Tompkins' testimony was considerably less incriminating than Wilkerson's account of it or the version Boyle printed in his newspaper story. When she looked at Mansfield, she said that she didn't know if he was the man near the slaughterhouse that day. Of all of the witnesses called, only two gave any kind of credible evidence against Mansfield: Ralph Thorpe and Alice Willard.

Thorpe was a restaurant owner from Shenandoah who had been traveling by train on the day the murders were discovered. He said two men boarded the train in Clarinda and sat in front of him. Their actions and conversation aroused his suspicions, particularly when they jumped off the train in a small town a few miles down the line. His story had been investigated back in 1912, but it didn't lead anywhere until, years later, Wilkerson showed him a photograph of Mansfield and he identified him as one of the men on the train. Thorpe stood by the identification when he saw Mansfield in person.

Wilkerson had never met Alice Willard before she testified before the grand jury. He recounted in the courtroom that someone had given him her name, that she lived near the Moore residence, and that she knew something pertaining to the murders, but Wilkerson was busy with other witnesses and sent Boyle to talk to her. Boyle met with Willard and learned that, at the time of the murders, she was married to a railroad employee but was not living with him. They were later divorced and her reputation around town wasn't good. She was casually involved with a traveling salesman from Chicago named Ed McCrae.

Boyle took her to see Wilkerson. He spoke with her, took some notes, and then the three of them went to see Gillett. Her story was, as promised to reporters, an "amazing" one and Gillett wasted no time in getting her in front of the grand jury.

Willard testified that on the Saturday night before the murders she had been riding in a car with McCrae and a woman named Mable Freeman when McCrae's car broke down. They walked down the alley behind the Moore house and saw several men engaged in a conversation. She said that they hid in some bushes and listened to the men – one of whom was Frank Jones – talk about a crime. She heard one of them say "get Joe first and the rest will be easy." She then pointed out William Mansfield and said that he was in the group.

The story was certainly incriminating, but the jury didn't believe her. There was no supporting evidence to back it up. Ed McCrae couldn't be found. Willard said that she heard he'd been killed in a car accident, but there was no proof of that, or that he even existed. Mabel Freeman had died of natural causes a few months before the grand jury hearing. As far as anyone knew, she'd never mentioned the incident to anyone. And, of course, neither had Alice Willard, until four years after the killings. She never spoke up about it until Jack Boyle came to call on her. This alone made her story look suspicious.

Newspapers reporters saw Willard when she left the courthouse and assumed that she was the woman who had sensational testimony to offer, but she refused to speak to them. The proceedings had been closed and the public and the press had to wait to hear her story.

On July 21, the grand jury returned a unanimous decision not to indict Mansfield and he was released. Sheriff Jackson took him to Omaha, where he boarded a train and returned to Kansas City.

The failure to indict Mansfield caused a considerable amount of unrest in the county, partly because the proceedings had been secret and people were left to guess, assume, or believe whatever they were told. Wilkerson was, of course, spreading the story that Jones had either bought off or intimidated the witnesses. Many people were quick to believe it, but who can blame them? They had read the news of Mansfield's arrest, saw his mugshot in the paper, and read Boyle's account spelling out his certain guilt. They wanted a trial and a conviction that would bring an end to four years of fear, horror, and uncertainty. Then, after five days behind closed doors, Mansfield was suddenly a free man. When Wilkerson said the whole thing was crooked and that Jones had used his money and influence to win sympathizers on the grand jury and to intimidate the witnesses, there were far too many who believed it.

But this would not be the last that the people of Villisca and Montgomery County would hear of William Mansfield.

16. THE SLANDER TRIAL
FRANK JONES FIGHTS BACK

The primary elections of 1916 caused a change in the cast of characters in the Villisca murders investigation. George Cosson failed in his bid for the governor's nomination. Horace Havner, a lawyer from Iowa City, took the Republican attorney general primary and went on to win the November election. In Montgomery County, a young farmer from Stanton named Bob Dunn earned the nomination for sheriff. Gillett actually got more votes for county attorney than either of his challengers, but the rules required that a candidate receive at least 35 percent of the primary vote to be on the ballot in November. Failing this, the selection went into the hands of Republican county delegates. The inexperienced Gillett proved to be unpopular with them, and after three ballots, the delegates gave the nomination to Oscar Wenstrand, a 28-year-old lawyer from Red Oak. Wenstrand had obtained his law degree from the University of Iowa and then went to Utah, where he worked at a bank for three years. He returned to Iowa in 1915, joined a law firm in Red Oak, and then ran for the county attorney's office. The job was a part-time position and the pay was hardly worth the problems that came with it, but it was a high-profile spot that could help a young attorney make a name for himself. It also offered a lot of courtroom experience and Wenstrand was soon going to need it.

The 1916 primaries had brought humiliation for Frank Jones. He was not only embarrassed by his defeat, but the wide margin by which he lost. He blamed Wilkerson and was determined to do something about it. Jones had announced that if any man publicly accused him of the murders, he'd take him to court. The *Villisca Review* printed this threat two times. Jones kept his promise and prepared to sue Wilkerson for slander. He also began an investigation of his own, hiring first Thomas O'Leary, and then other detectives, to dig up dirt on Wilkerson and possibly connect him to the anonymous letters that had been mailed out before the primary.

He picked two attorneys to handle his lawsuit: R.W. Beeson and Ralph Pringle, both from Red Oak. Both men were battle-hardened veterans. Beeson had been practicing law for 40 years and had served several terms as county attorney in the 1890s. Both men thought the case was a bad idea. They knew slander would be difficult to prove and that it would give Wilkerson a wide door to attack their client, but they failed to convince Jones not to go through with it.

Wilkerson had been focusing on Jones as a murder suspect since he had arrived in Villisca two years before. For at least a year, he had been attracting a small but loyal group of followers, conducting meetings, gathering information, and soliciting money. He continued telling people that Jones was guilty, and why. What he was alleging was public knowledge, but for the lawsuit, Jones' attorneys wanted something that was not only public, but recent and documented. They didn't have too long to wait. On August 3, Wilkerson called one of his outdoor meetings in a cow pasture south of town, likely belonging to Joseph Stillinger, who had become one of the detective's biggest supporters. Interested parties were publicly invited to attend. At the meeting, with a few dozen people attending, Wilkerson made specific accusations against Jones and the members of the grand jury who had failed to indict William Mansfield. He invited others to make their own accusations, and several did so.

The lawsuit, filed in early October 1916, named not just Wilkerson, but several of his closest supporters, including Ross Moore, W.H. Willett, W.W. Arnold, J.L. Gourley, Ed Northrup, A.D. Silverthorn, L.B. Penton, and Reverend Wesley Ewing. The petition stated that on August 3, 1916, and "at other diverse times before and since," the defendants "did conspire and confederate together with intent falsely and maliciously to cause and procure the plaintiff to be indicted and prosecuted for an offense, to-wit, murder, of which he is innocent."

Jones, or perhaps his lawyers, had second thoughts about bringing suit against people like Reverend Ewing and Ross Moore, and later re-filed the lawsuit, dismissing action against everyone but Wilkerson. They had narrowed the target to the out-of-state detective, a man who was not a family member of the victims, or a minister, or a respected local farmer or businessman. Even so, Jones would later say that the slander suit was the biggest mistake that he ever made.

The Burns detective agency was worried about the trial. It would be damaging to the agency's reputation if Wilkerson lost. To handle Wilkerson's defense, the agency hired a well-known trial lawyer from Council Bluffs named William Edward Mitchell. He was known for dominating a courtroom with his booming voice, masterful speaking skills, and caustic wit. He liked to refer to himself as "just a country lawyer," but the truth was Mitchell was smart, quick, and experienced and had been successful as both a defense attorney and a prosecutor. In preparing for the trial, he learned everything about Wilkerson's theory and would present it to the jury in a way that not only argued there was no slander because the detective had good reason to suspect Jones – he would convince them that Wilkerson's theory was true. He turned the trial into a prosecution of Frank Jones, and did it very convincingly. Before the trial, Jones had no idea of the depth of the investigation, of the people who would testify, or the incriminating things they would say. Instead of vindicating him, the trial turned into a disaster for him.

Tensions were high in Villisca and the surrounding area and the people of Montgomery County were anxiously awaiting the start of the trial. Wilkerson promised that he would defend himself by revealing the truth about Frank Jones and the murder plot. People traveled from all over the state – and beyond – to attend the trial, and area hotels quickly filled. Burns had assigned several detectives to stay in Red Oak to assist the witnesses and to run down any leads that developed while court was in session. Reporters flocked to town, excitedly covering the events for newspapers throughout the country. Clarence Miller, former editor of the Red Oak newspaper, was hired by the *Villisca Review* as a special correspondent. He was in the courtroom every day, taking notes and making observations. He would be accused of bias – rightfully so – since he was a Wilkerson devotee. Within a few months, he would be named secretary of Wilkerson's "protective association." His duties would include attending dozens of meetings, keeping records, and taking charge of fundraising to keep the investigation going. The *Review* responded to these accusations by saying it received an equal number of letters complaining that Miller showed favoritism toward Jones and, therefore, the paper considered his coverage to be fairly balanced.

The trial began on Tuesday, November 14. Attorney R.W. Beeson opened the proceedings on behalf of Frank Jones. His comments were aimed to the jury:

> *This address is not an argument, not to be accepted as evidence in the case at hand. Indeed, this is no ordinary case. It is one of the most important ever tried in this county. A case which involved the honor and good standing of one of the most prominent citizens of the county. Sometime during the night of June 9, 1912, there was committed at the home of Joe Moore in Villisca one of the most horrible murders in the history of Iowa. Whoever did it got away and the deed was not discovered until 8 o'clock the next morning. The defendant in this case has defamed the plaintiff F.F. Jones, by saying that he furnished the money to pay for that crime. We ask that Mrs. Jones be placed right as far as a verdict from this jury can place him right.*

Jones' attorneys filed a pleading on several separate causes for action. They referred to the meeting that Wilkerson had on August 3, during which he spoke out about Jones and the grand jury that had failed to indict William Mansfield. Wilkerson held another meeting that day at the home of the Montgomery family (Sarah Moore's family) and again denounced Jones as the instigator of the murders. He was quoted during this meeting as saying "I will give F.F. Jones $500 to bring suit against me." He added, "We have Mansfield, the man who wielded the ax, and F.F. Jones, the man who paid for the murder of Joe Moore." Beeson stated that such allegations were false and that Wilkerson acted as a "public denouncer" and not a detective.

Beeson also charged that Wilkerson went to a Mrs. Campbell in Villisca in September 1915, and told her that Jones wanted the Moores out of the way and was instrumental in doing it. He told this story repeatedly in other towns. "The evidence will show maliciousness and intent to injure Mr. Jones," he said. "There is not one bit of evidence to show that F.F. Jones ever had a thing to do with that murder."

Beeson then predicted what the defense would allege: They would claim that the murder plot was overheard by a woman near a slaughterhouse a year before the murder took place. He laughed and said that not even a three-year-old boy would believe such a far-fetched story. He said he knew that Wilkerson alleged that he had talked with Hank Horton, who said Frank Jones told him about the murders on the morning they were discovered, and before more than two or three people knew they had taken place. "We will prove there is no truth whatever in that story," he added. "The evidence shows that Wilkerson tried to get Horton to go before the grand jury and perjure himself, that Wilkerson stood at the door of the grand jury room and questioned the witnesses, and told them what to swear to. We will show that this man Wilkerson has worked two years to frame up a case and convict an innocent man."

Following Beeson's opening remarks, Wilkerson's attorney, William Mitchell, took the floor. He said he understood that this was not the time to argue the case, but he did want to present the facts as the defense knew them. He offered a detailed account of the Moore-Stillinger murders and stated that the killer was seen near the Moore house on the days leading up to the murders and had, at least once, gone into the Moore yard and picked up the murder weapon. Witnesses had seen the man and could connect him to the crime, he said.

Mitchell them pointed out that on the night of the murders, Frank Jones had attended services at the Methodist Church, but got up during the service and stayed outside for 15 minutes, and then came back in and sat down near the back.

He then turned his attention to the testimony of Vina Tompkins, who he alleged had been "kidnapped" by Senator Comfort Harvey Van Law of Marshalltown, a friend and supporter of Frank Jones, in order to keep her from testifying at the trial. He told about how she and her husband had been in Villisca during the street paving and that she heard men plotting against J.B. Moore behind the old slaughterhouse. Mitchell claimed one of the men was Frank Jones.

Frank Jones had many motives to kill J.B. Moore, Mitchell told the jury. The main one was business: J.B. Moore had become a rival when he quit working for Jones and opened a competing implement store. Mitchell said, "Time and again, F.F. Jones was heard to complain that business was not what it used to be for him."

He then cited the second motive: "The evidence will also show that certain charges can be made regarding the relations of a certain woman and Joe Moore, which led to an estrangement between F.F. Jones and Joe Moore. We will show you that these are motives that led to the plot. No claim is made by the defendant that the plan was to kill anyone but Joe Moore, but the murderer killed all in the house."

Mitchell promised to show that at 2 p.m. on the day of the murders, an automobile drove around the block near the Moore house two times and then sped away to the north. Furthermore, on Sunday night, Burt McCaul was in Villisca and was seen several times in the company of Frank Jones. He said the defense would also show that on the night of the murders, McCaul got his automobile out of Nelson's Garage and was not seen again in town until 9 a.m. the next morning. Earlier than morning -- between 4 and 5 a.m. -- McCaul was seen with Albert Jones several miles north of Villisca. Mitchell also promised to bring in a witness to "testify to an incident in the life of Albert Jones and Joe Moore."

Despite the fact that the grand jury had failed to indict William Mansfield, Wilkerson's attorney still insisted on drawing him into the case. In fact, he announced plans to bring in Ralph Thorpe, the restaurant owner from Shenandoah who claimed to have seen Mansfield on the train after the murders. He would also bring in Vina Tompkins, whom he said could identify Mansfield, as well as two boys named Nelson who lived between Villisca and Clarinda who also supposedly saw Mansfield that morning.

He closed by re-stating Wilkerson's accusations about the grand jury members being somehow biased. "How about that grand jury that would not indict F.F. Jones?" he asked, ignoring the fact that it was Mansfield, and not Jones, who was being accused. "First, the cashier of Mr. Jones' bank; second, Mr. Dirim, nephew of the vice-president of that bank; and third, Mr. Rusk, a warm friend of Mr. Jones." He then added:

I ask you men to give candid attention to all the evidence to be submitted and to bring in a verdict according to what you believe is just and right.

At the conclusion of Mitchell's remarks, the court took a short recess and then adjourned a few minutes later, since it was close to 5 p.m. During the break, the courtroom was disrupted by a disagreement between the three lawyers. Not surprisingly, Wilkerson was involved. Beeson had been speaking with Gillett, who was still county attorney, when Wilkerson walked in and interrupted them. Beeson took offense and told Wilkerson to get away from him and not to "poke his nose in" when he was talking. The judge called for order and Beeson angrily replied that there would be order and plenty of it if any fourth-rate detective got funny with him. Mitchell interrupted and said that he thought the detective could take care of himself and that he had as much right there as Gillett had. Beeson warned Mitchell to take care of his detective and to keep him out of his way. Mitchell barked out a laugh and told Beeson that he had better look out for himself because he might be in a worse state of mind before the trial was over. Needless to say, the spectators in the courtroom were highly entertained by the exchange.

Court was back in session on Wednesday, November 15. Beeson called a number of people who testified that they heard Wilkerson state that Jones had paid to have J.B. Moore killed. They also reported that Wilkerson spoke about the slaughterhouse murder plot, told stories about Jones' cheapness, about McCaul taking his automobile out on the night of the murders, about McCaul and Jones spending time together, and of Wilkerson vowing that he would see to it that Jones lost the election. Most of the day was spent with witnesses like this, all of them testifying to damaging things that Wilkerson had publicly said about Jones.

In his column about the trial, correspondent Clarence Miller noted that Vina Tompkins was in the courtroom on the second day of testimony. Wilkerson had previously told the press about how Tompkins had been "kidnapped" by Senator Van Law. In his opening remarks, Mitchell had told the jury that Tompkins was changing her story after being influenced by Van Law. Miller noted that the "kidnapping" plot was a fabrication on the part of Wilkerson and his attorneys. Tompkins had been staying at the Griffith Inn the night before, Miller wrote, and could have been found at any time. No one had kidnapped her. It was more likely that she was refusing to speak to Wilkerson after the blatant lies that he made up about her past testimony.

The trial continued on November 16. The courtroom was filled beyond capacity with spectators arriving hours before the courthouse opened so that they could get good seats. They sat on benches and chairs. Those who couldn't find seats stood up. Many of them sat on the floor, just a few feet from the judge's bench.

The first witness on Thursday morning was A.W. Hill, a longtime friend of Frank Jones. Hill testified to attending a meeting on the John Montgomery farm north of Villisca, where Wilkerson spoke out against Jones and accused him of hiring J.B. Moore's killer. He testified that Wilkerson said he did not want to injure any innocent man but then went on to find fault with the grand jury and the county attorney, as well as Frank Jones. Hill also related a new story that Wilkerson was spreading about his meetings with Vina Tompkins. This time, the detective claimed he had thrown a photograph of Jones into her lap, at which point she supposedly threw up her hands and cried, "Why, that's one of the men I heard plotting the murder of Joe Moore!"

Lester Scott, Jack Seefeldt, and C.M. Orr also testified against Wilkerson. They had attended one of Wilkerson's meetings and heard the detective state that Jones was behind the murder plot. Villisca photographer John W. Noel testified that Wilkerson had attempted to purchase a photograph of Frank Jones from him.

Charles Callahan, a livestock dealer from Red Oak, testified he had heard Wilkerson accuse Jones of involvement in the murders. He said he also heard Wilkerson claim the grand jury had not been unanimous in its decision against indicting William Mansfield. Even if this was true, grand jury proceedings were closed and Wilkerson had no actual knowledge that this was the case.

O.R. Osborn of Villisca also testified to attending one of Wilkerson's meetings and corroborated most of what had already been told by other witnesses. However, he added that Wilkerson claimed to have "evidence" that Jones furnished the money to have J.B. Moore murdered – evidence that he had not produced at the time of the trial.

Al Davis, a farmer who lived near Stanton, testified for Jones and also spoke of attending one of Wilkerson's meetings. When cross-examined by Mitchell, though, he said that he could not remember the exact words that Wilkerson had used with regard to Jones and the murders. He further testified that he heard Wilkerson say that he had no malice toward anyone and that there was a vote during the meeting that pledged support to Wilkerson as he continued his work.

Elmer Hyde, a farmer who lived northwest of Villisca, testified to attending two of Wilkerson's meetings. In addition to corroborating what the other witnesses for the plaintiff had said, he told the story of the Cosson letter that Jones allegedly produced for Bell, the newspaper writer, when he tried to extort money from Jones for Wilkerson and Boyle. Wilkerson told the story of the extortion attempt at the meeting that Hyde attended, except that he told it in a completely different way than it actually happened. In his courtroom notes, Clarence Miller wrote:

A detective had called on F.F. Jones and claimed that he had wanted to sell him some very valuable evidence in regard to Jones' part in the Moore murder. Mr. Jones is alleged to have told him to wait, that he would think it over. Then the fellow said that he would go to Denver and return in a few weeks to see Jones again. He did so, but by this time Mr. Jones didn't want to buy the information at all, said that he had assurance the matter would be dropped, and he pulled out a letter purporting to be from Attorney General Cosson, and handed it to the detective to read. It was addressed to Senator Jones and stated that as far as the attorney general was concerned the prosecution of the Moore murder would be dropped and was signed by Mr. Cosson. The story is that the detective made a mental copy of the letter and handed it back to Mr. Jones. The evidence which he had tried to sell to Mr. Jones was priced at $500, and that it was the amount Mr. Jones agreed to pay if he decided to take it all.

Readers who recall the basic facts behind the story will quickly realize that Wilkerson was telling a "white-washed" version of the incident at his meetings, trying to make it look like it had not been an extortion attempt, but rather a sanctioned method of investigation. For starters, Bell was not a detective at all. He was a newspaper crony of Boyle's who had been convinced to offer Jones evidence in exchange for $25,000 – a far cry from the $500 that Wilkerson claimed had been offered. Bell had met with Jones three times, the final time in his home. This was when Jones allegedly produced the letter from the attorney general. Of course, there is no evidence that such a letter existed. No one could produce it (the extortionist supposedly made a "mental copy" of it) and Jones never spoke of it or showed it to anyone. Even if the letter existed, Cosson would never have promised to close the Villisca investigation. Most likely, any such letter would have simply been a character reference for Jones, probably expressing doubt from the attorney general's office that the highly esteemed citizen had been involved in the murders.

Little was written about the trial on November 17. Witnesses for the plaintiff continued to testify, each telling of being at one of Wilkerson's meetings and hearing him make further charges against Frank Jones.

The attorneys for Jones rested their case on Friday morning, November 18, and the trial was turned over to the defense. Mitchell called Dr. J. Clark Cooper, who related the particulars about the Moore-Stillinger crime scene and what he saw at the house in June 1912. Attention was given in the questioning to ensure that he described the marks in the ceiling that had been made in the upswing of the ax. He was not cross-examined.

The next witness was Sylvester "Ves" Cooney, who told of being hired to remove the bloody bedclothes from the house. He repeated his previous accounts of gathering up the bloody clothing, along with pieces of bone and flesh, rolling it all up in a mattress, wrapping the mattress with wire and burning it at the city dump. Mitchell made sure that he pointed out to the jury that Cooney was convinced that he had removed all of the pieces of bone from the house.

The next witness called by the defense was Lee Van Gilder, a nephew of J.B. Moore and a grandson of John Montgomery. He told of going to the Moore house on June 10, after the murders had been discovered and finding his grandfather already there. He also described walking through the house after the bodies had been removed. Van Gilder said that he had found a name tag from a key ring in the front pocket of J.B.'s trousers and that the key ring and keys had been forcibly removed from it. He also testified that as he and his grandfather had passed the Jones store on the way to dinner that day, Frank Jones had come out and said to Montgomery, "John, this is an awful thing. There is lots of talk around here about me being mixed up in this thing. You don't think there is anything to that, do you?"

Van Gilder also testified that Jones had visited him a few weeks before the trial and asked if there was anything that he could do for him. Van Gilder said no, and then Jones went on to tell him about hiring Thomas O'Leary to see if he could determine who sent out the anonymous letters before the primary. Jones said that O'Leary had some circumstantial evidence that the mailing had been done by Wilkerson. Jones assured him that he had nothing to do with the murders, that he and J.B. had been friends and that it was he, Jones, who had convinced the attorney general to hire a detective to look into the case.

In my opinion, Van Gilder's testimony can hardly be called harmful to the plaintiff. Instead, the references to Jones seemed to show a man who was concerned not only about his reputation, but in the well-being of the Montgomery family. On the day the murders were discovered, Jones was expressing worry about the family. He also wanted to make sure that John Montgomery, whom he had known for many years, did not think that he was somehow involved in the deaths. There is no mention of Montgomery's reply, but he almost certainly told Jones that there was nothing to worry about and that he didn't think that Jones was involved. Montgomery's later interest in Wilkerson's theory probably had more to do with the fact that Wilkerson was at least doing *something* with the case. After more than four years, he had undoubtedly become frustrated and tired with the lack of movement in the investigation. He was ready to believe in anything at that point. As with Van Gilder, I get more of a sense that Jones was worried about the young man than anything else. He asked if he needed anything, which is not an uncommon question from an older man to a younger one. Jones also wanted to assure him again that, despite the rumors, he had not been connected to the murders.

The next person brought to the stand was Ralph Thorpe, who claimed to have seen William Mansfield on the train to Clarinda on the morning after the murders. Beeson objected throughout his testimony, which is not surprising since the grand jury had already dismissed it and had chosen not to indict Mansfield, based on the exact same evidence that Mitchell was now offering. The objections led to a heated exchange between the attorneys. The judge rebuked them both and allowed the testimony to be received.

Following Thorpe on the stand was Otto Wiltte, the chief of police from Blue Island, Illinois. He took the stand carrying an ax wrapped in heavy paper. He told the court about the Blue Island murders and the similarity between them and the Villisca murders. During his testimony, the ax was unwrapped and it was shown, still covered in dried blood, to the jury as the murder weapon. He did mention that Mansfield was working in Milwaukee at the time his family was killed, but he said he believed that he could have taken a train to Blue Island, committed the murders and then returned in time to make it to work the next morning. Wiltte did not mention that someone else had already confessed to the murders and had been locked up. In fact, no one mentioned that it had already been proven that Mansfield could not have committed the murders in Blue Island or Villisca or that a grand jury had already failed to indict him. Since the Iowa grand jury proceedings had been secret, Mitchell knew that the current jury was not aware of these details.

After that, the court was adjourned for the weekend. On Monday, November 20, the most highly anticipated defense witness in the case, Vina Tompkins, took the stand. She first gave her basic background information and then told of the slaughterhouse incident. She described the three men she heard plotting, stating that one of them had a beard. When Mitchell pointed at Jones and asked if the man's beard had looked like his, she said, "A little longer, I think, and a little wider under the chin." She said one of the men was heavy and Mitchell pointed out Albert Jones and asked if the man was as heavy as Albert was. Tompkins said that he was "not quite so heavy, but short like him." She was asked if she could make out what they said. She said the tall man had asked how they were to get money and the man with the beard replied that he could get it, but not all at one bank. The men spoke of some "job" and there was a remark about what would be done about "the girl." The man with the beard answered, "We will have him out of the way anyhow." She said one of the men asked about when it would be done, and one of the others replied that it would not be right then, but some time later.

During cross-examination, she said that she had told others about the three men, but Wilkerson was the first to hear the whole story. She claimed that she was reluctant to talk about it because someone who had murdered eight people likely wouldn't hesitate to kill her too if they found out that she had told. She admitted that the only reason she told Wilkerson about the details of the incident was because a fortune-teller told her to do so. She then claimed that she had not told everything she knew to the Mansfield grand jury "because she was not asked to."

Beeson then produced a typewritten transcript of an interview that she'd had on November 4, with Senator Van Law. This was a confusing part of the trial because Mitchell and Wilkerson claimed that Van Law had kidnapped Tompkins to keep her from talking. The plaintiff's lawyers, of course, had a different version of events.

Comfort Harvey Van Law had served with Jones in the senate, but they were not personal friends. Van Law, disturbed by the allegations against a fellow senator, had gone to see Tompkins on his own. Jones was not aware of his visit until later. Tompkins told Van Law that she had seen three men near the slaughterhouse but had never gotten close enough to hear what they were saying. She told Van Law that she had not seen the face of the older man, but that she did hear the word "money" mentioned and assumed they were gambling. She also told Van Law that she had been threatened by a detective and had been told exactly what to say in court. This version of events completely discredited her earlier story (which had been greatly inflated by Wilkerson) and blew a huge hole in Wilkerson's theory of the case.

But the defense wouldn't be damaged so easily. When questioned by Mitchell, she claimed that she had lied to Van Law and had not been under oath. Wilkerson had told her, she said, that if questioned, she should never tell the truth about the case. She said that Van Law had accompanied her and her husband to Red Oak and told her not to see anyone or say anything to anyone before she went on the stand. She also acknowledged that she had told the same story that she told to Van Law to attorney Ralph Pringle, but claimed again that it was all a lie.

During her questioning by Mitchell she also added that she remembered the men at the slaughterhouse had said something about leaving the money "where old man Whipple was shot." She said that she had never been threatened or offered a bribe by Wilkerson and had been questioned by Marshal Horton and Mayor Lewis, but had lied to them too. Tompkins said that this was because one of the men at the slaughterhouse had said that the marshal was "fixed."

By my count, this is (at least) the fifth time that Vina Tompkins' story had been changed, either by Wilkerson or by Tompkins herself.

The next witness called was another highly anticipated one, even though once again, her testimony had already been dismissed by the grand jury. The public didn't know this, however. Alice Willard took the stand and told the jury that she lived with her father, one block south and one block east of the Moore home. On the morning of June 8, she said she saw two strange men walk past the Moore house. She saw them again that night around 9 p.m. Willard said that later that night, after an automobile ride with a salesman from Chicago named Ed McCrae and her friend, Mable Freeman, the three of them were walking toward Willard's home. At the north corner of the Moores' yard, they saw three unknown men coming from somewhere near the house. She said that she and her friends (for unknown reasons) hid behind a clump of bushes just west of the corner and waited for the men to pass by. The men, however, climbed over a fence and went across the Moore yard to the northwest. There they met two men who had come from the west whom Willard identified as Frank Jones and Bert McCaul. The five men proceeded to have a conversation but she could only hear bits and pieces. There was something said about "Sunday night" and "get Joe first and the others will be easy." Willard said that she heard those words clearly and would be haunted by them for the rest of her life.

Willard also testified that she had received some threatening letters after testifying before the grand jury and that Frank Jones had come to see her in August. He said that he had heard about the letters and offered to have his detective find out who sent them.

The courtroom was packed even tighter that day and with so many people crowded in to hear Willard's testimony, Judge J.B. Rockafellow announced that from then on, no one except those connected with the case would be allowed inside the railing. Only those who could find seats in the gallery would be allowed in the courtroom. It had gotten so bad that during the noon recess, spectators had even taken the attorneys' chairs.

On Tuesday, November 21, it was announced that Alice Willard had become ill during the night and would be unable to return to the stand that day. Fourteen others testified in her place, all called by the defense to show that Wilkerson had good reason for saying what he had about Jones.

The first witness was a Mrs. McCoy, who lived about two blocks from the Moores at the time of the murders. She testified to seeing two strange men on the afternoon of June 9. Later that evening, she saw them again, walking past the Moore home. The cross-examination centered on how she could have possibly remembered seeing two random men four and a half years before. No clear explanation was offered.

Margaret Landers, who lived across the street to the east of the Moores, also testified to seeing two strange men on June 9. She said that they had gone into the Moores' back yard and picked up an ax. They looked at it and then put it down and walked away to the north. She also claimed that, during the night, she heard a woman that she thought was Sarah Moore screaming and crying, "Oh dear! Oh dear! Don't, don't, don't!" This statement had never been heard before and it almost seemed as though the neighborhood was vying to see who could come up with the best story.

Lige Nelson was next on the stand. He testified that he had operated a garage on the north side of the square in Villisca at the time of the murders. He said that on the night in question, Bert McCaul, who kept his Ford at the garage, came in about 9 p.m. to get his car. He said that he remembered the incident because he had to move a disassembled vehicle out of the way so that McCaul could get his car out. He said that he did not see the car again until about 8:30 a.m. the following morning, when it was parked in front of McCaul's pool hall on the south side of the square. Nelson also said that, about two months later, McCaul and Frank Jones came to the garage in a new car and that McCaul said the car belonged to him. McCaul told Nelson to bring the bill for the old Ford to his place, and when Nelson went upstairs over the post office to McCaul's room a few days later, he found McCaul and Jones sitting at a table with a bottle of beer between them. He added that he never saw Jones drink any of it. He said that McCaul paid the bill of about $20 and still had money left over. Nelson said that Jones had spoken to him before the Mansfield grand jury met, asking him what he planned to tell them about McCaul getting his car from the garage that night. He claimed Jones also questioned him afterwards and asked if he told them about seeing him and McCaul drinking beer in McCaul's room.

Jones' attorneys pointed out several inconsistencies in Nelson's story, namely, why the garage owner had collected $20 from McCaul when the ledger showed that the bill with the garage was actually only $7.

W.R. Tilson, the county treasurer from Maryville, Missouri, was called to the stand and gave his account of the man alleging to be Mansfield, who came into his office a few days before Mansfield was arrested and asked for money being sent to him from Villisca. Reporters who talked to Tilson after his grand jury testimony were clear in saying that Tilson looked at Mansfield and said that he was not the man. During his testimony in the slander trial, though, he was shown a photograph of Mansfield and said that while he could not be positive, it resembled him very much.

J.C. Briggs, who owned a sawmill a few miles south and west of Villisca, said that on the morning of June 10, 1912, he saw a man walking through the woods near the mill, heading south. He was shown a picture of Mansfield and he said that he thought it was the same man. Aside from the fact that Mansfield was nowhere close to Villisca at the time of the murders, Beeson asked him how, after seeing a man's face for a few seconds from a distance of at least 60 feet, he could possibly identify him four years later from an old photograph. Briggs said that he thought he could do so.

Three men testified to having seen Albert Jones and Joe Moore having a conversation in the alley that separated their two homes on the Sunday evening of the murders.

An older man, "Admiral" George Rhue of Grant, took the stand next. He was extremely hard of hearing and Mitchell had to shout his questions at him. Rhue testified that he had seen Albert Jones on a sidewalk in Grant at about 6 a.m. on June 10, 1912.

Jim Birdwell, also of Grant, said that he saw both Albert Jones and Bert McCaul in Grant at about the same time. Birdwell was a disagreeable witness during the defense's cross-examination, shouting his replies at Beeson. At one point he responded to a question by asking what difference it made anyway.

Although it was by accident, Birdwell raised an interesting point – what difference did it make if McCaul and Albert had been in Grant that morning? There was no question that they had left Villisca early on the morning the murders were discovered. They called on a number of clients and were north of town, only a few miles south of Grant, when informed about the murders. Wilkerson maintained that they took an earlier trip, going 30 miles north to Atlantic to take someone involved in the killings to the railroad depot. In 1915, three years after the murders and after Wilkerson held one of his meetings in Grant, several men, including Birdwell, said that they suddenly recalled seeing McCaul and Albert in Grant that morning. Grant was seven or eight miles farther north than Jones and McCaul said they had gone. There was really no reason for them to lie about being in Grant since Jones had a number of customers there and routinely called on them. But he and McCaul both denied it and this became important to Wilkerson's case because if he had lied about being in Grant, the detective asked, what else did he have to hide? In addition, Wilkerson needed the Grant witnesses because he was unable to produce anyone, at the Atlantic depot or anywhere else, who could support his belief that the two men had taken the killer to meet a train outside of town.

The next witness, M.V. Selley, told about Jones' behavior at the Methodist Church on the evening before the murders occurred. He recalled him sitting in the back and then leaving for a few minutes during the service.

Lee Van Gilder was recalled to the stand and said that he was in the Villisca National Guard unit that was called to guard the Moore house following the murders. He related that Bert McCaul had come to the house on Monday and insistently tried to go inside. He said McCaul made such a pest of himself that a big Swedish guardsman named Axel Joneson grabbed him by the collar and threw him into the street.

On Wednesday, November 22, Alice Willard returned to the stand. She testified that two of the men who met Jones and McCaul at the Moore house that night were William Mansfield and Harry Whipple – Wilkerson's favorite suspects.

During the cross-examination by the Jones defense team, she said that the woman friend who was with her that night was now deceased. She said Ed McCrae, whose car they had gone for a ride in, was a traveling salesman for a Chicago novelty company. She said she had not seen him in a couple of years. She said the encounter took place around 10 p.m. The sky was clear at the time, but there was no moon. She swore again that Harry Whipple was there, but she was less certain about Mansfield. She hesitated when asked if she was sure that one of the men was Frank Jones. She was asked several times and, after her initial hesitation, maintained that she was sure that it had been him.

Beeson was as skeptical about her story as the Mansfield grand jury had been. He said that it was absurd that she could have positively identified the men from hiding, at a distance of more than 20 feet, on a dark night with no streetlights (they were shut off that night) and with no moon. She was asked to explain how, if she could see them so clearly, they were unable to see her. Willard replied that it was likely because she had seen them approach and then had hidden. She said that McCrae had recognized Jones too – begging the question as to how a traveling salesman from Chicago could identify Jones – but the judge ruled this inadmissible. She was also asked to explain why she had never told this story to anyone and then decided to tell Wilkerson. She said she had kept the secret until the previous August and then after receiving the threatening letters (which she had not mentioned to the grand jury), she had contacted Wilkerson.

The next witness was Mrs. Fred Shipper, who was the next person that Wilkerson wanted to use to place McCaul and Albert Jones north of where they claimed to have been. She said that she lived about 10 miles north and a little east of Villisca and said that she heard about the murders from a telephone call that morning. She said that she went to tell her husband about it and found that McCaul and Jones were at her house. Her husband followed her to the stand and said that he had not yet gone to work in the field when McCaul and Albert Jones pulled into his drive. He said they had talked for a while and then his wife came outside and told all three of them about the murders. Albert Jones then asked: "Which Joe Moore was it?" (There were two Moore families in the Villisca area and both included a man named Joe) Shipper said that Albert Jones did not seem excited about the news but McCaul said. "For God's sake," and told Albert that they had better get back to town.

Roy Dunn and George Baker testified to having seen McCaul and Jones traveling north toward Grant on the morning of June 10. They estimated the time to have been around 5 a.m. Mrs. Andy Devine testified that Albert Jones had stopped at her home north of Villisca on the morning of June 10, but did not know what time it was. She did say that it was before she heard about the murders. When cross-examined, she admitted that Wilkerson had interviewed her before the Mansfield grand jury and asked her to fix the time that Albert had arrived at her house. When she still did not recall, he suggested that she just say that it had been 7 a.m.

Mr. and Mrs. J.B. Kimmel took the stand, one after the other. Mrs. Kimmel said that Albert Jones had stopped at her house about 11 miles north of Villisca at 8 a.m. on the morning when the murders were discovered. She said he was looking for Ira Stickler and she directed him to a nearby field where he was working. Mr. Kimmel said that he saw Jones talking to Ira Stickler in the field that morning.

Dr. R.B. Smith, a Villisca dentist, testified that on the morning when the murders were discovered, he went to the Moore house and saw Frank Jones sitting in an automobile across the street. He had a conversation with Jones, and Smith made a remark to the effect that if the bloodhounds were to do any good in tracking the murderer, there shouldn't be so many people allowed to tramp through the house. Jones allegedly replied, "That won't make any difference."

Walter March, who operated a restaurant near the Villisca train depot, testified that he had been in McCaul's pool hall on the day after the funerals. He said that he saw McCaul go to the cigar case and bring out what he claimed was a piece of J.B. Moore's skull. He described the object as a long piece of bone about one-quarter of an inch thick, two inches long and about one and one-half inches wide. It still had blood on it. March said the fragment was shaped like it might have come from the back part of a man's skull. He named several other people who were there at the time, all of whom had seen the piece of bone.

Henry Gourley also testified to seeing the gruesome trophy and added that McCaul told him that he "got it when they were cleaning up over there." George Sparger confirmed the testimony, saying that he had been shown the bone about two weeks after the murders. Harry King also testified, saying that he had been in the pool hall in December 1912, and had seen the bone. He said that he asked McCaul about it and McCaul gave it to him. King took the piece home, but his wife objected to him having it in their house, so he threw it away.

Wilkerson's theory had it that the piece of bone had been picked up by the killer at the time of the murders and had been taken to Frank Jones as proof that the deed had been done. Cooney's earlier testimony was intended to show that the bone fragment wasn't there when he cleaned up the house after the murders, therefore, it could not have been found later and carried away from the scene as a souvenir. The other witnesses' testimony had been set up to show both that McCaul had the bone and that it was purported to be part of J.B.'s skull. Another damning bit of testimony was given by Charles N. Fessler, the Villisca undertaker who prepared J.B. Moore's body for burial. Fessler said there had been little left of Moore's skull; that it was beaten to a pulp and that small fragments of bone and flesh were strewn over his pillow. He said that he had gathered them up in a basket and removed them to city hall. But there is little doubt that McCaul *did* sneak into the house on the afternoon of the day the bodies were discovered. He was allowed into the house by Captain Casey, his drinking and gambling buddy, who was in charge of the local National Guard unit. It was at this time that McCaul likely stole the piece of bone that was later displayed at the pool hall. McCaul was unquestionably a loser, but he wasn't part of a murder plot, no matter what Wilkerson claimed.

William Wright of Villisca was the last witness of the day. He testified that he had been at the Moore house shortly after the murders were discovered and that Dr. Cooper and Marshal Horton were also there at the time. Wright said he arrived only a few minutes before Frank Jones and he overheard Jones asking if he could go inside. According to Wright, Dr. Cooper replied, "No, Frank, you had better not go in, for you will see something you will never forget."

The proceedings continued on Thursday, November 23, with the attorneys battling it out over the admissibility of some of the testimony about the bone fragment. After nearly two hours, the judge finally decided it would be allowed and would stand in the record.

After this, Alice Willard returned to the stand. This time, she testified about a visit that Frank Jones paid to her home on August 12, 1916. She said that Jones asked her if she had received a threatening message signed with his name and she told him that she had received some letters, but nothing with his name on them. Apparently, she had visited Jones' store and told several employees, including Albert Jones, about the letters. Frank Jones called on her after that time. She also admitted that he had asked her the names of the men she had seen behind the Moore house on the day before the murders and that Jones remarked that he didn't know how she could identify them by photos four years later.

J.B.'s brother Ross Moore followed her on the stand. He testified about the telephone call that he had received from Mary Peckham and the events that led up to the discovery of the bodies. He described how Marshal Horton had come out of the house and gasped, "Something awful has happened. There is somebody dead in every bed!" Moore said that he nearly collapsed and went directly to the Peckham house and lay down on the couch. He came back about a half hour later and Frank Jones met him in the yard and shook hands with him, offering condolences.

Hank Horton also testified about the events of that morning in June 1912. He said he was in the Moore house while Dr. Lomas, Dr. Cooper, and Dr. Williams examined the bodies. He returned to city hall at about 9:20 a.m. and Frank Jones was there and asked him if he knew where Lee Van Gilder (the father of J.B's young nephew) was. Horton said that Jones told him there had been some trouble between J.B. Moore and Van Gilder and this ended in the separation of Van Gilder and his wife. Jones told Horton that he should look him up and that he had heard that Van Gilder was in Galesburg, Illinois.

Sheriff Jackson was the next witness and murmurs rippled through the courtroom as he brought the murder weapon with him on the stand. He testified that he and Wilkerson had met Vina Tompkins at the Pilgrim Hotel in Marshalltown and that she had been shown a picture of Frank Jones. He quoted her as saying,

"That is one of the men I saw at the meeting on the banks of the Nodaway." He further testified, over objections from Beeson, that Ralph Thorpe had seen Mansfield in jail during the grand jury session and identified him as one of the men he saw on the train on the morning after the murders.

One of the letters that Alice Willard had allegedly received told her to come to Red Oak on the night of August 29, and if she retracted her statement about the men she had seen in 1912, there would be "monetary considerations" available to her. This led up to Mitchell calling Harry Faunch, the day clerk at the Johnson Hotel in Red Oak, to the stand. Faunch produced the hotel register from August 29, which showed that Frank Jones, Thomas O'Leary, and his wife were registered at the hotel that night. He also stated that he had seen Jones eating dinner there that evening. Of course, there was nothing to prove that Jones and O'Leary were meeting anyone that night. Jones had already hired the detective to investigate Wilkerson and had gone to Red Oak. The hotel register could have been altered at any time.

James Wilkerson's testimony had been anxiously awaited by his supporters, although it turned out to be somewhat anti-climactic since the story had already been told. The people packed into the courtroom hung on every word of his seven-hour testimony, which started with his statement that Marshal Hank Horton was dishonest. Horton, he claimed, originally told him that Frank Jones had approached him before word of the murders became public knowledge and said he should look for the senior Van Gilder, but that Horton had since changed his story. Objections to his testimony came fast and furious, but were largely overruled. He managed to give a detailed account of his investigation and why he had been led to conclude that Frank and Albert Jones had planned the murders. He went through all of it, including his belief that Dona Jones was carrying on multiple affairs and Frank Jones, already angry that J.B. Moore was hurting his business, became enraged when he learned that J.B. was one of her lovers. Mitchell led him through this testimony and he told of meeting Vina Tompkins and her identification of a photograph of Frank Jones as one of the men seen at the slaughterhouse that day. He told of Thorpe and his identification of Mansfield as the man he saw on the train. He spoke about Bert McCaul and his role as the part of the plot, namely assisting with the killer's escape. He described McCaul's new automobile, obtained a few weeks after the murders, and said he believed that Jones had given him the car as payment for his part in the crime. Wilkerson said that after learning about the early morning trip of McCaul and Albert Jones, he grew suspicious and had gotten Albert into a hotel room and had questioned him about it. He also made much of the fact that Albert claimed to have stopped at Ira Stickler's house that morning to speak to the farmer about a used binder and that he had been in his hay field at the time. Stickler agreed that they had talked about a binder but said that he had been in a cornfield, not a hay field. Wilkerson also told of a visit that he and Sheriff Jackson had paid to Bert McCaul in which they called him a liar and accused him of being involved in the murders and the killer's escape. He said McCaul responded that *they* were damned liars. Wilkerson claimed that as he and Jackson pressed him, McCaul started to cry, but maintained his denial.

After that, he turned his attention to Mansfield and the Blue Island murders. He said that he believed that shortly after Mansfield was arrested, Frank Jones had hired Pringle as his lawyer. He said that County Attorney Gillett had put little effort into the Mansfield indictment. "He could not be persuaded to exert himself to any great degree," he sneered.

He then produced a clipping of an article from a Des Moines newspaper containing an interview with Frank Jones. In the interview, Jones said efforts to locate the killer were turning out to be a farce and that a detective had offered to sell the senator evidence regarding the case. When Jones had discovered it was a blackmail attempt, he had thrown the man out of his office. Jones was also quoted as saying that detectives hired to work the case were mostly frauds who "after collecting $200 apiece usually spent it and then begged for money with which to get out of town." Jones added that Vina Tompkins' story had been investigated two years earlier and found to be utterly false. He concluded by saying, "It is my opinion that it will be a mere accident if the murderer is ever caught." The interview really had nothing to do with the case, but Wilkerson was obviously angered by it and used it to show that Jones had a bias against him. Of course, there was little that could measure up to the bias that Wilkerson maintained against the senator.

Wilkerson then testified about the grand jury that failed to indict Mansfield, strongly intimating that the jurors were biased in favor of Jones. He said the panel included a cashier at Jones' bank, a nephew of a vice-president of the bank, and another man who was a "warm, personal friend and co-worker in the Methodist church with Mr. Jones." He said that he didn't ask for an indictment against Jones at that time, just of Mansfield and Harry Whipple. After the jury failed to indict Mansfield, Wilkerson said that he had a private conversation with an unnamed local judge who told him, "In my opinion, the man who furnished the money for that murder is more important than the man who did the murder. Keep on after the man who furnished the money and you'll get him yet."

Wilkerson was cross-examined by Ralph Pringle, who didn't keep him on the stand for long. In response to Pringle's sarcastic questions, Wilkerson coolly replied that he had never attended acting school and had never been on the stage except as a public speaker. He said he thought that the Burns agency had spent about $7,000 on the case, although only $5,000 had been paid.

After Wilkerson, Ed Landers took the stand. He had some pretty sensational claims to make. Landers was the son of Margaret Landers, who had testified earlier that she saw two strangers in the Moore's backyard before the murders and then heard what sounded like Sarah Moore screaming on the night of the murders. Lander was a real estate salesman from Shenandoah. He and his wife, Ethel, were staying with his mother in June 1912. The elder Mrs. Landers lived across the street from the Moores. He testified that he was returning to his mother's house shortly before 8 p.m. on June 9, after eating dinner downtown. He said he was a block west of J.B. Moore's house when he saw a man walking ahead of him. When the man reached the Moore house, he turned and went inside. When Landers was asked if he recognized the man he replied that he did, but he refused to say who it was. He sat on the witness stand in silence, refusing to speak for almost five minutes. When the judge finally ordered him to reply, he said that he thought the man was Albert Jones, whom he had known since childhood. He said he had been about eight feet away and could see the man clearly as he went into the Moores' house.

After prompting from Mitchell, Landers said that he had been in his sister's restaurant in downtown Villisca on June 8, and had seen a man with a scar on his throat. Mansfield had a scar on his throat, but Landers couldn't say for sure if it had been him. During cross-examination, Landers said that he had never told anyone this before because he "didn't want to give such damaging evidence until [I] was absolutely sure about the exact night the occurrence had happened." The defense attorneys produced a transcript of the testimony that Landers had given at the coroner's inquest more than four years before. He had said nothing about seeing Albert Jones entering the Moore house. When asked about this, he repeated that he had not mentioned it then because he wasn't sure about the date. He insisted that he was sure now, though, that Albert had gone into the house while the Moores were still at church that night.

J.B.'s brother Ross Moore was recalled to the stand, this time by the defense. He was asked to recount the details of a trip that he made with a few other men to an abandoned slaughterhouse just two days after the murders in 1912. He had been contacted by a clairvoyant from Red Oak known as "Auntie" Hamilton who was said to possess what the newspapers called "occult powers." He said the psychic described the murderer as a large man with a dark mustache, roughly dressed and wearing a slouch hat. (Readers may recall this is almost the same description given of a suspect in the Colorado Springs murders in 1911.) She predicted that he would give himself up in two weeks. Local reporters didn't take her seriously, but many people did, and her psychic predictions made interesting reading. Apparently, she didn't know that the murder weapon had been left at the scene because she told Ross Moore that it would be found near a slaughterhouse. Ross got a couple of friends to go with him and they went out to the abandoned building on the banks of the East Nodaway River to look around. They found nothing of interest, but their search made the newspapers. During Ross Moore's testimony at the slander trial, attorney Pringle suggested that the search, which had been reported in the newspapers, inspired Vina Tompkins to concoct her story about overhearing the murder conspirators plotting at the slaughterhouse.

A number of other people followed Moore on the stand, including an osteopath from Villisca, a traveling salesman, a farmer and several businessmen. All of them had been called to testify concerning the reputation and moral character of Alice Willard, one of Wilkerson's star witnesses. They did not speak favorably. Oscar Wenstrand, who by then was the county attorney-elect and on hand to observe the trial, later wrote about the proceedings. After hearing the testimony against her, came to believe that Alice Willard was a prostitute, willing to sell herself and her testimony.

H.A. Glackemeyer, a neighbor who lived between the two Jones households, testified of seeing a stranger in town at about 8:30 p.m. on the evening of the murders. He said the man had approached his house, but when he saw

Glackemeyer sitting on his porch, he quickly turned and started walking south. He said that he didn't know who the man was and had not seen him since. He also testified about the vacant lot where Alice Willard claimed to hear the "Get Joe first" conversation. He said that the lot was rye grass with some hogs pastured on it and that the grass along the fence was only about a foot high. There was no brush or trees where she and her friends could have hidden. There was only one small tree on the northwest corner. He said he saw Albert Jones feeding his chickens at about 7 p.m. that evening. Later, when he was playing in his yard with his children, he saw through the dining room window that Albert and Dona were at home. So Albert could not have been going into the Moore house that night, as Ed Landers claimed. If anyone had been seen going inside, it was the strange man that Glackemeyer had seen on the street.

On Wednesday, November 29, Albert Himiller, who lived south of Villisca, testified that on the night of the murders, he was calling on a young lady who lived on the northeast side of town. He said that he returned home that night, passing through the downtown area around 11:30 p.m. At the corner of First Street and Fourth Avenue, he saw two men standing close together on the sidewalk. He turned his flashlight toward them but they had their backs turned and he did not see their faces.

The next witness was Mrs. John Montgomery, who testified that she and her husband lived at the corner of Fourth Avenue and Fifth Street and that, at the time of the murders, Bert McCaul lived across the street to the south of her home. She said that at about 2:30 a.m. on June 10, she heard someone across the street call out, "Bert!" She said the call was repeated three times. She got out of bed and looked out the window to see a man standing in the street in front of McCaul's house. She said that no one responded to the calls and the man left, walking west toward the Hopkins feed barn on the corner. She said that Hopkins and McCaul were often seen together and seemed to be friends.

Bert Marvick was called to the stand to rebut the testimony of Lige Nelson about McCaul getting his car out of the garage on June 9. Marvick said that he managed the garage in 1912 and had employed Nelson as a repairman. He said that the south end of the garage was never used to store disassembled cars and that he never saw one there. He also testified that Nelson had never collected a bill from McCaul that he was aware of.

Alice Willard was recalled by Beeson, who asked her if, at the Mansfield grand jury session the previous summer, she had told a number of people, including Hank Horton, Mrs. Lew Pierce, F.P. Greenlee, and Frank Jones, that she could not identify Mansfield as the man she had seen on the streets of Villisca at the time of the murders. She stated that she had never said any such thing.

Mrs. Lew Pierce was then brought to the stand. She testified that when she and Alice Willard were in Red Oak at the time of the grand jury session, Willard had told her that she could not identify Mansfield. Pierce stated that she had introduced Willard to Wilkerson. She also acknowledged that Frank Jones had talked to her after the grand jury and asked about her testimony. She said that she had told him, "What I said would not help or hurt anybody very much." She also said that Jones told her that he had heard Wilkerson coached the witnesses before they went before the grand jury.

Finally, Bert McCaul took the stand. He told the jury that he was currently living in Missouri Valley, Iowa, and that he had moved there four years ago after living for eight years in Villisca with his wife and two children. While living in Villisca, he had operated a billiard hall, sold cars, and operated an automobile livery service. During his time as an auto dealer, he sold Ford, Regal, and Jackson automobiles and was assisted in his business by Albert Jones.

After some general background, the attorneys steered him toward the days of June 9 and 10, 1912. He said he had made previous arrangements to take Albert Jones on a business trip north of Villisca on the morning of June 10. After rising early, he had breakfast at the Postonian Café and then went to the Jones store, where he met Albert. They departed at about 6:50 a.m. McCaul traced the trip north, recalling seeing and then overtaking the Davie brothers, and making their first stop at the farm owned by Andy Devine. Andy wasn't home so they went on north through Sciola and then stopped at the Kimel farm looking for Ira Stickler. They found him in a field and Albert spoke to him. From there they went to the Shipper farm, where they heard about the murder. According to McCaul, they returned to Villisca on the same route, arriving back in town around 9 a.m. He denied being in Grant at any time that morning. He also denied that he had been in the vacant lot behind J.B. Moore's house on the night of June 8, when Alice Willard claimed she had seen him. He said that he did not see Frank Jones on June 8, and stated that he did not take his car out of the garage on June 9. McCaul said that he had purchased the car himself – it had not been a payoff from Frank Jones – and had driven it home from Omaha. The only connection that the Joneses had with the automobile was that Albert had purchased it through the Jones store and then McCaul had paid the store. He said he paid with a certificate of deposit for $630, leaving a balance of $260 for which he made payments to the store. He denied that he told Wilkerson that the car had been paid for any other way. Beeson took McCaul point by point through earlier testimony that had tended to implicate him and he denied all of it.

McCaul was aggressively cross-examined by Mitchell, who tried to confuse him and get him flustered. At one point, he even caused McCaul to forget his wedding anniversary. He asked him if his real business was poker, not billiards, and McCaul said that he played poker "just for recreation." He admitted to often playing cards at Tom Bradfield's room at the Sandel Building. He was unable to remember what he had been doing on June 8, 1912 – it was more than four years ago – but assumed that he had been at his place of business. He acknowledged that he had been at the Knights of Pythias hall on Sunday, June 9, to play cards and named several people who were there, including Captain Casey. He thought he had played cards until about 11 p.m. that night. He didn't recall where he had been the previous Sunday night, but imagined it was the same place, with mostly the same people. He admitted that he had tried to cross the National Guard line and enter the Moore house, been turned back, and then later was allowed inside by Captain Casey. When questioned about the bone fragment, he claimed that he had picked it up in an alley because it looked just like a piece of bone that he saw in the Moore house. He said he had taken it into his pool hall and stuck it in the cigar case. He alleged that he had never told anyone it was a piece of J.B. Moore's skull, but a lot of people came in to see it and ask about it. He said he kept it for a few days and then threw it out. Mitchell badgered him about the bone, and he repeatedly denied taking it from the house and denied telling anyone it was part of anyone's skull.

McCaul told Mitchell that he had no idea that he was a suspect in the murders until he received a letter from Frank Jones a few weeks before the trial. He admitted that Wilkerson had accused him of being part of some plot a long time before, but McCaul said he "didn't rely on anything Wilkerson said."

Beeson returned to ask McCaul a few more questions and he stated again that he had picked his car up no earlier than 6:30 a.m. on Monday morning. There was no one at the garage at the time, but he had his own key. He said he couldn't be sure if the car was in the garage on Sunday night, but he hadn't used it, and wasn't aware of anyone else using it.

Hank Horton was recalled to the stand by Jones' attorneys. He testified that he had spoken to Alice Willard about Mansfield after the grand jury session. He said that she told him that Mansfield "might be the man, but I couldn't swear to it." Horton also testified that Ed Landers had never told him of seeing anyone go into the Moore house until the fall of 1912, and then he said he thought the man walking in front of him was Ross Moore until he turned around, and then he didn't know who it was. Horton stressed the fact that Landers had never told him it was Albert Jones.

Horton also testified that he and then Mayor Lewis had gone to Marshalltown to talk to Vina Tompkins and she told them that all she knew about the Villisca murders was what she read in the newspapers. She had none of the "secret knowledge" that she had when Wilkerson came around and started promising her things in exchange for her testimony.

The marshal did mention one strange event that took place on the night of June 9. At around 10 p.m., Horton said he was in the city park talking to night watchman Henry "Mike" Overman when they saw a man walk by them in the shadows. Horton called out to him, but the man never turned around. He said he told Overman, "Mike, I've got a notion to make that fellow face around." Horton didn't shine his light on him, or call out to him again, and the man disappeared into the darkness.

On Friday, December 1, L.E. Lewis, the former mayor of Villisca, was called to the stand. He testified, as Horton had, about going to Marshalltown to interview Vina Tompkins. He also said that she knew nothing about the murders at that time, other than stories that she had seen in the newspaper. When cross-examined, Lewis, who was an attorney himself, admitted that he had told Frank Jones what Tompkins had told them and that he had been employed a few days before by Jones' attorneys to serve a few subpoenas. One of them was to Harry Whipple. Lewis also acknowledged that he had been paid by Ross Moore for the trip to Marshalltown to interview Tompkins.

The next witness called by the defense was Harry Whipple, who would likely have had some interesting testimony to give – if he had actually been asked to offer any. Whipple was, according to Wilkerson, an essential part of the murder plot. He had (with Vina Tompkins' testimony) depicted him as an outlaw and killer of the worst kind and had placed him inside of the house while Mansfield was slaughtering the Moore family. A few weeks earlier, Wilkerson had taken Alice Willard to Carbon, where Whipple lived, and she had positively identified him as one of the men she had seen with Mansfield on June 8. Ralph Thorpe had claimed that Whipple was on the train with Mansfield on the morning after the murders and another witness saw someone matching his description walking south from Villisca earlier that same day. Whipple had been subpoenaed by Jones, supposedly to establish that he had been nowhere near Villisca at the time of the murders.

Whipple was a tall, rough-looking man who had been sitting in the courtroom for nearly a week, expecting to testify each day. He was accompanied by several other men, the assumption being that they were there to confirm his alibi. He finally took the stand on December 1, was sworn in, and then Mitchell asked for a recess to consult with Wilkerson. Whipple's testimony was postponed until after lunch but when court reconvened, Mitchell asked that John Warren Noel be called to the stand instead.

Vina Tompkins had been seen during the lunch break talking to Mitchell and Wilkerson, and then talking with her brother. No one knows what transpired next but Whipple and his friends left the courthouse and didn't return. Fortunately for Wilkerson, he never testified. If he had been put on the stand and had provided a convincing alibi, the detective's case would have been badly damaged. As it turned out, we will never know what Whipple might have said that day.

John Noel's return to the stand surprised many in the gallery. He was listed as a witness for Frank Jones and early on, had told the jury that Wilkerson had tried to buy a picture of Jones from him. That was all he expected to testify to.

Noel was placed under oath and he proceeded to tell about a strange conversation that he happened to overhear. (It seems people were always overhearing disturbing conversations connected to the Villisca murders.) The photographer said that at the time of the incident he had lived in Villisca for about three years. He and his wife occupied a house on the southeast corner of the block on which the Jones house was located. He said the house was about 14 feet from a warehouse that belonged to Frank Jones. He said that on May 26 or 27, 1916, a few days before the primary elections, he returned home from his studio at 10:30 p.m. His wife told him that she had heard voices coming from the warehouse and Noel went outside to listen. He described the building as a large wooden structure with openings in the sides. There was a gap between the double doors, and that is where Noel said he stood, looking inside and listening as the four men inside talked. Mitchell asked him if he knew any of the men and Noel replied that he did – Frank and Albert Jones and two other men, one of whom he later learned was Bert McCaul. They were in the dark but were smoking cigars and the dim light from the burning tobacco illuminated their faces.

He claimed that he heard Jones say that he had to win the primary election or he would "not have the political pull to put down this thing." One of them also said that they had to get rid of Wilkerson, "We have to get rid of that son of a bitch if we have to kill him." They also allegedly mention Landers testifying against them and that "they knew about Mansfield."

Noel said that they discussed either paying off Vina Tompkins or using Senator Van Law to scare her away. One of them also mentioned a trip to Grant, mentioning the names of two of the men who claimed to see McCaul and Albert Jones in Grant on the morning of the murders. They also brought up Attorney General George Cosson. Noel said, "I heard them say something about Cosson being with us, and that County Attorney Gillett was easily fixed."

Noel said that he had listened outside the warehouse until almost midnight but could not make out most of the conversation. It was a fantastic – and preposterous story – much like Vina Tompkins' story, and Wilkerson undoubtedly had his hand in it. It was more than a coincidence that Noel's story nicely contained all of Wilkerson's theories. What is unknown is why Noel had waited so long to come forward with it, especially with Wilkerson's life supposedly in danger. Most of the reporters on hand treated the tale with skepticism, but it was still big news.

Beeson took up the cross-examination, asking why he had waited six months to tell about what he heard. Noel had no good answer, only that he thought "it would be for the good of humanity to tell it now." Beeson forced him to admit that he knew Jones held him responsible for the fire in the bank building in December 1915, and that he had been "sore" about it. He also admitted that he had been in his studio with Wilkerson, Mitchell, and some other men on the night before he testified, going over what he was going to say. He denied that Wilkerson had paid him for his testimony. Beeson cast some doubt on Noel's fanciful story, but there was no way to know if it was enough.

Court adjourned for the weekend and on Monday, December 4, Albert Jones took the stand. He answered questions about the day the murders were discovered, describing his activities that morning as he always had. He said that on Saturday, June 8, he and his wife had gone to Clarinda to visit friends, Mr. and Mrs. Robert Crisswell. He said he and Dona spent the night and most of Sunday with the Crisswells and then returned to Villisca on Sunday evening around 6 p.m. He said that he went to the store, returning home around 7 p.m., and did not leave the house the rest of the evening.

On Monday, Albert said he got up, did some chores, had breakfast, and then went to the store and waited on an early customer. He telephoned McCaul to make sure he was still coming to pick him up, waited for him a short time, and then made the trip north with McCaul driving, stopping several times to call on customers. He said they were at the Shipper farm when they were told that Joe Moore had been murdered. Albert said that he had asked which Joe Moore had been killed and when Mrs. Shipper told him that several children had been killed too, he knew it was his neighbor. He said he and McCaul returned immediately to town at that point. He denied that they had been in Grant that morning. He said that he often hired McCaul to drive him around and that they were friends. He confirmed that they had been partners in an auto dealership, but added that they had not done well with sales. He denied that the conversation in the warehouse described by Noel ever took place.

Mitchell cross-examined him with several random-seeming questions. He asked if he had moved recently and when Albert replied that he had, he asked if it was because his home was so close to the Moore house. Albert said that it wasn't, that he had got a good price for his house. He acknowledged that the Saturday night before the murders was the first time he and his wife had stayed with the Crisswells, but said his wife and Mrs. Crisswell were old friends. Mitchell also asked him if he had ever gone ice-skating on the Nodaway River east of town, or had done any hunting there. Albert said he had done neither, and denied knowing anything about the slaughterhouse where Vina Tompkins said she had seen him.

John Palmquist, an employee at the Jones store, testified about the interior of the warehouse and stated that it was rarely used by Albert and Frank Jones. He produced a cash register record from June 28, 1912, which showed receipt of payment from W.B. McCaul for "$890 for auto, gas $1.50" and a deposit slip for the same transaction. When Mitchell cross-examined him, he was forced to say that he did not know who made out the deposit slip, so it was ruled out as evidence. Palmquist also told him that he had tried to confirm a rumor that he had heard that Alice Willard had been sick in June 1912, and was confined to her house, making it impossible for her to have heard or seen what she claimed.

D.H. Meyerhoff, an attorney from Corning who had known Jones for almost 30 years, was sworn in next. He said that on the morning the murders were discovered he had traveled to Red Oak for business on the early train and was traveling back around noon. While on the train between Red Oak and Villisca, he heard people talking about the murders and thought he overheard someone say that Frank Jones might be involved. Meyerhoff testified that he got off the train in Villisca and walked uptown. He saw Jones on the southwest corner of the square, where Jones was overseeing construction on his new bank building. They spoke briefly, Meyerhoff said, and it was then that he told Jones what he had heard on the train.

The next witness was Frank Jones. Beeson took him through a series of questions that allowed him to talk about his background, his career in teaching, farming, banking and in the farm implement business. He also spoke of his involvement in his church, his terms on the city council, three terms in the Iowa House of Representatives, his Senate career and appointment to the state board of education. Beeson then began asking him about every allegation that had been made against him – the slaughterhouse plot, Alice Willard's story, Harry Whipple, Mansfield, the Noel testimony -- everything. Jones denied being connected in any way with the crime.

He said that on the night of the murders, he had gone to church, admitting that he had not taken his usual seat in front. The Holy Rollers were conducting their service that night and he wasn't sure that he was going to stay, so he sat in the back. Jones said that there were some boys making noise outside during the service, so he stepped out long enough to tell them to quiet down. He went home after the service, he said, and did not leave his house again that night.

He said he found out about the murders while he was at the construction site of his new bank. A man named Rose came running down the street and told him. Jones said that he then went to the Moore house and, seeing Ross Moore sitting on the porch of the Peckham house next door, went to him and shook his hand. He saw Dr. Cooper coming out of the house and asked him if the news was true. He said he told him that it was, there were eight people dead inside, and that he didn't advise going inside. He said that it was around noon when he saw Dennis Meyerhoff, who told him that he was a suspect, although he denied telling John Montgomery that. He said that he did talk with Montgomery that day and had asked where Van Gilder was. He said Montgomery replied that he did not believe Van Gilder would have done such a thing, and had asked where Jones heard his name mentioned in connection to the crime. Jones replied that Van Gilder had been mentioned at city hall and Jones said he also admitted that he had been among those who speculated about Van Gilder's feelings toward Moore.

He said that on the morning the bloodhounds were brought in, he had been talking with a farmer named Harry Willett who said there were suspicions concerning a man named Bartlett being involved with the murders. Jones said he replied, as a joke, "They have me among the suspects too." He also said that he did not remember saying anything to the effect that all of the people walking around the house and yard wouldn't make any difference to the bloodhounds. He denied the entire story that had him in a room with McCaul drinking beer, declaring that he had never drank a beer in his entire life. He said that he had been in an automobile with McCaul only once, when he took a short ride around town to try out the younger man's new Regal.

Jones confessed that, prior to the trial, he had gone out of his way to talk to several people who had made incriminating statements about him. He said he had talked to Lige Nelson about his claim of seeing Jones and McCaul drinking beer and Nelson, after a long hesitation, denied that he ever said it. Jones said that he had talked to Alice Willard about Wilkerson's claims that she had received threatening letters with Jones' name on them. He said that Willard told him that she had received no such letters and knew nothing about the story. Jones said that a few days later, Willard and her sister came into his store and told him that she wanted to set the story right. She admitted to having received some threatening letters, but none of them had Jones' name on them. She also told him that she had seen some strange men near the Moore house around the time of the murders. Jones asked her why she didn't tell the investigators about it at the time and she said she didn't know why, but she had told her neighbors. Jones said she also told him that she had identified a photograph of one of the men she had seen that night, but when Mansfield was in Red Oak for the grand jury, she saw him and knew it wasn't him.

Jones firmly stated that he had never sent letters of any kind to Willard. In addition, he had never heard of William Mansfield until the anonymous letters were sent out just before the primary elections. He denied planning or paying for the murder of J.B. Moore. He said that he did not assist Mansfield with his defense and he did not put up any of the money for his bond.

Mitchell began his cross-examination with a sarcastic question. "How many witnesses have you impeached in your testimony thus far?" Beeson objected but Mitchell continued, "About twelve, I have it."

He then asked Jones if he had taken a great interest in the case and Jones admitted that he had. Mitchell asked him if he had asked any of the grand jury witnesses about their testimony and Jones said that he had not.

"When was the first time you heard Mansfield was connected with the murder?" Mitchell asked.

"When I saw it in the *Kansas City Post* some months ago," answered Jones.

"When did you first learn that Wilkerson was investigating this case?"

"About a year ago this fall, at the time of the Old Settler's Reunion, I believe."

Mitchell continued with a lengthy list of questions, mostly wondering when Jones became aware of certain things. Mitchell then asked if it was true that Wilkerson introduced himself to him at church about 18 months before and Jones said he didn't recall. He said he often met strangers who were just passing through while at church. When asked who was present at city hall on the morning of the murders while telephone calls were being made, Jones could only remember Hank Horton, Captain Casey and himself.

Mitchell spent hours grilling Jones, wrapping up the testimony for the day. The aging senator was visibly shaken when he finally left the stand, but he felt good about his testimony. He had denied any connection to the crime and had set the record straight, finally dismissing the idea that he had anything to do with the murders. After this, he believed, the rumors would finally stop.

Or so he thought at the time.

On December 6, Robert Gourley, Jones' long-time barber, took the stand. He testified that Jones' beard was no longer or wider than it had been in 1912, which had been claimed by Vina Tompkins when she allegedly identified him.

After this, Frank Jones was called back to the witness box. He was asked when he first heard about Vina Tompkins. He replied that it was June 12, 1916, when he received a letter from Senator Wallace H. Arney, who told him about Tompkins and her story. Jones wrote him back and both letters were admitted into evidence. Mitchell pointed out that in Jones's letter, he wrote to Arney that Tompkins did not testify at the grand jury like he wanted her to. Mitchell asked Jones how he had obtained secret grand jury information and Jones replied that Wilkerson's landlady had told him. Later in the letter, he referred to Wilkerson as a "first-class rascal." Mitchell asked Jones how and when he reached that opinion and Jones said it had been in July 1916. He pulled a letter from his pocket from H.W. Stubbs, the county attorney of Grant County, Kansas. Mitchell took it from him and read it, his face turning bright red. He immediately objected to it being admitted as evidence. The judge agreed and the jury never got to hear what Stubbs had to say about Wilkerson and the Nellie Byers murder case, although we can rest assured that it was not flattering.

Mitchell then called Mary Moore, J.B.'s mother, to the stand. The elderly woman was carefully escorted to the witness box by James Wilkerson. The detective held her arm, comforted her and helped her to take her seat. Mitchell asked Mrs. Moore her name and established the fact that her son, Joe, had been working for Jones when one of his and Sarah's children had been born. Beeson asked her no questions, likely wondering why Mitchell had called her as a witness, and she was excused. Wilkerson hurriedly went to her side and escorted her from the courtroom.

Alice Willard returned to the stand on December 7, and it would be testimony that would send an electric shock through the courtroom. Her earlier testimony that she had seen Jones, Mansfield, Whipple, McCaul, and others planning the murders had been stunning enough, but that she came forward only after receiving anonymous threatening letters, that the only people who could corroborate her story were either dead or missing, that Beeson and Pringle had managed to portray her as a whore who would sell her testimony and her body, all combined to make her a tainted sort of celebrity in the area. She was the center of attention by this point of the trial and the subject of more gossip than anyone else involved, save for perhaps Frank Jones himself. And now, as most people thought the trial was nearly over, she was back on the stand again. The lawyers knew what was coming, as did many of Wilkerson's cronies, who had spread the word to get to the courthouse early to get a good seat, but everyone else was taken by surprise.

Mitchell put the story together for the court using several witnesses:

After court had adjourned on Monday, December 4, an attorney named Chevalier Junkin, who belonged to the same law firm as Pringle and had been seated with Jones' attorneys during the trial, had rented a car from the Petty Auto Co. in Red Oak. A man named Emory Penry was hired to drive the car from Red Oak to Villisca. Penry testified that it was Junkin who rented the car, but that the passenger he was supposed to take to Villisca was a man he identified as Jim Atkinson. He said Atkinson told him to drive to the Evans Hotel and that he went inside and came out a few minutes later with a woman. The woman was Alice Willard, although Penry admitted it was dark and he didn't get a good look at her. Penry said the woman and Atkinson got into the back seat and as he drove he overheard parts of her conversation. He claimed to hear her say, "They got that backwards" and later, "No, I seen what I saw that night." Penry said that he drove, as instructed, to a house in Villisca. When they got there, the woman was crying and didn't want to get out. He was told to drive around for a few more minutes. When they got back to the house again, both passengers got out. Atkinson returned a few minutes later. Penry said they left the car at a garage in Villisca, ate supper, then caught a westbound train. Atkinson got off in Stanton and Penry returned home to Red Oak.

Mitchell brought in other witnesses to corroborate the auto rental and to confirm that Jim Atkinson and Alice Willard were seen in it. He then called Alice Willard back to the stand.

After being reminded that she was still under oath, Willard stated that she had left the courtroom on Monday and had gone to the local depot, but missed the train to Villisca. She said that she met Atkinson there and he offered her a ride. She had known Atkinson and his wife for years, considered them friends, and accepted his offer. She said that as they were driving to Villisca, Atkinson asked her what she was getting in exchange for her testimony against Jones. She replied that she had received nothing, and that she knew the Moore boys for years and they had always been friends. Atkinson said that she should have asked for money because if she had testified for Jones, she might have been able to get as much as $2,000 for it. Willard then told Atkinson that she knew what she had seen that night and that money would not buy her testimony. She told the courtroom that Atkinson reminded her that she had no one to back up her story about seeing Frank Jones behind the Moore house that night – her friend Mabel Freeman was dead and no one knew where McCrae was. Atkinson then allegedly told her that Jones had plenty of witnesses to say that he wasn't there and that many of them would say he was in Des Moines that night. His lawyers would make her out to be a liar and she was liable to go to prison for perjury.

Willard admitted that she began to cry after this and was crying too hard to get out of the car when they reached her house. She then claimed that Atkinson told her that she would be well paid if she agreed to retract the statement she had made about Jones.

Mitchell smiled smugly at the end of the story, knowing that he finally had Jones right where he wanted him.

The plaintiff's attorneys, not surprisingly, had an entirely different version of the encounter between Atkinson and Willard. They knew Atkinson, had him on their witness list, and planned to use him to further destroy the reputation of Alice Willard. Atkinson's story was that he knew Willard very well and that on Memorial Day 1915, they had met in the park in Villisca, where they sat on a bench and talked. He said she told him about being out on the Saturday night before the murders and seeing three men, but didn't know who they were. One of them, she said, had looked like her ex-husband. Atkinson said that she told him that Wilkerson had offered her $500 to give him a statement saying that two of the men were Jones and McCaul, but she was holding out for $1,000.

Atkinson had been present for most of the trial, waiting to testify, and had seen Willard several times during the past week. He said that he thought she was worried about what he might testify to and that on Monday after the trial, she told him that she needed some advice and suggested he take her home in a car. Atkinson not only didn't have a car, he said he didn't know how to drive, but he thought if she needed to talk, it might be important. Among those also waiting at the depot were Hal Hausen, a banking partner of Jones, and the lawyer, Chevalier Junkin. Atkinson told them of his conversation with Willard and arrangements were made to rent a car and driver. After the trip got underway, Atkinson asked her what she wanted to talk about and she replied that she was worried about the evidence she had given and wondered if Jones could prove an alibi. Atkinson told her that he didn't know, but if she wasn't sure that it had been Jones she saw that night, she needed to tell the court. Atkinson denied he offered to pay her to change her testimony and he contended that he had been set up. In hindsight, he realized that Willard had raised her voice only at a time when she said ambiguous things like "I know what I saw" and "I'll never do it." She had intended the driver to overhear and the words had been taken out of context, he claimed. Her crying in front of her house, Atkinson said, was all part of Willard's show for the driver.

With that in mind, Beeson cross-examined Willard, but it did little good. She denied everything that Atkinson charged and swore that he had tried to bribe her. Beeson did get her to admit that the first person she told about the controversial ride with Atkinson had been James Wilkerson.

Mitchell called Atkinson, who seemed to be a reluctant and uncertain witness. As he told his story, Wilkerson was sitting at the defense table, glaring at him, and passing notes to Mitchell. He spoke about what he believed Alice Willard had done to entrap him, but Mitchell pretended to be dubious of his story. He managed to bring out that the bill for the car rental had gone to Pringle's office. Atkinson said he'd straighten that out and pay the bill himself but by this time, the damage was done.

It's not hard to see now that Atkinson had been tricked by the cunning woman, likely with advice from Wilkerson, but at the time, there were many who believed her story and believed that Frank Jones had tried to buy off an incriminating witness. This would turn out to be one of the final nails in the coffin of Jones' lawsuit.

More testimony followed, including conflicting accounts about the warehouse behind the Jones store, where Noel claimed he had heard McCaul and the Joneses making plans. Some witnesses said that there would not have been enough space in the gap between the doors for Noel to see inside, that the flame from a cigar would not have been bright enough to see their faces, and that there was too much farm machinery inside for three men to have stood where Noel said they were. Jones never used profanity, they said, and Noel's story was a complete sham. Then others came to the stand who said there would have been plenty of room between the building's slats for Noel to see inside, and an aisle in the shed would give three men plenty of room to stand. The jury looked at photographs of the building and even took the train to Villisca to take a look for themselves.

Hank Horton was called to the stand once again, becoming the last witness in the case. He described how Wilkerson had taken him to task a few days earlier for "leaning toward Jones." He said that the detective told him that he (Wilkerson) was the authority in the case and would see to it that Horton lost his badge. Beeson used this testimony to show how Wilkerson had bullied and tried to intimidate the Villisca marshal.

But when Mitchell began questioning him, he took another approach:

"Hank, you agreed with Wilkerson, didn't you, that you ought to take off that star?"

"No, I didn't," Horton replied.

"Now, Hank, right down in the bottom of your heart, don't you think Wilkerson was right?"

Horton was never allowed to answer. Mitchell dismissed the witness and with that, the testimony came to an end.

Closing arguments in the case were heard on Saturday, December 9. The courtroom was packed and extra spectators were allowed to fill the aisle, line the walls and squeeze into spots on the floor. Every available space was taken, and after court convened, the doors were locked to keep anyone else from coming in. Pringle was to start the arguments, followed by Mitchell, then Beeson, and finally, jury instructions.

Beeson began by citing the accusations that had been made against Frank Jones and then summing up the character and reputation of James Wilkerson:

You will see that this defendant has organized one of the most assiduous campaigns to destroy the reputation of Mr. Jones. I insist the work of J.N. Wilkerson has not been fair. All of his cunning has been used to fasten this crime on F.F. Jones. He would thus gain fame by having hung the crime on a man of statewide reputation. He first poisoned the minds of the people before he sprung his charges so their minds would be prejudiced against the real truth.

He talked about Mansfield and how the only evidence against him were statements made by Wilkerson. He asked why, if Mansfield was guilty of the Blue Islands murders, as Wilkerson claimed, authorities in Blue Island had made no effort to extradite him, or even question him. He had already been cleared by those closer to the Blue Island case than Wilkerson would ever be. Beeson also expressed disbelief in the testimonies of most of the defense's witnesses, adding, "The tales of Huckleberry Finn or Tom Sawyer don't depict more childish things than the story of this defense." And it wasn't just his opinion, he reminded the jury, quoting from the coroner's inquest and earlier accounts by the defense witnesses. None of them matched and every story had been expanded or exaggerated – always under the control of Wilkerson. He paid special attention to Vina Tompkins:

Mrs. Tompkins gave every evidence of being a woman who is easily influenced. How this defendant had such an influence over her, I will not venture to say. She said on the stand here: 'I don't know today whether it was F.F. Jones or not' and 'I didn't know when I was before the grand jury.' Her testimony shows the finished work of the detective.

Beeson went on to criticize Noel's story, which came out after the witness spent an evening with Wilkerson. He also called into question the ridiculous nature of the claims that Bert McCaul and Albert Jones were farther north than they were supposed to be on the morning after the murders. Not only did Beeson say that he doubted the story, he couldn't understand the reason the defense was bringing it up. He wrapped things up by again attacking Alice Willard's questionable testimony – and reminding the jurors of the 13 witnesses who had disputed it. He also accused her of creating a libelous story about Atkinson that she could use to frame him. After nearly three hours, he closed:

In conclusion, there is no evidence to show that F.F. Jones had any reason to kill Joe Moore. It is all framed up, dramatic, unbelievable. Scandal loves a shining mark. All this evidence is fictitious, constructed, the growth of imagination and falsehood. Do what your conscience prompts you to do in this instance.

After Beeson was finished, Mitchell took his place, starting off by calling Beeson's argument both "disgraceful and outrageous." He then turned to Alice Willard, a woman whom he characterized as a respectable woman who had been unjustly insulted. He said she had been "hounded and subjected to torture by attorneys for this plaintiff and their agents." He then turned to an attack on Jim Atkinson, criticizing him for claiming that a "weak, frail woman" like Willard could possibly take advantage of him. He then chastised everyone associated with the Atkinson-Willard car ride, particularly Pringle. He said he was ashamed of those who faulted Willard's character and expressed the opinion that they should be brought before God to answer for their horrible behavior.

According to Mitchell, the murders had been planned by a "master-mind" and carried out by a hired killer. Mitchell gave his rationale for everyone in the house being murdered by saying that either Albert Jones or Bert McCaul was present when Mansfield committed the crimes and someone in the house saw and recognized them. Therefore, everyone had to be killed. He defended Ed Landers and ripped apart Hank Horton, who he called a "henchman of F.F. Jones." He gave the jury something besides the slander suit to consider when he said:

If you want the murderer to be caught then give a verdict that will encourage men who are trying to ferret this thing out. Bring in a verdict for Jones and this thing will remain unsolved forever.

Mitchell concluded his arguments at a few minutes before 6 p.m. Court adjourned for dinner until 7 p.m., after which Beeson was given the final word on the case. He showed no mercy in attacking Wilkerson and the various witnesses for the defense. Wilkerson, he said, was a pathetic man and a publicity hound. Beeson reminded the jury of the detective's demeanor during the trial. While Frank Jones had attended the trial each day and sat quietly, minding his own business, Wilkerson constantly circulated throughout the courtroom, smiling at the ladies, slapping backs and shaking hands like a low-rent politician. Beeson added, "It will take more than him and a loud-mouthed Council Bluffs lawyer who gets up here and twists the facts to convince you in this case."

Beeson started his discrediting of the defense witnesses with Vina Tompkins and laughed about the various versions of her slaughterhouse story. He also pointed out that Ross Moore had gone to the same slaughterhouse after the murders – looking for an ax that a fortuneteller told him he would find there – and testified that there were no trees within 70 feet of the building behind which to hide, as Tompkins said she had. Beeson suggested to the jury that the whole slaughterhouse plot story had evolved from newspaper accounts of Ross Moore's innocent wild goose chase.

Beeson called Ed Landers "a queer kind of duck," and said his story was absurd and had been thoroughly impeached. Noel, Beeson said, was even more ridiculous than Landers. He told the jury that the photographer's testimony was pure fiction that had been concocted by Wilkerson.

Alice Willard was the most unbelievable of all. Not only was her reputation questionable, but her testimony had clearly been for sale. She could not have seen anyone in the darkness that night well enough to identify him, particularly Mansfield and Whipple. She had never seen them before, but yet claimed she could identify them from a distance of 15 or 20 feet on the darkest night of the year, using photographs shown to her several years later.

Beeson also wanted the jury to remember that Willard had claimed she heard Frank Jones say "get Joe first and the rest will be easy." If they were to believe her story, then the jury had to believe that Jones had not only wanted his business competitor killed, he fully intended that his wife and four children be murdered too. Beeson described the enormous horror of the crime and then spoke about how it was at odds with Jones' long track record of public service and upstanding reputation. Beeson then added:

Gentlemen, before you convict a man of murder, you certainly want better evidence than this. I say a verdict against Frank Jones will be hailed everywhere as an accusation of murder. Are you going to say that this man of over 60 years of age was a party to this horrible murder? They are hinting here and now that he will be indicted for murder if this verdict goes against him.

This remark turned out to be the biggest misstep that he could have taken. It was tantamount to saying that a verdict against Jones was the same as an indictment for murder. Beeson intended it as a way to show the jury that a verdict against Jones was a ridiculous idea, but instead it returned to haunt Frank Jones for many years afterward.

By the time the judge finished giving the jury their instructions on Saturday evening, court did not adjourn until 11:35 p.m. He suggested that the jury members retire for the night and then take up the debate in the morning. The jury, however, had been in the courtroom almost every day for the last four weeks and was anxious to get things over with. They had a brief discussion and then cast their first ballot. The vote was split with half for Jones and half for Wilkerson. They gave up for the night.

On Sunday morning, the jury voted again. This time, one of those who had voted for Jones moved over to Wilkerson's side. Over a dozen votes were taken that day and one by one, those who favored Jones gave in to the pressure and voted for Wilkerson. By 5 p.m., only one holdout remained and at his request, a message was sent to the judge asking: "If we find for the defendant, will that indict the plaintiff for murder?" The judge ignored the message. At 8 p.m., he called to the jury room and asked if they had reached a verdict. They had not, so he told them to continue their deliberations. After a short time, the judge recalled them and addressed the question about whether or not a verdict in Wilkerson's favor was an indictment of Jones. That issue, the judge said, was not for them to consider and should not be a factor in their decision. He told them that if they found that the defendant had made the statements as charged and that the evidence against Jones did not merit the statements, then the verdict should be for the plaintiff. If the defendant had established a basis for truth in his charges, then the verdict should be in Wilkerson's favor.

The one lone juror holding out for Jones did so until after midnight. It was later reported by people who passed by the jury room (or more likely, tried to listen at the door) that loud arguing and shouts were heard that night. In the end, the holdout was finally worn down and the jury found for Wilkerson.

The slander trial had turned into a full-fledged disaster for Jones. The trial turned the whispered rumors into front page news. William Mitchell began publicly proclaiming Jones' guilt. Much was made, then and later, about Beeson's closing remarks, and County Attorney Oscar Wenstrand was forced to pay attention to it. At the time the trial ended, he was faced with the realization that a finding in Wilkerson's favor was only the beginning. The slander trial jury had no authority to indict Jones, but as their verdict gave credence to Wilkerson and his wild theories, Wenstrand felt the obligation to take the matter before a jury that would be able to do so.

17. VILLISCA GOES TO WAR

On April 6, 1917, the United States joined its allies – Britain, France, and Russia – to fight the Great War on the battlefields of Europe. In the cold, snowy months of early 1917, the war was already filling the newspaper headlines. It had been grinding on with no end in sight for several years and Villisca's Company B had been activated to spend the winter in South Texas patrolling the Mexican border. It was clear that the soldiers would soon be much farther away from the fields and small towns of Iowa.

But the fighting was not confined to just the battlefields of the war. There was plenty of conflict in Villisca, Red Oak, and the towns and farms of Montgomery County. All of it surrounded a nearly five-year-old murder case and the man who some believed was getting away with murder – Frank Jones. Everywhere that people gathered, whether it was a restaurant, a church, or around the pot-bellied stove at the local general store, debates, arguments, and fistfights over the Villisca murders were common. On one occasion, an argument at the Villisca train depot escalated into a gun battle that sent bullets flying. Luckily, no one was hurt.

The slander trial, which ended in December 1916, had created an intense interest in the case again and James Wilkerson used that to his advantage. He continued to hold his public meetings and made frequent requests for financial support to continue his investigation. The small, private meetings that he had held before the Mansfield arrest, which had included guards to keep out the unwanted, were now large, public events that were widely advertised. They became popular at a time when there was little else to do during the Iowa winter and more and more people flocked to see the increasingly charismatic speaker.

The meetings in early 1917 largely concerned the unpaid investigative bill for $2,800. The Burns agency felt that Montgomery County was obligated to pay the tab, but the board of supervisors disagreed. The original agreement with Burns was that the relatives of the victims, along with Dr. Kelsey, put up a portion of the money needed to hire a detective. Attorney General Cosson had obligated the state to pay for a part of the preliminary investigation, which the state did with growing reluctance for some time. But after Wilkerson and Boyle accused Cosson of making a deal with Jones to protect him from prosecution, state funding for Wilkerson came to an end. Bills from the Burns regional office in Kansas City were submitted regularly, with some being paid by citizens' groups and some by the county, but by January 1917, nearly $3,000 was outstanding and the Burns agency wanted it.

Oddly, Montgomery County was not, and never had been, part of the original agreement with Burns. They had legal advice that not only were they not obligated to pay any bills the agency sent to them, but that they did not have the authority to use taxpayer's money for this purpose. However, Wilkerson's supporters felt that if the county supervisors wanted to pay the bill, they would find a way. Wilkerson had a meeting in Red Oak in the middle part of January to urge citizens to ask the supervisors to find the money. The bills had to be paid, he told them, in order for the investigation to continue and for justice to be found for the innocent victims.

He held a meeting at the Beardsley Theater in Red Oak on January 10, that attracted almost 1,200 people. Many of those who attended had a genuine concern about the bill and wanted to see it paid. The majority, though, were curiosity-seekers who read about the goings-on at the slander trial and wanted to see Wilkerson for themselves. Wilkerson spoke at length about the grand jury proceedings and the recent slander trial, of the great trust he put in the citizens of Montgomery County, and how he hoped they would allow him to continue his work to see that justice was accomplished. He told them:

I want to see public sentiment rightly directed in this manner and public sentiment rightly directed will be a power against which no man can fight successfully. I want you to know the facts. I shall not tell you what to do. You will know what to do... I will quit this task if you want me to. I can get much less dangerous work to do. I believe that the man who lives for money alone had better not have lived at all. The man who has a gift or power to accomplish a thing is a recreant to his trust if he does not keep on.

Wilkerson's statements would have been almost comical – based on his lies, concoctions, bribed witnesses and travesties like the Nellie Byers case – if so many people didn't believe in him. He knew how to exploit the gullibility of the public and turn it to his advantage. But sometimes we have to wonder if it was Wilkerson who was the gullible one. Had he said the same things over and over so many times that he had started to believe them himself? Were his claims against Frank Jones merely to gain fame and fortune for himself by taking down a highly regarded public figure? Or had he appointed himself a crusader for justice and so fervently believed that Jones was guilty that he would do anything to prove it, even if it meant lying and paying off witnesses? We may never know, but whatever the case, Wilkerson had managed to get many members of the public on his side.

He continued the meeting by bringing in several others connected to the case and allowing them to speak. One of them was Ed Landers, who told the "real" reason for his testimony at the slander trial. He said that he was so offended that the plaintiff's attorneys tried to impeach his dear, old mother's testimony that he'd decided to tell what he had been keeping to himself for years – that he had seen Albert Jones go into the Moore house on the night of the murders. He told the group at the theater that some people (he didn't identify them) had tried to get him to change his story since the trial but that he would "fearlessly tell the truth."

A well-known Red Oak attorney named Thomas J. Hysham, who had agreed to represent Wilkerson's interests in presenting the bill to the county, was in the audience and spoke for a few minutes. He had an interest in being part of any other legal action that developed and played up his part as an "impartial citizen," even though he obviously wasn't. He made a number of remarks and then received applause and shouts of approval when he concluded: "I think it ought to be investigated to the end, and I don't care whether the end reaches down to the realms of the devil or up to the throne of the Almighty! I don't care! Only that I want them to get the right man!"

The meeting served its purpose. More than 50 people committed to paying the bill for Wilkerson's services if the county refused to do so. They were all confident that their numbers would grow over time and they proved to be right.

The board of supervisors met about the matter on January 22, and Frank Jones was among those in attendance. He asked to address the board and was allowed to do so. Jones was quite possibly in the midst of the lowest point of his life. His political career had been ruined and he was the subject of rumor and scandal, but no one would have known this to look at him. On the surface, he was cool, calm and collected, seemingly above the fray. His business interests were still strong. He had undoubtedly lost some of his implement and bank customers in recent months and yet, he remained one of the wealthiest men in the county. This was one of the things that Wilkerson tried to use against him. He gained support for his crusade against Jones by exploiting class warfare. Take a look at the wealthy senator, he said, the rich Republican who has more money than you, has a nicer house than you, has important friends, and owns a bank – he can get away with murder! If it were you accused of such crimes, you'd already be in jail. He urged his supporters to show Jones that the common people could take him down a notch. Jones tried not to let this get to him, or at least that's how it appeared, but deep down, he must have been suffering from tremendous stress. He tried to strike back with futile efforts like the slander trial because he wouldn't – and didn't even know how to – stoop to Wilkerson's level.

When Jones stood before the county board, he said that if the bill to Burns was owed, then it ought to be paid, and if the county had an honest obligation, then it should be fulfilled. On the other hand, if it were not due or was not appropriate for the county to pay, then they should refuse. Jones said he had no problem with it either way, but that he believed that Wilkerson and the Burns agency should not be allowed to continue the investigation. He produced letters from officials in Kansas City and elsewhere who were harshly critical of Wilkerson's methods. He said that Burns himself had recently been indicted by a grand jury for stealing valuable papers, for wire-tapping, and dishonestly using recording devices. Jones also quoted a Georgia judge who "openly proclaimed that W.J. Burns is a menace to the country."

Jones asked that a fair-minded man be put in charge of the investigation and said that if this were done, he would help pay the cost himself. He went a step further by offering to leave the state while the investigation was conducted, if Wilkerson would do the same. He also said that if the citizens wanted, he would convene his own public meeting and answer all of their questions.

Jones had scored a number of points with the board members and with the people attending the meeting, but then he went a step too far and crossed over into the sort of character assassination that "Agent 33" engaged in. He couldn't resist adding that according to a document filed in a recent Kansas City court proceeding, Wilkerson was living with a woman in Villisca who was not his wife. Jones had spent a lot of money to dig up dirt about his nemesis and he apparently didn't want to miss the chance to use it.

Wilkerson got up to say that he had not intended to speak but would not have Jones assail the character of Mrs. Wilkerson. He dismissed Jones' allegation as a lie. He spoke of Jones keeping him tied up in the Red Oak courthouse for four weeks "trying to drag me down, and now he brings up what he could not get into court." Wilkerson concluded his remarks by turning to Jones and saying that if he was allowed to continue the investigation and found anything in Jones' favor, "I shall pursue it and without a cent of charge to you, and if I find it not in your favor, I shall follow it up just the same."

Jones' attorney, R.W. Beeson, told the board that in his opinion, payment of the Burns bill was not legal and further that Wilkerson was "a man of but one idea. He gets a track and then pays no attention to anything else." He went on to say that Wilkerson had been working the case for two and a half years and it was no closer to being solved than it was before he started.

For the next four hours, the board heard arguments both for and against the use of further county funds to satisfy the Burns bill. In the end, they settled on Beeson's advice that they were not authorized to use taxpayers' money for payment because the balance far exceeded the amount that had been previously approved. However, before the meeting was adjourned, an announcement was made that prior to the public session, the board met with the sheriff and county attorney and had agreed to pay $700 to continue the investigation, with Wilkerson remaining in charge.

Jones was embarrassed by this development. He had spoken out against his enemy, had lowered himself by questioning the detective's marital status, and then was told the decision to keep Wilkerson on the case had already been made. Jones stood up, apologized to the board for wasting their time in arguing a matter that had already been resolved, and walked out of the room.

The hearing might have been a low point for Jones, but he also received some good news that day when he learned that one of the men responsible for his political downfall was in jail. Jack Boyle, the unscrupulous reporter who had written the Mansfield story in 1916, and likely had a hand in the anonymous letters that were sent out before the primary, was picked up on drug charges in Kansas City in January 1917. Boyle and his wife were arrested during a drug raid and charged with possession of opium. The arrest marked the end of Boyle's involvement in the investigation.

The decision reached by the board of supervisors meant that the group of citizens who had pledged support to Wilkerson had to pay the detective agency's bill. Wilkerson realized that the $700 appropriated for his future services would not last long, so he made plans for more fund-raising meetings. On January 31, he traveled to Villisca, where nearly 800 people turned out on what proved to be the coldest day of the winter. With a thick blanket of snow on the ground, they began arriving by car, buggy, train, and on foot. A group of men from Nodaway, fearing that the passenger train might not get them there in time, hopped a freight train and made a nearly five-mile ride on an open flatcar in driving snow and wind.

The meeting was held at the Villisca Opera House, an elaborately built structure just off the town square. The audience had come for free entertainment to pass a bitter winter's day and to see Wilkerson continue his attack on Frank Jones, a man who was richer, more famous and, undoubtedly, happier than they were. They wanted scandal and excitement and Wilkerson was there to give it to them. He knew how to work the crowd and knew what buttons to push. Newspaper accounts report him being in fine form that day. Reverend Ewing offered the opening prayer, not only because he was a Wilkerson supporter but because he had been the Moores' pastor. Wilkerson took the stage after that and began by introducing some of the day's participants, as well as some of the supporters who had pledged financial help, a category that he hoped many of those present that day would join. He added that the people of Montgomery County were the best in the world. No matter what the future held for him, he declared, he would never forget them.

One of those present was Ed Peterson, a Red Oak area farmer who had signed on to help pay the cost of retaining Wilkerson. Another was photographer John Noel, another Wilkerson advocate who continued to tell his story of the late-night conversation he overheard in the Jones warehouse. Also seated on one side of the hall with a stenographer beside him was Frank Jones, who was determined to exact some kind of retribution against Wilkerson. At one point during his speech, noting the stenographer's presence, Wilkerson shouted, "Take it down, Mr. Jones!" Later, he proclaimed, "Anyone who can censure me, stand up." After a brief silence, Wilkerson again called out to Jones, "Mr. Jones, you have done that repeatedly, stand up!"

Jones rose out of his chair. "Why yes," he said mildly, "I'll stand to that. Thank you."

"Now sit down!" Wilkerson commanded. "The people are against you!"

The rest of the discussion that night was about money – how Wilkerson needed it and how the attendees were supposed to come up with it. The speakers that were introduced all basically said the same thing. One speaker, L.B. Penton, took the stage to say that there were now four types of people in Villisca. There were the "knockers," who discredited the investigation and wouldn't put any money into it. There were the "cowards," who were afraid to get involved. The "good people" were those who contributed to the cause and, lastly, there were those few men who were willing to do the actual work. He ended his speech by saying, "When we appear before St. Peter and tell him how we used to live in Villisca and he asks us if we helped to clear up the mystery of this tragedy, it seems to me our chances will be mighty slim if we can't say 'we did our best.'"

The program went on for more than two hours. Eventually, Wilkerson returned to the stage and spoke about the investigation he was conducting and how dangerous it was, what a great service it did for the people, how good he was at it and, of course, how he needed money to keep it going. He claimed that many people were afraid to tell what they knew about the murders and would only come to him in secret. Because they would not talk publicly, he said he was unable to use what they told him, due to the fact that he was an impeccable and honest investigator. Anyone who claimed that he brought questionable evidence into the case, he told the crowd, was lying.

Wilkerson was interrupted several times by applause. While he was talking, he walked off the stage and entered the audience. He continued his speech as he moved among the people, walking up one aisle, across the back of the theater and coming back down the other. Heads turned and people stood up to see him better. They burst into applause as he came close to them. It was a tactic that would be familiar to any of today's viewers of sleazy TV talk shows, but to the people of rural Iowa in 1917, it was novel and thrilling. He shouted as he walked. "I am only earnest in the extreme in this case. It is the principle I am after. I can face any man or woman. I can hold my head up and pass among you without fear of anything or anybody!" He was near Frank Jones at this point. Glaring at him, he shouted, "Thy sins will find you out!" The applause erupted again and Wilkerson returned to the stage.

He stood at the edge of the stage in silence, letting the moments pass and making the audience strain to hear his voice as they waited in anticipation of his next words. Finally, he spoke. He said that he had been asked why he wouldn't continue the investigation without money and his answer, he said, was "Why doesn't the bank loan money without interest?" Wilkerson said he needed money because he had several mouths to feed but "if I was pursuing this for money alone, I would have quit this job a long time ago. I would not be out of a job if I left this case at once. The Burns people have not received as much money with this case as they have put into it." He needed their moral support to succeed in solving the case, he told the audience, and their financial support to pay the cost of continuing.

Wilkerson received an ovation when he took his seat. Dr. R.B. Smith, a Villisca dentist who had been seated in the front row, jumped to his feet. Smith was clearly in Wilkerson's camp. He had testified during the slander trial that he had heard Frank Jones remark that the bloodhounds brought in to search for clues following the Moore murders were going in the wrong direction. His reaction to Wilkerson's speech could either be attributed to him being overwhelmed by the excitement of the moment or, as some cynics suggested, he had been coached to stoke up the fever pitch of the meeting. The dentist waved his arms as he turned to face the audience. "We've lived in this reign of terror long enough!" he cried. "It's time, by gosh, to raise the money and get after this thing, by gosh!" He walked over to Ed Peterson, extending his hand and shouting, "Put 'er there!" Then to Wilkerson, "Put 'er there, by gosh!" He then turned to the crowd again and cried, "Let's get busy and raise the money!"

Wilkerson left the stage at this point, saying he would "leave the rest of the meeting to the people." Like a faith healing minister who had successfully gotten a man to rise out of a wheelchair and walk, he withdrew from the theater to cheers and applause. Back inside, Peterson began passing the hat through the crowd.

Before the meeting was over, he had collected about $250 in contributions.

18. MANSFIELD EXONERATED!
THE ASSAULT TRIAL AGAINST JAMES WILKERSON

After leaving the adoring crowd in Villisca, Wilkerson returned to Kansas City to prepare for something that he had hoped to avoid: his trial for assault. Jacob Detweiler, the local attorney who had read about Mansfield's arrest in the newspaper and offered to defend him for no charge, had filed suit against Wilkerson some months before. He had asked the courts for $5,000 in damages, which would be paid by the Burns agency if Wilkerson lost. The agency hired a trio of attorneys from Kansas City, led by a man named Brady, for the detective's defense.

The trial began on February 8, 1917, and William Mansfield was the first witness on the stand. He testified about his arrest, saying that he was told that someone wanted to see him and then being taken to a room where several men were waiting. He didn't know them, but the man he later learned was James Wilkerson said to him, "Hello, Insane Blackie." Mansfield told him that he must be mistaken; that he'd never been known by that name. No one listened and he was taken to the main city jail in downtown Kansas City. He was placed in a cell shortly after 5 p.m. on June 13, 1916.

About an hour and a half later, he was taken from the cell by Captain Thomas Fleming and placed in the back seat of an automobile. Wilkerson, along with Jack Boyle and a driver, rode along as Mansfield was taken to Station #4. Mansfield stated he was threatened several times during the drive and at one point, as they crossed a river bridge, Wilkerson said, "Let's stop this machine and throw this son of a bitch in the river." He also allegedly threatened, "I will kill you, God damn you, right here! I won't take the trouble to take you to trial." He then struck him hard in the ribs with his elbow. At that point, Mansfield said he still didn't know why he had been arrested. After arriving at the station, he was placed in an interrogation room where police officers questioned him all night and into the next morning. He said that at one point, Boyle had offered to get him a drink of water but Wilkerson told him not to. A drink of water, Wilkerson said, "would steady his nerves." When questioned specifically, Mansfield later acknowledged that Detective Fleming did allow him to have a drink.

At some time later in the night, he was told about the murders in Villisca.

Mansfield told Wilkerson that he had nothing to do with them, but Wilkerson said he was lying. If he didn't confess, the detective added, he would "beat the hell out of him." During the interrogation, Wilkerson also grabbed an ax, held it threateningly over Mansfield's head, then laid it against his face and mouth, saying he would kill him the same way that the people in Iowa had been killed. Mansfield said that Wilkerson punched and slapped him several times, but always when Fleming or other actual police officers were out of the room. He said that he stood up once and Wilkerson pushed him backwards with such force that he fell over his chair, bruising his back and ribs. By the time he was finished, Mansfield maintained that he was unable to eat for three or four days, he was spitting up blood and several of his teeth were loose.

Mansfield said that Wilkerson struck him again two or three days later. This assault occurred following a meeting during which Jacob Detweiler served notice to Kansas City police officials that his client was withdrawing his waiver of extradition. According to Mansfield, after Detweiler left, Wilkerson, Sheriff Jackson, and County Attorney Gillett arrived. Fleming broke the news to them and Wilkerson became so angry that he struck Mansfield in the face. Mansfield said that Fleming objected, stating that he did not allow prisoners to be abused and Wilkerson apologized, telling Fleming, "I was a little excited."

Afterwards, Mansfield was taken from the police station to the county jail, where he was allowed to see a doctor. According to records, his teeth were knocked loose in the front of his mouth, his lip was split, and one side of his face and one eye was bruised. He had pain in his back for two or three weeks, and after being taken to Red Oak, was treated by a doctor for stomach and side pain.

Mansfield was then cross-examined by Brady, who took him through his biography, starting with his naval enlistment at age 16, his desertion a few months later, and his enlistment in the Army at the age of 21. He told of leaving the Army and later turning himself in. He was sentenced to four years at Leavenworth, but was released after serving two. He had married Martha Mislich on Thanksgiving Day, 1912, and had lived with her for seven months. Martha had been pregnant when he left her and Mansfield was forced to admit that he had never made any arrangements for the care of the then-unborn child.

Detweiler objected frequently during the questioning. He claimed that matters of Mansfield's military desertion and his treatment of his wife had no relevance to the assault charge. The lawyers for Wilkerson argued that they were needed to demonstrate Mansfield's credibility as a witness.

Mansfield was asked about Kate Romanofski, whom he referred to as his common-law wife. He admitted that she had become pregnant while he was married to Martha and that, in fact, both of his children had been born almost exactly at the same time. He was evasive in his answers to questions about when Martha was murdered and when he learned of it, but finally acknowledged that he believed that she, her parents and the baby had been killed in July 1914. Further questions let the jury know that the murder weapon had been an ax, the same as the Villisca murders. Brady then took a final shot by forcing Mansfield to roll up his sleeves and show the jury his American-themed tattoos, which included a flag and a naval anchor. He also had a dagger, a dove, a broken heart, and others. Brady disparaged his patriotic tattoos since he was a deserter from two branches of the armed forces. The attorney walked away, shaking his head in disgust, when Mansfield remained silent.

Detweiler returned to his witness and his questions revealed that Mansfield did not know his wife had been murdered at the time he was arrested. The police in Blue Island had traced his whereabouts to Milwaukee at the time of the murders, but by then Mansfield was gone. He was cleared of his role in the deaths of his wife, child, and in-laws, and he had not even known they were dead. After his arrest, his sister had contacted him and told him about it. He said the reason that he had not stayed in contact with his family was because he was afraid they would tell Martha he was in Kansas City.

Detweiler tried to introduce a letter into evidence that was written to Mansfield from Martha's sister and her husband. The letter was favorable to Mansfield, saying they understood why he left and telling him that another man had confessed to the murders. The letter had been written in June 1916, again after he had been arrested. The defense argued that the letter should not be admitted and that the in-laws were unable to exonerate Mansfield, a man that Brady insisted was "guilty of adultery, bastardry, desertion, and non-support." The argument was a lengthy one, but in the end, the letter was not admitted.

The next witness was J.H. Barnes, who said he was a recovering drug addict. He had been in the county jail when Mansfield had been transferred there. He said that he had gone to jail because he had stopped using morphine and had asked to be locked up to prevent a relapse. He was now recovered, he said, and had not used drugs for more than seven months. He was questioned about Mansfield's physical condition when he arrived at the jail. The defense immediately objected on the grounds that Barnes was not qualified to offer a medical opinion, but Detweiler submitted that the witness was qualified to testify in what Mansfield looked like and what was said to him.

This was not the only reason that Detweiler wanted him on the stand. Barnes had been on the streets while he was using morphine and he knew a man named "Insane Blackie." He was ready to testify that William Mansfield was not the same man. Detweiler explained to the judge that Barnes had been called to not only confirm the injuries that Mansfield sustained, but also to show malice --- Wilkerson knew Mansfield was not "Insane Blackie" within days of his arrest, but continued to say he was and took him to Red Oak to try and get him indicted anyway. Brady countered this argument by saying that the suit was about assault and had nothing to do with whether Mansfield was "Insane Blackie" or not. He also protested that Barnes was not a competent witness. The judge was apparently not sure how to rule, so he asked the witness to step down until he could look into it further.

After a short recess, Barnes was recalled to the stand, but Brady was still not satisfied with the judge's ruling. He again objected to the witness, at one point referring to him as a "dope fiend." Barnes interrupted to ask that he not be called that, saying that he had been one at one time but had worked very hard to reform himself and didn't deserve to be disrespected in such a way. Detweiler had agreed not to bring up the "Insane Blackie" issue, but said the witness should be allowed to testify to seeing Mansfield spit up blood and complain of pain. Brady again maintained that the witness could not speak about medical matters. The judge finally sided with the defense and Barnes, who was only allowed to answer an insignificant question or two, was excused.

The next witness called was C.C. Hedrick, a security officer at the Swift and Company plant where Mansfield had worked in Kansas City. He testified that he had seen Boyle's article in the June 12 edition of the *Kansas City Post* and on June 13, had called the Burns agency to tell them that Mansfield had recently worked at the packing plant and that he knew his present whereabouts. Wilkerson arrived within an hour and together, they went to find Mansfield. Hedrick later went to city hall and the police station and was at station No. 4 when Mansfield was being questioned. He said that he did not see anyone strike Mansfield and further claimed that the prisoner had been given something to eat at midnight. Detweiler cross-examined him, probing him about reward money that he had been given by Wilkerson. He also forced him to admit that there had been times when neither he, Fleming, nor any other officers were in the room with Wilkerson and Mansfield.

Detweiler had saved his best witnesses for last. Doctors Smith and Fulton were Kansas City physicians who treated prisoners at the county jail. Both of them had seen Mansfield during the time he was incarcerated there. Smith took the stand and said that he had seen Mansfield on June 20. At that time, he testified, Mansfield had a swollen lip, a cut inside his mouth, a contusion above one eye and complained of sharp pains in his right shoulder and stomach. Smith also said that several of Mansfield's teeth were loose.

Dr. Fulton testified that he saw Mansfield between eight and ten times during his time at the jail. He examined him thoroughly and had kept careful records of the examination, which he produced for the jury. According to his notes, Mansfield's injuries included, "Right side of the face bruised and somewhat swollen, lower lip inside cut by two teeth. Upper lip not cut, but two upper teeth injured. Bruised on right shoulder, dark in color, not swollen, painful on motion of shoulder. Bruised across back and middle third, not swollen, dark in color. Pain in bowels, constipated, looks bad, not nervous."

Detweiler had no further questions and Brady was unable to score any points for the defense with the two doctors. He finally gave up and began asking questions that intended to raise the possibility of drug use by Mansfield. Detweiler objected since the questions had not been raised during the direct questioning, but Brady argued that they were appropriate and Dr. Fulton was allowed to answer. He said that he did not believe that Mansfield was a drug user, although he was forced to admit that it was possible he had used drugs at some time in his life. The best that Brady managed to do was to get Dr. Fulton to say that constipation in prisoners was often simply the result of being incarcerated. On that small note, he excused the witness.

Detweiler rested his case and the defense began their side by calling James Wilkerson to the stand. The detective testified that the main questioning of Mansfield lasted from 8 p.m. on June 13, and ended around 5 a.m. on the following day. He said that during this time, he was never alone with Mansfield. He said that the suspect was treated well, given a big lunch, and that he had all the water he asked for. Wilkerson said that Mansfield drank so much water that at one point he told him to be careful or he'd "rust his constitution." He said that he absolutely never hit Mansfield or pushed him and that he never called him a "son of a bitch" or used any other kind of profanity. Brady questioned him about every allegation that Mansfield had made and Wilkerson denied doing anything that could be considered inappropriate. While testifying, Wilkerson managed to make it clear to the jury that he had good reason to believe that he was interrogating a brutal mass-murderer, and if he got a little rough treatment, well, he deserved it. However, he continued to deny that he had abused him in any way.

Detweiler had only started his cross-examination when he realized that he was dealing with a clever and manipulative witness when it came to Wilkerson. The detective got the chance to make Detweiler look foolish and he did so with great delight. Detweiler was pushing the malice angle. He wanted the jury to see that not only was Mansfield taken from his job and family, interrogated, abused and beaten, but that he was arrested simply because Wilkerson insisted he was "Insane Blackie" and kept him in custody even after it was established that he was not. It was a great plan, but the problem came when Detweiler forgot that Red Oak was in Montgomery County.

He asked Wilkerson, "Did you attempt to secure an indictment against Mansfield in Jefferson County, Iowa?"

"No, I did not," Wilkerson replied with a smug grin.

"Did you take him before a grand jury in Jefferson County, Iowa?"

"No, I did not."

"Did you ask him to waive extradition and be taken to Jefferson County, Iowa?"

"No, I did not."

"When he withdrew the waiver, did you not seek to have him extradited to Jefferson County, Iowa?"

"No, I did not," Wilkerson smirked again.

It was a bad moment for Detweiler. The case was being heard in Kansas City and probably most of the people in the courtroom had no idea what county Red Oak, Iowa, was in, and those who did know certainly weren't going to help him. Wilkerson relished the idea of making Detweiler look incompetent. Finally, Detweiler asked him if he had taken Mansfield to Red Oak, without naming the county, and Wilkerson admitted that he had. Detweiler finally realized his mistake and now, shaken and upset, he asked Wilkerson if he had taken the prisoner to Montgomery County, Iowa. Wilkerson said that he had, but quickly added that it was to the grand jury there, where Detweiler had given perjured testimony, further stunning the attorney.

Detweiler thought it best to get off the subject and asked Wilkerson if he had held the ax against Mansfield while he was being interrogated. Wilkerson said that he had not. Detweiler asked him where he had heard about "Insane Blackie." Wilkerson said that it was from some hoboes that he had questioned. The attorney pressed on, trying to get Wilkerson to admit that he knew that Mansfield was not

"Insane Blackie." Wilkerson answered by saying that William Mansfield was a multiple murderer, regardless of whatever name he had used. Knowing that he was getting nowhere with Wilkerson, Detweiler excuse him from the stand.

Thanks to Dr. Fulton's extensive records, as well as Dr. Smith's testimony, the jury had very convincing reasons to believe someone had severely beaten Mansfield and that someone was James Wilkerson. They found in favor of the plaintiff and Mansfield was awarded $2,500 in damages from the Burns Detective Agency. Burns later appealed to the state Supreme Court, claiming that the agency could not be held liable for Wilkerson's actions. The court again found in favor of Mansfield and the Burns agency was forced to pay.

Between the expense of the slander trial and the assault case, Wilkerson had cost the agency a sizable amount of money. Burns was finally fed up with "Agent 33" and they would soon part ways.

Despite all of Wilkerson's claims, Mansfield was finally cleared of any connection to the murders. The written records and sworn testimony that said he was working in Milwaukee during the Blue Island murders and had been in Montgomery, Illinois, during the week before and after the Villisca murders, was finally accepted as the truth. Contrary to Wilkerson's accusations, Mansfield had never been suspected of using drugs, had never been known as "Insane Blackie," could not be placed in Villisca at any time, and had never met Frank Jones.

With his unsavory past finally behind him, Mansfield made another name for himself in history as a labor union organizer. He spent the rest of his life working for the packing house workers union and was considered an esteemed and integral part of the organization. He died in the 1950s in Milwaukee, honored by the union and free of the troubles that had plagued him in the 1910s.

19. THE PURSUIT OF REVEREND KELLY

While the assault trial was taking place in Kansas City, Iowa Attorney General Horace Havner and Montgomery County Attorney Oscar Wenstrand, both recently sworn into office and anxious to delve into the Villisca case, were preparing to take Wilkerson's conspiracy theories to a grand jury. It would turn out to be one of the most volatile proceedings in the state's criminal history. It would exonerate one suspect (at least from a legal standpoint, if not in the minds of many locals), point the finger at another and, finally, show James Wilkerson to be the liar and fraud that he was. The fabricated case that he had built against Frank Jones would soon come tumbling down.

Havner and Wenstrand joined forces for the grand jury. Havner had the authority to take over the proceedings on behalf of the state and Wenstrand welcomeD his help. They both expected there to be as many as 100 witnesses called before the grand jury. Hundreds of pages of reports, letters, and depositions had to be read, studied, and analyzed. It was going to be a job for several attorneys. Wenstrand knew that men would have to be hired and he was limited to only what the Montgomery County board of supervisors would pay. With the state stepping into the proceedings, though, it would pay for many of the costs that would otherwise be the responsibility of the county. Wenstrand needed Havner's help and, fortunately, the two men got along well.

Havner began by hiring a special counsel named Frederick F. Faville, who had been an advisor to Attorney General George Cosson. Faville was an accomplished trial lawyer from Storm Lake and a former U.S. Attorney for Iowa's Northern District. He was an excellent prosecutor and would play an important role in the grand jury proceedings and the subsequent trial. Faville began learning the case, knowing he would be there when the attorney general couldn't be present. He would also make many of the important decisions during the investigation that followed and worked to assemble the evidence in the criminal case that came out of the grand jury hearings.

Havner had another resource that would help with the grand jury, which none of the earlier prosecutors possessed – the legislature had finally approved special investigators that were assigned full time to his office. He no longer had to rely on the use of private detectives. These special agents worked for the state, not the county, but with Havner so deeply involved in the investigation, he had them at his command. Two of these agents, Oscar Rock and James Risden, would figure strongly in events that later unfolded and both later became directors of the Iowa Bureau of Criminal Investigation.

Havner and Wenstrand were determined that the proceedings to come were going to be the most thorough ever attempted with the Villisca murder case. Both men wanted to get to the bottom of the crime. Both of them had political aspirations beyond their current offices and they wanted to make sure that everything was done correctly. For this reason, even as they prepared to present the Wilkerson conspiracy to the grand jury, they decided to take a fresh look at Reverend Kelly, the strange little minister who had embroiled himself in the case early on. They must have wondered why, with allegations against Kelly that included his talking on the train about the murders before they were discovered, that he'd sent a bloody shirt to the laundry a few days afterwards, that he was a sexual pervert with an unhealthy interest in young girls, and his admission to lawmen in South Dakota that he had committed the murders, their predecessors hadn't been more interested in him as a suspect? Havner and Wenstrand managed to keep their interest in Kelly away from the press, but even as the grand jury hearings began, Havner was directing his special agents to find out more about him.

Soon after the Mansfield assault trial concluded in late February 1917, an early morning break-in occurred at the Jones store in Villisca. The details of the attempted burglary were kept quiet but rumors began to circulate almost immediately that Wilkerson was involved in some way. What he might have been trying to do inside the store is unknown, but he still maintained his vendetta against Frank Jones. He considered himself an integral part of the proceedings that were about to begin and was sure that he was about to finally bring Jones down for good. Despite the setback of the assault verdict against him and the problems with the Burns agency, he was still quite sure of himself and felt the case he had created against Jones was ironclad.

The grand jury proceedings began in early March and not surprisingly, problems with James Wilkerson almost immediately cropped up. Wenstrand had gotten to know Wilkerson through conversations with attorneys and others who had dealt with him. He also had some first-hand experiences with him during the slander trial and he knew he could be controversial to work with. Havner had a staff that had remained from the Cosson term of office, so both men were wary of Wilkerson from the start. But they had no choice but to work with him. His so-called "Dope Sheet" was the blueprint that had been used to build the case and the county board of supervisors had appropriated the funds to retain him as their investigator.

Still feeling uncomfortable about Wilkerson, Wenstrand and Havner set out to call his witnesses while keeping the detective at arm's length. Predictably, Wilkerson took offense. He wanted to make sure that he was still front and center in the case and wanted all of the credit when Jones was finally indicted. With his Burns job now in jeopardy, he needed the notoriety of solving the Villisca case to ensure his future income. On March 7, Wilkerson met with 15 or 20 of his most hard-core supporters at the Johnson Hotel. After the meeting, he let the press know that they had backed a guaranteed fund to retain him now that he was being ignored by the state. William Mitchell, the Council Bluffs attorney who had endeared himself to Wilkerson supporters during the slander trial, stood next to the detective when he spoke to reporters. Wilkerson allies had retained him to look out for their interests during the new grand jury proceedings and, in anticipation of the Jones indictment, they hoped to have him assist with the prosecution.

Mitchell met with Havner and Judge Arthur to discuss the problem, which was essentially that Wilkerson did not like being ignored but there was little the judge could do. He advised Havner to meet with the detective and try to work out their differences. Havner had a short meeting with Wilkerson and the two called a temporary truce, hoping they could work together throughout the proceedings. The truce would not last for long.

By the middle of March, it was apparent, even though the grand jury proceedings were kept secret, that everyone was in for a lengthy ordeal. Wilkerson had started his "Dope Sheet" well before the slander suit and had continued adding to it in preparation for the grand jury proceedings. The typed, double-spaced pages, prepared by a detective who was a much better talker than a writer, was a lengthy record of everyone that Wilkerson had found over a three-year period who would say anything bad about Frank Jones or who would lend credence to Wilkerson's often changing theory. But as the jurors compared the "Dope Sheet" to actual testimony given by the witnesses, they began to realize something that Havner and his agents had already discovered – that what Wilkerson said people had told him and what they said while under oath were often two very different things. The witnesses that were the most damning to Jones were, for the most part, the least credible. To believe what Vina Tompkins, Ed Landers and Alice Willard had to say, jurors had to accept that these people had been aware of vitally important information about the murders, but had not told the authorities for years, even denying they knew anything – until James Wilkerson came along. And even after Wilkerson obtained their stories, those stories had a habit of changing. One of these changed stories even managed to land Wilkerson in jail.

During the proceedings, Alice Willard repeated her story about how she went for an automobile ride with two friends on the Saturday night before the murders. The account she told the grand jury was pretty much the same as her testimony during the slander trial: they went for a ride, the car broke down not far from the Moore house, and as they were walking down the street, they saw three men coming toward them. They hid and the men stopped near them and had a conversation that Alice said was "so degrading and vulgar I won't repeat it." She repeated some of it, though, including some new material that she had never included before. She said this time, the conversation included a graphic account of plotting to tie a man up while they took turns mistreating the woman, after which they would "perform an act of castration on him." She then testified that two other men approached and had a conversation with the first men that included the words "money," "closet," and the infamous "get Joe first" line. Just as she had at the slander trial, she said the group included Frank Jones, W.B. McCaul, John Oviatt and Harry Whipple.

The grand jury could read Wilkerson's report for themselves, but his version of the story was different. According to the report, Willard told him that she had gone out with Ed McCrae, accompanied by her friend Gertrude Lott and Maurice McCrae, Ed's brother. Now she was testifying that Gertrude Lott was already dead at the time, but that Mable Freeman was Ed's date, and that Maurice wasn't with them. In her original statement, written out by Wilkerson, she allegedly said that Albert Jones was one of the men she heard talking behind the Moore house, but during the Mansfield grand jury, she had not included Albert in the group.

The changes were of particular interest to attorneys trying to judge the credibility of Willard and Wilkerson. The grand jury focused on specific lines in the Wilkerson report that had Willard including Albert Jones among the conspirators. They noticed that later, after Albert and Dona had been able to establish that they were in Clarinda on June 8, the account had changed and it became Frank Jones that she had seen instead of Albert. Had Wilkerson misunderstood what she told him? Or had Willard changed her story? And if she had, did Wilkerson coach her to do so? While the presence of Frank Jones and Bert McCaul, as well as the "get Joe first" phrase was consistent in her testimony, much of the rest of it differed from Wilkerson's report. Her story could be taken as incriminating, but the inconsistencies raised serious doubts.

Wilkerson was called to the stand to try and clear things up. Faville, on behalf of the state, began a series of questions dealing with what exactly Willard did, or did not, say to Wilkerson in her original statement. Wilkerson could see the trap he was walking into – either he was going to be perceived as having misunderstood Willard, or deliberately misstating her, or as telling jurors she had changed her story. Apparently feeling that neither option was good, he refused to answer. Faville asked a specific question about which McCrae brother had been present that night and he again refused to answer. He was asked again and still would not provide an answer. Instead, he spoke to the jurors and told them that the question was intended to destroy the veracity of Alice Willard and put him in a position of perjury. He asked to be allowed to delay answering until he could consult with his attorney, William Mitchell. Havner, who was overseeing the hearing, refused to allow the delay. Judge Woodruff happened to be in town and Havner contacted him about the legalities involved. Woodruff convened court and the question was officially asked again. Wilkerson again refused to answer. Woodruff, irritated and not in the mood to deal with foolishness, found him in contempt of court and sentenced him to spend a day in jail.

Wilkerson refused to go quietly. He told the judge that his "Dope Sheet," which was on Havner's table, had cost him a great deal of money and time. It had been confiscated and he wanted it back. He left the stand and made a move to grab it off the table, but Havner pulled it out of his reach and handed it to Faville. Wilkerson made another grab for the papers and Sheriff Dunn, recently elected to office, stepped between them. Banging his gavel, Judge Woodruff called for order and Wilkerson, insisting that the day ended at midnight and that's when he should be released, was taken away to a cell.

Wilkerson's cronies were outraged. At midnight, about 20 of them showed up at the jail for his release, but Sheriff Dunn had told his deputies not to let him go. Judge Woodruff had stated that since the prisoner had been locked up at 4 p.m. on Saturday, he wasn't getting out until the same time on Sunday afternoon. When Wilkerson's supporters found this out, they marched over to the Johnson Hotel and roused the Attorney General from bed. He initially refused to meet with them at that hour, but after they rang his room several times, he changed his mind, put on his robe and went downstairs to meet them. The group demanded Wilkerson's release, accusing Havner of trying to whitewash the investigation and impeaching the witnesses. Havner told them that the judge had sent him to jail for one day, and that's what he meant. He was handling the grand jury so that it was fair to all parties and he would continue to do it the way he thought was best. The group disagreed, but finally went away. Wilkerson remained in jail until 4 p.m. on Sunday afternoon.

On Tuesday, Wilkerson was back before the grand jury. He was again asked to explain the inconsistencies between his report and Willard's account and he again refused to answer. Court was convened again and this time, Judge Arthur was on the bench. He told Wilkerson that, prior to sending him back to jail, he would give him a chance to make a statement about why he wouldn't answer the question.

Wilkerson gave a lengthy account about Willard and what she had told him, saying that part of the evidence was being misinterpreted. He said her first statement to him was a partial account and that he had gotten the final, verified statement at a later time. This is why it seemed to be a different story, he said. He added that he had expected to be consulted by those conducting the grand jury proceedings and he was going to explain everything to them. He couldn't, though, because now they were ignoring him. Wilkerson then began to complain again about how he was being treated badly. He said that Wenstrand had correspondence that he wouldn't share with him and that as an investigator for the county, he should have access to it. He also complained about Attorney General Havner, accusing him of "shyster practice." Wilkerson asked that Havner subpoena William Mitchell and Havner replied that he could issue subpoenas without advice from Wilkerson. Wilkerson said that he knew that, but he wanted the grand jury to know that he'd requested it.

Wilkerson continued to complain and bellyache for over an hour and when he finished, Havner asked to make a few remarks for the record. Judge Arthur consented and Havner said that when Wilkerson gave him the "Dope Sheet," he said that it was correct, and that he would add to it from day to day as the investigation progressed. Havner said Wilkerson had sworn before the grand jury that his account was correct and accurate and because of his assurances, the county was spending hundreds of dollars to verify it. He said that over 125 witnesses had been heard, some traveling from Montana, North Dakota, Oklahoma, and distant parts of Iowa, and in most cases, their testimony did not match what Wilkerson had put in his "Dope Sheet." He explained that the information that Wenstrand had not shared with Wilkerson were letters between

Reverend Burris and Frank Jones concerning a deathbed confession, and that Wilkerson had entered the county attorney's office and took them without permission. Wilkerson, he said, denied taking them but when given 24 hours to return the letters, they mysteriously appeared on Frederick Faville's desk.

After Havner was finished, Faville was given the opportunity to go on the record. He also had plenty to say about Wilkerson, noting that the attorneys involved, as well as the grand jury, had worked hard for several weeks and had more to do, all of which had been, and would be, accomplished with Wilkerson's instruction and assistance. He said that he had been practicing law for 24 years and knew what he was doing. Wilkerson had been given the opportunity to name witnesses who could shed light on the matter and all of them had either been, or would be, brought to the stand. The detective had not been required to do anything else. No matter how much he wanted to be in charge of the proceedings, they were able to do it without his help.

Faville also explained the reason Wilkerson was asked to answer the question about whether Alice Willard had told him Maurice McCrae was along that night was to definitely determine if there were two other living people who had heard the conversation. Ed McCrae was still being sought, but had yet to be found. If there was someone named Maurice McCrae who was present that night, Faville wanted to know and his investigators would begin an all-out search to find him.

Judge Arthur asked Wilkerson if he was now prepared to answer the question. He said that he would, but he first wanted to see a transcript of the statement he had just made so he could look it over and correct any errors. This effectively meant that he would take several more days to answer the question and in the end, he managed to delay answering it until after the indictment decision on Frank Jones was made.

The jurors had plenty of reasons to be disgusted with Wilkerson. They had read his "Dope Sheet" and they understood the importance of the question that he was being asked about Willard's original statement. His refusal to avoid the question was causing an unnecessary delay and the jury was left to speculate about the reason.

Wilkerson had first come before the grand jury very early in the proceedings. He brought his investigation report with him and had sworn: "Where this statement shows what the witnesses have said, it is a correct statement of what these witnesses have said to me and what they knew about the case." Havner was correct when he told Judge Arthur that many of the witnesses in the report were not testifying to the same things that Wilkerson claimed. Another example besides Alice Willard was Dan Stillians. According to the "Dope Sheet," Stillians told him that about midnight on the night of the murders he passed by the southwest corner of the block where the Moore house was located. He saw three men standing there and shined a flashlight on them. He said, according to Wilkerson, that the three men were Albert Jones, Bert McCaul, and a third man that he later identified from a picture that Wilkerson showed him as being Harry Whipple.

The statement was supportive of Wilkerson's conspiracy plot and seemed as though it would go a long way in incriminating Frank Jones. However, when

Stillians traveled from where he was now living in Great Falls, Montana, he told the grand jury a much different story. He said that on the night of the murders, he had gone to church, after which he accompanied a girlfriend named Fern Crowe to her home. He said that he was with her until 10:30 p.m. and then he walked downtown and spent a half hour at Van Camp's Restaurant. He went home after that, telling the jury that he might have seen some men on the street, but he didn't remember seeing anyone that he knew or recognized. He specifically said that he never told Wilkerson or anyone else that he had seen Frank Jones, Albert Jones, Harry Whipple or Bert McCaul that night, and he never said that he saw anyone on the corner near the Moore home.

In fairness to Wilkerson, he did have at least some basis for thinking that Stillians might have seen something incriminating. Of course, being Wilkerson, he had taken the rumor and run with it, bending it and shaping it to match his theory without ever confirming it with Stillians. Apparently, Wilkerson had been told by Goldie Hunt, the sister of another one of Stillians' girlfriends, that Stillians told her that he had seen Frank and Albert Jones looking into the window of the Moore house on the night of the murders. Hunt testified to the grand jury that Stillians had indeed told her this, and she stuck to the story even after Stillians had been brought into the room. Stillians then denied under oath that he had ever told Hunt of seeing anyone at the Moore house that night. Wenstrand, along with the grand jury members, were quick to realize that had happened – the young man had made up the story to impress the girls and when Wilkerson heard about it, he put it in his report as fact.

In his report, Wilkerson made much of the conversation between Albert Jones and J.B. Moore in the alley that separated their properties. There was no doubt that the conversation took place. People had seen them talking and Albert had readily acknowledged it. Albert said that they had chatted about business and generally talked in a friendly way, as they often did. He said that he didn't actually hear Sarah call J.B. and tell him to get ready for church, but J.B. said that she did and that was the end of the conversation.

Wilkerson, though, reported the conversation as being anything but friendly. In his report, he made it sound as though the men had quarreled in the alley and the detective noted that a witness named Lawrence Gridley could confirm the argument. Gridley was called by the grand jury, as were two other young men who were with him that evening. Gridley and the others testified that they saw or heard nothing that looked like a quarrel. Moore and Jones, they said, were talking when Gridley put his horse and buggy in a barn that belonged to a relative who lived southeast of Albert's house. They said that Albert, who had sold them the buggy, walked over to the barn and commented on it. Moore also came into the barn, looked at it and agreed that it was a nice rig. This was, Gridley and others assured the jury, the extent of the conversation. It was a pleasant exchange and Moore and Jones seemed to get along very well.

Even Vina Tompkins didn't testify the way that Wilkerson planned. Although, again, in fairness to the detective, her story had changed so many times over the past few years that it would have been nearly impossible for it to match any of her previous statements. She told the grand jury the story she had told others before Wilkerson came along – that she was at the slaughterhouse picking up kindling and had overheard some conversation between three men, but now said she heard nothing at all about plans for a murder. She thought one of the men might be Jake Weems (one of the leaders of the alleged criminal organization), but she said she didn't know the other two. Wilkerson had her telling him that she heard the older man say it would take him a while to get the money together but in front of the jury, she said she never heard this and never told Wilkerson that she had. Wilkerson also claimed that she told him she overheard the men discussing a getaway, some going north and some south, but Tompkins said this wasn't true. She also allegedly told him where the men would meet to be paid for the murders, but she stated that this was not true either. She also denied telling Wilkerson that a local police officer was "fixed" and that her brother Harry Whipple told her that he had a job "croaking a man for a rich banker." It seemed that nearly all of Tompkins' statements that Wilkerson had built his case on were now said to be untrue.

Heads were likely spinning on the grand jury as other witnesses were called to the stand and were disputing the statements in the "Dope Sheet." There were witnesses who agreed with Wilkerson's claim that Dona Jones might have been having an affair with J.B. Moore, but nothing that would confirm his claim that she was a "nymphomaniac" and carrying on several affairs at one time. Wilkerson listed men like Bert McCaul, Albert Davie and even her father-in-law, Frank Jones, as being sexually involved with Dona. One of the stories he wanted the grand jury to hear was that Albert had once returned home and caught Davie in bed with his wife. Gossip in town said that a fight had taken place and the telephone receiver had been knocked from the hook. This allowed the operator listening in on the line to hear the quarrel taking place. She heard a gunshot, the story claimed, and the bullet severed Davie's thumb. The true story was that Davie had indeed lost his thumb – but it happened when it was tangled in a rope that was attached to a horse that bolted. Another rumor claimed that Dona was having an affair with her doctor because she was seen slipping into his office through a back door. She had also been seen, Wilkerson claimed in his report, going into a farm shed with J.B. Moore.

When testimony was presented about Dona's affairs, however, only the telephone operators could be called and they could only say that Dona and J.B. spoke several times on the telephone, but that was all. If the jurors believed that an affair had taken place, they apparently felt that it was not a motive for murder.

Among those who testified before the grand jury, but did not appear at the slander trial, was Reverend J.J. Burris, who traveled from Oklahoma to tell his story. He said that he had been the pastor of the Church of Christ in Radersburg, Montana, in 1913, and was called to the bed of a dying man. Reverend Burris said the man, who he believed was dying from liver failure brought on by excessive drinking, told him that he had murdered eight people in Villisca, Iowa. Burris said that the man asked for the sake of his family members that his confession be kept secret unless it was needed to protect an innocent person. Burris wrote the man's name down in a book, but he later lost the book and was unable to remember the name. Then, the previous fall, he had seen a newspaper article about the investigations and had written to Frank Jones. He exchanged correspondence with Jones for a few weeks, but had not heard from him since. When Jones was called to testify, he said that he had turned the letters from Burris over to Wenstrand, assuming that the county attorney would follow up on the vague lead. Wenstrand apparently did nothing with the information until the time of the grand jury, issuing a subpoena for Burris. Authorities in Montana were contacted and investigators looked into Burris' story, but there was little they could do. They confirmed that Burris had lived there, that he was a minister, and that he had a good reputation, but without knowing the name of the man who had confessed to murder, there was nothing they could tell the Iowa officials.

The proceedings continued until April, when the grand jury finally issued their long-awaited report. They wrote:

We, the grand jury of the county of Montgomery, having had under consideration the matter of the investigation of the murder of Joe Moore, his family and two Stillinger girls at Villisca, Iowa, on the ninth day of June, 1912, would respectfully report to the court as to our doings in said matter the following:

As a grand jury we commenced the investigation on the fifth day of March, 1917, and have prosecuted said investigation practically continuously since said day, and have given to said investigation the most careful, painstaking, thorough, and conscientious consideration of which we are capable.

Realizing the heinousness of the crime that was committed and the importance of a proper solution if at all possible, to the community and the state, we have spared no effort and no expense to ascertain the truth and to, if possible, bring to justice the person or persons guilty of the offense.

For more than two and a half years one J.N. Wilkerson, an operative of the Burns Detective Agency, has devoted at least one-half of his time in an attempt to solve the mystery connected with this crime and to secure the evidence necessary to punish the person or persons guilty of the offense.

Prior to commencement of this investigation before this grand jury Mr. Wilkerson was requested to furnish the attorney general and to the county attorney for their use and the use of this grand jury a list of all of the witnesses whose names he had secured in connection with all of his investigations with a written statement of what Mr. Wilkerson said was a true statement of the facts to which such persons would testify to. Every material witness named in said list has been produced before this grand jury for examination and in order to accomplish this it has been necessary to call witnesses from many different states at a great distance and at great expense and every one of said witnesses, after having been daily sworn, was subjected to a thorough, searching, careful examination: not only by attorneys representing the state, but by members of the grand jury themselves. So that no fact or circumstances known by such witnesses would fail to be disclosed.

In fact, in view of the peculiarities of the case and the circumstances surrounding it, the grand jury extended its inquiry in great latitude and to a great extend in hope that, even by hear-say testimony (although incompetent in court), some clew might be discovered through which they could secure substantial evidence of the guilt of some person or persons. Notwithstanding the careful and painstaking manner in which the investigation has been pursued many of the material witnesses mentioned by Mr. Wilkerson when found and summoned before the grand jury either wholly failed to testify as stated in said statement regarding said witnesses, disclaimed or denied the statements attributed to them. This is not true of all witnesses.

It is a well known fact that since the commission of this crime there have been reported rumors of various kinds purporting to be clews as to the identity of the person or persons who committed this offense. We have not discredited these rumors without giving each and every one of them a thorough, full and complete investigation in the hope that we might thereby secure some tangible evidence of guilt on the part of some party.

Every available clew that we have discovered or have been advised of either by Mr. Wilkerson or any other person that has come to our knowledge from any source has been thoroughly pursued and investigated. We have spent twenty-four hours a day in this investigation and have brought before us and examined under oath 160 witnesses. No feature of the case that has come to our attention from any source has been overlooked, disregarded or slighted in the least degree. At all times in connection with said investigation we have tried to keep in mind the importance of finally ascertaining the truth, but up until this time we have been unable to discover any sufficient credible testimony upon which we would be warranted in returning an indictment against any person or persons which in our judgment would warrant any jury under the last in returning a verdict of guilty against any person or persons.

In other words, the grand jury stated that they were unable to return an indictment against Frank Jones – or about the person for which there had been "rumors of various kinds purporting to be clews as to the identity of the person or persons who committed this offense" --- because the witnesses that James Wilkerson brought to them changed their stories and were unreliable. Wilkerson himself had turned out to be sadly unreliable, as well.

What everyone who read the report from the grand jury in the newspapers realized was that Frank Jones had finally won a major victory in the fight to clear his name. Wilkerson could always try again with additional evidence -- and he would -- but any realistic chance that he had of convicting Frank or Albert Jones had disappeared. There were still twists, turns, and unexpected events to come, but Wilkerson's reputation had been shattered.

And he wouldn't be alone. One of the grand jurors who signed the report was Scott Smith, a Villisca hardware salesman who had supported Cosson's request to the legislature to hire state agents in 1913. He'd had a strong interest in the case since that time, was an outspoken juror, and subsequent events would indicate that some of his activities during the proceedings were questionable, if not illegal. But none of that was generally known until later, and neither was the fact that Frank Jones had hired a detective to report on Smith's relationship with Wilkerson.

This information would not help Wilkerson's reputation and neither would the events that immediately followed the release of the grand jury's letter. His credibility was damaged even more when the grand jury convened the day after the letter was printed. The detective took the stand to answer the question that he had spent a day in jail to avoid. He was again asked if Alice Willard told him that Ed McCrae's brother was along on the Saturday night before the murders and Wilkerson said that yes, she did tell him that. The answer made little difference at that point since the jury had already dismissed Willard's story. She, along with dozens of other star witnesses, had managed to destroy the veracity of Wilkerson's "Dope Sheet." So, why bring Wilkerson back to the stand even after the grand jury had declined to indict Frank Jones? Attorney General Havner wanted the chance to put Wilkerson, a man he now strongly disliked, on the stand and embarrass him into answering a question that he didn't want to answer.

After Wilkerson's last trip to the stand, the grand jury was dismissed, but not discharged. They probably knew when they left the courthouse that day that they would soon be back to hear what witnesses had to say about another suspect and hear about another investigation that had been secretly percolating for weeks.

In mid-April, Wilkerson submitted a bill for $595.29 to the county board of supervisors, which raised the amount he had billed since early January to more than $1,300. As expected, the meeting to debate the new bill drew quite a crowd. Ed Peterson asked that Wilkerson be retained to continue the investigation, and also that supervisors hire William Mitchell to present future evidence to the grand jury. R.W. Beeson repeated his case against doing so, referred to Wilkerson as a grafter and a bitter loser after the grand jury rebuked him and dismissed the concocted stories of his witnesses. A number of Wilkerson's still-loyal supporters were present and the meeting became loud and angry.

Wilkerson asked for the floor and produced a signed statement by Alice Willard. In the statement, she claimed that she was subjected to a three-hour "grilling" by Attorney General Havner, Special Prosecutor Faville and Special Agent Oscar Rock prior to one of her appearances before the grand jury. She said Havner had tried to force her to say that her story was not true, that she had told different stories at different times, and that she could not have seen the men she claimed to see in the dark. She said in her statement that Havner reminded her that she could be charged with perjury and sent to prison. The statement said that Willard fainted before the interrogation had been completed, and she had to be taken to a hotel and placed under a doctor's care.

Honestly, I'm not sure what the point of the statement was since the grand jury had already decided that Willard was an unreliable witness, and even if the three officials had "grilled" her, everything that they told her was the truth. Willard's story changed numerous times and she admitted in front of the jury that she did not say many of the things that Wilkerson attributed to her in his report.

The reminder that perjury was an offense that would send her to the penitentiary apparently worked, because she had greatly changed her story when she appeared during the grand jury proceedings, lessening the impact against Jones. But whatever power Wilkerson had over her, he flaunted it during the April meeting, producing a statement that made it look as though she had been intimidated into changing her story once again.

After Wilkerson produced the statement from Willard (it seems strange that she did not attend the meeting), other supporters spoke up on behalf of the detective and against the way that evidence had been presented to the grand jury. The board said that the direction of the inquiry would be up to County Attorney Wenstrand, who was present at the meeting but chose not to comment. The bill from Wilkerson was approved and the meeting was adjourned. Oddly to many, Wenstrand was not unhappy about the direction the meeting had taken. It was a small price to pay to keep Wilkerson happy, still chasing his lost cause, and too busy to look into what the grand jury was investigating now. Everyone was working hard to keep the new direction of the investigation secret and the best way to do that was to keep the publicity-seeking Wilkerson far away from it.

Later that week, an announcement was made that Wilkerson was holding another of his meetings at the Beardsley Theater on Saturday afternoon. About 600 people showed up, a smaller number than before. Joseph Stillinger acted as chairman and seated on stage with Wilkerson were a half dozen of his biggest supporters, including Reverend Ewing, Ed Peterson, his financial backer, and John Noel, whose motives were a mystery.

Wilkerson made his usual appeal for money, but gave it a new twist, telling the audience that the meeting was not actually about money, even though things were getting tight since by now he had lost his job with the Burns agency. He went on to say, as he often did, that the authorities were trying to keep him from telling the true story. This time, he added some new material to the show. He claimed that he had been told not to speak or he would have to leave the state. He noted that he had been put in jail for not talking, and now they were threatening him with jail if he did talk.

Wilkerson did say that he had an interesting revelation while in jail, however. He said that while sleeping on the jail cell's iron cot, a "phantom woman" appeared to him, clinging to his neck. He said that he tried to push her away, asking what she wanted from him. She replied that she had come to kill him but had changed her mind and at the same time, he saw an ax on the floor of the cell. Leaving the audience to do their own dream interpretation, Wilkerson moved on to a subject that he always included – the danger involved in his valiant investigation. He vowed that he would stand by those who stood by him, "even by shedding blood if necessary." He also told them that he would stay with the case as long as he was needed and his friends wanted him to – although he might be forced to stop at any time, which was a rather confusing promise to make.

When Wilkerson had told his supporters that he had been warned not to hold a mass meeting, he should have told them that this was only while the grand jury was in session. Although an admission of that would have made his dire warning seem much less dramatic. A warning against this kind of activity during grand jury proceedings was part of a piece of legislation that came to be known as the Thompson Bill, named for the Des Moines county senator who sponsored it. The bill was introduced near the end of the legislative session (about the time the grand jury was completing their evaluation of the case against Jones) at the request of Attorney General Havner. The bill provided that "any person attempting to improperly influence, intimidate, impede, or obstruct any petit juror, grand juror or other officer in a civil or criminal action or by any public speech improperly influenced the administration of justice" would be guilty of a felony and subject to a fine and imprisonment. In urging the passage of the bill, Senator Thompson specifically referred to Wilkerson, saying that he was slandering members of a grand jury, attacking the attorney general and the prosecutors and they were powerless to stop him. He added that many detective agencies hired unprincipled and dangerous rogues and that innocent people were serving time in prison because of them.

The bill passed, but would only take effect if Governor William Lloyd Harding signed it. Wilkerson, and a small delegation of his cronies, went to Des Moines to see the governor. The detective argued that the bill violated his Constitutional right to freedom of speech and would make it impossible for his investigation to continue. This seems to highlight the problem with the very nature of Wilkerson's investigation. There was no reason why he couldn't continue to investigate without harassing and threatening grand jury members and public officials. But perhaps he knew what kind of latitude that law enforcement officials would be given when it came to his meetings and public statements. They could shut him down for almost anything, whether he followed what he believed the rules were or not. Regardless, he argued the point with the governor, who heard him out and promised to study the matter closely before he made a decision.

Governor Harding had 30 days to decide what he wanted to do, but he didn't take nearly that long. On April 26, he signed the bill into law. It was a law that Wilkerson couldn't help but break, which set the stage for more problems with the detective in the days ahead.

Meanwhile, the grand jury had been, as expected, called back to work. They were soon to hear evidence that they found much more believable than the case that Wilkerson had presented against Frank Jones. The new focus of the inquiry was the Reverend Lyn George Kelly, but before they could get started, there was unfinished business left over from the previous session.

On April 30, Ed Peterson came before the jurors and wanted to read affidavits concerning the "grilling" of witnesses by Havner and Rock. He asked that Havner be excluded, but the attorney general refused to leave. Peterson left to get some legal advice and when he returned later that afternoon, Havner was not there. In this way, Peterson got what he wanted, which was to read Alice Willard's statement to the grand jury without Havner present.

The incident created a question that the jurors wanted answered. Scott Smith, the only member of the grand jury from Villisca, made it a point to ask Judge

Woodruff if the jury had the power to force the attorney general or the county attorney to leave the room while they questioned witnesses. The judge gave them a confusing answer. Woodruff said that he believed the jury had the authority to exclude the prosecutor, but the law permitted the prosecutor to be present while testimony was being taken in order to be aware of what the testimony was. Taking this to mean that "maybe" they could exclude the prosecutor, Smith then asked if a vote from the majority of the jurors could exclude them. The judge either didn't know, or didn't want to say, because he simply directed the grand jury to work together with the prosecutors to ensure a good outcome.

Smith's questions indicated that he perceived (or more likely, was encouraged to perceive it by Wilkerson) a degree of bias on Havner's part, as if he had come into the grand jury proceedings with the opinion already formed that Jones was innocent. Later, it appeared that Smith had a bias toward Jones, thanks to his association with Wilkerson, but in the end, the grand jury, including Smith, agreed that there was not enough evidence to justify indicting Jones.

Unfortunately for Havner, the allegations brought by Peterson and expressed by Smith did not go away. The grand jury, in the next term, heard from Peterson and Alice Willard and actually considered an indictment against Havner for misconduct in office. No matter how badly his reputation had been tattered, the specter of Wilkerson refused to go away.

The grand jury liked the case against Reverend Kelly. They had spent weeks slogging through the confusing jumble of Wilkerson's conspiracy but it took only four days to indict the minister. Havner had every reason to keep the indictment secret, at least for a while, but Wilkerson found out almost right away. The detective hired by Frank Jones learned that Scott Smith told him.

Jones wanted to bring down Wilkerson almost as badly as Wilkerson wanted to hurt Jones, and in that regard Jones and Havner had something in common. The attorney general frequently heard from Jones, starting well before the grand jury convened, but by all appearances he tried to keep him at a distance. In early 1917, only a few weeks after taking office, Havner responded to a letter from Jones by writing that he appreciated his offers of assistance, but he needed to independently investigate the case, "no matter where it went." Jones recognized the problem (he was the main suspect in the grand jury investigation after all) but Havner's attitude changed toward the former senator after the grand jury handed down the "no credible evidence" decision. The two men began corresponding on a regular basis.

In 1917, Jones's detective, who was also a freelance reporter who used the name J.H. Moore, went undercover among Wilkerson's circle of supporters, ingratiating himself with the leaders of the group. He was to find out whatever he could, keep tabs on Wilkerson, and report back to Jones, which he did on a sporadic basis. Jones then passed on the information to Havner. J.H. Moore met regularly with Wilkerson and his allies and was taken into their confidence. He informed Jones that Scott Smith and Wilkerson were meeting regularly while the grand jury was in session. Moore said that he was present when Wilkerson chastised Smith for failing to indict Jones, to which Smith responded, "You men had no case." Moore, who signed his letters "JH," wrote to Jones and told him that he had seen Wilkerson go to Smith's house and spend three hours there in the evening before the Kelly indictment was handed down. He returned the following night for another visit. He believed that Smith was perhaps making up for the lack of a Jones indictment by continuing to keep Wilkerson informed about the secret proceedings of the jury.

As it turned out, J.H. Moore was correct in his belief that Wilkerson knew that Kelly had been indicted. Although his motives were curious, Wilkerson immediately set out to find the minister and arrange for his legal defense. It seemed that the detective would do anything to make sure that no one else was found guilty of a crime that he believed Frank Jones had committed.

Wilkerson knew about the indictment, but the general public did not. For days, the newspapers speculated about what was going on with the grand jury. They knew the grand jury had completed their work and the reporters heard rumors that someone had been indicted. However, no one would make a public statement about it. Havner was waiting things out, trying to keep the indictment secret while Faville prepared behind the scenes for a trial. Frank Jones wrote to Havner, telling him what his detective had found out about Wilkerson, but there was little the attorney general could do about it.

Havner was focused on tracking down Reverend Kelly. At the time of the indictment, he was preaching in Sutton, Nebraska, but he left town soon after. He wasn't trying to hide because he had no idea that he had been indicted or that anyone was looking for him. Havner sent an agent named Theodore W. Passwater to find Kelly, but gave him instructions not to arrest him until he was told to do so. Passwater went to work and discovered that Kelly had left Nebraska. He also learned that he had then gone to St. Louis to visit friends. He headed to St. Louis – not knowing that Wilkerson had gotten there first. Wilkerson had no idea of Passwater's assignment, but he did know that the state would soon be looking for the little preacher. He went to Kelly, told him what was going on, and then spirited him out of St. Louis to the small southern Illinois town of Alto Pass.

Passwater was close behind Wilkerson. He wrote to Havner on May 1, and told him that he had located the minister in St. Louis. The following day he wrote to say that he'd learned Kelly had gone to Alto Pass. He located the boarding house where Kelly was staying, still with no idea that Wilkerson was mixed up in the hunt, and waited for orders. On May 4, while Passwater was waiting in his hotel room, Wilkerson, who had spent a considerable amount of time with Kelly by now, went to the railroad station and shipped Kelly's personal belongings to a storage warehouse in Kansas City. He paid the bill in cash and then signed the receipt for the Southern Express Company "F.F. Jones."

Passwater wrote to Havner again, now impatient with knowing Kelly's location and not being able to act on it. Alto Pass was a small, rather boring town and Passwater was tired of cooling his heels in a hotel room. Havner wrote back and assured him that it would not be much longer and then added that Passwater would be given credit for the arrest in hopes this might ease the agent's irritation. Kelly's arrest would attract considerable attention, thanks to the magnitude of the crime he'd be charged with, and Passwater decided to be patient.

Passwater's boredom apparently got the best of him and he failed to watch the boarding house as closely as he should have. On May 9, he wrote to Havner to tell him that Kelly's mail was being returned – the minister had vanished from town. After asking around Alto Pass, he wrote Havner again on May 10, to tell him that Kelly had suddenly left town, leaving no forwarding address. Wilkerson, perhaps finally learning of Passwater's presence, not only took Kelly out of town, but arranged for an attorney for him, as well.

A.L. Sutton from Omaha agreed to represent Kelly during the proceedings to come. Sutton had been a candidate for the Nebraska governor's office and was known as a skilled but bombastic defense attorney. Wilkerson had contacted him soon after he had located the minister but nothing happened quickly. If Iowa did have an indictment against Kelly, the state was certainly taking its time to find him. Sutton thought that it was simply a stall for time to prepare for trial, but Wilkerson's inner circle speculated that the state's motives were more sinister.

Once a grand jury handed down an indictment, the jury could not indict anyone else until the accused stood trial. Even if Wilkerson produced some actual evidence against Frank Jones, the grand jury couldn't indict him until Kelly was tried. Wilkerson undoubtedly pressed this theory on his followers as the reason for supporting Kelly and helping him find an attorney. He didn't want so see an innocent man suffer, he told them, for the sins of Frank Jones. However, his motives were almost surely not that pure. Thwarting Havner's case would be a small bit of revenge for the embittered detective and it's clear that Wilkerson would do anything to keep his name in the newspapers. Becoming a part of the Kelly investigation – from either side – would certainly serve his purpose.

Regardless of why Kelly had not yet been arrested, Sutton decided that the best thing for his client was for him to turn himself in, get the facts of the case, and then move for a speedy trial. Wilkerson helped the minister and his wife get their affairs in order and then they traveled together to Chicago to meet with Sutton. The news that he had been indicted should not have come as a surprise to Kelly, who had been telling people for years that the authorities were after him for the murders. He agreed to take Sutton's advice and return to Montgomery County. Following the weekend in Chicago, where his defense was discussed at length, Sutton and the Kellys made an overnight train trip to Red Oak, arriving at about 6 a.m. on Monday morning, May 14.

Sutton and the Kellys arrived in town nearly two hours before the courthouse opened for the day and so they walked around town after having breakfast in a restaurant on the town square. They waited a few minutes for the courthouse to be opened for business and then went to see the sheriff. Sutton was told that Sheriff Dunn was out of town, so he then took Kelly to Oscar Wenstrand's office. Wenstrand was caught completely off guard. News that Kelly had been indicted a few weeks earlier was a closely guarded secret. The last time that Wenstrand had heard from Havner, a state agent was watching the minister in a small Illinois town, and Havner was going to have him arrested when the time was right. Now their suspect was standing in his office! He asked the group to take a seat, put out a call for Sheriff Dunn, and then fumed while telephone operators tried to track him down. Dunn was eventually found in the eastern part of the county, but couldn't get back to Red Oak until after noon. Finally, more than six hours after arriving in town to give himself up, four hours of which were spent waiting in the county attorney's office, the man charged with Iowa's most infamous mass murder was taken into custody.

Havner was shocked by the news of Kelly's surrender and was enraged when he learned of Wilkerson's role in the debacle. The state was not ready to have the minister arrested, let alone take him to trial. So, Havner decided to engage in some dirty tricks of his own. He put together a shockingly detailed statement about Kelly's arrest for the newspapers, clearly violating the new Thompson Law in the same way that he had accused Wilkerson of doing just weeks before. The statement not only praised the grand jury for their indictment, but it also made a great attempt to influence the jurors of Montgomery County in the trial to come.

Lyn George Jacklin Kelly was born in England in 1878 and came to America with his wife Laura around 1904. He was obsessed with becoming a minister and eventually joined the Presbyterian Church. He was a bizarre character, plagued by weird habits, and was certainly a sexual deviant. Few knew him well and those who did were being kind when they referred to him merely as "eccentric." But was he a murderer?

In 1912, Kelly was preaching on alternate Sundays at a small country church outside of Macedonia. About three weeks before the murders in Villisca, a reputable witness testified that Kelly was discovered looking into the bedroom window of his house, where his wife was changing into her nightgown. It was probably not the first time he had done it – or the only window he "peeped" in – since he was often seen wandering around town at night.

Later in June, Kelly was present at the Children's Day program at the Villisca Presbyterian church on the night of the murders. His presence there, his departure from town during the early morning hours on June 10, and his strange behavior following the crime led to his indictment.

Kelly traveled to Villisca to preach and then to attend the program. He planned to stay overnight at Reverend Ewing's home on Sunday evening. When Kelly arrived in Villisca on Saturday, Seymour Enarson, the son of Henry Enarson, met him at the train depot. He was driven from the depot to the home of Louis Enarson, Seymour's uncle, for supper. After that, Kelly was taken to Henry Enarson's house to stay the night.

According to Enarson family accounts, Kelly acted very nervous when he arrived at their farmhouse six miles north of Villisca. Almost immediately, he began pacing the living room floor and at one point, ordered Mrs. Enarson and the children to leave the room because they were too noisy. Kelly spent the night in a small downstairs bedroom, and Mrs. Enarson was so alarmed by his strange behavior that she wrapped herself in a blanket and spent a sleepless night on the stairs leading to the upstairs bedrooms, listening carefully for any sound the preacher might make.

The next morning, Henry and Seymour Enarson took Kelly to the Pilot Grove Church for a picnic. Prior to lunch, Kelly gave a sermon that Seymour later described as "the strangest he had ever heard." Kelly returned to the Enarsons' for supper and then Seymour drove him to Reverend Ewing's home. That was the last time that the Enarsons saw him prior to the murders but they always believed that he had something to do with the killings. They later heard that the minister confessed to the crime on the train going back to Macedonia and that he had committed the murders because he had a vision that told him to "slay and slay utterly," a phrase that allegedly came from the Bible. The Enarsons had no reason to believe that the man who had behaved so oddly at their home was not guilty of the crimes that he was accused of.

Before he became a major suspect in the murders, Kelly seemed to be doing everything possible to make himself look guilty. When he arrived back in Macedonia on Monday, the day after the murders, he told several people details of the murders and of the number of people who had been killed. He claimed that he had actually heard the thud of the ax as the slaying took place and was one of the first people on the scene after the murders were discovered. He told this story in Macedonia between 8:30 and 9 that morning --- at the same time the bodies were being discovered in Villisca. This is information that he should not have known unless he was the killer, although later in the book, I'll explain why I think he knew about the murders, even though he was not the murderer.

According to material that Havner and his investigators collected, Kelly also took a bloodstained shirt to a laundry in Council Bluffs. The package of clothing containing the shirt had been left at the Bluff City Laundry without any name or identifying mark on it, only a slip of paper that requested a shirt in the basket of laundry be returned to Macedonia. Laundry worker Cora Marquard reported that there was a shirt in the package that someone had tried to wash by hand, since it was still damp, that had been soaked with blood. The laundry was sent back to Macedonia unmarked and Kelly came to the drug store where the delivery was made and claimed it. He had anxiously waited for it to arrive and had made several trips to the store to check to see if it was there.

Kelly became obsessed with the case and talked about it to anyone who would listen. This often caused incidents and problems, as was recounted earlier when he frightened a number of people in the lobby of a Villisca hotel with a vigorous re-enactment of the crime. He began writing letters to police officials and detectives, offering theories on the murders and sometimes implying that he was involved. Rumors claimed that he said things that only the killer would know and that he had been heard uttering on a train the ominous phrase "slay and slay utterly," which made his fellow passengers suspicious of him.

Kelly went back and forth to Villisca, claiming to be investigating the murders. At first, he stayed with Reverend Ewing, but later started staying in hotels when even the kindly Ewing began making excuses not to have the man in his home. He wrote a letter to Ross Moore, claiming that he had seen a strange man at the train depot on the morning after the murders that he believed may have committed the crime. The man supposedly spoke to him and Kelly recognized him as a man he had seen wandering the streets of Villisca during the early hours of the morning. Kelly did not explain what he himself had been doing roaming around at such an odd hour. As he closed the letter, he asked Ross if he would be allowed to work on the case as an investigator.

Kelly continued working as a minister in Macedonia for some time after the murders and witnesses later recalled that he constantly talked about the crime in Villisca. Late in the fall of 1912, he resigned from the church in Macedonia and from another small church near Villisca and moved to Carroll, Iowa, where he found a position as minister. Amazingly, as strange as Kelly was, he always managed to land preaching jobs.

Soon after moving to Carroll, he advertised for a class in stenography (shorthand) and then sent out another advertisement – looking to get young women to pose in the nude. His mental state continued to deteriorate. Witnesses later recalled Kelly not only talking about the murders, but asking unusual questions, too. One of them, a physician in Carroll, said that Kelly asked him if a man who committed murder could be punished if he was insane. The doctor told him that he could not. He also started to become paranoid, watching and following any strangers who appeared in town. He would make inquiries about them to find out if they were detectives. He was sure that the authorities were looking for him.

At some point in 1913, Kelly left Iowa and moved to Winner, South Dakota, where he preached, arranged revival services, and offered stenographic work. In late December he ran an ad in the *Omaha World Herald* seeking to employ a stenographer to pose as a model for pictures that would be used in a "literary and artistic work" he was writing. The book, the ad went on to say, would be "high class." A woman in her early thirties from Council Bluffs answered the ad and Kelly wrote back to her. In his first letter, he asked what experience she had as a typist. He also told her that anything exchanged between them had to be kept in secret for professional reasons. Then he began peppering her with personal questions: Was she free to travel as she pleased? Could she go out at night if she wanted to? Could she meet him in Omaha? Did she have a boyfriend? Was she engaged to be married? He said he needed to know these things because the woman he would hire as a stenographer and typist for an important book that he was writing had to be able to work late, without having to worry about returning home to her fiancée at a certain time. He also told her that his last stenographer (who of course, didn't exist) met him in the evenings and had dinner with him before they went to work. He said that their work would be done in a private home, where no one would bother them.

His letters soon became even more unsettling. He asked the woman to tell him frankly what she thought of a number of classic paintings, all of which were nudes like "September Morn," "Venus," and "Bath of Psyche," and whether or not she had any objection to art that depicted undressed figures. He eventually got around to asking what was really on his mind: would she be willing to pose nude for him in a place where they would be "absolutely secret and alone," where nobody would know them or what they were doing?

The young woman who received the letters turned them over to her pastor, who in turn gave them to Deputy U.S. Marshal William Groneweg in Council Bluffs, who ordered Kelly's arrest for sending obscene materials through the mail. When he was placed under arrest, he told the officers that he knew where they were going to take him – he was wanted in Villisca for the murders there. Confused, the agents told him that they were there to take him into custody on an obscenity charge, not for murder. Kelly first denied knowing anything about the letters, but then admitted that he had written them.

Kelly was placed in jail in Sioux Falls, where he was alleged to have made lewd advances to fellow prisoners, claimed to be guilty of murder, and generally acted irritable and deranged. Finally, tiring of the constant trouble he was causing, the jailer convinced a judge to charge Kelly with insanity and got him sent to the federal hospital in Washington, D.C., where he remained for several months. According to the records at the hospital, he was an extremely troublesome prisoner, going into fits of insanity, attacking attendants and patients, and screaming out profanity. He also had a habit of hiding food in his pockets and in his room, but with no apparent plans to eat it. As time passed, though, he seemed to calm down and eventually, he was released.

After his release, he was sent back to Sioux Falls and indicted in federal court on the obscenity charges. Soon after, the indictment was dismissed because of his mental condition. He was paroled into the custody of a "gentleman in Sioux City, Iowa."

His condition had not improved much, although he no longer seemed to be raving mad. He did make several overtures to young women, asking them to pose nude for him, and for this, he was arrested again and taken back to Sioux Falls. He remained in jail a brief time and then was released back to Sioux City, where he got into the same trouble over again. During this time, he still continued to talk about the murders in Villisca, but was no longer claiming he committed them. He told the man that he stayed with that the shirt he had taken to the laundry had been stained with blood as the result of a shaving accident.

After he left Sioux City, Kelly went back to work preaching in Sutton, Nebraska. A doctor that knew him in Sutton later testified that he would often come into his office and nervously inquire about strangers in town and whether or not they were detectives. Witnesses also testified about Kelly wandering about the city at night – just as he had done on a dark night in Villisca in June 1912.

20. REAPING THE WHIRLWIND
WILKERSON AND THE SUMMER OF THE STORM

The news release sent out by Attorney General Havner was essentially a summary of all of the incriminating evidence that had been gathered by the grand jury. There was plenty in it for A.L. Sutton, acting as Kelly's attorney, to be upset about. He threatened to have the attorney general charged with violating the Thompson Law and let the press know that there were other things going on that he believed were unfair to Kelly. The warrant for Kelly directed him to be imprisoned in Des Moines pending trial, which Sutton strongly disagreed with. At the preliminary hearing after Kelly's arrest, Sutton pleaded with the court to keep him in Red Oak, or at least within the judicial district, instead of taking him to Des Moines, which was 130 miles away. It was too far, Sutton said, for Kelly to have reasonable access to his lawyers and far too convenient for Havner and his state agents. Sutton used the hearing to not only try and convince the court to change the jail where Kelly was held, but also to disparage the prosecution. Wilkerson's many supporters packed the courtroom and loved every minute of Sutton's diatribe. Their applause and laughter whenever they felt that Sutton had scored a point against the prosecutors caused Judge Woodruff, who had tired of Wilkerson in the past and had sent him to jail once for contempt, to warn that he would clear the courtroom if their antics continued.

Havner explained to the court that he had asked Kelly to be incarcerated in Des Moines because a number of people had recently broken out of the Montgomery County Jail. The facility in Des Moines was the best constructed and cleanest in the state and was a better place for a high profile prisoner like Kelly. He was concerned, he said, that someone might try and take the law into his own hands, and keeping Kelly out of the county seemed to be the best course of action. Havner stated that he had no objections to other jails in the judicial district, but did not want it to be Council Bluffs, which was the home of Kelly's lawyers.

Red Oak attorney Thomas Hysham, who had represented Wilkerson when he tried to get his bill paid by the county, was included in the defense team. He brought up the charge that Havner had broken his own law about influencing the public when he released his statement about Kelly. He also mentioned the claims about how Havner had grilled the witnesses during the previous grand jury, reiterating the fact that he could not be trusted to legitimately practice the law. He suggested that the real reason that the attorney general wanted to keep Kelly in Des Moines was so state agents could "break down his mind and put him in an asylum." Both Hysham and Sutton pressed the judge for a speedy trial.

Judge Woodruff heard both sides and ruled that Kelly would be held in Logan, a city about 80 miles northwest of Red Oak. He did not set a date for the trial, but promised that he would soon. Kelly's defense team made no objection to relocating him to the county jail in Logan, but they were perhaps unaware that one of Havner's best agents, James Risden, lived in Logan. Risden would, in the months to come, spend more than a little time with Kelly.

Wilkerson was not present at the hearing. He had remained in Chicago for a few days after Sutton and the Kellys left for Red Oak. When he returned to Iowa, he stopped in Des Moines and realized that his growing celebrity status had extended beyond Montgomery County when the local press sought him out. Wilkerson, who was always happy to get his name in the newspapers, told reporters that he didn't believe the charges against Reverend Kelly. He also said that he had quit the detective business and planned to practice law in Red Oak. He had already started the paperwork that was necessary for him to make an application to the Iowa bar, but he apparently had not taken into consideration how he was going to get approved, considering the animosity that existed between him and the state attorney general. Wilkerson did open an office in Red Oak, but he did not actually practice law -- not in the conventional sense, anyway. For the remainder of 1917, he used the office as a base of operations for the Kelly defense team, and in 1918, it became the headquarters for his own run for elected office.

The Kelly trial was set to begin on June 18, but a few days before, the state filed for a continuance until September. In his motion, Havner acknowledged that the authorities had not been actively seeking Kelly immediately after the indictment because they were not ready to go to trial. Kelly had come in demanding to be arrested, which caught them off guard. It was a complex case, he said, involved a five-year-old crime and the prosecution needed more time to prepare. Havner also said that Faville, who would continue to serve as special counsel for the state, was scheduled to have surgery and would not be available until sometime in July. In addition, Havner had to spend June fulfilling his duties as chairman of the board of examiners that reviewed applicants for admission to the state bar. As if those reasons weren't enough to justify a delay, Havner was also having trouble locating one of his witnesses. This person was out of state, but was expected to return in early July.

Not surprisingly, Sutton objected to a continuance. Kelly was in poor health, he said, and had already been confined for six weeks. It was the state's own negligence that caused them to be unprepared for trial, and it should not be delayed.

The judge disagreed and the continuance was granted. The public was disappointed, but there would be plenty of things to keep them engaged in the coming months, including the arrest of Wilkerson at the end of June.

One Saturday morning around 9 a.m., he was arrested in Red Oak and then taken before a judge in Corning, in nearby Adams County. He posted bond and returned to Red Oak in time for one of his meetings at the Beardsley Theater. When he arrived at the theater, the law was waiting for him again. As soon as he took the stage, Sheriff Dunn served an injunction to restrain him from talking about the Kelly case in a public meeting. The injunction was something that Wilkerson and his lawyers considered to be a first amendment issue, one that he would use to gain sympathy from his supporters, but the initial arrest was another matter.

The arrest had to do with the attempted break-in at the Jones store, which took place just before the grand jury proceedings began in late February. The authorities had little doubt that Wilkerson was behind it. It was probably Jones' private detective, J.H. Moore, who tipped off Frank and Albert. But regardless of how they found out, they knew the burglary was coming and stood guard at the store for several nights in a row. When the bungled attempt occurred, it was just a matter of putting together the details to pin the crime on the detective. Wilkerson later claimed that his objective with the break-in was to obtain evidence for the grand jury, which he said was hidden in Jones' safe, but Jones believed that Wilkerson had a different motivation.

A couple of weeks before the burglary, Wilkerson met with a police officer in Atlantic whom he knew and trusted. He told him that he was looking for someone to "do a job" and was referred to Ed "Brick" Boiler, 25, who had a criminal record and a collection of burglary tools. Wilkerson, according to Boiler's subsequent confession, told him that he had a job for him, gave him $15 and promised him $100 when the job was completed. They traveled to Red Oak and met in Wilkerson's room at the Johnson Hotel. There, Wilkerson talked extensively about the Villisca case, why he thought Jones was guilty, and what Boiler's role would be in bringing the former senator to justice. Boiler said that not only did Wilkerson assure him that the break-in was legitimate detective work, and if arrested he would be released when it became known that he was acting as a detective, but that Wilkerson offered to make him a full-time Burns operative if the plan worked out. Wilkerson also solicited Boiler to make a side trip to see Harry Whipple and present him with a story that Wilkerson hoped would cause Whipple to make an admission of guilt.

Boiler spent a couple of days in Villisca and Red Oak and then went back to Atlantic to recruit an assistant for the break-in, a pal named William "Squint" Walker. The two cased the Jones store, buying a couple of small pieces of hardware from Albert, and then set a date for the burglary, which was postponed when Wilkerson missed his train out of Red Oak. He told the two burglars that he needed to get out of town before they broke in, so he could establish an alibi for himself. Of course, they should have wondered why Wilkerson needed an alibi if what they were doing was perfectly legal, but if they wondered, they apparently didn't ask. They planned the break-in to occur on the night of February 27.

While waiting for the date to arrive, they recruited another friend, 17-year-old Harry "Red" Nave, who traveled with them to meet Wilkerson in Corning on

February 26. They spent the night there, going over details and making final plans. Wilkerson would provide them with a car and a revolver, and then, when they reached Villisca, they were supposed to capture the night watchman and lock him up in the town jail. That way, they could break into the store without interference. Boiler supposedly knew how to crack a safe, and they were supposed to take whatever documents were inside.

On the evening of February 27, Nave and Walker remained in Corning, while Wilkerson and Boiler took the train to Creston, about 25 miles to the west. The complexity of this ridiculous plan was typical of Wilkerson, who came up with schemes that had as many twists and turns as those that he attributed to others. Instead of just giving the gun to Boiler, he put it in a suitcase and placed it in the car that the burglars were supposed to use. He didn't even take Boiler to the car. He just told him where to find it. As Boiler left for Corning, Wilkerson set up his own alibi by checking into a Creston hotel. Boiler made it to Corning around 11 p.m., picked up his accomplices, and headed for Villisca.

During the dark drive to Villisca, the three would-be burglars began getting nervous about the scheme. Nave and Walker didn't know it, but as they neared the town of Nodaway, Boiler tried to abort the plan by flooding the engine of their rickety Maxwell automobile. He worked in a garage and knew how to do it without causing suspicion. He could cancel the plan and no one would find out about the uneasiness that he was feeling. His friends, who rode in nervous silence, likely would have gone along without question. But whatever he tried to do with the choke and accelerator didn't work and the car puttered on through Nodaway. Not far outside of town, Boiler took a wrong turn and lost the Villisca road. They had to turn around and backtrack. They got back on course, and then the car ran out of gas. It was nearly 2 a.m. when Walker and Boiler started walking back to Nodaway to look for gas. They found a building with a gas pump out front, got the proprietor out of bed, and borrowed a can of gasoline. It was nearly 4 a.m. when they finally reached Villisca. None of them wanted to seem like cowards, but they all knew things were not going well.

And things were about to get worse. There were three men with shotguns waiting inside the Jones store.

They parked the Maxwell on the north side of town and walked to the square, keeping an eye out for the night watchman. Boiler held the revolver, tightly gripping it in his pocket. He was determined to go through with the plan, but was glad that they didn't see the watchman. They needed to get into the store, get out with the documents, and get on their way. They approached the front of the store and looked around. No one was on the street. No one was watching. The plan was to quickly jimmy open the door, but if they couldn't do it, they would break the glass on the back door in the alley. As he stepped up to the front door, Boiler thought he saw someone at the window but when he turned on his flashlight, no one was there. The reason he didn't see anyone was because town Marshall Hank Horton, who had been waiting in a chair by the window, saw the three men and quickly ducked out of the way. He alerted Albert Jones, who had been watching the back door.

Horton had his shotgun in hand and was about to return to the front door when two of the burglars arrived at the rear. Boiler had decided that the front door was too exposed and had continued around the side of the building, still looking out for the watchman. He waited at the entrance to the alley, telling Walker and Nave that he would keep watch until they got the door open. As the two reached the window that they intended to break, Horton raised his weapon. Unaware that anyone was inside, the two burglars pressed their faces to the glass, shining their flashlight around the interior of the store. Suddenly, they realized that they were looking down the barrel of a shotgun! Horton, at point-blank range, pulled the trigger – and the gun misfired. Walker and Nave, terrified that they were about to be shot, ran away down the alley, shoving past Boiler and flailing madly as they tried to get away. Horton had no chance to get off another shot.

Albert and Horton gave chase, but first they went to the jail, thinking that the night watchman had been locked up. This was what was supposed to happen according to the plan that they had been tipped off to. The watchman, a man named Greaves, wasn't there and didn't show up until later. Most likely, he made himself scarce, not liking the idea of being locked up by men with guns. Not finding Greaves where they thought he would be, Albert and Horton started searching for the burglars on their own. A few minutes later, a car that Albert recognized as a Maxwell came toward them down the street. They chased the auto on foot and almost got off a shot when Boiler turned into a dead-end alley and had to back out. The car sped north past the square, where the driver got his bearings and sped out of town in the direction they had come from. They refueled, dropped off the gas can in Nodaway, and arrived in Creston around 7 a.m.

Wilkerson, roused from bed, was disappointed when he heard their story. He purchased train tickets for Nave and Walker, and went with them to Red Oak. Nave went from there to Atlantic, while Walker was given $5 to go to Villisca and hang around for a few days to see what the talk was about the attempted break-in. Boiler, as had been arranged, took the car and went in search of Harry Whipple. After finding him, he told Whipple what Wilkerson had coached him to say: that he had been seen on the streets of Villisca on the night of the murders, that detectives had the goods on him, and he had better talk.

Whipple may not have been the murderous outlaw that his sister, Vina Tompkins, had made him out to be, but he was a rough, rather sinister character from a tough little town called Carbon, a coal mining community reputed to be home to some of the hardest men in the state. He was also an amateur wrestler who took on anyone in the days when brutal, no-holds-barred matches were held in the street. Whether Whipple's reputation as a tough guy had anything to do with Wilkerson sending Boiler to confront him rather than going himself is unknown, but the strategy didn't work out. Whipple glared at the young man, told him that he had no idea what he was talking about, and suggested that he get the hell out of town. Boiler quickly went, probably realizing that he was lucky to have left Carbon in one piece. He decided that he would rather go back to being a mechanic than become a detective, so he returned the borrowed car and caught a train for home.

Wilkerson told the three failed burglars to keep silent about the botched crime, but the need to share the details of their adventure was too great for them to stand. Within days, authorities in Atlantic had heard about what had happened. There is no clue as to why it took nearly four months for an arrest warrant to be issued, but perhaps it was because so many other things were taking place at the same time. Iowa state agent Rock spent a little time on the case, but detectives hired by Jones did most of the actual work. Havner's busy schedule kept him from delving into the issue for some time and when he did, he had to admit that the case was not as black and white as Jones considered it to be. Even though the law didn't go as far as Wilkerson had stretched it, it did give private detectives considerable latitude when seeking to obtain evidence. Havner and Faville agreed that getting a Montgomery County judge to convict Wilkerson of the break-in attempt would be difficult. They also knew that any legal action against him would give him the opportunity to tell the press, the courts, and the public that Jones was guilty of murder and that he was being thwarted in his efforts to prove it. But Havner was blinded by dislike when it came to Wilkerson and he moved ahead. He planned on exercising the Thompson Law against him too, so why not pursue a burglary charge as well?

On June 26, Frank and Albert Jones and their wives, along with Hank Horton, traveled to Des Moines. They were there for two days, spending at least part of that time at the attorney general's office. What happened behind closed doors is unknown, but shortly afterwards, Havner moved ahead on the criminal case against Wilkerson and the arrests soon followed. Havner, hoping to avoid the problem of Wilkerson's popularity in Montgomery County, figured out a way to file the charge in Adams County. Wilkerson and the three men from Atlantic had spent the night before the burglary in Corning devising their plan, so the attorney general opted to charge them for conspiracy to commit burglary in Adams County.

Walker, Nave and Boiler were rounded up. Once in custody, they not only confessed, but talked openly about what had taken place to newspaper reporters. With confessions in hand, Havner and Rock went to Corning and secured a warrant for Wilkerson.

The preliminary hearing was held in Corning on July 9, and a bitter battle began between Havner and Wilkerson. With Judge Shepard presiding, Wilkerson waived the preliminary examination, meaning that he would not testify or question witnesses. This left everything to Havner, who planned to examine his prosecution witnesses and then send the case to the grand jury. Frank Jones was one of the main witnesses and he testified as to the contents of his safe, which had been Wilkerson's target with the break-in. He listed everything that it contained in a three-page document, including many items that would have proved embarrassing to Wilkerson, including court papers from Wilkerson's divorce case; charges against John W. Noel for theft and a case against him for slander; letters about Wilkerson's behavior during the Nellie Byers case; a letter from the police chief of Blue Island, Illinois, clearing William Mansfield of murder; and a stack of correspondence, reports and photographs that were used as investigative tools against Wilkerson. There was nothing in the safe that might have incriminated

Jones, but plenty that made Wilkerson look bad.

After the final witness testified, Havner concluded by reminding the court that Wilkerson had waived preliminary examination and, therefore, did not have the right to make oral arguments in court that day. At this, Wilkerson jumped to his feet with a cry, accusing the attorney general of violating his rights. Wilkerson's supporters cheered and applauded, only quieting when Wilkerson indicated that he wanted to continue. He disparaged Havner and, as usual, accused him of a cover-up. When Havner stood up to object, Justice Shepard silenced him, stating that not only did the audience want to hear what Wilkerson had to say, he wanted to hear it himself. At that moment, Havner must have wondered if he had made the right decision in orchestrating the case to be heard in Adams County.

Wilkerson went on at length. At one point, he walked over to where Frank Jones sat in the gallery and shook his finger in his face. He thundered, "Who is Frank Jones that he has got so great that it becomes a crime to try and get evidence that he has been responsible for the murder of eight innocent citizens of Iowa, that he can evoke the mighty arm of the state of Iowa?"

Havner again objected to the court allowing Wilkerson to continue, but Shepard, now regretting that he opened the door, was unable to close it. Urged on by a cheering crowd, Wilkerson continued to ridicule Havner, state agents, and many officials of Montgomery County, claiming that they were part of a political scheme to protect their friend, Frank Jones. At one point, Jones rose to his feet and looked as though he planned to confront Wilkerson, but Havner intervened. Then Albert jumped from his seat and went for Wilkerson, intent on pummeling the smirking detective. Havner grabbed him around the chest and held him back. The courtroom was in chaos and Havner shouted over the din to ask the judge if they were in a court of law, or in the midst of a vaudeville routine. Wilkerson continued on and Havner, realizing that Shepard had lost control, gave up, sat down, and waited for the tirade to run its course. When it did, 30 minutes later, the judge bound the case over for the grand jury. Wilkerson had lost. Bond was set at $1,000. "Fix it for $10,000!" shouted Wilkerson's money man, Ed Peterson, who was standing nearby with his checkbook in his hand.

After Wilkerson was taken into custody, it was John Noel who drove to Corning to be there when he was released and then rush him to Red Oak in time for the meeting at the Beardsley Theater. When the meeting began, Sheriff Dunn walked onto the stage and served an injunction, prohibiting the event under the provisions of the Thompson Law.

The injunction was issued following a petition filed by Havner in a second strike against Wilkerson. In the petition, he pointed out that the detective had conferred with Reverend Kelly in St. Louis and a few days later in Alto Pass, where he informed the minister that an indictment had been issued. Havner then detailed how Wilkerson had paid many of Kelly's bills and, using the name F.F. Jones, paid to have his possessions shipped to a storage site in Kansas City. He accused Wilkerson of paying for the relocation of Kelly and his wife to a hotel in Chicago, as well. He also stated that Wilkerson's meetings had been arranged to influence grand juries, that the detective had broken into Wenstrand's office and had taken files and records that pertained to the grand jury and that he had made threats and had tried to improperly intimidate and influence those who would be assigned to the jury, as well as witnesses, during the Kelly trial. Havner asked that Wilkerson be barred from holding the public meeting on Saturday, June 30, 1917, and be further restrained from any action that would improperly "influence, obstruct or impede the due administration of justice."

Sheriff Dunn handed the injunction to Wilkerson, who read the two pages signed by Judge Woodruff out loud to the audience. Wilkerson announced that he was not one to violate the law, asked the chairman to continue the meeting, and left the stage.

Havner had beaten him not once but twice. The attorney general finally had the Thompson Law serving the purpose that it had been created for – controlling the actions of James Wilkerson. But the wily detective was not finished yet.

Not surprisingly, he managed to use the injunction to his advantage. He left the stage when the document was served, but he immediately made it clear that he was being unfairly victimized. The meeting went on, and before it was over, $700 had been collected for Kelly's defense fund. Wilkerson and a few of his closest supporters – Peterson, Noel, Stillinger, Miller, and Ross Moore – arranged for a meeting in Omaha the next Saturday. All week long, flyers were circulated stating that there was "no gag rule in Nebraska." Over 1,000 attended the Omaha meeting, although few of them traveled from Montgomery County and southwest Iowa. A special train had been booked, but it was canceled when not enough tickets were sold.

The meeting was opened with a prayer from Reverend Ewing and then Joseph Stillinger took the stage. Part of his performance that night may have been theatrics since he had, after all, been part of Wilkerson's stage show since the beginning, but there is little doubt that Stillinger was a different man in 1917 than he had been in 1912. On the stage in Omaha, he often broke down in tears and spoke emotionally to the audience about waving goodbye to his two little girls as they went off to church that morning. He presented a far different picture than the miserly, profane, and work-driven man that the first detectives in Villisca had found him to be. He had never been one to show emotion but the tragic death of his two daughters and the growing realization that no one would ever be punished for the crime had changed him. He sobbed audibly as he spoke, taking long pauses as he fought to regain his composure. On the stage that day, the rough Iowa farmer made an indelible impression on the crowd.

The rest of the meeting was typical, with Wilkerson ranting on stage for two hours about the "petty tyrant" Havner and how, by indicting Reverend Kelly, he was "trying to railroad a poor nut." The show went on and on, continuing the now-familiar theme of the Frank Jones murder conspiracy. Wilkerson closed the evening with a plea for contributions and volunteers passed around collection plates. The city folks may have found the performance entertaining, but one reporter wrote that when the hat was passed "the audience melted away like mist before a morning sun."

The presentation in Omaha raised very little money -- not even enough to cover expenses -- and so Wilkerson decided to take the meetings back to Iowa. In the new legal climate, he was careful about the injunction – at least in the beginning. He did not personally speak about Reverend Kelly, starting the first few meetings by speaking about justice and fairness and then turned any talk about a frame-up of Kelly to other speakers. He later told his supporters that he had found a loophole in the Thompson Law, which he called the "Wilkerson Law" and sometimes the "Stop Wilkerson Law," and said that he didn't think Havner could enforce it. He may have been right, because as the meetings continued, he became bolder and bolder in his remarks, stirring up public opinion like he had never done before, but he was never arrested for it.

Soon, Wilkerson began formalizing an organization, appointing officers, adopting an oath and, of course, requiring a $10 membership fee to join. Oddly, by then, the entire organization had become more about the Villisca murders *not* being solved. If the killer was caught, the group would dissolve and the cash flow would end. The whole purpose of the meetings, lectures, and endless pursuit of the murderer had been turned on its ear.

The money collected was supposed to go toward the defense of Reverend Kelly, but it was supporting Wilkerson, as well. Notes taken by the group's secretary tell of large, enthusiastic crowds who pledged money and joined the group, making the required donation. Hundreds of dollars poured in, although at one meeting on July 21, only 30 people attended, so the membership fee for that night was lowered to $2.

In late July, Wilkerson began posing his "100 Questions" to the crowd. This was a list of questions that he had created much earlier in the investigation that he demanded that Frank Jones answer. They had been edited and altered by 1917, but mostly dealt with the murder conspiracy and cover-up that he claimed that Jones was involved in. The questions were all couched in such a way as to imply guilt, and Wilkerson twisted them to his own devices.

The questions became a staple in his new Iowa show. He made sure that they were widely repeated and talked about, not only to spite Jones and Havner, but to get them into people's minds on the eve of the Kelly trial. It was a relatively safe way for him to convey his message because making a statement accusing someone of criminal conduct was potentially more difficult to defend from legal action than asking a question – no matter how inflammatory that question might be. He refused to actually print the list for distribution and thanks to this, the questions were often changed and re-worded.

Wilkerson's "100 Questions" were popular with his followers, but at least a few newspaper editors were beginning to perceive his entire campaign as outrageously prejudicial. The largest and most influential newspaper in the region, the *Des Moines Register & Leader*, had taken Wilkerson's side on the Thompson Law, pointing out that it was aimed at one individual and was a violation of freedom of speech, but it took a dim view of the "100 Questions." The newspaper published an editorial urging the public to condemn Wilkerson's actions as a detective, "for never in the history of crime was pursuit of anybody conducted in this way by a sane man who had honest motives."

Wilkerson, of course, didn't let up. He liked the format of his new show so much that he prepared another 100 questions for Havner and had them printed in pamphlet form, which he sold for a dime apiece. The questions for Havner were just as suggestive, misleading, self-important, and senseless as those that had been written for Frank Jones.

When Wilkerson read them aloud to the delighted crowds that packed his presentations, the audiences stood and cheered. In the various meetings, night after night, Wilkerson hammered out his message: that Frank Jones had planned the murders and hired the killers; that corrupt county and state officials, including the county attorney, two attorneys general, and other elected officials going all of the way to the governor's office were protecting Jones; that Reverend Kelly was being framed only because Wilkerson was onto the Jones' conspiracy and convicting the minister was the only way to clear Jones of the crime.

By this time, other newspapers were starting to get wind of Wilkerson's antics and roundly condemned them. Kelly's arrest, and the approach of what promised to be a sensational trial, had attracted media attention from all over the Midwest. With downtime between the arrest and trial, the reporters had little else to cover but Wilkerson's meetings. The local newspapers, with subscribers on both sides of the issue, tried to remain neutral, but those outside of Montgomery County began to finally express what they had been thinking for quite some time.

In July 1917, the *Storm Lake Pilot-Tribune* wrote: "Wilkerson will not be accused of being ashamed of himself. So much of his stuff is so utterly silly that it would not be given credence except by those who are living under the spell of extreme excitement. The situation in Villisca and Red Oak is as terrible as it is absurd. Wilkerson should be banished."

The *Shelby County Republican* published their own editorial: "That Wilkerson fellow who has been on the Villisca murder case a few years ought to be jailed or retired. He is acting dead wrong. The place to try murder cases is in a courtroom before a judge and a jury – not in an Omaha opera house... All Wilkerson's talk is bosh and an outrage against Jones, the courts, the juries, the attorneys, the legislature, and the state of Iowa. Wilkerson ought to be made to put up or shut up."

F.A. Turner, the editor of the *Avoca Journal-Herald,* added: "While every good citizen is and should be most deeply interested in the punishment of the Villisca ax murderer or murderers, a condition has arisen down in Montgomery County that every good citizen should and does deplore. And it is a condition for which there is no excuse. It seems to be the results of one J.N. Wilkerson who claims to be a detective... the sooner the state rids itself of him the better it will be, for not only Montgomery County but the whole state of Iowa. He seems to have woven a lot of circumstances together and labeled them evidence in establishing the guilt of a well-known citizen of that county. Some of these circumstances bear evidence of fabrication and should be accepted with a great deal of allowance. But Wilkerson does not seem to possess the kind of mind that can do this. And the result is that he now seems to be putting himself in the position of one who tries to justify his acts and conclusions by questionable methods, such as appealing to the passions and prejudices of those who, regardless of his shortcomings, impose confidence in him, a confidence that he could not have obtained under ordinary circumstances... Wilkerson should be eliminated, and the people of the state should firmly demand it. If he is acting in good faith he has lost his usefulness by his foolish and unreasonable conduct."

The editorial that ran in the *Massena Echo* ran about a week before the Kelly trial began called Wilkerson a statewide disgrace: "The greatest disgrace that has ever fallen upon southwestern Iowa is the present "rage" of Detective Wilkerson, whose activity in the Villisca ax murder mystery has now assumed the aspect of a real menace to that community.... Wilkerson's activities should be stopped at once, before more murders are committed, and before some crazy firebugs begin their work. It ought to be possible to convict and punish the man or men who committed the terrible ax murders. But it can't be done by the methods of Detective Wilkerson. He had decided who is guilty and is now trying to work up a lot of ignorant prejudice and feeling to insure his success in sending to the gallows men whom he does not like and who seem to stand in Wilkerson's way of getting a big money consideration for convicting someone of this heinous crime. Let the courts of justice decide this case. The people's sentiment – after being manufactured as Wilkerson is manufacturing it – is of no value at all and is only a menace to the welfare of the community. It is assuming the proportions of a statewide disgrace."

The *Des Moines Register*, which had already criticized Wilkerson, added more fuel to the fire by coming out in defense of Havner and former Attorney General George Cosson: "That both these men would violate their official oath to shield anybody for such an offense as the killing at Villisca is so absurd that it needs only to be suggested to be condemned."

Wilkerson continued to hold his meetings right up to the time of the trial. He took the show to dozens of small towns, and if the numbers kept by his cronies were accurate, he was heard by as many as 10,000 people between July 17, and August 13. Jones' mysterious "J.H." was still on the payroll and was still working as a news reporter and an undercover agent within Wilkerson's camp. He attended many of the meetings and passed the news to Jones and then to Havner that people were becoming more inflamed and more enraged by Wilkerson's speeches. There was good reason for the concern about violence breaking out, as noted by some of the newspaper editorials of the time. There seemed to be no way to find an impartial jury for the Kelly trial.

Special prosecutor Frederick Faville, who had been operated on at the Mayo Clinic and then sent to Colorado Springs to recuperate, was using his time to prepare for the trial. On August 17, he wrote Havner, conveyed his thoughts about the "100 Questions," and expressed a belief that the trial was likely lost before it even began. He wrote:

I have no doubt that the Wilkerson sentiment is on the increase. This kind of proceeding is the most subtle and insidious that he could possibly think of. The form of question is the old resort of the slanderer who claims that he makes no charge for which he can be called to account by merely asking questions. He knows that he cannot be indicted for libel for this form of writing unless he makes some statement with sufficient innuendo to charge a crime and of course this he is careful to avoid.

Now as to the thing to do – I dislike to express an opinion definitely without going over the situation with you. One thing I am quite convinced of is that a conviction of Kelly in that county is an impossibility, unless some miracle happens. But I do not think we are responsible for what a jury may do with the evidence in the Kelly case, if we present it all fully and fairly as possible.

Faville also advised Havner about what to do with Wilkerson and the Thompson Law:

What he wants to do is draw you into a controversy and make it a personal matter between you and him, and he thinks he is "solid" in Montgomery County, which is probably the case. I do not think it is advisable to use the new law against him. The court might hold that it would not apply merely to the asking of questions of an officer. If the court should refuse an injunction it would place you in a bad situation and I do not think I would try it. Even if you enjoined him, it might do more harm than good.

Wilkerson's meetings continued and Havner simmered over them, but he followed Faville's advice. According to the treasurer's accounts from Wilkerson's organization, the detective was being paid $5 per day during the summer of 1917, plus ten cents per mile and all of the proceeds from the sale of the pamphlets. There were also a few other incidental expenses, but revenue exceeding those expenses was supposed to be set aside for the Kelly defense fund. It was no surprise that questions would be raised later about where all of the money had gone.

The trial was set to begin on September 4, and as the date got closer, the grand jury was back to work again. Because some of those called were witnesses in the Wilkerson slander trial, rumor had it that new evidence was being heard. This was not the case. The jury was actually hearing about testimony from an earlier session, namely claims by Alice Willard that Attorney General Havner had tried to get her to change her testimony. Havner knew what was happening with the grand jury and could only hope for the best.

Letters written by Havner before the trail indicate that he truly believed Reverend Kelly was guilty, but he knew there were problems other than those started by Wilkerson. He could prove opportunity, the bloody shirt and the testimony that Kelly had talked about the murders before they were discovered. He could also show that Kelly was a pervert with an unhealthy interest in young girls, that he walked the streets at night and that he liked peeking in windows. He could also produce witnesses who would tell of the minister trying to get girls to pose nude for him and prisoners who claimed Kelly had groped them and tried to perform oral sex on them. He could also show that Kelly was obsessed with the ax murders, had spoken about them continuously over the years, and even claimed to have committed them on various occasions.

But he knew there was no way that he could prove the substance on Kelly's shirt had been blood, or even if the shirt belonged to the minister. The five-year period between the murders and the trial posed obvious problems, since witnesses were bound to remember things differently. Former Sherriff Jackson and former County Attorney Ratcliff were expected to testify and both of them would say that they had looked closely into Kelly and found no reason to charge him.

Havner also had to deal with the fact that several Villisca residents had gotten onto the train with Kelly on the morning after the murders and none of them saw blood on his clothing, or heard him talk about the murders. It was only after Kelly changed trains at Henderson that he allegedly talked about the crime and made his incriminating "slay and slay utterly" statement. He was also aware that even though Kelly was obviously disturbed, it was going to be hard to prove he was a murderer. Just because Havner believed it, it didn't mean that he could convince a jury.

It was not a strong case and given the mood of Montgomery County residents that year, Havner knew his chances were as poor as Faville depicted them. He needed something else and even though it was a risk, he decided to take a chance.

According to Special Agent Risden, Sheriff Myers, Deputy Atkins, and the prisoner who shared Kelly's cell at the jail in Logan, Kelly was ready to confess to the Villisca murders. He had already made several verbal admissions, but wanted a promise from the attorney general before signing a full confession. Havner really wasn't in a position to offer Kelly anything but a trial, plus there was a major problem for Havner if he heard his confession. The grand jury was already considering an indictment against him for coercing Alice Willard and Havner knew full well how his obtaining a confession from Kelly would be seen. But he was trying to find the miracle that Faville told him it would take to get a conviction, so he had little choice but to follow through.

At that point in his career, Havner was considering a run for governor. First, though, he needed to get re-elected in 1918. He was making as many public appearances as his schedule permitted and was slated to be in Magnolia, a few miles from Logan, for an Old Settlers' picnic on August 30. Havner contacted Risden a few days in advance of his trip and preparations were made at the jail. Risden assured the attorney general that Kelly was ready to confess and Havner was determined to get everything into the record. After Havner's speech in Magnolia, he went to Logan and met Reverend Kelly for the first time. A court reporter named Fannie Longman was on hand and Havner had attorney J.J. Hess and another court reporter brought in from Council Bluffs. Paul Roadifer, the Harrison County Attorney, was present, along with Sheriff Myers and Agent Risden.

The questioning of Kelly began around 10:30 p.m. and continued through the night. Hess and the second court reporter, J.J. Ferguson, arrived at 2:30 a.m. The entire session was taken down in shorthand and later transcribed. When it finally ended, Roadifer, with Risden doing most of the dictating, typed up Kelly's admission. Kelly read it, made some corrections, watched it being retyped and then signed it. His signature was notarized by County Clerk Lynn J. Irwin.

Reverend Kelly had just confessed to one of the most horrendous murders in Iowa history and the long nightmare was finally over --- or at least that's what Attorney General Havner thought at the time.

21. TRIAL BY JURY
THE MURDER TRIAL OF REVEREND KELLY

Reverend Kelly was brought from Logan to Red Oak on September 3. Representing him was Thomas J. Hysham of Red Oak, A.L. Sutton of Omaha, John A. McKenzie of Omaha, and William E. Mitchell of Council Bluffs. At the prosecution table were Attorney General Horace Havner, County Attorney Wenstrand, Frederick Faville, and J.J. Hess of Council Bluffs. Hess had been added to the team on the suggestion of Faville, who feared that his own health issues might interfere with the trial. Hess was a good trial attorney and Faville had asked Havner to add him to the team a few weeks before. The judge presiding over the trial was W.D. Boise of Sheldon. Iowa's Chief Justice Frank R. Gaynor had gone outside of the judicial district when he assigned the trial, choosing Judge Boise because he had a reputation for running a fair and tight proceeding. Everyone was well aware of the attention the trial was going to get and the way that related hearings had gotten out of control in other courtrooms. The chief justice thought Boise could handle any problems that came about.

Just as jury selection was getting started on September 4, Attorney General Havner was arrested on a grand jury indictment charging him with "oppressing" Alice Willard as a witness. Havner's arrest on the first day of a high profile trial was not a good sign, but he had no choice but to push ahead. He was in the delicate position of trying to convince the people from which the jury would be made up that Kelly's confession had been fairly obtained while still dealing with the fact that he had been arrested for tampering with another witness. He posted a $1,000 bond and went back to work. Perhaps hoping to keep attention away from his own situation, he decided to speak with reporters about Kelly's confession.

Risden would later state that Kelly had welcomed the opportunity to confess and Roadifer agreed. All of those present at the confession – with the exception of Kelly – later swore that no grilling, no third degree, no promises, and no threats were made at any time. Both court reporters, along with their transcripts, supported this, but Kelly's lawyers painted a very different picture of the treatment of their client.

When the cluster of reporters camping at the Red Oak courthouse heard the news of a confession, they went into a frenzy. But Kelly's defense team heard about it before the reporters did and they were stunned. John McKenzie was the first of Kelly's lawyers to meet with him after the admission, and when he left the minister's cell, he was quick to announce that the confession had been retracted. McKenzie said that Kelly told him he had been given the third degree by Havner and six others all Thursday night and Friday morning and he had finally broken down at almost 4 a.m. He claimed that Kelly had been told that a lynch mob was waiting for him in Montgomery County, but there were 20,000 National Guard soldiers that would save him in Des Moines if he confessed. He also said that Kelly begged to have his attorneys present, but was denied.

Sutton, after meeting with Kelly, said almost the same thing, telling the press that Havner had threatened Kelly with lynching and only promised to protect him if he confessed. He said that Kelly had been sick, unable to eat, and that he was in a weakened state when Havner and the others took him from his cell and frightened him into reading the statements of 85 witnesses who were going to appear against him. Kelly was completely innocent, Sutton said, the confession was worthless.

Defense attorney William Mitchell agreed that the confession was laughable. He said that the minister once told him that he had sunk the *Lusitania* and that, given the right time and place, Kelly would confess to anything. He said Havner should have known better. Kelly obviously had a number of problems and his confession should never have been taken seriously.

With Kelly's confession now discarded and the prosecution's case in shambles, the opening days of the trial did not go well. But the defense suffered, too. Juror after juror was questioned, challenged, and excused. The prosecutors asked every prospective jurist if they had attended any of Wilkerson's meetings, or had been otherwise influenced, and found very few who had not. Wilkerson had spread his message far and wide, and finding an unbiased juror was just as difficult as Faville had predicted it would be. Judge Boise was tough on both sides, but he took special time to admonish Wilkerson, who was more animated than the judge thought he should be at the defense table. By mid-week, the supply of jurors was running low, and it became necessary to draw from the 75 additional names that had been collected just for that reason.

Even with the stern hand of Judge Boise, courtroom disruptions frequently occurred. Sympathetic citizens often crowded around Kelly to shake his hand and offer encouragement. On the first day of jury selection, the judge told the bailiff not to let it happen again. When it did — many times as the week passed — Boise told the bailiff that if he allowed the public to approach Kelly one more time, he'd be replaced by someone "who would do his duty." Unfortunately, Boise used his "one more time" threat far too many times, leading people to suspect that he was not as tough as his reputation had made him out to be. Disruptions continued throughout the trial.

With the confession in tatters, Havner had to rely on other evidence to make his case. The prosecution essentially relied on four points, and during closing arguments, Havner's team would tell the jury that any of the first three, independent of other evidence, was sufficient for a conviction. They had the confession (which Havner maintained was legitimate), testimony that Kelly had talked about the murders before they were discovered, and the bloody shirt. Fourth, they would try to show the jury that Kelly was a pervert with an unnatural lust for young girls. Havner had to be careful with this approach. He was trying to secure the murder conviction of a preacher in the most religious part of the county. He was also maintaining that only a madman was capable of the crimes that had been committed, but that Kelly, who was insane, had been rational and truthful when he confessed.

The biggest issue was that, regardless of the evidence, it was hard for people in small town Iowa during the early 1900s to conceive of anyone committing a crime that was so unspeakably horrible. This was one reason why the conspiracy theory created by Wilkerson captured people's attention in the way that it did. To believe in his story, it was not necessary to believe that Frank Jones himself had taken an ax and bashed out the brains of the sleeping family and their small guests. It was only necessary to accept that he had felt emotions that everyone was capable of -- namely bitterness and anger -- and then allowed his anger to get control of him, starting a chain of events that ended in murder. The killers themselves were faceless strangers – the proverbial "boogeymen"—who had no connection to anyone in southwest Iowa. More than a dozen people were implicated by Wilkerson and it was easier to accept that each played some small role in the whole thing and that no one person was responsible for it all.

Havner's task was to convince a jury, aware of Wilkerson's theory whether they admitted it or not, that the crime was the act of one man. He had to show that Kelly was not just mentally unbalanced, but that on one night in June 1912, his madness, religious fervor, and sick sexual desires caused him to become something other than the frail little man who was sitting slumped over the defense table. Havner and his team would produce witnesses to demonstrate that Kelly, in the years after the murders, was obsessed with the desire to see naked girls and young women, at least one of whom he tried to solicit to pose nude. They would also show that he had a history of window peeping and would walk the streets late at night. They believed that these sexual desires were what pushed him over the edge that night in Villisca. Havner believed that the preacher had left the Ewing home that night, had walked to the Moore house, saw a light in the bedroom window on the first floor and watched the Stillinger girls getting undressed for bed. Either as he was walking up to the window or leaving it, he stumbled onto the ax. He heard voices -- God was talking to him – and as he stood there in the yard, his insanity overwhelmed him. He entered the house carrying the ax, found a lamp and lit it, and took it from room to room, killing everyone inside.

Havner believed that Kelly then returned to the bed of the Stillinger girls and draped cloth over the mirrors. Ina, the youngest was next to the wall. Lena, nearly 12, who was described as physically mature for her age, was on the side closest to the killer. Kelly pulled the covers back, and tugged her body down in the bed. Her nightgown was pulled above her waist and her underwear, if she was wearing any, was taken off and dropped on the floor. Her knees were pulled apart, opening her the way that Kelly needed her to be posed. Kelly then masturbated, or attempted to, and his rage finally passed. But he still had work to do.

He took Lena's underwear from the floor, wiped the blood from his hands and the ax, and then placed the ax next to the wall. He covered his victims with sheets, rinsed his hands in the basin, and wandered about the house, moving and touching items. Finally, putting out the lamp and locking the front door behind him, he departed. Kelly then returned to the Ewing house where he had left his suitcase. He buttoned his coat so that the bloody stains on his shirt were hidden and walked down to the depot to await the arrival of the morning train.

This was Havner's theory, and I believe this is *almost* exactly what happened that night – except for the fact that Kelly was not the one who wielded the ax.

As the prosecution began to put together their case, they had to admit that they couldn't be certain of the exact sequence of events or all of the details of the murderer's acts. No matter how they presented the timeline of that night, the deeds they attributed to Kelly were profound, almost unimaginable. It was going to be hard for the rural jury to believe. Havner could only hope that the image of the crime that he put into the juror's minds – supported by a string of witnesses and Kelly's confession – would be enough to see the man convicted.

He opened the prosecution's case with a number of witnesses who testified to Kelly's obsession with the murders immediately after they happened. They came from almost every town where Kelly had lived between the time of the murders and his indictment. Some claimed that Kelly told them he was a detective investigating the case, others said that he was afraid of strangers that he claimed were detectives on his trail. He told others that he had been the first in the house when the bodies were discovered or that the murderer had left a bloody shirt at the laundry in Council Bluffs. Some testimony even came from South Dakota law enforcement officials who stated that Kelly told them that he had committed the crime.

Max Stempel of Macedonia testified that on the Monday afternoon of the murders, Kelly told him that he had spent the previous night in Villisca, that he had not felt well, went out on the street and heard thumping sounds coming from the house where the murders were committed. He told Stempel that it sounded like someone hitting a pig in the head with an ax."

Havner called witnesses who traveled on the morning train with Kelly who distinctly heard him say that there had been an awful murder in Villisca the night before and that he was going to apply to work on the case as a detective. This was between 7 and 7:30 a.m., an hour or more before the murders were discovered. They weren't alone. A parade of witnesses passed through the courtroom, each of them testifying that Kelly seemed to know about the murders long before news of the discovery had broken.

The impact of most of these witnesses was dampened by cross-examination. Their testimony was weakened by that of others who were present but either hadn't seen Kelly or hadn't heard him speak of the murders until the afternoon. Some of the state witnesses, it was learned, were not even sure of the exact time and date. One of them, an elderly man named Sam Barnett, testified that he'd heard Kelly talking excitedly about the murders that morning in Macedonia, but the defense produced a witness who said Barnett had told him that it was actually much later in the day – or maybe another day altogether. But even under the most intense cross-examination from Mitchell, witnesses on the train that morning stuck to their story of hearing Kelly murmuring "slay and slay utterly." But on what date? They were sure it was a Monday in June, and thought it was the 10th, but Mitchell elicited from them the admission that they could not be completely certain of the date. At this point, good detective work and accurate record keeping by the railroad allowed the prosecution to reinforce the testimony. The witnesses said they had purchased two tickets on the Burlington line that would take them from Sidney to Carson. There were several stops on the way, including one in Hastings, where Kelly left the westbound train to catch a train going north. Records of ticket sales were generally not well kept, but the Sidney depot was apparently the exception. The agent, W.R. Daniels, had sold hundreds of tickets in June 1912, but after going through all of them he found only two that had been purchased on a Monday with a starting point of Sidney and a destination of Carson. Both had been purchased at the same time, early in the morning on June 10. The defense objected to the admission of the records, but Judge Boise overruled it. The best that Mitchell could manage was to get the station agent to say that the ledger entry had been hand written and that whoever wrote it could have made a mistake.

Havner was then ready to offer Kelly's confession. Judge Boise had denied the defense motion to suppress, and so it was slowly and deliberately read to the jury and into the record. Listening in the quiet courtroom, interrupted only by the sobs of Reverend Kelly, even those who felt that he was being framed were forced to reconsider.

In the confession, Kelly detailed his movements in Villisca before the Children's Day program at the church and then spoke of going to stay with the Ewings at their home. Unable to sleep that night, he got out of bed and went outside. He claimed he was working on a sermon on a text called "Slay Utterly." He went over and over it in his mind and as he walked, he claimed that he felt a grip on him that he did not understand. God wanted him to "slay utterly," he believed, but he did not know where he was going or what he was supposed to do. The voice kept calling out to him to "slay utterly" and Kelly replied, "Yes Lord, I will." As he walked, he wandered into a yard and stumbled across as ax. He picked it up and began to call out to a shadow that he believed God had shown him and wanted him to follow. He went to the front door and the voice commanded, "Go in, and do as I tell you; slay utterly." Unable to control himself, he went into the house and followed the voice, walking through rooms and not knowing why he was there – only knowing that he was driven by an impulse and a voice.

Kelly stated that the voice told him, "Suffer the little children to come unto me." Kelly replied, "They are coming, Lord." Before he knew what he was doing, he "started sending those children somewhere, I did not know and I had to do as God told me and slay utterly... and so to obey God, I used the ax."

Kelly confessed that after killing the children, he went into the room where the parents were and he killed them, too. "My head was all wrong and I kept hearing voices," he said. He said that he then wanted to rest and went downstairs to another bedroom he had seen and found that two children were in the bed. "More work yet," God told him and before he knew what he was doing, he "continued my sacrifices." By killing the two little girls, Kelly said he believed that he was offering more blood sacrifices to God.

"To the best of my memory, I left the ax in the house and returned to the Ewing home, and went back to bed." He finished the statement, signing it on August 31, 1917.

By present-day standards, Kelly's "confession" was absurd. Not only would it not meet the standards of evidence today, no prosecutor would accept such a vague statement that was lacking in details the way that Kelly's was. Basically, he said that he was crazy, heard voices, and killed the Moores and the Stillinger sisters, never offering anything that he could not have read in the newspapers. I have no doubt that Kelly was connected (in a way) to the crime, but he most certainly did not commit the murders. Even the chances of the slight, scrawny little man being able to swing a heavy ax with the force needed to commit the eight murders are preposterous.

Havner presented further evidence from the transcriptions that were made by Fannie Longman and J.J. Ferguson on the night of Kelly's confession. These statements, which came in the form of questions from Havner and answers from Kelly, were meant to bolster the prosecution's theory of the crime. Of course, they did this by using only selected, incriminating passages, which the defense also did when it came their turn to present their case. The defense attorneys also maintained that Kelly was mistreated, under duress, and was coerced into confessing. They claimed he asked for his lawyer several times, but his request was denied. It's unlikely that Kelly was mistreated or forced to confess. What's more likely is that the "confession" was another product of his deluded mind. As one of his own attorneys stated, Kelly would confess to just about anything if he was given the chance. The prosecutors should have never taken it seriously, whether they believed he had committed the murders or not. Even prosecution witness J.J. Ferguson described Kelly as "rather nutty."

As the prosecution continued, laundry worker Cora Marquard testified that on the Wednesday after the murders, a man thought to be Kelly dropped off a white shirt to be cleaned. He gave no name and asked that it be returned to W.C. Miller's drug store, the laundry's pick-up point in Macedonia. It was unusual, Cora replied when asked, for a customer not to leave a name when dropping off his laundry. The shirt was damp and stained with what the cleaners thought was blood. She testified that it appeared as though someone had attempted to wash it by hand.

C.W. Miller, the druggist in Macedonia, testified that Kelly stopped in several times to see if the shirt had been returned. The druggist's wife, Laura Miller, testified that she heard Kelly talking about the murder many times over the years, often offering theories of the crime at her husband's store. She said he often stated that the killer had first stunned the victims by hitting them with the flat side of the ax and had returned later and chopped them to death. He had also said that the girls in the downstairs bedroom were hardest to kill because one of them woke up. She said Kelly claimed that the killer had been interrupted in his work when he heard the voices of two people walking past the house and that he had gone to the kitchen porch and listened until they were gone.

Other witnesses were called to say that Kelly told them about the shirt many times over the years, sometimes saying that it was stained after he cut himself shaving, while others said he claimed he had spilled hair tonic on it.

The defense didn't argue about the shirt being taken to the laundry, but pointed out that there were no tests to confirm the stain was blood. Even if it were, they said, it didn't prove anything. Reverend Kelly's wife later was offered as a rebuttal witness. She said that her husband was wearing the same clothing when he returned that he was wearing when he left for Villisca. There were no stains on his shirt when he came back.

The prosecution brought witnesses who testified to the presence of a bloodstain just above Lena Stillinger's knee. Hank Horton told the jury, "It looked like it had been made by a man's hand, stained with blood." Under cross-examination, though, he admitted that he couldn't be certain that it was made by a hand, but it looked like it. Several other witnesses, including doctors, agreed that the mark was a smear of blood. The testimony that followed became graphic, dealing with blood and the possibility of sexual assault. Jurors were told that Lena had not reached puberty and was not menstruating. Other than the positioning of Lena's body, there was no indication that she had been sexually violated in any way.

Doctors with backgrounds in mental illness were called, but their testimonies almost seemed to cancel each other out. Those called by the prosecution told the jury that Kelly was capable of murder and his confession could be valid, while those for the defense felt the suspect was hopelessly insane, would admit to anything, and was unlikely to commit a crime of violence. The jury must have been confused as they listened to doctors who swore that Kelly was in his right mind when he gave his confession, only to have those words refuted by doctors with equally impressive backgrounds who said he was not.

When the state rested its case against Kelly, the defense began theirs with the prosecution of Frank and Albert Jones. They called Ed Landers, who had now told his story so many times, between the slander trial and Wilkerson's meetings, that he could do it in his sleep. He left the restaurant, he said, walked with his wife to his mother's home, and as he passed by the Moore home a few minutes after 8 p.m., saw Albert Jones walk up to the front door and go inside. His mother was called and she repeated her testimony of hearing Sarah Moore scream in the night.

Faville attacked their testimony, going back to the fact that they had both testified at the coroner's inquest and never told these stories, only bringing them up years later. He forced them to admit that Landers' wife had been with him that night and never saw Albert Jones. Witnesses were called who swore Landers was at the restaurant until later than he claimed and, therefore, could not have seen anyone going into the Moore house. One of them, J.H. Bartlett, who had a shop near Moore's implement store, said he was absolutely sure that Landers had been at the downtown restaurant until at least 10:30 p.m. that night. He was sure of the time because he was on medication and took a dose at exactly 10:30, then stepped out of his shop and spoke to Landers and his wife as they walked past.

The defense called most of the same witnesses they had used in the slander trial – people who talked about Albert Jones and Bert McCaul's trip north; the slaughterhouse story; Alice Willard; Ralph Thorpe; John Noel and others. Judge Boise

Reverend Kelly and his wife, Laura, made a strange couple. Mrs. Kelly once confided to Oscar Wesnstrand that they had never had "normal sexual relations."

refused to allow some of them to testify, agreeing with the state's objections that their testimony was irrelevant to the guilt or innocence of Kelly. The ruling probably made little difference when it came to what the jurors did, or didn't, know. If they had not attended one of Wilkerson's meetings, then they read the reports of the slander trial in the newspaper. The state had run out of strikes to remove potential jurors long before the line of jurors had run out. It was impossible to think that they could keep every supporter of Wilkerson's theories out of the jury box. The trial was in its second week when the defense called Laura Kelly to the stand. She testified, in a prim British accent, that she and her husband had gotten married in London 12 years earlier, then she recounted the events of their life together up until the time of his arrest for murder.

She had been the one who packed his bag for Villisca, she said. There were toiletry items, something for him to read, but no extra clothing. When he returned on Monday, he was wearing the same clothes he had set out in, and she noticed no stains.

Laura was a sympathetic character to the people in the courtroom, especially those who agreed with Wilkerson that the minister was not guilty of the murders. The tall, slender, homely woman slouched when she stood or sat next to her five-foot-two-inch husband, deliberately trying to make herself look smaller. Kelly often cried out and sobbed at the defense table and she would put her arm around him, pat his back and wipe away his tears. As prosecution witnesses gave horrific evidence against him, he moaned and, with the top of his head just reaching her shoulder, she would pull him close and comfort him like a child. Laura often held his hand and whispered in his ear. Oscar Wenstrand later said that he sometimes looked over at her from the prosecution table and wondered if she had any regrets. He had interviewed her many times before the trial, trying to get some sort of insight into her husband's behavior. She once confided to him that she and her husband had never had "normal sexual relations." The county attorney inferred from this that they had engaged in some sort of sexual activity, but not what she considered normal. He would wonder, more than 50 years later, what kind of sex they must have had.

The defense also attacked the use of agents, posing as prisoners, who tried to extract information from Kelly while he was locked up in the jail in Logan. Planting someone to act as a prisoner was not only legal, it was a common tactic in those days, but the defense wanted the jury to see it as an underhanded way to trick Kelly, part of a scheme to get a mentally incompetent person to admit to a crime that he didn't commit. In truth, the prosecution had gotten little from this tactic, other than just making Kelly nervous and pushing him toward his unfortunate "confession."

Witnesses were called who had seen the ax marks in the ceiling of the Moore house. The defense used them to cast doubt on the idea that the diminutive Kelly, who weighed 120 pounds, was strong enough to have struck the ceiling with the backswing of the ax. Years later, people in the courtroom that day spoke of the dramatic impact when the ax was raised high and measured, of how Kelly cringed and looked away, and of the defense being successful in proving that Kelly couldn't have made the marks. The prosecution proved this was mistaken, though. Based on Kelly's height and the length of his arms and the ax handle, he could have swung it high enough. He could have – but it was very unlikely that he had.

Closing arguments lasted for two days, with several attorneys addressing the court. Hess took half a day with the initial presentation on behalf of the state, followed by slightly longer presentations by Sutton and Hysham for the defense. County Attorney Wenstrand deferred to Faville, after which Mitchell had his turn. Attorney General Havner spoke last.

Hess reviewed the details of the crime and told the jury that it could have only been committed by a madman, a moral degenerate, and a sexual pervert. He went into uncomfortable descriptions about Lena Stillinger and her "womanhood," trying to re-create in the jurors' minds the sensations that Kelly must have been feeling when he saw her. Unable to violate her, he took out his rage in other ways, Hess said. He reminded the jury of Kelly's obsession with the crime, the bloody shirt, and his attempts to get women to pose nude for him. He added, "We find him preaching a sermon one day, and the next day we find him trying to get his young woman stenographer to strip off her clothes."

He took time to ridicule Ed Landers and his testimony, citing his earlier and entirely different statements, and he named all of the witnesses who said his story was untrue. Finally, he closed with remarks about the confession, disparaging the defense claims that Kelly was mistreated. "I leave it to you, gentlemen, has he done it? Fifty-one times during the conversations held in the sheriff's office at Logan, Kelly was urged to tell the truth. Repeatedly Kelly begged the authorities not to turn him loose; 'I may do it again if you do.' And yet the counsel for the defense asks you to give this man his liberty."

When Hess finished, the jury took a break and Sutton took the floor. He began with a passionate discourse on the virtues of Reverend Kelly, a man who "felt his call to preach the gospel of the living Christ." He spoke of Kelly's mother in England, anxiously awaiting the results of the trial, and how his wife's heart had been wrenched as he she sat next to her accused husband during the proceedings. Sutton's emotions (or his acting skills) swelled to the point that he began to cry. When this happened, Kelly, who was watching him intently, also began to cry. Laura hugged him and dabbed at his cheeks with her handkerchief.

Sutton then got down to business. He said that the jury should disregard anything that Kelly said or wrote because he was insane. He added that the evidence did not support the state's claims that Lena Stillinger had been sexually assaulted in some way. The confession had only been taken after Kelly had been "abused for hours and hours."

The accusation was just the start of Sutton's attack on Havner, who he stated really didn't want Kelly – it was Wilkerson that he was after. "Havner wants to get Wilkerson," he told the jury, "whom Havner hates with all of the hatred of his nature." He said that the state offered too many motives for the crime – that Kelly was a pervert and that he was working on a sermon that told him to "slay utterly" – but that these motives furnished no reason for the crime. "If Kelly did this job in a fit of religious frenzy, then that does away with misconduct with the girl. They cannot reconcile the causes," Sutton said. He then went on, "If the attorney general can ever hold up his head again and walk the highways of Iowa, then he is a worse degenerate than he claims Kelly to be. Havner is full of revenge for Wilkerson, and Kelly is made the victim."

Wilkerson supporters in the courtroom loved it and Sutton banged his fist on the defense table and gave them more. He cried, "If the state had evidence enough they would not have gone down there in the darkness of night when honest people were in bed, and the confession obtained under mental suggestion. Havner was not satisfied and he called for Hess and a stenographer... They destroyed poor Kelly's reason until he babbled like a goose and then called for a stenographer! For this Havner should be removed from office and not be allowed to practice law until he has been punished for this crime against this poor insane man!"

Wilkerson supporters cheered and clapped until Judge Boise warned them that if there was another outburst, he would clear the courtroom.

Sutton continued by raising some of the weak points of the confession. Kelly said that he had gone back to the Ewings' and returned to bed for a time before leaving to catch the train, yet Mrs. Ewing found no evidence of blood on the bedclothes. Kelly said that he killed the children upstairs first, then the parents, then the girls downstairs last. Sutton said that this was impossible in a house as "flimsy" as J.B. Moore's without awakening everyone in the house. He said that it was likewise impossible for the crime to have been committed by one person, at least one as frail as Kelly. He wanted an acquittal, but he let the jury know that he would have no problem if they decided to send Kelly to a mental hospital. In fact, he really suggested it when he told the jury, "Kelly was not only a nut, but a carload of nuts."

Sutton concluded with one last shot at Havner, raising his voice and shaking his fist. "I would rather be a louse and feed on the carcass of a rotten mongrel than occupy the position of Attorney General!" Sutton chose those words wisely. He never actually said the attorney general was a parasite, but when he used the description and mentioned the office in the same breath, he knew the jury would understand his implication.

Hysham then took his place, describing how he thought the crime had been committed and why Kelly could not have done it. He said that the only way that eight people could have been bludgeoned to death with an ax as they slept without anyone awakening was for there to have been several people involved. They were, he suggested, hiding in the house when the Moores returned home from church. They were experienced criminals, he told the jury, who had carefully planned the crime. Perhaps, he said, the killers didn't originally intend to kill the children, but decided it was necessary in order to make their escape. He said that the parents had to have been killed first, and suggested that the screams of Sarah Moore – which Mrs. Landers said she heard – had awakened the children and doomed them to death. He told the jury that Havner had tried 50 times to get Kelly to say that he had killed the parents first because it was the only way that it could have been done. The killers were sane, calculating people and Kelly was anything but that. He snorted a sardonic laugh, "If Kelly would stand up here in the courtroom and confess, I would not believe him."

Hysham noted that the murders would have been impossible to commit in the way that Kelly claimed he had in his confession. He could not have climbed the stairs with an ax in one hand and the lamp in the other, passed within inches of J.B. and Sarah's bed and killed the children without waking them up. Hysham said Kelly did not confess – Havner had written the words and forced Kelly to sign. He said Havner had gone to Logan to get the confession with "malice in his heart and ambition in his mind."

William Mitchell had endeared himself to Wilkerson supporters during the slander trial and his cutting wit, commanding presence, and deep voice riveted the attention of juries. Mitchell had a folksy way of describing himself as "just a country lawyer" that belied his razor-sharp mind, and the press could always rely on him for good quotes. He was the perfect choice to sum up the defense's case, but his talk was not all that interesting because there was so little left to say. He spent two and a half hours reiterating what had already been said, but he did it in his own creative way. He referred to Kelly as a man "whose high calling in life was to blaze the way for his fellows in the inevitable journey over the river."

He compared the interrogation of Kelly to a court of inquisition presided over by Havner, a man with a hand as strong as the hated Kaiser of Germany. This was an ethnic shot at the attorney general, who was of Dutch descent, and meant to inflame a jury during a time when anti-German sentiment was high. At that time, "Dutch" and "German" were almost synonymous, especially in the midst of World War I, and Wilkerson often referred to Havner as "the Dutchman" during his presentations. It was not meant as a compliment.

Mitchell, like the other members of the defense team, reminded the jury that Kelly's confession was not valid because an admission was not considered legally valid if the person giving it was insane at the time. He urged the jury not to find Kelly guilty but, as Sutton did, gave them an option by telling them that, "if he did this, he is insane."

Mitchell praised Kelly, denigrated the confession again and made the attorney general and the state investigators into the real villains. He carried this off with the style and flair that Wilkerson supporters had come to expect.

After another break for the jury, it was Faville's turn, leading off his presentation with a shot at Sutton, referring to his closing as "the Fourth of July speech we all learned in the fifth reader years ago." He said that Sutton's remarks were pleasant to listen to, but they were no help in arriving at the truth. Faville proved that he was as witty as Mitchell, making humorous swipes at Hysham's closing remarks and the difficulty of imagining a scenario in which the killer had to have a light to commit the crime, yet could have passed the light over J.B. Moore's bed without awakening him. Hysham, Faville said, told the jury that the members of the household could not have been killed in the dark, but then they could not have been killed by the light of anything in the house. "The only conclusion," he smirked, "we can draw from the counsel's argument is that these people were not killed at all."

As to Hysham's remarks about Kelly not being able to commit the crime without awakening the victims, Faville said that Hysham apparently had no experience trying to get children out of bed in the morning for breakfast. Kelly was a small man, who could tiptoe easily from room to room without being heard. He defended Havner, stating that the confession was fairly obtained. There was no force, no coercion, no intimidation. When the confession was typed, Kelly read it, made some corrections, and finally, signed it.

Faville left the jury with a plea not to release a man like Kelly, who had said once that he would kill again if God told him to.

Havner had saved himself for last and he summarized the entire case against Kelly. He did this patiently and in great detail, defending the confession and going over the testimony that supported a conviction.

He concluded his nearly three-hour summarization with one grim thought. "Gentlemen, you're standing between this man and society. He has told you that he does not want to be turned loose. I am now done; my duty has been performed. I have done the best that I could."

Havner's final words to the jury seemed to show that he felt that his best had still fallen short. He and Faville had feared the worst before the trial had even started. As Faville wrote to him weeks before the trial began: "A conviction of Kelly in this county is an impossibility."

Judge Boise read the instructions to the jury, which included a careful explanation of the degrees of guilt available for their findings. They had five possible verdicts: first-degree murder, second-degree murder, manslaughter, not guilty, or not guilty by reason of insanity. The latter verdict, he explained, meant that the suspect had committed the crime but could not be held responsible because he was insane at the time the crime was committed.

The jury was sent out to deliberate on the afternoon of Wednesday, September 26. They worked for four hours before taking their first ballot. Eleven voted for acquittal and one voted for not guilty by reason of insanity. There was more discussion, more ballots, but the result didn't change. Beds were moved into the courthouse, but the jury didn't use them the first night. They debated until morning, but still, the only holdout, a man named T.C. Brown, refused to budge.

On the afternoon of the second day, a note was sent to Judge Boise saying that they could not agree and asked to be released. The judge sent back a note of his own, refusing the request. They were to work until they arrived at a verdict, he said.

As Thursday turned into Friday, the mood in the jury room turned dark. Some of the jurors were no longer speaking to one another. Brown refused to discuss it further and would not take part in another ballot. Observers outside the courthouse saw jurors standing at the windows for extended amounts of time, their arms crossed and their faces set in anger. Finally, the debate ended – eleven stood for acquittal, Brown for insanity – with no hope for progress.

On Friday afternoon, after 21 ballots and more than 44 hours of deliberation, the judge allowed them to give up. It was a hung jury, and if the state still wanted to convict Kelly, they'd have to do the whole thing over again. The defense team celebrated, never believing that the prosecution would go through all of it again.

But the pursuit of Reverend Kelly was not over yet.

22. TRIAL AND TRIBULATION

The jury was sent home, leaving Havner with a dilemma on his hands. He knew that the chance of a conviction in a second trial was virtually non-existent, but on the other hand he had brazenly -- and foolishly – told the newspapers that he was so convinced of Kelly's guilt that he would try him eight times if he had to, once for each of the victims. So now, like Frank Jones in his slander case, he was bound by his word to continue pursuing a lost cause. A second trial would be a waste of both time and money, but Havner and Faville truly believed that Kelly was the killer. They had an obligation to continue their pursuit of the "Little Minister," as he was known. If Kelly was released and he killed again, the blood of his new victims would not be on their hands.

In the meantime, Havner had other business to worry about. The charge against him for "oppression in office" for the alleged coercion of Alice Willard was still hanging around his neck, as was the grand jury hearing for the case against Wilkerson for the break-in attempt at the Jones store. Another event was unfolding during the trail of which Havner was unaware, but it would result in another violent death, and the consequences would lead to the final series of bitter confrontations between Havner and Wilkerson.

As the Kelly trial was getting ready to begin in the late summer of 1917, John Warren Noel's life was coming apart at the seams. No one -- not even his wife -- knew it at the time because he kept secret just how serious his problems were. That summer Noel bought a new Oldsmobile, causing people to wonder where he got the money to pay for it. He was far from wealthy and his photography business was in jeopardy, thanks to his devotion to Wilkerson and the constant distractions that kept him away from his studio. He was a vocal fund-raiser for the detective and he had attended nearly all of the meetings that Wilkerson held in 1917, working the crowds and soliciting contributions and pledges. When he was on the road he paid for his own food and lodging. With no earnings coming in, he started borrowing, using his photography equipment as collateral.

Within days after the end of the first Kelly trial, the sheriff and the county attorney were looking into allegations that Noel had written forged checks. Apparently, some of the people who had pledged money to Wilkerson's cause – or at least in Noel's mind had made a commitment – failed to pay. Noel decided to rectify the matter by writing their checks for them. And that was only part of the problem; businessmen who had loaned him money that was secured by his studio equipment found out that he had sold most of it to raise funds, something that was illegal. Worse yet, Wilkerson supporters Ed Peterson and Clarence Miller had a growing suspicion that Noel had not turned in a sizable portion of the money that he had collected at fundraisers. Noel would soon be found with a bullet in his head – but things were going to get even stranger before that.

During the Kelly trial, Wilkerson had kept a low profile, probably at the defense team's request, but on the day after the verdict was returned, he held a public meeting at the now-familiar Beardsley Theater in Red Oak. The meeting was to be the first step in raising funds for Kelly's second trial. Wilkerson again criticized Havner, telling the attendees that the attorney general would be up for re-election the next year and when the voters saw his name on the ballot, they should remember the slogan "Slay Utterly." A petition was passed demanding Havner's resignation. It didn't name Jones, but it charged Havner with associating and consulting "with a man whom the public has reason to believe was implicated in the Villisca murder." Juror Tom Brown also came under fire at the meeting. The man who hung the jury had, literally overnight, become a very unpopular figure in the community. Brown attempted to redeem himself by speaking to the newspapers. He told them that he had been unfairly accused of being good friends with Frank Jones, but this was not true; he hardly knew the man and had spoken to him only once in the 10 years before the trial. Brown stated that he went into the trial with an open mind, and that, having found the confession believable, was convinced of Kelly's guilt and simply could not in good conscience, vote any other way. Of course, none of that mattered to Wilkerson fanatics, who became enraged all over again as the second trial approached, blaming Brown for the fact that it was taking place at all.

In October 1917, the Villisca National Bank made a brief announcement. Frank Jones, after a 22-year career that saw his advance from teller to cashier to president, was stepping down and ending his association with the establishment. His stock in both the Villisca bank and the branch that he had opened in Morton Mills was being sold and his longtime friend and bank vice-president, Bert Dirrim, was replacing him. Jones was 62 years old by this time, in excellent health, and had no plans to retire. Under other circumstances, he would have continued on at the bank indefinitely. But the specter of suspicion that was created and fueled by J.N. Wilkerson, month after month and year after year, had ruined his political career and was now hurting the bank as well. Jones wanted to do what was best for the bank and steeping down seemed to be the right thing to do.

Using the proceeds from the sale of his stock, Jones bought a farm on the north edge of Villisca and he and Albert went into the business of raising purebred Poland China hogs. Jones continued to manage the implement store, but he did this mostly from his office at home. Albert and Dona moved out to the new farm, where Albert began spending his days with the livestock rather than at the store.

Frank and Albert had stopped being the high-profile figures they once were. It just seemed best to go about life as quietly and carefully as they could.

The date for Kelly's re-trial was set for late November. The minister had higher hopes for the second trial and he was certainly in better spirits. He had grown accustomed to life in jail and his newly found friends in Montgomery County had supplied him with a canary for company, as well as a typewriter and a supply of paper on which to write his life story. Reporters who visited him in jail said that he was able to use the corridor outside of his cell, making his living arrangement more like a small apartment than a jail lock-up. As his canary sang, Kelly told the news writers that he hoped to publish his autobiography after he was acquitted. For the odd little preacher, who spent most of his career living hand-to-mouth and traveling from one church position to another, living in jail was probably better than the outside world.

Wilkerson was doing what he could to ensure that Kelly was acquitted the second time around. He continued his fundraisers and was scheduled to speak at one on a cool, wet night in Nodaway. John Noel planned to be there and before leaving, he called John Montgomery, Sarah Moore's father, and offered to give him a ride. Montgomery had not been as vocal as most of Wilkerson's supporters, but he was a steady worker and had provided a sizable amount of money to the cause. His only goal was to live long enough to see his daughter's and grandchildren's killer brought to justice. He attended a number of Wilkerson's meetings and occasionally spoke, always briefly and eloquently. He agreed to go along with Noel that night.

Noel, driving his new Oldsmobile Eight, picked up Montgomery at his farm north of Villisca around 6 p.m. They first drove to the railroad depot in town, where Noel said they might meet Wilkerson and save him from riding the last few miles to Nodaway on the train. Wilkerson wasn't there, so Noel said he would probably be on the next train. He and Montgomery left, traveling east on the old Nodaway Road, a former wagon trail that intersected with the railroad and the East Nodaway River about two miles outside of Villisca. Both the road and the tracks ran in a straight line, crossing each other about one-half mile west of the river. West of the overpass, the road went over, and the railroad went around, a steep rise known as Boot's Hill, named for a farmer who had once lived there. From the top of the hill, there was a sweeping view of the railroad, the overpass, and the river bridges.

It was starting to get dark when Noel and Montgomery reached the hill. As they started down the east side, they saw a light that, as it got closer, appeared to be on the railroad tracks between the overpass and the river bridge. Noel wondered if someone might be injured. He stopped the car, climbed the fence alongside the tracks and went to investigate as Montgomery waited in the car. He said Noel went only a short distance before coming back to get a flashlight. This time, he asked Montgomery to come along and the older man followed him over the fence and down to the tracks where they had seen the light.

Suddenly, Noel saw – or claimed to see – two men running away from them. He gave chase, taking a .32-caliber revolver from his coat and firing off two shots.

In a statement later given by Noel and Montgomery, they said that they found a wooden railroad tie chained to the tracks and worked quickly to remove it before the train carrying Wilkerson came through. Noel told Montgomery then, and others later, that he was sure they had ruined a plot to derail the train into Nodaway for the purpose of killing Wilkerson. After removing the chain and the wooden tie, Noel and Montgomery drove into Nodaway and told the station agent what had occurred.

Other authorities were contacted, including Sheriff Dunn, railroad detectives from Creston, and a work crew from Villisca. They went out to the scene to investigate and found a log chain by the tracks, as well as several discarded railroad ties, but little else to suggest that the incident that Noel and Montgomery reported had taken place. There was a general skepticism about the story – which increased when Noel began, almost immediately, to suggest that he should be eligible for a reward for averting a train wreck. A number of people who knew Noel told railroad detectives that he had been acting strangely and it's likely that Sheriff Dunn told them about the photographer's deepening financial problems.

If Noel had been alone that night, it would have been easy to pass the whole thing off as a hoax perpetrated by the photographer to make him look like a hero and more importantly, earn him a reward. It would have also been a great publicity stunt for Wilkerson, allowing him to "prove" that he was really in danger as he so often claimed to be. It would have also given credence to Noel's claim that he overheard Jones threaten the detective's life in 1916. Noel had been on hand and was ready to testify at Kelly's trial, but Judge Boise wouldn't allow it. With a new judge, he hoped to take the stand in the second trial.

The only thing that gave credence to the Noel's story was the presence of John Montgomery. The farmer was a respected citizen and a longtime resident of the area with a reputation for honesty. He initially swore that the events had occurred. People who knew Montgomery found it difficult to believe that he would have gone along with the story if it wasn't the truth.

Regardless of John Montgomery's claims, railroad detectives were convinced that Noel had engineered the whole thing to try and collect a reward. When they questioned him and brought up his financial problems, Noel became jittery and agitated. He knew about the sheriff's investigation into the forged checks, but he denied making up anything about the railroad incident. Soon after, Peterson and Miller confronted him about the missing money from the fundraisers. Noel's house of cards was starting to collapse. Desperate, he sold his car, then went to the insurance company and told them it had been stolen. They refused to pay and he didn't pursue it.

A week or so later, he went to an insurance agent in Red Oak and tried to take out an additional life insurance policy on himself. He was denied because he was already heavily insured. He was then carrying $32,000 in life insurance – the equivalent of his anticipated salary for the next 25 to 30 years. The policies had a 12-month suicide exemption, but they'd been in effect for more than a year.

On Wednesday, October 31, Noel hired a driver to take him to Nodaway. The driver later said that Noel seemed to be in a fine mood and told him that he was going to Corning. At the depot in Nodaway, Noel mailed a special delivery letter to his wife. He then took the train to Corning, where he had a short and unremarkable conversation with an acquaintance, then boarded another train and continued traveling east. He stopped at the railroad office in Creston and asked about the investigation of the Nodaway incident and was told that it was completed and was now being reviewed to see what actions were appropriate. He got back onto the train and continued on to Albia. There were later unconfirmed reports from this leg of the trip that said Noel was seen drinking whiskey straight from a bottle.

If Noel had traveled straight through, he would have arrived in Albia early that evening. Instead, the next few hours remain a mystery. At 7 a.m. the next morning, he was found on the platform of the freight depot with a .32 caliber bullet through his head. The bullet had entered just behind his right ear and had exited the upper part of the left side of his head, lodging in the wall of the depot building. The revolver was beside him and his wallet, which contained $29, was lying on the platform a few feet away. When he was found, he was unconscious, but still alive. He was rushed to the Albia hospital where he died later that morning.

Before receiving word of her husband's death, May Noel had gotten the letter that he had mailed to her before getting onto the train. May, a pretty young woman with three small children, one an infant, was stunned by the letter. She had supported her husband in the work that he did for Wilkerson, but she was unaware of his recent legal and financial difficulties. The letter was later submitted at the coroner's inquest. It read:

My dear wife – I am in the hands of some men who said they were railroad men, they got me on the train and said they wanted me to take a trip with them. I don't know where they are going to take me and I know that I am in a bad bunch as they are bad men and I am afraid something is going to happen. I don't know who any of them are but they have threatened to kill me if I didn't keep my mouth shut and go with them where they wanted me to, they are watching me now but if I can get this to a porter and slip him a dollar he will mail this for me.

I hope that I get back to you all right, but I am afraid that they know that I have that money on me keep that to yourself about that money that I got if this is a railroad bunch they may use that to get me into trouble on.

Fairweather and Burke have followed me all day and I believe they planned this deal on me, if I shouldn't get back all right Jack Conway at Creston can probably help find out who these fellows are, I have always tried to do the best I could for you little girl, and oh god if I only had the last two years of my life to live over if I shouldn't get back try to raise our dear baby as best you can, I wish I could tell you what a condition I am in but I can't explain it, I've been working for about three hours to get this wrote and maby [sic] this will work out all right any way if you get this letter don't worry until you hear from me. I am going to try and get another slip in this letter for you alone to read and then hide or destroy but keep it to yourself.

Gorden must have gone back on me or else somebody else is puting [sic] us to a job as he and Willet and Peterson think that I have done something crooked

but I have not.
With all my love to you and my dear father and mother and babes,
Yours most lovingly,
Warren

Less than an hour after the letter arrived, May received a telephone call from the hospital in Albia, telling her that her husband was critically wounded. Noel's mother accompanied her on the next train, but he was dead before they made it to Albia.

John Warren Noel was only 27 years old. The coroner's jury, hearing testimony about his financial problems, his legal issues, the letter to his wife, and the opinion of the attending physician, ruled his death a suicide.

But of course, Wilkerson publicly stated that this was not the case. It was murder, he said, another in a series of violent deaths that could be traced back to the slaughter of the Moore family and the cover-up that followed. Wilkerson and his supporters claimed that Noel had received threatening "black hand" letters threatening retaliation against him for having testified against Jones. They pointed out that Noel's wallet was found several feet from his body. Why would a man about to commit suicide take out his wallet and toss it? They also made much of the fact that he had been shot in the right side of the head, while the gun was found next to his body on the left side. There was also the additional insurance policy that he applied for shortly before his death. It had a one-year suicide clause, so why apply for it if he planned to kill himself a few days later?

They failed to explain this reasoning since Noel was turned down for the policy. They also failed to account for Noel's final hours, but insisted that he had not taken the trip to Albia to kill himself. Someone had followed him there, taken his gun away, and killed him with it.

There is no question that Noel's death was mysterious. What had become of him between Creston and Albia, a trip that should have only taken a few hours? Why was his body not found until the next morning? Why had he taken such an unusual trip, just to kill himself outside of a freight depot? There are many unanswered questions about his death and so it's no surprise that his friends questioned everything about it, including whether it was suicide or not.

Within a few days of Noel's death, John Montgomery had second thoughts about sticking to his version of events about the night on the way to Nodaway. He went to the authorities and told them that in the excitement of the moment, with Noel shouting and firing his revolver, he had allowed his imagination to convince him that things were other than they actually were. He hadn't seen anyone running away, wasn't sure about the light that Noel claimed to have seen, and had not actually seen the railroad tie on the tracks. Montgomery apologized, saying that he had not meant to give a false statement, but that he had allowed himself to be taken in by Noel.

This seemed to close the book on the investigation of the incident – and on Noel's death as well. No matter what Wilkerson and his friends might say, another blemish on Noel's reputation leaned everyone further toward being convinced that he had taken his own life. If not, he had certainly not been killed by one of the "Villisca conspirators."

If John Warren Noel did not commit suicide that Halloween night, I'm afraid that the reasons behind a possible murder would have less to do with the slaughter in Villisca and more to do with the trouble that the young man had managed to get himself into on his own.

As all of this strangeness was taking place, a bit of legal strangeness was occurring elsewhere. Attorney General Havner was now a defendant in a jury trial in the western part of the state. He had managed to get a change of venue in his case since there was no way that he could stand trial in Montgomery County. Judge Boise had granted his request and sent the trial to Logan. An attorney from Glenwood named Clyde Genung was hired by the country to assist Wenstrand in the prosecution.

The trial itself was a bizarre set of circumstances. Havner was at Logan as a defendant in the same courthouse where he had obtained the Kelly confession. He was being prosecuted by a team of attorneys led by Oscar Wenstrand, with whom he had just worked during the first Kelly trial and was preparing to work with him again during the second. And to top it off, Kelly himself was lounging in his cell just a stone's throw away from where Havner was being tried.

If Havner was found guilty of oppressing the witness, Alice Willard (who, ironically, was not believed by anyone anyway), he could face a hefty fine, some jail time, and even disbarment. This was bad for any attorney, but fatal for an attorney general with designs on becoming governor someday. Havner was, however, not without support. A number of prominent trial lawyers from around the state, men who had followed the attacks waged by Wilkerson against Havner and Jones, offered their services *pro bono*. Even Oscar Wenstrand was apologetic for his role in the trial, but Havner knew – and insisted – that the young county attorney was only doing his job. Havner accepted a couple of the offers for help in his defense, although he paid their expenses out of his own pocket.

Alice Willard's complaint against Havner was based on Havner's alleged actions during the grand jury proceedings the previous spring, during which he pointed out the glaring discrepancies in her earlier testimony, as well as substantial differences in the original statement that she gave to Wilkerson. The grand jury's questioning of Willard took place over several days, while she was staying at the Johnson Hotel in Red Oak. She claimed that Havner asked her to go into a meeting room with him on a day before she was to testify. There, she alleged that he asked her to change her testimony. Willard said Havner told her that unless she did so, he would prosecute her for perjury, and that perjury was an offense punishable by imprisonment. According to her account, she refused but Havner persisted. She began to feel ill, she said, and moved toward a window to open it and get some fresh air, but Havner stepped in front of her and closed it. Willard claimed she then blacked out and when she came to, she was lying on a couch. Her coat and hat had been removed and her face and breasts were soaked with water. She asked to go home, but Havner would not let her leave. She said that Agent Oscar Rock was there and offered her whiskey, which she declined. She asked to be permitted to use the bathroom instead. After some hesitation, Havner called Sheriff Dunn and directed him to take her to the ladies room, located on the floor below. When she got there, she told Dunn she was sick, and he took her across the street to her room at the hotel.

The entire story was questionable, especially with the case being pushed forward by Wilkerson, but Willard was not so deep into it that there was no way out. It was a simple case of her being caught lying with her earlier, wildly fabricated, testimony, and when Havner tried to warn her about the penalty for perjury, she piled another lie on top of all of the others, hoping to injure the reputation of the attorney general. At Wilkerson's prodding, she had filed the original charge and then told this story again to the jury in Logan.

After Willard, the prosecution called Dr. L.O. Thompson, who attended to Willard after she returned to the hotel. He said that he found her in a nervous state and offered an opinion that her condition was likely the result of being grilled by the attorney general. This statement was objected to and sustained, especially since she could just as easily have been frightened by Havner's promise that she would go to prison if she didn't stop lying. During cross-examination, Dr. Thompson admitted that he had been brought to Logan to testify by Ed Peterson, further eroding his credibility.

Another poor witness was Frank Jones' private investigator Harry Moore, who said he was a newspaper reporter from Des Moines. Moore stated that he was in the courthouse on the day in question and asked to be admitted to the room where Havner and Willard held their conference. He was turned away, he said. He said that he saw Dunn take Willard out of the courthouse later that afternoon. He further testified that on February 28, just before the grand jury convened, he was on a train leaving Red Oak and that Havner and Ed Northrup were on the same train. He said that he overheard their conversation and that Havner told Northrup the Willard testimony was a "myth and a lie."

Ed Northrup was called and testified that Havner did indeed make that statement to him. But when cross-examined, he added that Havner also told him he "was going to get to the bottom of the case, no matter who was implicated."

Witnesses for the defense included Frederick Faville, who testified that it was he, not Havner, who asked Willard into the room to discuss her testimony. He said that initially, Havner was not even there; only Willard, Faville and Rock. He said that he asked her about the significant discrepancies between what Wilkerson claimed she said in his report, and what she later testified to. He said that she should tell the truth to the grand jury, no matter what was in Wilkerson's report. Faville said that Willard then asked him what would happen if she changed her testimony and he told her that he couldn't say for sure. At that time, Faville said, she asked to see Havner. Since the attorney general was in the building, he went into the meeting room with Willard and Rock and Faville left. He said that about 10 or 15 minutes later, Havner called him back into the room. Willard was sitting on the floor with her back against the couch. Her eyelids were moving, Faville said, and she was conscious. He said he helped her to her feet and suggested that she take off her coat and hat. She did this without assistance and then lay down on the couch. Faville said that she rested for a few minutes and then asked to use the bathroom. It was he, Faville said, not Havner, who summoned Sheriff Dunn. He said there was no objection to her leaving the building when she felt well enough to do so.

Agent Rock followed Faville to the stand and corroborated Faville's account, adding that he did not at any time offer Willard a drink of whiskey.

Havner was sworn in after taking the witness stand. He testified that when he entered the room, Willard asked him what would happen to her if she changed her testimony. He said that he told her that he wasn't sure, but in any case, she should tell the truth. He said that he did not threaten her with a perjury prosecution (although he would not have been out of line if he had), or say that she could be sent to prison. The defense attacked him, claiming that no matter what Agent Rock said, Havner was alone with Willard in the room. They also claimed that he did not give her appropriate assistance when she was on the floor.

Judge Shelby M. Cullison, who presided over the trial, finally stated that he had heard enough. When the defense moved for a dismissal, he allowed the state and the defense to argue the merits of the motion for two hours, and then ruled "the charge in the indictment was not proven and even if it had taken place as alleged no crime was committed." He told the jury that they were excused and directed a verdict for Havner. After less than one day of testimony, the trial was over.

Havner won in Logan and Wilkerson also won his own case in Adams County. Three confessions and several witnesses left little doubt as to the facts behind the break-in attempt, but the grand jury inexplicably refused to indict Wilkerson. They listened patiently as the prosecutor presented the case, called witnesses, and took them through the events, but they would not indict the detective. It's thought that perhaps the trial simply did not belong in Adams County. If the account of events leading up to the attempted break-in was accurate, Wilkerson conspired in not just Adams County but in Cass, probably in Pottawattamie, certainly in Montgomery and the case was delivered in Union County. The Adams County grand jury just didn't want the responsibility for it. Trials involving Wilkerson tended to be expensive and the jurors had no interest in bearing the cost.

Somehow, the wily detective had one more victory.

Reverend Kelly was a different man when he came to Red Oak in early November for his second trial. Gone was the morose, weird little man. He had been replaced by a fellow who was animated and smiling during jury selection, which went better than the first time around. There were 140 jurors questioned for the first trial and there would have been even more if both sides had not exhausted their assigned number of strikes. The second time, though, it only took two days and 88 people to put together a new jury. After they were seated, Judge Arthur had a lecture prepared for them and for Tom Brown, who was a spectator in the first row of the gallery. The jury was told they were expected to get along, to communicate, resolve their differences, and to treat each other with respect.

The judge told them that when they cast their ballots, the majority was usually right, and the greater the majority the more likely they were of being right. He was letting them know that there would be no 11-1 hung juries this time around.

To the onlookers in the courtroom, the judge was even more blunt. There would be no "one more time" warnings. He required complete silence from the spectators and anyone who violated that rule would be escorted from the courtroom. He also posted an officer at the door with directions that no one would be allowed to enter or leave except when the court was in recess. Arthur was determined to keep tighter control over the proceedings than Judge Boise had, and he did so. It was a comparatively short, orderly trial, but in fairness to Boise, the audience was neither as large nor as emotional as it had been the first time around. The case and the participants had been on the front pages for too long. The need to get a glimpse of those involved had largely been satisfied and it was a general opinion that the outcome of the trial was not in doubt. There was no jockeying for seats in the courtroom this time around. In fact, on many days, empty chairs were scattered throughout the gallery.

The trial was shortened even more when the state decided not to use the controversial confession. The prosecutors had debated this at length, mostly feeling that the confession had been turned against them in the first trial. Its use had created sympathy for Kelly and made Havner look like a brutal interrogator. On the other hand, the one juror who believed Kelly was guilty said that he felt this way because of the minister's guilty admission. In the end, Havner decided not to use it. He and Faville still needed a miracle and he wasn't sure that the confession would produce it.

The opening arguments were essentially shortened versions of the ones from the first trial. The trial produced only a handful of new witnesses. The state did use some evidence that it had left out the first time, including a reading of the letters that Kelly had written to the Council Bluffs woman whom he wanted to pose nude for him. When the first letter was written, it was turned over to the postal authorities and they answered it, pretending to be the young woman, acting interested. It was the start of a lurid exchange as Kelly's letters quickly progressed to graphic depictions of sexual acts. The letters were read out loud to the jury during the second trial. Many watched Laura Kelly closely during the readings and while the minister made faces and squirmed in his chair, his wife listened calmly, showing no emotion at all.

The state offered an additional witness who swore he'd heard Kelly talk about the murders on Monday morning, and another witness, W.H. Fulweider of Winner, South Dakota, an auto dealer who lived in Winner while Kelly was living there. Fulweider said that he once drove Kelly to another town for a sermon or lecture and during the drive, Kelly spoke at length about the murders, claiming that he was tracing a man who took a bloody shirt to a laundry in Council Bluffs. He knew who the shirt belonged to, he said, and when the authorities found him, they would have the guilty man.

The other witnesses for the state were the same ones from the first trial. Lawyers on both sides repeated the same questions they had asked before. A few new ones were attempted, but no new information was gained. Closing arguments, except for the fact that the confession wasn't mentioned, were nearly identical. Jury selection for the trial had started on November 12, and the case went to the jury on the afternoon of Saturday, November 24. In less than five hours – with only one ballot – Reverend Kelly was acquitted.

The minister was finally a free man. During the trial, Kelly had said he expected to stay in the area and finish his autobiography, regain his strength, and enjoy the company of his many new friends, but he didn't stay long. He moved to Omaha within a few weeks and delivered a few lectures, but he didn't stay very long there either. He and Laura left less than three months after they arrived, telling friends they were going to Boston and then back to England.

Something changed his mind, though, because a few months later, he was in Chicago, writing to people he knew in Montgomery County and asking them for money. He needed it, he told them, so that he could hire attorneys to sue the state of Iowa for false arrest. The lawsuit was filed, but dismissed soon after and Kelly later vanished into history.

It was said that Reverend Kelly eventually returned to England and years later, some of the Enarson children claimed that Kelly wrote to their father and asked him for money to help him return to the United States. The Enarsons ignored the letters but many believe that Kelly managed to return anyway. It's been said that he lived in Kansas City, Connecticut, and New York, but the remaining years of his life, and final resting place, are a mystery.

James Wilkerson stayed on in Montgomery County, becoming an official resident. Until the trial ended, and perhaps for some time after that, he was drawing from the funds raised to defend Kelly and continue the investigation, but that account was quickly depleted, and since Kelly had been acquitted, new cash would be difficult to raise. He had lost his position with the Burns Agency months before, and he was no longer interested in continuing his career as a private detective. Wilkerson was unable to live on contributions any longer. He needed a job and a regular source of income and to achieve it, he came up with a new plan – he would run for the position of county attorney.

Wilkerson had practiced law in Texas and he certainly knew his way around a courtroom. In addition, he was also one of the best-known -- and most eccentrically popular -- figures in the county. He announced his candidacy, which was a typically brazen thing for him to do. He had been criticizing local law enforcement officials for years, calling them incompetent and criminal, and making a general nuisance of himself. Now, he was running for the top law enforcement job in the county – and doing so knowing full well that he did not meet the minimum qualification that required a county attorney to be a member of the Iowa bar. Wilkerson was not licensed to practice law in Iowa and to do so, he had to deal with the attorney general, knowing that Havner would fight him until the end. But Wilkerson also knew the final decision on his admittance rested with the Iowa Supreme Court and he must have believed that he had a fighting chance with them. He sent in the nomination papers, applied to the bar and prepared for the battle to come.

On March 24, 1918, Reverend Wesley J. Ewing passed away in a Des Moines hospital where he was recovering from a minor operation for a nasal problem. He was a well-liked, albeit notorious, man known not only for being the pastor for the Moore family, but for his hosting Reverend Kelly and his advocacy of Wilkerson and his crusade. His presence had loaned a degree of respectability to the often rancor-filled public meetings. His surgery was thought to be successful, but something went wrong and his heart stopped, suddenly ending his life.

In April, Wilkerson filed his formal request for admission to the bar. Havner, knowing that it was coming, filed an objection offering seven reasons why Wilkerson should be refused, including that he would not maintain proper respect for the courts; that he was guilty of acts that showed he was not of good moral character; that he was guilty of acts that showed he would seek to mislead judges; that he would encourage the commencement or continuance of actions from motives of passion or interest; that he had violated court orders; that he had been guilty of acts of moral turpitude while a resident of Iowa; and that he had been guilty of willful violation of the duties of an attorney.

The seven reasons were made public and the voters had to wonder about Havner's comments concerning "moral turpitude" and his "moral character." They would learn a lot more about Wilkerson after the primaries, and as the primaries drew closer, Wilkerson went on the attack. The medium he used best was public meetings and he already had a network in place. He had staunch supporters all over the county and most of them were happy to set up the gatherings and solicit people to attend. Wilkerson also had the advantage of a weak opposition. Oscar Wenstrand had let it be known that the ongoing war in Europe and military service were on his mind. He did end up running in the primary, but whether or not he'd actually return to the office was in doubt. Other candidates had declared, but none of them were experienced like Wenstrand or well-known like Wilkerson. The former detective went straight to the people, promising real law enforcement and investigations that were free of influence from people with powerful connections like Horace Havner and Frank Jones.

Wilkerson campaigned vigorously, quickly becoming the front-runner. Many predicted an easy victory – and then Montgomery County election officials dealt him what appeared to be a fatal blow. Candidates had to fill out a form that requested, among other things, that the candidate attest that he is "eligible" to hold office. Wilkerson had drawn a line through those words and wrote in "would be eligible," and then checked the box. Based on this, officials debated about whether or not his name could legally appear on the ballot. Because he had not yet been admitted to the bar, the decision was made that he not be permitted to run.

But Wilkerson had never let anything as superficial as a legal ruling stand in his way. Once again he cried foul, claiming the powers that be were out to get him. He again went to the people, stepped up his public meetings, cried out against corruption in high places, and appealed for write-in votes. He also provided an insight into just how he planned to manage county law enforcement by revealing that his chief supporter and heaviest contributor, Ed Peterson, would be his candidate for sheriff. Clarence Miller, another close supporter, was running for county supervisor. The prospect of Wilkerson and two of his top lieutenants holding three key offices deeply concerned many voters, but they turned out to be in the minority.

As the June primaries approached, Havner began putting together an operation that was designed to destroy any chance that Wilkerson had of practicing law in Iowa. Frank Jones, not surprisingly, was doing all that he could to help. Over the years, Jones had gathered quite a lot of information about Wilkerson, most of which he had not been able to use. He paid for a lot of the information gathered by detectives, but even more of it came from people who read about his persecution by the former detective and wrote or called to tell him what they knew about Wilkerson and his methods. Jones had piles of information locked in his safe, including affidavits on the Nellie Byers murder, the Blue Island murders and other cases that Wilkerson had worked. There were also documents about his association with Jack Boyle and a lengthy file on Wilkerson's previous divorces and marital status, including the apparent fact that he'd lived in Villisca for a time with a woman who was not his wife.

To Jones, the election was important. He despised Wilkerson for what he had done to him, believed him to be devious, immoral and unworthy of holding political office. In addition, it's plainly obvious as to why Jones would not want Wilkerson holding a law enforcement position in Montgomery County: once in office, his persecution of Jones would never end. Jones wanted Wilkerson brought down and he did everything he could to make it happen. Eventually it happened, but it was not Frank Jones or Horace Havner who brought about his ruin, it was Mae Noel, the widow of Wilkerson's supporter, John Warren Noel.

Havner took the information that Jones gave him, and included much of the material that he had submitted to the state supreme court. He also used the state agents that had been assigned to his office. The supervisor of these agents, who worked general criminal investigations and special assignments, was Oscar Rock, who answered directly to the attorney general. Rock had spent considerable time on the Villisca case and probably wanted Wilkerson as badly as his boss did. He did some traveling that spring to look into the former detective's background. It wasn't long before Rock and his men began hearing about what Wilkerson was up to.

As a candidate and applicant to the state bar, Wilkerson was supposed to follow a different set of rules than he had as a detective, but he was either unaware of it or didn't care. In gathering what turned out to be a voluminous file for the Iowa Supreme Court, Havner took a series of affidavits from farmers and businessmen who could attest to Wilkerson's activities either during his investigation, or during his campaign for office. The witnesses spoke of the way that he divided the county in hostile factions; that he used fraudulent and unfair means during his public meetings, and had denounced the courts, the officers of the courts, and the state officials of Iowa. During his 1918 campaign, the affidavits stated, he had "openly and publicly advised Democrats to call for Republican ballots and vote the Republican ticket for him, without further advising them that it would be improper and unlawful for them to do so unless they changed their party affiliation."

The affidavits went on, accusing Wilkerson of damaging the credibility of the primary election, polarizing the county and inciting terrorism, and even defaming the Farmer's National Bank in Red Oak. Exactly what the bank had done to anger Wilkerson wasn't reported, but one of the bank's directors was present during a campaign speech and attested that the former detective had advised his audience to pull their money out of the bank because the president and the active manager were dishonest and embezzling the money that had been entrusted to them. Wilkerson was "an agitator, and a disturber of a very bad character," the bank director reported. "During the past two years in this county, [Wilkerson] has bred discontent, suspicion, disrespect, and dishonor in the minds of his followers for court officials and constituted authority."

The affidavits were collected by Havner to be presented to the court, and it's unlikely that most voters were even aware of them as they prepared to cast their ballots. Even if they had known about them, it's unlikely that many would have cared. These were mostly old charges that had been leveled at Wilkerson for years and those who believed in him were fiercely loyal – which was revealed by the vote. In one of the last elections in which women were not allowed to vote, the men of Montgomery County came out strongly for Wilkerson. There were 987 voters who wrote in his name on the ballot for the position of county attorney, while Wenstrand came in second with 790 votes. Wilkerson even received enough write-in votes on Democratic ballots to win the nomination for that party too, along with three write-in votes for sheriff, one for county recorder, and one for clerk. Ed Peterson swamped his opponent and would go on to become the next sheriff. It was a huge victory for Wilkerson and his cronies and their "slay utterly" campaign against state officials captured the public's attention. While the state as a whole would re-elect both Havner and Governor Harding, both of them lost by substantial margins in Montgomery County.

As the dust settled from the primary, it was clear that Frank Jones' fears were justified. If Wilkerson won the general election – and after the primary, it was assumed he would – he knew that Wilkerson would be absolutely committed to charging him with eight counts of murder. With county resources, a longtime ally as sheriff and a grand jury at his disposal, Wilkerson would undoubtedly resume his attempt to put Frank and Albert Jones on trial. After the Kelly indictment, it seemed that the Jones family was finally safe from Wilkerson, but the primary elections of 1918 sent a stab of terror into the heart of Frank Jones.

The Iowa Supreme Court moved forward in the process to make a decision about Wilkerson's application, designating Oscar Wenstrand as the commissioner to take depositions on the court's behalf. Wenstrand began hearing testimony in mid-June, starting with Ed Peterson and Clarence Miller. He wanted to get the details of Wilkerson's fund-raising from them, as well as testimony about the defiance of the injunction and a copy of his "100 Questions." Wenstrand apparently wanted to show the court that Wilkerson had been retained by the county to investigate the ax murders, and then sought and accepted employment with the "Citizen's Investigating Committee," an association Wilkerson himself took the lead in forming. The committee was also used to raise funds to defend Reverend Kelly. For someone to receive county money to investigate the murders while also raising funds to defend someone accused of the crimes was, in the opinion of Havner and Wenstrand, highly unethical. Witnesses produced records showing the inflammatory nature of Wilkerson's speeches, his derogatory remarks about the attorney general and other officials, and his frequently public airings of the affidavit that Alice Willard filed when she claimed to be "grilled" by Havner.

Wilkerson was allowed to cross-examine the witnesses, and his questions were designed to give Peterson and Miller the opportunity to state for the record, over and over again, that Wilkerson wanted nothing more than truth and justice for everyone; for the guilty to be punished, and for everyone to know that he was even-handed, fair and honest in his dealings. Wilkerson asked questions of Peterson and Miller, particularly about the Willard affidavit, which were designed to bring Havner's conduct into question. The hearing wasn't about the attorney general, and Wilkerson knew it, but as he had always done, he tried to deflect negative attention away from himself and onto those he felt were conspiring against him.

Havner objected to nearly every question asked by Wilkerson, but the validity of the questions would have to be determined by the court. Havner just wanted to make sure that his objections were made for the record. It finally got to the point that Havner's objections became so repetitive that he merely signaled the court reporter to note on the record each time he objected. Peterson and Miller parroted anything that Wilkerson wanted them to say, but Havner hoped he could wear down the court with his objections. He was not only doing this verbally, he was doing it with piles of documents as well. Havner dumped statements and court records from Kansas, Missouri, and Texas on them, along with the transcripts of the entire 1917 grand jury inquiry. The clerk who weighed the box containing the massive accumulation of paperwork stated it weighed 49 pounds.

But all of this would soon be irrelevant. Soon after his nomination, with the court still pondering a decision about whether or not he was eligible for office, Havner's agents caught Wilkerson in a darkened hotel room with Mae Noel and arrested him for adultery. Wilkerson had made a foolish, reckless mistake, one from which he would never recover.

Even though there would be some who would argue about exactly what was going on in the hotel room that night, the arrest itself was pretty straightforward. One fact known for certain was that Mae Noel had received $32,000 in insurance benefits as a result of her husband's death a few months before. She said that she had traveled to Albia and Ottumwa to loan her brother-in-law $1,600. She had the cash and was prepared to make the loan, but wanted her late husband's trusted friend, James Wilkerson, to accompany her on the trip to advise her about collateral and repayment. She made arrangements for her two older children to be cared for in Villisca, but took the 14-month-old baby along with her. The three traveled by train to Albia and spent part of the day on business there before boarding a train for Ottumwa that evening.

It was dark and close to 11 p.m. when they arrived. The first hotel they stopped at did not have suitable accommodation, so Wilkerson and Mae, carrying the baby, walked down the street to the Frazier Hotel. Wilkerson asked for adjoining rooms, one for Mae and the child, and the other for himself. He registered under the name "L.R. Johnson of Centerville" and signed in Mae and the baby as "Mrs. N. Norton and baby of Albia."

Two state agents, W.A. Potter and H.W. Terrell, had seen them enter the hotel. The officers had been working the Wilkerson case for several weeks and in addition to investigating his movements, followed him throughout the region. They trailed the trio through town, secured a room across the hall from Wilkerson's adjoining rooms, and summoned a third agent, L.A. Fisher. Terrell moved a table to the door of his darkened room and stood on it, watching through the glass transom over the door.

Shortly after arriving, Wilkerson called the bellman to his room, and then sent him out to buy two bottles of "near beer," a non-alcoholic beverage that tasted like beer. Wilkerson drank one and then, a few minutes later, went to Mae Noel's room. He was only there for a few minutes before leaving the hotel, returning later with some fruit. Wilkerson dropped off the fruit in Mae's room, and then returned to his room. Moments later, when he stepped back into the hall he was clad in a nightshirt. As an undoubtedly delighted Agent Terrell watched, Wilkerson went back into Mae's room. The agents hurried to the door and one of them pressed his ear against it. The baby fussed for a few minutes and then quieted. The lights were turned off. Terrell's report stated that the agents then heard the sound of creaking bedsprings, which was enough to convince them of what was going on.

The agents had already identified themselves to the desk clerk and informed him that a crime of a carnal nature was in progress. The clerk went to the door, knocked, and asked for Mr. Johnson. There was a short delay before Wilkerson, wearing the nightshirt, opened the door of Mae's room. The agents pushed their way inside, the desk clerk right behind them, and turned on the lights. Mae Noel was in the bed, wearing a green robe, her face turned away from the men. The agents identified themselves, called Wilkerson by name and placed him under arrest. He was taken to his room where he was allowed to dress, and then taken to jail. He was released the next morning after posting a $300 bond. The charge against him was adultery, a felony in Iowa at the time, for which he could face as much as three years in prison.

At the preliminary hearing, Wilkerson's defense stated that the charge was not in the information filed. This may – or may not – have been a mistake. The agents originally charged adultery, but after talking to Havner, it was amended to conspiracy to commit adultery, which they felt was more appropriate. The original charge was dismissed and Wilkerson and Mae were immediately re-arrested for conspiracy to commit adultery. There was a scuffle when Terrell made the arrest and he and Wilkerson nearly came to blows. Needless to say, there was a dispute about what happened. Terrell said Wilkerson resisted arrest and Wilkerson claimed the state agent mishandled and practically assaulted him.

Wilkerson quickly announced that he had been framed. State agents had been trailing him for weeks, he said, hoping to get something on him, which was why he had registered under a false name. The baby had been sick and crying and he had simply gone to Mae's room to try and help quiet the child. There had been nothing inappropriate taking place; he had simply been sitting on the edge of the bed, rocking the baby, which explained the creaking of the bedsprings. The story didn't convince anyone since Mae had no explanation for why she was in her nightclothes or why the lights were turned off. Wilkerson didn't have an excuse for those things either – or why, if he believed that state agents were following him and trying to frame him, he would place himself in such a compromising position.

Havner actually had been following Wilkerson and Jones had his own agents at work as well. It's possible that either Jones or someone else suspected that a relationship existed between Wilkerson and Mae, found out about the trip to Albia and tipped off Havner, who made sure his agents were in place.

Daily reports from the agents dispute this, however. They stated that they had been working on a bootlegging case and just happened to be near the depot when Wilkerson and Mae came in on the train. Ottumwa was a rough town at the time. It was home to several packing plants and industries and attracted more than their share of bootleggers and prostitutes. The reports filed by the agents at the time showed that they had been working in Ottumwa for several nights before Wilkerson arrived. There is nothing to indicate that these particular agents were looking for Wilkerson, and at the trial they maintained that they were not, but they recognized him and knew that Havner and Rock had him in their sights. Terrell had also seen the former detective with Mrs. Wilkerson and knew that the woman with him was not she.

The trial would not be held for months, but the news made it to Montgomery County within days of the arrest. The incident in Ottumwa made front page news and Wilkerson's supporters began to abandon him. The thought of the 52-year-old, married former detective romancing the 25-year-old widow of a man who had been loyal to him was repulsive to everyone. Wilkerson denied everything, but his denials were dismissed in the face of the cold, hard facts that emerged about that night. There had been rumors about Wilkerson and women in the past, including some of his witnesses, including Vina Tompkins. He spent hours with her and she confided things to him that she told no one else. And there was Alice Willard, a woman of questionable reputation who took overnight trips with him to Sioux City, Carbon, and Missouri Valley when he went to question Bert McCaul. There were merely gossip, rumors and suspicion – just like the whispers about Dona Jones and J.B. Moore – but to many, the incident with Mae Noel suddenly made the stories believable.

The county convention was made up of delegates who would cast their votes in a manner that was similar to the electoral college system in national elections. While delegates generally voted in accordance with the popular election, they had the authority to resolve disputes and to elect candidates in situations where none of them received at least 35 percent of the primary vote. The delegates were also authorized to rule on the candidates' eligibility, which was bad news for Wilkerson.

A few days after his arrest, the convention gathered to hear a petition that had been filed by 18 delegates claiming that Wilkerson was not qualified to be the party's nominee and, therefore, should be ruled ineligible. The petition did not mention his arrest, but it was undoubtedly filed because of it. The allegation that was made stated that because he had not been admitted to the bar at the time of the primary election, he should not have been able to run. That meant the write-in votes that had been cast for him were invalid and so could not be counted at all.

It was a contentious meeting, but this time, Wilkerson was outnumbered and he no longer had the vocal support that he'd once had. Attorneys Pringle and Beeson, who had been against Wilkerson from the beginning, represented those who wanted him disqualified. They submitted that he was not eligible, that he did not file an affidavit, as required by law and that the Republicans were entitled to field a candidate in October who was already eligible, not someone who "may be eligible" at some future date.

Wilkerson was present for the meeting and was allowed to speak on his own behalf. As usual, he was arrogant and insulting. He referred to the board as the "chief justice" and "associate judges" and called the witnesses "party bosses." He asked if the will of the 18 objectors was superior to the will of the people, whom he maintained wanted him to take office. He pointed out that the Iowa constitution made no reference to a candidate being admitted to the bar, and told the convention that they had no business getting involved in what he saw as a constitutional issue.

When the debate was over, the convention voted 96 to 25 against Wilkerson. A note was entered in the record: "That in view of events which have occurred in this county and elsewhere, it would be a disgrace to the county, to this state and to the legal profession to permit one J.N. Wilkerson to occupy any position of public trust."

The incident in Ottumwa was never mentioned in the public documents or in the debates, but it was never far out of the committee members' minds.

Wilkerson had finally suffered a serious defeat. He'd been given a taste of his own medicine and he didn't like it. He had to face the fact that he would not be able to run for county attorney and there was nothing he could do about it. No public meetings, threats or innuendoes were going to change the public's minds. There were other things he could do, however, and after exploring his options he filed a $195,000 slander lawsuit in early September that named 33 men who provided affidavits against him to the state supreme court. He also withdrew his application to the Iowa bar, changed his residency to Omaha, and applied for admission to the Nebraska bar.

Wilkerson was in Villisca on Christmas Day, 1918 – which marked an odd last encounter with Frank Jones. Wilkerson's purpose in town that day is unknown, but he may have been there to visit Mae Noel. Charges against Mae had been dismissed and she would be among the witnesses who would testify for the defense. The adultery trial, after several delays, was set to begin in January 1919. A few days before Christmas, Wilkerson learned that his application for admission to the Nebraska bar had been denied, and he had given up on the slander suit. He never filed the necessary papers and the case was eventually dismissed.

When Wilkerson saw Jones on the street that Christmas day, the man he hated so much was on his way to the City Bakery. Wilkerson approached him and spoke. No one knows what was said, but an argument ensued, although no blows were struck. Jones turned away and went into the bakery. Wilkerson followed and there were more harsh words. Angry, Jones drew back his foot and kicked Wilkerson in the leg. He could have struck him in a number of ways, or worse since he often carried a revolver in his pocket. Instead, he chose to kick him like a dog.

A farmer named R.E. Gilmore was in the bakery and he stepped between the two of them. Jones turned in disgust and walked out. Wilkerson watched him go, and started to follow, but Gilmore grabbed the former detective by the arm, told him that it was over. The two of them watched as Frank Jones disappeared down the street.

The adultery trial was as nasty as one might imagine. Havner would have been wise to drop the case and save himself the trouble and the taxpayers the expense; there was little to be gained from it. Havner had been re-elected and Wilkerson was now as politically ruined as his nemesis Jones. His support was gone, he couldn't raise any further money for the investigation and his chance to gain admission to the bar was gone. A conviction in the case would be hard to come by and even if the state won, it was unlikely that Wilkerson would face any real penalty. Havner was kicking him when he was already down, hoping to put him away for good with a felony on his record and the public snickering about how he went into Mrs. Noel's hotel room in his nightshirt to "help her with the baby."

The preliminary motions would have been amusing if they had not been so pointless. The defense filed a motion that conspiracy to commit adultery was not actually a crime; the act either took place or it didn't. The law, they argued, was to punish people who committed adultery, not those who thought about it. If that was illegal, then half the state would be in jail. Havner, who was prosecuting the case himself, disagreed and produced precedents to support that a conspiracy to commit was still a crime. The judge agreed and the case moved to trial.

Wilkerson was just as aggressive in his defense as he had always been. He started the trail by petitioning the judge for a bodyguard, claiming that his life was in danger. He specifically pointed out Agent Terrell, who was on hand to testify, saying that Terrell had assaulted him and he feared for his life. The judge said that he really didn't think there was any need for concern, but assigned an officer to watch over him during the trial.

The prosecution presented its case in one day, relying on the testimony of the agents and hotel employees. The defense was just as brief. Mae Noel's doctor testified that she had recovered from measles a short time before the trip with Wilkerson and was likely still in a weakened condition. He also said that the baby was coming down with measles around the same time, which is why he had been so fussy. Bank papers confirmed that the trip did have a legitimate business purpose. Wilkerson didn't testify, but Mae did. She said that she was feeling frail and exhausted when they arrived in Ottumwa and that Wilkerson had carried both of their bags and the baby to the hotel. She said that the baby had cried and Wilkerson heard it from his room next door and offered to help. He had, she said, gone out for fruit, helped her while she fed the baby and finally got the child to sleep. Nothing else had occurred, she said; there were no advances by Wilkerson and nothing that would be considered inappropriate. Mrs. Wilkerson watched her testimony while seated in the courtroom, but what she may have been thinking about the incident is unknown.

Understandably, the jury largely rejected the case. The idea of someone actually being charged with "conspiracy to commit adultery" likely sounded far-fetched to them. The jurors were uncomfortable with the idea of state agents lurking outside of hotel rooms listening for creaking bedsprings. They began their deliberations with a ballot of 10-2 for acquittal, soon moved to 11-1, but got no further. As with the Kelly trial, there was one holdout and there was no convincing him. They debated for 46 hours, and then gave up. The jury was hung and Havner wisely chose not to try the case again.

James Wilkerson never returned to detective work. He apparently also made no further attempts to run for office or to practice law. Instead, he purchased part interest in the mummified remains of a an old man who purported to be the real John Wilkes Booth. This was an odd story in itself.

The body was that of an Oklahoma man named David E. George, who claimed to be Booth. He had allegedly escaped from Washington after the Lincoln assasination with help from fellow conspirators who covered up the fact that he had not been killed. George died in 1903, but years earlier, when he believed that he was dying from an illness, he confessed his identity to several people, including Finis Bates, an attorney from Texas. After his death, a few newspapers carried the story about his claiming to be Booth. Bates, who was living in Memphis at the time, traveled to Enid, Oklahoma, to view the remains. He discovered that the body was that of the man who told him that he was Booth several years before.

The body was unclaimed for several years and remained on display at Penniman's undertaking parlor. Eventually, Finis Bates purchased the mumified corpse and had it tested to try and prove that it was really Booth. Oddly, when it was examined at the University of Chicago, researchers found a silver ring that had been lodged in the corpse's stomach cavity. Although badly tarnished, the initials "JWB" were etched into the ring. This discovery prompted Dr. Otto L. Schmidt, president of the Chicago Historical Society, to write, "I can say safely that we believe Booth's body is here in my office."

The identity of the mummy was never accepted by mainstream historians, which is likely what got the attention of James Wilkerson. During the 1920s and 1930s, Finis Bates leased the mummy to Wilkerson and a carnival promoter, who toured the country and charged 25 cents to view the "Assassin of President Abraham Lincoln." Wilkerson toured with the mummy and delivered lectures about the Lincoln assassination and why he believed that it was the result of a conspiracy that reached into the highest levels of the government. In effect, it was the same old song sung to a different tune.

The mummy was displayed until the early 1940s, when Wilkerson's partner went bankrupt and moved to Idaho. He placed the mummy in a chair on his front porch and charged visitors a dime to take a look at it. Eventually, the mummy disappeared; it is rumored to be in a private collection somewhere, but no one knows for sure.

As for Wilkerson, he suffered a severe stroke in 1943 and never recovered. He died a year later, an old and broken man, haunted by the events of the past.

Horace Havner continued on with his distinguished career. He worked on many important cases, including a series of school and church fires and an attempted bombing against members of the Dutch Reformed church in the New Sharon area. Members of the congregation had obtained conscientious objector status and as the war dragged on, resentment against them led to violence. After months of investigation, Havner and his agents made several arrests and the agitators were successfully prosecuted. Hoping that the publicity he received for solving the "Hollander Fires" would be beneficial, he ran for governor in 1920. He lost in the primaries and returned to private law practice in Marengo.

Albert Jones settled into a quiet life after the stormy years of trials, accusations, and political intrigue. He farmed and spent time at the implement store until suffering a series of strokes in the early 1930s. He was an invalid for some time, but he eventually recovered enough to be able to walk downtown on his good days. He was happiest when at the implement store, talking and visiting with the staff and with old friends who stopped by. His recovery was short-lived, though, and after suffering another massive stroke in the summer of 1935, he became bed-ridden and unaware of his surroundings. Frank Jones was at his son's bedside on August 2, 1935, when Albert died. He was only 49 years old.

Dona Jones later remarried and left Villisca for good.

Frank's daughter, Letha, left Villisca shortly after the murders. She enrolled at Columbia University in New York and later taught at colleges in North Carolina and Florida. She eventually returned to New York and taught at the Maxwell Training School for Teachers. She spent many summers with her parents in Villisca and traveled to Europe with them. She inherited Frank's farm property and that, along with her retirement income, allowed her to live comfortably in New York until the end of her life.

Letha never lived in Villisca again. She loved her family and her friends, but she never really forgave the townspeople for the fact that they were willing to believe the worst about her father, a man who had always done good things for the community.

Letha died in New York on June 3, 1973. She is buried with her parents and brother in the Villisca Cemetery.

Frank Jones remained unbowed by the pressures that had been placed on him and by the destruction of his political career. He may have been pushed out of office, but his influence in the state of Iowa did not end. He had many friends and supporters and for several years after his defeat in 1916, it was not unusual for politicians looking for endorsements, ideas, or furthering causes to write or call upon Frank Jones. He may have lost his political influence in Montgomery County, but he was still a man to listen to in Des Moines. He also continued on the state board of education, filling a vacancy in 1915, and was later reappointed by the governor for a six-year term. His work on the board of education, by all accounts, was exemplary. As a fiscal conservative, he dealt with trimming expenses at the state universities and worked with educators to receive their appropriations. He attended, and was honored at, countless college graduation exercises and was present for many retirements and the induction of new university presidents. Long after his term on the board expired, he continued to get letters from those he had worked with, thanking him for his support and guidance.

The attacks by Wilkerson took their toll on Jones; there was no question about it. His once-wide circle of friends became considerably smaller, but those who knew him best remained fiercely loyal. He still taught Sunday school, still visited and dined with close friends and still spent a lot of time at the store. But he never forgot that a significant segment of the community believed, or at least suspected, that he was a murderer. Many of them were suspicious about everything that he did, and that suspicion never really went away. As mentioned by Roy Marshall in his comprehensive book on the case, some locals even believed that Jones stayed close to the dying Albert's bedside because he feared his son might offer some sort of confession about the murders. They refused to see Frank as merely a loving parent, blinded by grief over the loss of his son.

By the late 1920s, Frank's correspondence with politicians and educators had dwindled. He had faded from the public eye and perhaps that was for the best. He enjoyed traveling and for the next decade, he and Maude took numerous extended trips. The Depression affected his finances and as he and Maude got older, they began staying home more, edging toward complete retirement. Finally, in 1937, he sold the implement business. He was now 81 years old and still in good health. He self-published his memoirs in 1940 and wrote that he had never taken a drink of liquor, did not use tobacco, had excellent hearing and eyesight, and had all but one of his own teeth. Around this time, he planned his funeral, making detailed notes of how he wanted the service to be conducted.

Frank Jones passed away in his sleep on February 6, 1941. There were many in Villisca who believed that he took the secrets of the Moore-Stillinger murders to his grave.

After his death, the contents of his study were donated to the Villisca Public Library. They would not be sorted out until 1968. There were letters, notes, and grand jury statements about the case, but no shocking secrets were ever found. Years later, a couple who purchased the Jones home discovered all of Albert's old diaries and papers in the attic. They destroyed them without letting anyone else read them, simply stating that there was nothing relevant in them. Whether or not they held any answers to the Villisca murders will remain a mystery. If Frank and Albert Jones were innocent of any involvement in the murders, then they, too, became victims in one of the most horrible crimes in Iowa history.

For the most part, this brings the story to an end. It's a story of lives created and of lives broken and lost, all swirling around a series of murders that have never been solved. The impact of eight of those murders -- those in Villisca -- is still being felt today. In that sense, the story will never end.

The people of Villisca were never given the justice they deserved. The hatred that was fostered by the dispute between the pro-Jones and anti-Jones factions split the town and it festered there for generations. Villisca, even today, has never gotten over it. Many of the residents would rather it was forgotten, but it refuses to go away.

The murders still haunt the town, lingering in large part because the killer was never caught.

23. BLOOD ON THEIR HANDS
WHO COMMITTED THE VILLISCA AX MURDERS?

When looking back on the murders committed in Villisca – and in the other locations across the Midwest during this same time period – we find that the case offers no more clues about the identity of the killer, or his motives, than it did to the authorities back in 1912.

By all accounts, the Moores were well liked and seemed to get along with just about everyone. Everyone. There seemed to be no reason why anyone would want them dead or why anyone would have been targeting Joseph Stillinger by slaying his daughters. The only person in town who seemed to have a grudge against any of the victims was Frank Jones, and despite the campaign concocted against him by Wilkerson, the idea that he would kill someone over a business dispute was almost laughable. But, as mentioned previously, this was the suspect and motive that seemed to be the most appealing to the people of Villisca. It was simply because it presented motives that they could understand – jealousy, greed, and envy. When you add in lust and the alleged affair between Dona Jones and J.B. Moore, you have an almost biblical motive that anyone could sink his teeth into.

Unfortunately, I don't think things were that simple. The residents of Villisca at that time – just like the residents of other small towns where death came calling – wanted closure, an easy remedy for the horror in their midst. They didn't want to consider something even more horrific and sinister – that the murders might be the work of a random stranger, with absolutely no motive at all.

SEARCHING FOR A KILLER...

In the days that followed the murders in Villisca, there were at least four suspects mentioned in every edition of the newspaper. However, leads were quickly exhausted, alibis were established and possibilities began to dwindle. The local police, state investigators, private detectives who were working for pay, and even amateur detectives hoping to collect the reward all combed the town and the surrounding region, following every clue that was presented. Dozens of theories were pursued, but each time the investigation seemed to be getting close to a breakthrough, it all fell apart again.

On the second day after the discovery of the murders, a clairvoyant from nearby Red Oak, a woman called "Auntie" Hamilton, made her views known in the newspaper. Using what she called her "occult powers," she proclaimed the killer to be a large man with a dark mustache, roughly dressed and wearing a slouch hat. She predicted he would give himself up in two weeks. She also foretold (not realizing the ax had been found at the scene) that the murder weapon would be found near a slaughterhouse. The local newspapers didn't take her seriously, but others did. Ross Moore got a couple of men to go with him to look for clues at the abandoned slaughterhouse on the banks of the East Nodaway River, but as we know, there was nothing there that had any connection at all to the murders.

Two early suspects were disgruntled relatives of the Moores'. Both of them were living out of state and it was easily established that they had not been in Iowa at the time of the murders. Among others who attracted attention that first summer was a man named Charles B. Soward, a stranger who had bought a hand ax in Clarinda. It would seem odd that something so simple could draw attention, but not in light of the frenzy of suspicion and speculation that swept the countryside immediately after the murders. In addition, Soward's behavior was a bit on the unusual side. He was seen sharpening the ax as he walked down the street, and a few people claimed that he made some disturbing remarks. He spoke about the Villisca murders, saying that it would have been no trick at all to plan the crime, "crack the victims over the head," and then go to the river and wash off the blood.

Soward was quickly arrested and began telling the authorities a bizarre story. He was, he claimed, "Head Chief of the U.S. Indian Police" and showed them a badge that designated him in that position. He said that he had been appointed by Judge C.A. Hanford of Seattle, Washington, and had a staff of 50,000 men working for him. The authorities learned that there had been a Judge Hanford in Seattle, but that he had recently resigned during impeachment proceedings and was difficult to reach. Soward was the cousin of Dr. Erastus T. Farrens of Clarinda, but Farrens told the press that his cousin was insane and that he hadn't seen him for 20 years or more.

Whatever his mental state, Soward seemed to enjoy the attention he was getting. He was held on a federal charge and transferred to Union County. While in jail, he made jokes, answered questions, with questions and generally made a fool of anyone who tried to question him. Among the detectives who interviewed Soward was Thomas O'Leary. He later told the newspapers that he didn't think the man had anything to do with the Villisca murders. Soward baited his interrogators, but it was soon established that he was in Colorado when the murders occurred, 500 miles from Villisca, and he couldn't have committed them.

Another suspect that summer was a man named Andy Sawyer, who came to the attention of the authorities through a Burlington Railroad bridge foreman named Thomas Dwyer. He had become convinced that Sawyer had committed the murders and contacted Sheriff Jackson in late June 1912. The story he told was a plausible one.

Dwyer said that on the Monday after the murders, Sawyer approached him in Creston looking for work. He said that Sawyer was wet to the knees as if he'd been wading in the river and his shoes were covered with mud. Sawyer told him that he was good with an ax and was given the job of sharpening piles, which were timber pieces used for the bases of wooden railroad bridges. By late afternoon or evening, Sawyer was talking about the murders and didn't seem to want to talk about anything else. He told Dwyer that he had been in Villisca on Sunday night and wondered if he might be a suspect. A day or two later, Dwyer was with him when Sawyer took a handkerchief out of his pocket, saying that he had a lot of them, having picked up a dozen or so in Villisca.

Dwyer said that Sawyer was the fastest man with an ax that he had ever seen. He spent a lot of time sharpening it and even took it to bed with him at night. A few days after Sawyer started with the crew, Dwyer saw him bent over, rubbing his head with both hands. Dwyer approached him from behind and although he didn't mean to, he startled the other man. Sawyer leapt to his feet and shouted, "I'll cut your God damned heads off!" and began wildly swinging his ax.

Dwyer had seen enough. He went to Red Oak and talked to Sheriff Jackson, who went looking for the itinerant railroad worker. He found Sawyer with a railroad crew in Cumberland, called him aside and asked a few questions. Sawyer denied that he was involved in the crime. He said that he had hopped a freight train from Osceola, about 60 miles east of Villisca, and had ridden it to Creston on the night the murders took place. He spent the night in Creston and on Monday morning, asked Dwyer for a job. He hadn't been in Villisca at all, he said. He heard about the murders in the newspaper and was only interested because he had once lived near Villisca and knew some extended members of the Moore family. Jackson heard him out, but didn't think there was anything to pursue and went back to Red Oak.

After Jackson left, Sawyer was allegedly very agitated. He returned to the boxcar where the crew slept, gathered his belongings and walked away. Dwyer was unhappy with the lack of an investigation and took his story to the newspapers, which printed his belief that Sawyer was the killer. Jackson didn't know where Sawyer had gone and hadn't checked his alibi, so he took some heat over it. Several weeks passed before Thomas O'Leary finally traced Sawyer to a farm near Lark, North Dakota, but it was not until the fall of 1912 that Montgomery County Attorney William Ratcliff took a Burns detective named W.S. Gordon with him to interview Andy Sawyer.

They traveled by train, resorting to renting a horse and buggy to make the last leg of the trip to the isolated little town. The weather was cold in early October and rain turned to sleet before they arrived at the small tarpaper shack where Sawyer lived with his family. He was not home when they arrived but Sawyer's wife, according to Gordon's report, fainted when she saw them. After she recovered, she told them where Sawyer was. They found a place to stay the night and tracked him down the next day. He gave a more detailed statement than he had given to Sheriff Jackson and the two investigators returned to Iowa to check out his story.

Sawyer's account was so seedy that it had to be the truth. He had left his wife the previous spring, went to Des Moines, got drunk, was arrested, was thrown in a "pest house," was released, spent a few nights with a prostitute, rode the rails, was run out of Osceola by the police, and eventually arrived in Creston on Sunday, June 9. Gordon set about verifying the story and while much of it couldn't be confirmed, he was able to place Sawyer in some of the places that he claimed he was in. Gordon soon became convinced that Sawyer could not have been in Villisca on the night of the murders.

Lunatics seemed to be everywhere that summer.

Harlan Burge, a farmer from nearby Gravity, came to see the authorities in Villisca late that summer to show them some threatening letters that he had received. Four years earlier, Burge had hired a man named John Bohlen to help him with the corn picking. Burge did not get to know Bohlen well, had no idea where he lived, and did not see him again until January 1912. One winter's day, Bohlen came to see Burge and accused his startled former employer of trying to hypnotize him. At first, Burge didn't recognize him, but when Bohlen told him that he had once worked for him, Burge recalled the hired hand. Bohlen again asked why Burge was trying to hypnotize him and the farmer insisted that he wasn't. Bohlen seemed satisfied with that response and drove away in his buggy.

That was the last that Burge heard from him until a month after the murders. At that time, he received a 40-page letter from Bohlen, followed by another a few days later. Both letters rambled on about the "Garden of Paradise... being cast out of the east door of the temple... a mark to be placed on the head of the righteous to prevent them from being slain," and more – for page after page after page. The letter was postmarked Nebraska City, Nebraska, so the well-traveled Detective O'Leary set out to make sure the man had not been in Villisca at the time of the murders.

Another odd letter was sent to Sheriff Bradshaw of Ellsworth, Kansas, which he copied and sent to Sheriff Jackson. The letter read: "Sorry you students of crime are puzzled about the ax men according to Matthew 3rd chapter 10th verse and Josiah 9th chapter 24th verse the ax users viz, the Gideonites are inhabitants of Lincoln, Nebraska, and surroundings of the country and of the same city. If you will follow my advice examine all Nebraska people living in your city and if you fail to find the ax men I may write again. Be sure and do what I am telling you and you will find your man. The above is a prophecy went into force since 1911, May the 18th, and it will continue. Axmen for four years – after four years then the criminals will use fire to destroy human life. Yours for Humanity and God." The letter was signed "Masar Shallal Rash Bass."

Sheriff Jackson heard from people who recalled the assault conviction of a man named Joe Briggs in Page County seven years before. Someone had the idea that J.B. Moore had identified a knife belonging to Briggs, which led to his conviction. Briggs, as the story went, had been released a few days before the murders and had sworn revenge.

Another "lead" given to Sheriff Jackson had to do with the only murder that had ever taken place in Villisca before the summer of 1912. A man named W. Thiele had become aware of his wife's relationship with a traveling man and had stabbed her to death. He was found guilty, but because of the circumstances, he was given jail time rather than being hanged. A rumor in the summer of 1912 was that J.B. Moore had been on the Thiele jury and that Thiele had promised to get back at the jurors. According to the story, he had escaped a couple of days before the murders occurred.

Jackson checked out both stories, but of course, they led to nothing.

Detective O'Leary had dozens, perhaps hundreds of letters to read during his investigation. He had to look over every one of them, deciphering some, discarding others and determining what should be done about the "information" they contained. For weeks after the murders, they flooded into the post offices at Villisca and Red Oak. Most of them were written by people who sincerely thought they had information that would help with the case. Others were from psychics, religious lunatics, and cranks. O'Leary read them all, making notes on everything that warranted follow-up.

It was a tedious job. Just figuring out the handwriting on some of them was a challenge. Several letters blamed the crime on a gang of Negroes who were killing white Midwesterners as vengeance for lynchings that were occurring in the South.

Other letters, such as one connecting the crimes to "The Whirlwinds of Ezekiel," reinforced the theory held by some (including Sheriff Jackson) that a group of religious fanatics were responsible for the crime. This is not as far-fetched as modern readers might think. The early 1900s in America was a time when a great number of religious cults, sects, and movements began to form, alarming the staid Baptists, Presbyterians, and Methodists of the nation's small towns and farm communities. The presence of the "Holy Rollers" in Villisca on the night of the murders signaled to many local residents that perhaps some sort of murderous religious nuts had been at work.

O'Leary had particular interest in the "Whirlwinds of Ezekiel" letter. It was postmarked from Kansas, where other ax murders had taken place, and rambled on at length about scripture, vengeance, and axes. The writer identified himself as the "Miss Tree of Life" and wrote that "death upon earth is Errette." Other passages read, "if you listen to the voice in my words you will find me" and "the neighborhood, the press where these killings take place, seldom record or take note of the root, for God will Show Man. Is it murder without money incentives that excites us? Are those in murder without money behind it necessarily insane? ... The Whirlwinds of Ezekiel, blessed art thou, Villisca. God's hand hath touched thou as Christ was murdered upon the cross of the world head down on the Cross of Nay Shun. It is only More for the Errette still in you. Sweet babes hear the shaking of a Nay Shun sacrifice of heaven." The letter was signed "Eli Eloi."

O'Leary puzzled over some of the words in the letter, believing that if the writer was not the killer, he had some knowledge of the crimes. O'Leary was one of the proponents of the idea that the killer had murdered before in Kansas, Colorado Springs, and elsewhere. He felt the words "Show Man" were a play on the name Showman, the family that had been murdered in their beds in Ellsworth, Kansas, in 1911, by someone wielding an ax. He felt "More" referred to the Moore family and that "Miss Tree of Life" and Nay Shun" were obvious, but he never figured out the meaning of the word "Errette."

No additional letter came from the writer and the "Whirlwinds of Ezekiel" were eventually forgotten.

In time, the principal suspects in the case became a wealthy banker and politician and a deranged minister with a taste for young girls. Despite what many believed was strong evidence against them, some of the detectives who worked the case were unable to ignore other, similar killings that had occurred in the Midwest around the same time as the Villisca murders. These cases were outlined in the early pages of the book.

It is my belief that a serial killer was at work in the Midwest at the time. In those days, such terminology was not used, but one newspaper referred to a "transient butcher." There was certainly reason for this possibility to be considered. In fact, I feel that this is the most likely explanation as to who killed the Moore family and the two Stillinger girls. Readers will recall my numerous references to "Billy the Axman," as he was dubbed in one newspaper story. Despite the humorous name, there was nothing funny about this harbinger of death, who traveled by rail throughout the Midwestern states, bringing horror along with him.

I believe this killer visited Villisca in June 1912. I also believe that he was not the only person to enter the Moore house on the night of June 9, and the early morning hours of June 10. Reverend Kelly may not have been the killer, but he certainly was not without blame.

"BILLY THE AXMAN"

In September 1911, a series of bloody ax murders began in Colorado Springs, Colorado. Like a plague, the killer traveled the Midwest, likely by rail, seeking victims in Kansas, Illinois, and Iowa. He moved silently, leaving almost no trace behind. Each of the murder sites was remarkably similar to the others and the crimes were carried out in almost the same way. The "transient butcher" murdered his victims in their beds, crushing their skulls with an ax. The bodies were covered, the windows draped, and lamps were found with the glass chimneys removed. In some cases, he washed up after his grim task. Other times he consumed food found in the cupboards. He continued to kill until 1914, when he apparently vanished without a trace.

The newspapers called the killer "Billy the Axman," which is the closest we have ever come to giving him a name. His true identity has never been learned, but there were several attempts to identify him. There were a number of detectives and police officials who believed that a serial murderer was responsible for not only the murders in Villisca, but for the other Midwest murders as well. Every one of them was hot on the trail of the killer for a time, although in the end, he was never captured.

Billy the Axman was first "identified" by the Chicago police in the summer of 1912. They believed the killer was an escaped lunatic named Galasko Enchevy who had been arrested in early 1910 for allegedly killing a former schoolteacher named Jennie Cleghorn in Chicago's Englewood neighborhood. In January, her beheaded corpse was found on the street and Enchevy had confessed to the crime – or at least he had babbled, "Yes, I killed her. I killed her but it wasn't my fault." He was arrested and committed to an insane asylum, from which he later escaped.

Chicago Assistant Chief of Police Herman Schuettler, a well-known and experienced officer who had been involved in the famous Luetgert murder case in 1897, wrote a letter addressed to the "Villisca City Marshal" about Enchevy and suggested that he might be the "transient butcher" who had been killing people throughout the Midwest. Schuettler had been researching Enchevy and noted that the 1911 and 1912 murders occurred after he escaped from the asylum. He wrote, "In every case, the murderer – it seems to be one man – unlocks the door to enter and fastens it after the crime, proceeding as quietly as possible, just like Enchevy did. I believe Enchevy is traveling all over the country killing people. He is a maniac that changes with the moon. He loses control over himself and is irresponsible."

There were some things to like about Enchevy as a suspect: he had committed an earlier crime, he was from the Midwest, he was an escapee from an asylum, and no one seemed to know his whereabouts. There was also speculation about why the articles of clothing in Villisca and the other murder scenes had been draped over mirrors and windows. Some believed that it was a superstition from Romania or Bulgaria, stemming from the idea that if you saw your own reflection in a room where a dead person lay, you would also soon die. People from Eastern Europe, like Enchevy, often pulled down window shades and covered mirrors while the dead lay in state.

In addition, Enchevy was obviously insane, as many investigators believed Billy the Axman was. But was Enchevy *too* insane to have gotten away with so many murders? Yes, I believe he was. I also believe that Captain Schuettler was wrong in his analysis of the Axman being a crazed, out-of-control killer. The murders were all very organized and while obviously the work of a psychopath, they were not the work of a disorganized one, as Enchevy definitely was.

The authorities in Chicago and Villisca would have definitely liked to have talked to Enchevy, even though hard evidence linking him to the murders was basically non-existent, but he was never found. Eventually, he was forgotten.

Another Billy the Axman suspect was a man named Henry Lee Moore, who was no relation to the Villisca victims. The details of his crimes were mentioned earlier in the book, but basically, Moore was convicted of the ax murders of his mother and grandmother in December 1912, just months after the Villisca murders occurred. There was at least one detective who believed that Moore was responsible for the bloody rampage of death that wreaked havoc across the Midwest, including the slaughter in Villisca.

An unbalanced man who was prone to violent rages, Moore was prosecuted in December 1912, for the two murders in Columbia, Missouri. The possible connection between Moore and the earlier murders was made after authorities in Villisca requested federal assistance in investigating the June 1912 massacre. The police had the savaged bodies of the Moores and the Stillinger girls but had no clues or direction for their investigation. A federal officer, Matthew Wilson McClaughry, was assigned to the case and his investigation revealed that the Villisca murders were not unique. He connected the Villisca killer to the murders in Colorado Springs, the Dawson family in Illinois, and the Showman family in Ellsworth, Kansas. Just five days before the carnage in Villisca, the Hudsons were murdered in Paola, Kansas. These murders were carried out in the same way as the earlier crimes and the scene seemed to be duplicated again in Villisca a short time later. No suspect had ever been identified in any of the killings and rumors of a "romance angle" in the Hudson case produced no leads. McClaughry believed that he was dealing with a transient maniac after the Villisca murders, but even so, clues were in short supply.

Mathew McClaughry was a bit of an anomaly among the investigators of his day. His father was the warden of the Leavenworth Penitentiary and his brother was in charge of the Iowa State Reformatory. He started his career as a records clerk at Leavenworth and went on to lead the U.S. Department of Justice's Bureau of Criminal Identification when it was moved to the penitentiary in 1907 to serve as the nation's repository for fingerprint evidence. He became a special agent for the Department of Justice (a forerunner to today's F.B.I.) and studied the Bertillon fingerprint system under its creator in France.

Readers may remember McClaughry's less than illustrious arrival in Villisca after the murders. When he arrived in town, he was so drunk that Dr. Linquist forced him to leave the Moore house and go to his hotel to sleep it off. When he sobered up, he returned to the house and wrote a detailed report of the scene. He also spent the next two days attempting to find fingerprints in the house. He examined lamp globes, mirrors, panes of glass, the bloody wash basin, the ax -- anything that might have been touched by the killer -- but he found no fingerprints that were usable.

McClaughry continued investigating the case, but it was coincidence that pointed him in the direction of Henry Moore. Prison officials in Missouri sent a letter to Leavenworth to ask about Henry Moore's time spent at the Kansas Reformatory. Moore was now serving a life sentence in Missouri for the December 1912 murders of his mother and grandmother, and McClaughry's father informed his son of the imprisoned ax murderer. After comparing the evidence in all of the cases, capped by interviews with Moore, McClaughry announced on May 9, 1913, that the books had been closed on 23 Midwestern homicides. He theorized that Moore was responsible for crimes in Colorado, Kansas, Illinois, and Iowa based on the similarities between the crime scenes and the fact that the killings had started after Moore's release from the Kansas Reformatory in 1911, and stopped after his imprisonment in Missouri.

Moore had been born November 1, 1874, in Boone County, Missouri, and was the eldest son of Enoch and Georgia Ann Wilson Moore. Enoch Moore was a farmer and Civil War veteran and Georgia supported herself in later years as a nurse for families in the Columbia area. In the 1900 census, Henry Lee Moore was listed as a farmhand living in Franklin County, Iowa, with a family named Vaux, which included a young daughter named Martha. By 1910, the Vauxes had moved to northern Wisconsin, taking Martha and her daughter, Edna, with them. Martha was listed in the census as a widow, although it's likely that her daughter was fathered by Henry Moore.

Moore was not listed in the 1910 census because he was awaiting incarceration in Sedgwick County, Kansas, on a forgery charge. Even though he was 35, he convinced the authorities that he was much younger and was sentenced to the Kansas Reformatory School in Hutchinson. He was released from the reformatory on April 26, 1911, making it theoretically possible for him to have committed the crimes that started in Colorado Springs in September 1911. Testimony at Moore's trial indicated that he had lived with his mother and grandmother in Missouri during the winter of 1911 and the summer of 1912 before taking a job with the railroad. His employment with the railroad could have afforded him the chance to travel around the country, killing people, but in truth, he didn't start working for the Wabash Railroad until September 1912, long after most of the murders occurred. The other big problem with McClaughry's theory was that he stated the murders stopped after Moore's arrest in 1912, but this completely left out the nearly identical murders in Blue Island in 1914. Henry Moore, from prison, denied any involvement in the other crimes.

Other law enforcement officials did not seem to put much stock in McClaughry's theory. Officials in Columbia, Missouri, did not think Moore was connected to the other murders. Thomas O'Leary, who investigated the Villisca case, interviewed Moore in prison after his arrest to determine if he had anything to do with the Iowa murders. He went away believing that Moore was not the killer. As he wrote to Henry Sampson, "As you are no doubt aware, there was absolutely no connection between the Columbia and Villisca murders except that an ax was used in both cases and the names were the same."

Henry Moore was undoubtedly a murderer, but he was no "transient butcher." He was guilty of ax murder, but the crime in Columbia was so poorly executed that he was immediately arrested and unanimously convicted. Was it really likely that a man accused of killing people in cities across the Midwest and vanishing without a trace would return home and kill his remaining family members in such a haphazard and obvious manner?

Moore spent 36 years in prison before being paroled on December 2, 1949. He was 82 years old and had lived for eight years at the Salvation Army Men's Center in St. Louis, working as a tailor and earning $40 a month, when the governor commuted his sentence in 1956. When and where he died remains a mystery.

The last Billy the Axman suspect to emerge was the only one tied to the Blue Island murders in 1914. Although William Mansfield was investigated, he was eventually cleared, despite Detective Wilkerson's efforts to hang the crime on him.

A year after the murders took place, another suspect emerged. In July 1915, a man was arrested in Buffalo, New York, who confessed to the Mislich murder. His name was Casimir Arciszewski and he had once boarded with the Mislich family. He was alleged to be mentally ill and after making advances toward the Mislichs' daughter, and failing to pay his rent, he was thrown out. He dropped out of sight soon after.

After his arrest, Arciszewski told the police that he had roamed the country both before and after the murders, traveling by rail and drifting aimlessly. According to the time range of the murders, this would have made it possible for him to be Billy the Axman, although most likely he wasn't. Billy was an organized killer and while insane, it's likely that no one would have ever suspected that he was a bloodthirsty maniac. The same thing couldn't have been said for Arciszewski.

One day, he simply walked into a police station in Buffalo and confessed to the Mislich murders. Two Chicago detectives and the mayor of Blue Island traveled to New York and brought him back, intent on learning if he was connected to the string of other murders that had been taking place since 1911. If he was, he never told them. He was judged to be insane and incompetent to stand trial, and was committed to a mental asylum in 1915. After that, he vanished into history, leaving another mystery in his wake.

In time, the idea that a transient murderer was responsible for the Midwest murders, including Villisca, began to fade in popularity. In Iowa in the years that followed, most people were happy to believe that Reverend Kelly committed to the Villisca killings, or that Frank Jones was somehow involved. Kelly "confessed" to the murders, but was later acquitted, and Jones denied any involvement in the crimes until the day he died.

Over the years, the information collected by detectives like Thomas O'Leary and Matthew McClaughry was largely forgotten. McClaughry always maintained that Henry Moore was responsible for the murders and while I believe that he was wrong, I do believe that his investigation was on the right track.

The murders in Villisca remain officially unsolved; however, I think that I know what happened in the Moore house on the night of June 9, 1912 – leaving little reason to wonder why the house is haunted today.

"MURDERED IN THEIR BEDS"

The killer knew what happened in the Moore house that night.

One other man knew also, but he never really told everything that he knew, or everything he saw. He couldn't because if he had, he would have gone to prison, a fate that he narrowly avoided anyway.

Because we will never know for certain, what follows is pure supposition. I have never claimed to be an expert on the Villisca murders. I have pursued the facts in the case for many years and have also studied not only historical crime, but scores of ax murders ranging from the late 1800s to the 1920s, searching for links, clues and theories about the crimes. Based on my own research and about a dozen visits to the Moore house, I have tried to put together what I think occurred that night, from the murders themselves to the events that followed, which would lead to Reverend Kelly being placed on trial for murders that he didn't commit.

So, what happened on June 9?

I believe that the killer (whom I will just refer to here as Billy because I believe that he was the transient butcher who was also responsible for murders in Colorado, Kansas, and Illinois) entered the house through the back door, which opened into the kitchen. Why did he choose the Moore house? We will never know. None of the murders seemed to have a motive behind them. The families who were murdered had no enemies; no one had a grudge against them and they appeared to be chosen at random. I am convinced that the killer traveled by rail. All of the towns where he killed were "railroad towns," offering easy access into the community and an easy escape route. Villisca was no exception. The night of June 9 was perfect for a murder. As with the other cases, it was a Sunday night. Why the killer chose Sundays is unknown, but again, Villisca was no exception. What made this night even better was the fact that the streets were unlit thanks to the dispute with the local utility company. This made the killer's work even easier. As to why he chose the Moores, no one can say, but it's likely that Billy had reasons all his own – reasons that would perhaps make no sense to an ordinary person.

Billy entered the house through the back door and after prowling through the kitchen, saw the narrow stairway that led to the upper floor. He carried an ax that he had found in the backyard into the house with him; as was his usual method, he would later leave it behind at the scene. As he entered the kitchen, he picked up an oil lamp from the table. It was a common design that could be found in hundreds of thousands of homes across the Midwest. He quietly lit the lamp, turning the wick down as low as it could go.

Billy silently climbed the wooden stairs without disturbing anyone in the house. He was used to small houses – in every previous murder the house had been small and no one heard anything – and he knew how to be quiet. When he reached the top of the staircase, he could see the bed where J.B. and Sarah Moore were lying through the wooden railings. Before he entered the bedroom at the top of the stairs, he removed the glass chimney from the oil lamp. The dull light barely illuminated the scene, but Billy's eyes were used to the darkness and he could see everything that he needed to see. The stairs turned sharply to the left and moments later he was standing at the foot of the bed.

J.B. Moore was murdered first. He was the only victim struck by the sharp edge of the ax. It was necessary for the man of the house had to be killed first; he was the one most capable of fighting back. Moore was struck with savage ferocity, once, twice. Billy swung so hard that the backswing of the ax hit the ceiling. J.B. never stirred; he died instantly from the blows. The blows themselves brought only the sound of a solid strike, like that of a melon being smashed on a sidewalk. Even so, it was likely loud enough to cause Sarah to begin to awaken. She was a mother, used to coming out of a dead sleep when her children cried out from a bad dream.

She undoubtedly started to wake up when her husband was killed but the killer was prepared. Before she could scream, he brought the heavy head of the ax down on her skull. He hit her again and again until Sarah, like her husband, was dead.

Using the dim light of the lamp, Billy then crept into the south upstairs bedroom, where the children were sleeping. There were three beds in the room. Two of the children slept together and two others slept in separate beds. One by one, the murderer bludgeoned them all to death with the flat side of the ax, swinging and pounding as blood spattered the walls, the floor, and even the ceiling. Their small skulls were fractured savagely and all were killed without awakening the others. When he was finished, Billy pulled the sheets of the beds as high as they would go, carefully covering the faces and bodies of the dead. This was his ritual and he performed it just as he had done at the murder houses in Colorado, Kansas, and Illinois.

When he was finished in the children's room, he returned to the bed where J.B. and Sarah lay. He stepped next to the bed, accidentally moving one of Sarah's shoes that had been filling with blood dripping from her body. He looked down at the bodies that he had destroyed and as he had done in the children's room, he drew the bed sheets over their faces. He left his lamp on the floor under the dresser; he had no more need of it – his work was done. He had killed them all, he believed, and now he would wash himself before setting off into the night.

Billy descended the stairs into the kitchen and using the pump on the sink, he filled a pan with water with which to wash the blood from his hands and face. He dipped his hands into the water, turning it a reddish pink color. Now, he needed food. It didn't take him long to put together the pieces for a meal. He placed a plate on the table and prepared to sit down. He still had hours before the sun rose and he would be well on his way before then. But as he pulled out a chair and prepared to sit down, he heard the rustle of movement from the front of the house. There was someone else there – someone else who needed to be punished. He retrieved a second lamp, lit the wick, rolling it down until the light could barely be seen. Billy picked up the ax and silently crossed the kitchen and entered the front parlor.

To the right was a doorway leading to the small downstairs bedroom, the room where Katherine Moore usually slept. When he entered the room, he found two small forms sleeping on the bed. He removed the chimney from the lamp, dulling its glow and looked down at the two sleeping girls. He placed the lamp on the floor, hefted the ax and dealt another series of horrific blows. The two girls had also been punished. He pulled the bed sheets up over their bodies and leaned the bloody ax against the wall. His work was finally complete – but something was bothering him. Was it the fact that he had interrupted his work to wash and prepare to eat? Was it because his normally uncanny ability to search out all of the occupants of the house had failed him when he did not realize that there were two others in the house?

Billy the Axman was unsure, unsettled, and perhaps even had the distinct impression that he was being watched. As he felt the eyes of another crawl over him, he peered toward the darkened window that overlooked the backyard. Thin curtains hung over it, but he could plainly see the dark square of glass. He saw nothing outside, but could not shake the feeling that someone was there.

He left the food in the kitchen untouched and fled the house in silence. His bloody work was complete in this town, but there was more work to be done. The killer hopped aboard the next freight train passing through Villisca and vanished into the night.

He never returned to southwest Iowa again.

But Billy the Axman was not the last person to enter the Moore house that night.

Restless, unable to sleep and driven by desires that he could not begin to describe, Reverend Lyn George Kelly prowled the dark streets of Villisca. He was supposed to be sleeping in the guest room at Reverend Ewing's house, but it had been easy to slip away since the minister and his wife were sleeping in a tent in the backyard. Kelly wandered for a short time, looking for a house with a lighted window. He couldn't help himself – he was a window peeper. He liked looking at women and girls as they changed their clothing, or bathed or engaged in marital acts with their husbands and lovers. He couldn't stop himself from doing this and his desires sent him out into the midnight darkness of Villisca on June 9.

As he crept through an alleyway and into the backyard of the Moore house, he saw a faint light moving about in a downstairs window. He had no idea who lived there, but he felt a rush go through him when he realized that someone was awake and moving about. He managed to contain his excitement as he entered the yard and edged closer to the house. Then, he heard a strange sound coming from inside. It was a solid, thunking sound that was repeated several times. It seemed to be coming from upstairs and Kelly waited in the darkness to see what was going on. He could hear the quiet sounds of someone moving inside. There were footsteps on a staircase, then the quiet tread of boots in the kitchen. A faint light could be seen and then it was gone. He moved closer to the house and leaned in to peer into a downstairs window. It was a bedroom and there looked to be two small forms on the bed. He felt his pulse quicken as one of them stirred. The figure shifted position and the sheet fell away – it was a girl, a young, ripe little beauty, exactly what Kelly had been looking for. He felt himself stiffen and he nearly groaned aloud.

Moments later, a brighter light appeared in the doorway of the bedroom. The figure of a man approached, holding an oil lamp, but the light was so dim that Kelly was unable to get a good look at him. What he did see, however, was that the man was carrying an ax. The man placed the lamp down on the floor, swung the ax and pounded it into the two girls sleeping on the bed. As he struck the first girl, who was lying next to the wall, Kelly saw the second girl suddenly startle awake. Her hands flew up, but it was too late. The ax slammed into her skull and she collapsed back onto the bed. Kelly nearly screamed, his fist jammed into his mouth to keep from crying out. He was terrified, but he was unable to look away.

When he was finished, the dark figure in the room leaned the ax against the wall and stood there for a moment, gazing down at the small bodies on the bed. He covered them with a sheet and then stepped back. With a quick jerk, his head turned to the window. He seemed to look right at Kelly. The little preacher twisted away, ducking down below the sill and he waited there, terrified that he would be the next to be struck by the killer's ax. But no blow came. There was no cry of discovery, no panic from the killer. Kelly quickly hid, still worried that he might be discovered. A few moments later, he heard the soft click of the back door and he watched as the killer slipped away into the night.

A short time later, Reverend Kelly entered the house.

One of the main reasons why Kelly became a suspect in the Villisca murders is that he seemed to know more about the murders than anyone, aside from the killer. He spoke about the murders on the train back home the following morning and told people about them before the bodies had even been discovered. If he was not the killer, it was reasoned, then how could he have known such things?

I have become convinced over the years that Kelly saw the murders occur, or at least stumbled onto the scene as the killer was preparing to leave. It was a well-documented fact that Kelly was a window-peeker. By his own admission, he was unable to sleep at the Ewings' that night and so he walked around town. He was known for doing this in every town he lived in, and he likely saw more than his share of private scenes over the years. However, it's likely that in Villisca was the first time that he ever saw a murder. I believe that Kelly was either looking through the window when the Stillinger girls were killed, or he showed up soon after. Most likely, the sight of the dimly lit body of Lena Stillinger was too much for him to handle.

I believe that Kelly entered the house and likely walked all through it, which is how he knew how many people had been murdered. It may have been Kelly who accidentally moved Sarah Moore's shoe, changing the flow of the blood spatter and disrupting the scene. But it was in the bedroom where the Stillinger girls had been sleeping that Kelly left his greatest mark. I believe that it was he who covered the mirrors and the windows in the house with clothing. The covering of the mirrors was unique to this scene and had not been done in Colorado, Kansas or Illinois. The windows had been covered, likely so that no one would see the light moving around in the darkened house from outside. Kelly covered the windows, making sure they were completely blocked, because he didn't want anyone to see inside. He couldn't stand for them to see what he was about to do. He covered the mirrors so that he would not see his own reflection. He couldn't help himself but he didn't want to look into his own eyes while he was doing it, either.

According to the report from Dr. Williams, Lena Stillinger was found on the outside edge of the bed. Her nightgown was pushed up and she had no underwear on. Her body was drawn into an odd position. She was on her right side, her leg sticking out sideways from the bed and her right arm and hand under her pillow. Dr. Williams believed that she had been turned that way after her death because blood had already seeped through the pillow and onto the bed before her arm had been placed there. There was also a smear of blood on the inside of her right knee, suggesting that someone had turned the body slightly after she had been killed. Lena had not been raped, but the position of her body and the removal of her underwear led to the speculation that "sexual perversion" had occurred.

Detective Tobie, in a report that he wrote about interviewing Dr. Lindquist, the acting coroner in the case, was blunt about his suspicions concerning Lena Stillinger:

Dr. Linquist of Stanton, the acting coroner in this case was seen and interrogated; he states that in his opinion the murder was the work of a sexual pervert, that there was no semen in the vagina of Mrs. Moore or any indication of her having been assaulted, but that the condition of the body of the elder Stillinger girl was such as to indicate her having been fingered after rigor mortis had set in and that her vagina plainly showed this condition. It is not thought the penis entered the body, but that even after death this degenerate felt the body of the child during masturbation...

The report went on to make some pretty amazing claims as to the sexual interests of the killer, and it seems doubtful that Dr. Linquist actually used the words that Tobie attributed to him. The doctor would have known that rigor mortis sets in a few hours after death, hardly within the hour or so that the killer – or in my theory, Reverend Kelly – would have been in the house. And in subsequent legal proceedings, even under direct questioning, Dr. Linquist does not cite observing physical evidence of vaginal penetration after death. The sentiment of the statement, though, is consistent with Linquist's opinion. He would maintain for the rest of his life that an act, or acts, of sexual perversion had taken place after the killings.

As late as 1931, he was quoted in a newspaper interview as saying that the crime was committed by a sexual degenerate who "indulged his orgy." He also said in the same interview that the man who was guilty had gone to England.

While I don't agree that Kelly committed the murders, I do agree with Dr. Linquist that he was the one who committed "acts of sexual perversion after the killings." I believe that it was Kelly who moved Lena Stillinger's body and posed her so that her vagina was visible. When he did so, he got blood on his shirt – the same shirt that he took to the laundry in Council Bluffs. There was no evidence that he ever touched her and, based on his later acts and requests for girls to pose nude for him, physical touching was not what excited him. Kelly liked to look and watch. There is nothing to suggest that he ever engaged in sex with any of them. Even his wife told a prosecutor in his murder trial that she and her husband had never had "normal sex."

Kelly liked to watch and he was also likely a masturbator. It's likely that he masturbated while looking at Lena Stillinger's nude body, which could also explain why he covered the mirrors in the room. As distasteful as the suggestion might be, we must consider the slab of bacon that was found sitting in the kitchen by the investigators who later came to the house. It's possible that Kelly used grease from the bacon as a lubricant when he masturbated, something that was unfortunately common during that era.

As twisted as the explanation is, we now have a good idea about how Reverend Kelly came to know about the murders before the bodies were discovered and how he got blood on his shirt, which were the main reasons why he was suspected of the crime.

But explanations or not, my theories bring us no closer to knowing who committed the Villisca murders, or the killings in Colorado, Kansas, and Illinois. "Billy the Axman" simply disappeared into history, leaving death and despair in his wake. Unfortunately, this means that none of the murders will ever be solved and we will forever wonder how the killer chose his victims, what motivated him to claim their lives, and where he vanished to when his bloody spree was over.

I don't think Billy stopped killing because his lust had finally been satiated, I believe he was forced to so, either by death or imprisonment. The penitentiary seems an unlikely ending for a man who carried out so many murders and never left a clue behind, but the insane asylum does not. I think that one day, Billy finally snapped and he was locked away for good. What became of him after that is unknown, but if I had to guess, I would say that he is lying out there somewhere in the Midwest, in a pauper's burial ground.

Billy the Axman took his secrets to the grave.

24. GHOSTS!
THE HAUNTING OF THE MOORE HOUSE

During the dark night of June 9, 1912, a small wooden frame house in Villisca, Iowa, became the site of one of the grisliest massacres in Midwestern history when the family of J.B. Moore and two overnight guests were murdered as they slept. The house earned a place in American crime history and a place in the annals of ghostly legend, as well.

The house on Lot 410 in Villisca had been built in 1868 by George Loomis. It was purchased by J.B. Moore in 1903, and he and his wife Sarah, along with their four children, made their home there until their deaths nine years later. After the massacre, the house remained the property of the estate until 1915, when it was purchased by J.H. Geesman.

Over the course of the next 90 years, the house had seven different owners, including the Villisca State Savings & Loan, whose name appears on the title from 1963 to 1971. In 1971, the house was sold to Kendrick & Vance, a plumbing and heating company, and a month later, was sold again to Darwin Kendrick. He remained as owner, renting the house out to tenants until it was sold to Rick and Vicki Sprague on January 1, 1994. A few months later, a real estate agent approached local farmers named Darwin and Martha Linn about the possibility of them purchasing the house. At the time, the Linns already owned and operated the Olson-Linn Museum on Villisca's town square and they felt that purchasing the infamous house at 323 East Fourth Street would give them the opportunity to preserve an important piece of the area's history. The house was in poor condition and was in danger of being razed. If the Linns had not purchased it, it's likely that it would have been destroyed. They soon set about obtaining the necessary funds to restore the home to its condition at the time of the murders in 1912.

As Darwin and Martha began researching the house, they found that they had a lot of work ahead of them to make the restoration complete. Years of renovation followed and some paranormal researchers believe that it was the restoration work that followed that caused the house to become "active." In many cases of hauntings, an event may occur that leaves an impression on the atmosphere of a place. Such an event may include a traumatic occurrence like a murder or, in the case of the Moore house, eight murders. Often a haunting will lay dormant for many years before becoming active. The paranormal literature has reported a number of hauntings that were said to be generated by buildings being remodeled or renovated. This disturbance can often cause effects to occur that are related to the haunting -- including sounds like voices, footsteps and cries, as well as physical effects like doors opening and closing, widows rattling and even knocking and rapping sounds. Is this merely a "recording" of the past that has been activated again or could there be an actual ghostly presence that

The Moore House during the restoration years

generates the activity? In some locations, like the former J.B. Moore house, it may just be both.

As the Linns attempted to work on the restoration, they found that 13 previous owners were listed on the deed and that the house had often been used as a rental property. They started to compile a list of the tenants who lived in the house, but progress was slow because many of the renters stayed for only a short time. They did learn that between 1936 and 1994, the house had undergone extensive changes. The front and back porches were enclosed, plumbing and electricity were added. and the outbuildings were either removed or replaced. The house barely resembled the Moore house of 1912, but that was soon to change.

Using old photographs, the Linns began work on the house in late 1994. The restoration included removing the vinyl siding and repainting the original exterior wood. The enclosures to the front and back porches were removed, as was all the indoor plumbing and electrical fixtures. An outhouse and chicken coop were added to the backyard. Lastly, a small barn like the one that housed the Moores' horse and cows was moved onto the property. In keeping with their quest for authenticity, the Linns referred to testimony and records from the coroner's inquest and grand jury hearings to place furniture inside the house where it had been at the time of the murders. The furnishings that had belonged to the Moores had vanished many decades ago, so antiques were used to replace what was lost.

The Moore home was added to the National Register of Historic Places in 1998 and remains today as a colorful time capsule of 1912, the ghastly murders that occurred there and the mystery that followed. The walls hide many secrets and these secrets bring many visitors to the door. Some of them come hoping to experience the atmosphere of a house where the worst mass murder in Iowa history took place – but most of them come looking for ghosts.

Ever since the Moore house was opened to overnight visitors several years ago, ghost enthusiasts, curiosity-seekers, and diehard paranormal investigators have come there in droves, all seeking the strange, the unusual, and the haunted. Some of the bolder ones who have stayed there alone overnight have had perplexing experiences, like the Des Moines disk jockey who awoke in the night to the sounds of children's voices when no children were present. Others have come in groups and have gone away with mysterious audio, video and photographic evidence that suggests something supernatural lurks within the walls. Tours have been cut short by falling lamps, moving objects, banging sounds, and a child's laughter, while psychics who have visited the place have claimed to communicate with the spirits of the dead.

If even a fraction of the stories circulating about this place were true, I reasoned when I first heard about the so-called "Villisca Ax Murder House," then it would have to be one of the most haunted places in America. Its gruesome history certainly provided a possibility for the story of the haunting to be true --- but was it? I would find that out for myself in May 2005, when I joined a group that was staying there overnight.

I arrived in Villisca on the evening of my first stay at the house an hour or so before the sun went down. I met up with the rest of the group at Darwin and Martha Linn's museum on the town square. The museum is housed in two floors of the building that was once Frank Jones' implement store. It features a jumbled assortment of old cars, farm equipment, advertising signs, and historical records. There are so many displays and artifacts from bygone days that a visitor could spend hours there and still not see everything. I met Darwin and Martha for the first time and went on to cultivate a friendship with the wonderful couple that extended until Darwin's passing in 2011. I spent a little while chatting with them before Darwin introduced the group to the bloody history of the Villisca murders.

The next stop was the town cemetery, where Darwin showed us the burial places of the Moores and the Stillinger girls. The grave markers had been purchased from the sizable reward fund that had been collected in hopes of capturing the killer. Since the reward was never claimed, surviving family members donated the money to be used to purchase the tombstones. After leaving the burial ground, Darwin pointed out the once-grand mansion that had belonged to Frank Jones. He then led us back to the square, where we had dinner at one of the local restaurants. After dinner, we met at the Moore house, where we would spend the rest of the night.

Walking into the house for the first time was like stepping back in time. There is no electricity in the house; the only illumination comes from candles and kerosene lamps, and no plumbing either. There is now a bathroom in the barn, but at the time of my first visit there was only an old outhouse, which was authentic to 1912. The house is small and we entered through the back door, which let us into the kitchen. The parlor is located at the front of the house, with the bedroom leading off from it, where the bodies of the Stillinger girls were found. Just off the kitchen is a small pantry and the staircase leading to the second floor. At the top of the steps is the bedroom that belonged to J.B. and Sarah Moore. At the front of the house is the children's bedroom, where the blood-soaked bodies of the Moore children were discovered. There is also an unfinished attic that is reached through a door in the Moores' bedroom.

It had been a warm afternoon, fading into evening, when we arrived in Villisca. The heat of the day had generated a line of fierce thunderstorms, and soon after arriving at the house, we began to hear rumbles of thunder and see flashes of lightning above the distant, rolling hills. By 11 p.m., the rain began to pound down on Villisca, but it only lasted for a short time. In less than an hour, the storms had moved off, leaving the night warm and humid. The group that I had come with planned to thoroughly investigate the house. If there was any evidence of ghosts there, they hoped to find it. I had come to watch. I like to experience investigations and get a feel for the locations, but I usually prefer to stay out of the details of the experiments. However, sometimes, you become a part of your own story, whether you want to or not.

Two of the members of the group that night, Anney Horn and her daughter, Jada, had been to the Moore house on another occasion and Anney told the group about some rather strange happenings that she had experienced in the children's room on the second floor. She was convinced that Paul, one of the Moore children, remained behind in his old room and would interact with visitors in exchange for candy. She had brought along a pocketful of treats and suggested that the group try and make contact with Paul. Everyone agreed. David and Josie Rodriquez, from Omaha, set up an array of equipment in the south bedroom to record any strange events that might occur. It was a camera pointed at the closet that managed to capture the most dramatic happenings of the night.

Within a few minutes, most of the group had crammed into the children's bedroom. It was hot and crowded in there, so I chose to stay downstairs with David Rodriguez and watch what was going on through a monitor that was wired to the camera upstairs. After about 20 minutes of watching the video feed, I wandered over to get a drink and soon after, David called out to me; there was something odd going on, he said, and I should come and take a look.

I looked over his shoulder at the monitor. The picture and sound were being fed to a laptop computer, and we watched as the people in the bedroom tried to coax the "ghost boy" into performing on cue for them. They were asking him to close the closet door and as far as we could tell, the door was closing just as they asked it to! This happened several times in a row – the door opening and closing on cue. After watching for a little while, I decided that I had to see it for myself.

I hurried upstairs and walked into the south bedroom, which was now filled with very excited people. I squeezed in as they gave me a description of what had been happening. What they told me matched perfectly with what I had been watching on the monitor in the kitchen. I sat down and watched as Anney began to again try and coax "Paul" into opening and closing the closet door. To be honest, I was very skeptical about what was occurring. I had come upstairs not because I was expecting to marvel at the antics of a ghost who closed doors for candy, but to find a logical explanation for what was going on. There had to be a reasonable

The closet in the children's bedroom, which opened and closed in front of a number of witnesses – and was captured on film while doing so

answer for why the closet door was behaving the way it was, and I was determined to find out what that could be.

Anney called to Paul a few times and promised that she would leave some candy for him if he would make the closet door open and close for her. We all watched in silence as the door swung open about eight inches. Nothing happened for several beats and then, for no apparent reason, the door slowly swung closed. It did not slam closed but rather seemed to just gently close, as though someone was pushing it. There was absolutely no one near it at the time.

I'm not sure how I managed to do it but I convinced the guests to take a break and go downstairs for a few minutes. I wanted to check out the closet. I was dubious about the "ghost boy" and was sure that there had to be a reason as to why the door seemed to be performing on command. I looked at everything ---- I looked for wires, for slopes in the floor, for loose hinges, and even tried opening the door and pushing it closed several times. Could it be a draft? I went through the entire upstairs and closed all of the doors and windows so that I could be sure that there was no air current coming in. Could it have been the distance that the door stood open that allowed it to swing closed? Was it a coincidence? If the door was left alone long enough, would it open and close anyway? I sat and watched it for quite some time, much longer that it had been left with the room full of people, but it simply refused to do anything.

Close to an hour later, I was ready to try again. I called everyone back into the bedroom and instructed them to try and get the door to close now that I had sealed off the windows from any outside air. Everyone sat down and Anney once again called out to Paul, coaxing him to open and close the door. A minute or two passed, and then the door opened and swung shut again – something I had been unable to duplicate a short time before. There was no way that we could attribute it to air currents or drafts from the windows. The door continued to open and close over and over again, but only when Anney asked.

This happened several more times before I decided to try something else. If it was not an air current that was moving the door, would it open and close anyway if we waited long enough? I had waited several minutes, but perhaps that had not been enough time. Would the door just open and close? And if so, was it because the doorframe had settled over time and was slanted in such a way as to make it appear like it was opening and closing "on its own"?

We all left the room. We would not ask Paul to do anything with the door. Anyone who wanted to watch it could do so from the monitor downstairs in the kitchen. With that, we all went downstairs or outside to have a midnight snack and to wait around and see what might happen in the bedroom.

We waited for nearly two hours. No one went into the room during that time. Through most of the time, someone was watching the door from the monitor in the kitchen, or at least checking in periodically to see what was happening. During that entire time, the door never budged. Nothing had changed – except that no one was asking Paul to close it. It just remained there, unmoving and open a crack, apparently waiting for us to return.

Finally, at about 2 a.m., several of us filed back into the room. The door was just as we had left it. It had now been motionless for almost two hours.

Anney spoke out loud, asking Paul to close the door. "Paul? Are you there?" she called. "Would you close the door for us again? If you do, I'll leave some more candy inside the closet."

Seconds ticked by and then, with no one moving or speaking, the wooden door slowly swung open and then shut, latching with a soft click. It had not moved until someone politely asked it to do so. I would love to provide a rational explanation for why it happened, but I don't have one.

I think it was at this point that I realized the Moore house is haunted.

I have since visited the house many times, traveling there from Illinois to stay the night and experience the house, the town, and surrounding area. I have traveled there to work with film crews, meet ghost hunters, and to just soak up the atmosphere of this eerie and troubling place. And yes, I have had other encounters with the ghosts.

I have seen doors close by themselves; saw a child's ball roll across the floor, reverse direction and return to the person who pushed it and, most unsettling, heard footsteps follow me up the narrow stairs to the second floor. This might not have bothered me so much if I had not felt the distinct presence of someone standing watchfully nearby. I caught a faint odor of sweat and unwashed clothing and immediately went back downstairs. I instinctively wanted to get far away from whoever or whatever had been next to me on the stairs that night.

In the end, we have to ask: is the Moore house in Villisca really haunted? There are many who maintain that it's not. They say that many people lived in there in the decades following the slayings and none of them ever mentioned encountering any ghosts. It was not until the renovations began that visitors began to experience strange events within the walls of the "Ax Murder House." Are these events merely the products of overactive imaginations or wishful thinking? That's what some would like you to believe, but don't be fooled; I don't think the explanation for what happens in the house is that simple.

277

But don't take my word for it.

I have come to believe that the house is haunted solely because of what I have experienced within its walls. I hope the reader will reserve his or her own judgment until the time comes when they can spend their own night there. It's not a place for the faint of heart, but if you are looking for something special – whether it be ghosts or answers to a lingering mystery -- then make your own plans to journey to this historic -- and haunted -- place.

Troy Taylor
January 2016

BIBLIOGRAPHY

Burns, Stanley B. and Sara Cleary-Burns – *Deadly Intent;* 2008
Getting the Axe – Internet Blog, maintained by "Inspector Winship"
Hudson, Marilyn A. – *When Death Rode the Rails;* 2011
Klingensmith, Beth H. – *The 1910s Ax Murders*, Unpublished; 2006

Marshall, Roy – *Villisca*; 2003
Marshall's book is essential reading for anyone with an interest in the ax murders. After researching the case since the early 1970s, the author offers insight into the people and the community that cannot be gained from other sources.

Newton, Michael – *Encyclopedia of Unsolved Crimes*; 2009
Sifakis, Carl – *Encyclopedia of American Crime;* 1982
Taylor, Troy – *Dead Men Do Tell Tales*; 2008
--------------- - *The Haunted President*; 2009
-------------- - *So, There I Was*; 2006
Wilkerson, J.N. – *Dope Sheet* (1912 Villisca Iowa Murders) Edited by Tammy Rundle, Kelly Rundle & Edgar V. Epperly; 2003
Wright, John -- *Unsolved Crimes*; 2010

Personal Interviews & Correspondence

Newspapers & Periodicals
Altoona Mirror (Pennsylvania)
Colorado Springs Gazette (Colorado)
Columbia Herald (Missouri)
Daily Free Press (Carbondale, Illinois)
Denver Post (Colorado)
Des Moines News (Iowa)
Des Moines Register & Reader (Iowa)
Ellsworth Reporter (Kansas)
Iowa Recorder (Iowa)
La Crosse Tribune (Wisconsin)
Logansport Pharos-Reporter (Indiana)

Massillon Evening Independent (Ohio)
Miami Republican (Iowa)
Monmouth Review-Atlas (Illinois)
Riverdale Reporter (Illinois)
Salt Lake Tribune (Utah)
Sheboygan Evening Press (Wisconsin)
Villisca Review (Iowa)
Washington Democrat (Indiana)
Waterloo Evening Courier (Iowa)
Western Spirit (Miami County, Kansas)

Images & Photographs:
Burns Archives
Colorado Historical Society
Colorado Springs Gazette
Miami Republican (Iowa)
Montgomery County Historical Society
Private Collections
Villisca Historical Society
Villisca Public Library
Villisca Review (Iowa)
Wichita State University

Special Thanks to:
Lois Taylor: Editing and Proofreading
April Slaughter: Cover Design and Artwork
Lisa Taylor Horton and Lx
Orrin Taylor
Darwin & Martha Linn
Len Adams
Bill Alsing
John Winterbauer
Steven and Amber Tracy
David Rodriguez
Johnny Houser
Rene Kruse
Rachael Horath
Elyse and Thomas Reihner
Bethany Horath

www.ingramcontent.com/pod-product-compliance
Lightning Source LLC
Chambersburg PA
CBHW051414090426
42737CB00014B/2668